⇽ CATO ⇾
SUPREME COURT
REVIEW

2012 — 2013

CATO SUPREME COURT REVIEW

2012 — 2013

ROGER PILON
Publisher

ILYA SHAPIRO
Editor in Chief

TREVOR BURRUS
Associate Editor

ROBERT A. LEVY
Associate Editor

TIMOTHY LYNCH
Associate Editor

WALTER OLSON
Associate Editor

CENTER FOR CONSTITUTIONAL STUDIES

Washington, D.C.

THE CATO SUPREME COURT REVIEW (ISBN 978-1-939709-08-0) is published annually at the close of each Supreme Court term by the Cato Institute, 1000 Massachusetts Ave., N.W.,Washington, D.C. 20001-5403.

CORRESPONDENCE. Correspondence regarding subscriptions, changes of address, procurement of back issues, advertising and marketing matters, and so forth, should be addressed to:

Publications Department
The Cato Institute
1000 Massachusetts Ave., N.W.
Washington, D.C. 20001

All other correspondence, including requests to quote or reproduce material, should be addressed to the editor.

CITATIONS: Citation to this volume of the Review should conform to the following style: 2012-2013 Cato Sup. Ct. Rev. (2013).

DISCLAIMER. The views expressed by the authors of the articles are their own and are not attributable to the editor, the editorial board, or the Cato Institute.

INTERNET ADDRESS. Articles from past editions are available to the general public, free of charge, at www.cato.org/pubs/scr.

ISBN 978-1-939709-08-0

Printed in the United States of America.

Cato Institute
1000 Massachusetts Ave., N.W.
Washington, D.C. 20001
www.cato.org

Contents

Contents

FOREWORD

Equal Protection

*Roger Pilon**

The Cato Institute's Center for Constitutional Studies is pleased to publish this 12th volume of the *Cato Supreme Court Review*, an annual critique of the Court's most important decisions from the term just ended, plus a look at the term ahead—all from a classical Madisonian perspective, grounded in the nation's first principles, liberty through limited government. We release this volume each year at Cato's annual Constitution Day conference. And each year in this space I discuss briefly a theme that seemed to emerge from the Court's term or from the larger setting in which the term unfolded.

Clearly, the theme that ran through the major decisions the Court handed down during its final days was equal protection. The long-awaited decision in *Fisher v. University of Texas at Austin* was expected by many to put an end at last to the use of racial preferences in public higher-education admissions decisions. Instead, the Court vacated the Fifth Circuit's decision upholding the university's affirmative action scheme and remanded the case for further proceedings under scrutiny more strict than the lower courts had employed.

In another closely watched case with roots in the civil rights movement of the 1960s, *Shelby County v. Holder*, the Court found the formula for determining which state and local governments must comply with the preclearance requirements of the 1965 Voting Rights Act so out of date as to be unconstitutional, thus raising serious questions about equal protection as it concerns not only voters but state sovereignty as well.

* Vice president for legal affairs at the Cato Institute, founder and director of Cato's Center for Constitutional Studies, B. Kenneth Simon Chair in Constitutional Studies, and publisher of the *Cato Supreme Court Review*.

Finally, equal protection was squarely before the Court in a complex pair of same-sex marriage cases the Court decided on its last day, *United States v. Windsor* and *Hollingsworth v. Perry*, although the Court ducked the issue in *Perry*, holding that the petitioners had no standing to defend California's Proposition 8, which defined "marriage" as between one man and one woman, while in *Windsor* the Court found Congress's similar effort to define "marriage" in the Defense of Marriage Act unconstitutional on federalism, due process, and equal protection grounds.

Equal Protection's Difficult History

Over the years the Court has had no little difficulty deciding cases on the basis of the equal protection principle, often conflating equal protection and due process. Witness *Plessy v. Ferguson* and *Brown v. Board of Education, Bowers v. Hardwick* and *Lawrence v. Texas,* and especially "class-of-one" cases like *Engquist v. Oregon Department of Agriculture,* where the Court came up short. That's not surprising, first because equal protection as such is merely a formal principle, and second because we got off to a bad start with the idea, not only at the outset but even after we incorporated it at last in our constitutional firmament.

Grounded as we are in the natural-rights tradition—which emerged from natural law by emphasizing equality, as in Locke's theory of equal rights and Jefferson's premise of equality in the Declaration of Independence—we flinched when it came to drafting the Constitution. To ensure unity among the states, slavery was recognized, if only obliquely. The Framers knew the "peculiar institution" was inconsistent with our founding principles. They hoped that it would wither away in time. It did not. It took a civil war to end slavery and the passage of the Civil War Amendments to constitutionalize the change, thus instituting at last an express guarantee that states could not deny to any person within their jurisdiction the equal protection of the laws.

The proximate cause of that change, however, can be found in the pernicious Black Codes that Southern states passed shortly after the Civil War ended. They were met by the Civil Rights Act of 1866, which the 39th Congress enacted to protect "the natural rights of man," as members of that Congress said in so many ways during their debates. But in both cases, both in the Black Codes and in the

1866 Act, the language of racial classes—"black" and "white"—was explicit.

Thus, despite the fact that Section 1 of the final version of the Fourteenth Amendment speaks only of "citizens" and "persons," the understanding and application of the equal protection principle was colored from the start by a class-based approach when in truth the principle is deeper and more far-reaching. And the potential difficulties inherent in that approach were only exacerbated when brought to the surface by the "scrutiny theory" entailed by *Carolene Products'* (in)famous footnote four. For after that, not only did laws implicating different "classes" get different levels of judicial scrutiny—"strict" for racial classifications, for example, "heightened" for gender classifications—but laws employing most classifications—sexual orientation in most jurisdictions, for example, entrepreneurs everywhere—got effectively no judicial scrutiny because they were not "suspect classes," at least not until a legislature or a court recognized them as such.

First Principles

We've had, therefore, an "evolving" equal protection jurisprudence, much like our evolving and closely connected due process jurisprudence, which protects the unenumerated rights the Ninth Amendment tells us we "retained" only insofar as courts have recognized them as "fundamental" because "deeply rooted in the nation's history." By contrast, a jurisprudence grounded in First Principles—the nation's First Principles, as it happens—would go about the matter very differently. It would begin by recognizing the theory of political legitimacy implicit throughout the Constitution, slavery aside, as manifest most clearly in the Preamble and in the Ninth, Tenth, and Fourteenth Amendments, which taken together restate the Declaration's theory of legitimacy: namely, that we all have equal natural rights to property justly acquired (Locke's "lives, liberties, and estates"), to enter into contracts, to remedy wrongs regarding those rights, and to institute governments to secure those rights and do the few other things we've authorized them to do, as illustrated by the federal government's limited, enumerated powers.

Thus, equal protection under a government so limited, whether explicitly guaranteed as in the Fourteenth Amendment or implicit as through the Fifth Amendment's Due Process Clause, would not turn on class membership or recognition but rather would be a function simply of the larger background theory. Individuals would have a right to be treated by governments, federal, state, or local, not as members of particular classes but as abstract individuals—much like law students are graded, behind a veil of ignorance as to their particular characteristics. Not for nothing is Lady Justice blindfolded. In fact, she illustrates the clearest understanding of equal protection: because we all have equal rights, and because government belongs to all of us, it must treat all equally in all of its functions—legislative, executive, and adjudicative—notwithstanding our many differences.

In operation that means that if government does treat an individual differently than others, it must have not just a reason—we all have reasons for what we do—but a compelling reason related to the background theory of legitimacy. Thus, treating wrongdoers differently than others is perfectly legitimate; so too is discrimination that may be necessary for carrying out authorized governmental functions. And that presumption of equal treatment means also that the burden is on government to justify unequal treatment, not on the individual treated unequally to show that he has a right to equal treatment in the case at hand.

Facing Reality, Affirmative Action

But equal protection's difficult path into the Fourteenth Amendment and thereby into our Constitution more broadly does not alone account for our uneven equal protection jurisprudence. More recently, as we were employing the principle correctly at last to end Jim Crow segregation in the South we were faced with the legacy of that wretched institution and with the question of what to do about it. Strict adherence to First Principles would have prohibited only illegitimate *public* discrimination, of course, as just noted. It would not have prohibited "unreasonable" or "irrational" *private* discrimination, even though such discrimination could no longer be *imposed* through force of law, as under Jim Crow. So entrenched was that discrimination in Southern culture, however, that we decided—for better or worse, doubtless for better—to bend our principles, to limit *private* freedom of association, which we did by prohibiting unreasonable discrimination in most commercial and, over time, many other private associations on the basis of race, color, religion, sex , or national origin, grounds that have expanded over the years.

To enforce this desegregation there followed various kinds and degrees of "affirmative action," all of which required discrimination in the name of ending discrimination. Initially justified mainly as necessary to break the social hold segregation had in the South, affirmative action soon was rationalized as rectification for past wrongs—even though the individuals rewarded by the practice were often not those who'd suffered under segregation while those now discriminated against had not themselves engaged in discrimination. (Such are the distributional inequities that arise from "social justice" schemes.) More recently, however, rectification has been replaced by an even less justified rationale—diversity. Discrimination is needed, it is said, to ensure a more diverse student body, workforce, loan portfolio, housing unit, what have you. And so we come to our first case, *Fisher v. University of Texas*.

Fisher v. University of Texas

Fisher offers a good illustration of how equal protection has been ignored under current law. Start with the most basic question: Why is government involved in higher education at all—or even in education, for that matter? Like food, clothing, and shelter, education is a private good. It exhibits neither of the cardinal characteristics of public goods—nonexcludability and nonrivalrous consumption. And publicly subsidized *higher* education, which is enjoyed by only a portion of the population, is especially problematic from the perspective of equality: on balance, as economists have long noted, it constitutes a massive wealth transfer from the poorer to the richer parts of society, a point Justice Clarence Thomas explored in some detail in *Grutter v. Bollinger*. Thus, the initial inequality arising from such programs is between those who benefit from them and those who do not, even as they subsidize the beneficiaries through taxation.

But set that fundamental objection aside because it can be said about any redistributive program—the main business of governments today—and ask how, if we have such programs, they can be conducted, insofar as possible, consistent with equal protection, with treating all as individuals. Let's approach that question by starting with a simple, unproblematic example of discrimination by a public institution. Public fire departments use strength, among other criteria, to screen applicants for firefighter positions because that criterion is central to their purpose or mission, even though doing so has a "disperate impact" on female applicants, and even though an occasional woman may satisfy the standard. We accept that discrimination because the ground on which it is based is closely connected to the very reason we create a fire department in the first place. The discrimination is "rational," we say. No one wants to be protected by firefighters who are not up to the job.

Well what is the reason for which we create public universities and public law schools? Plainly, there are many reasons, not all of them praiseworthy, which is why the issue here is relatively more difficult. But unless such institutions are open to all, indiscriminately—and the existence alone of "flagship" institutions gives a lie to that—then discrimination in admissions will be required. Yet to be justified at all, that discrimination must be tied fairly closely to the core reasons that justify the institution in the first place, as in the firefighter example. Otherwise it risks being arbitrary or even "unreasonable."

Given the core educational business of universities, admissions officers have tended to focus mainly, though not exclusively, on a student applicant's aptitude as the main ground for discrimination, because there are relatively objective measures for that criterion and, more to the point here, because it is central to the basic purpose of the institution—again, much as in the firefighter example. By contrast, other criteria—legacy, athletic ability, life experience—may be less central to a university's core mission, while some criteria—race, ethnicity, gender, religion, appearance—may be irrelevant altogether.

Yet that, precisely, is where the diversity "interest" that was accepted in *Grutter* and assumed by Justice Anthony Kennedy in *Fisher* becomes problematic. In some way or at some level it *requires* admissions officers to focus not simply on forbidden grounds but on irrelevant grounds—and to treat applicants other than as abstract individuals. And note that it isn't simply, as under current law, that public officials must avoid certain class-based *forbidden* grounds— grounds that may vary from jurisdiction to jurisdiction—but that they must rest their decisions only on truly *relevant* grounds if equal protection is to be fully achieved, if even the appearance of arbitrariness is to be avoided. Barbara Grutter and Abigail Fisher applied to their respective institutions expecting to be judged behind a veil of ignorance, taking into account only those factors *most relevant* to the core function of those institutions. If it violates equal protection for

Lady Justice to lift her blindfold when deciding guilt or punishment, why is it any better for her to do so here?

If "social justice" is our concern, it would be far better, of course, if all universities were private and if they were free to discriminate as they wished. That would also solve the reverse-welfare problem, where below-cost legal education is provided, partly through taxation, to the mostly better off at the expense of those who never apply to such schools—for many reasons—or, if they do, are unable to get in. That remains the fundamental equal protection problem. And just to be clear, that is not a mere "political" problem. It is a constitutional and hence a legal problem as well, its roots in the rise of the redistributive state the Constitution was meant to guard against, the failure of which has unleashed the dynamic that public-choice economists have explained in so many domains, public higher education being only one, but an especially pernicious one given the economics of the matter.

On remand, therefore, one hopes that the court below reaches beyond Justice Kennedy's narrow-tailoring instruction: "The reviewing court must ultimately be satisfied that no workable race-neutral alternatives would produce the educational benefits of diversity." Far better it would be if that court turned instead to Justice Thomas: "The Equal Protection Clause guarantees every person the right to be treated equally by the State, without regard to race. 'At the heart of the [guarantee] lies the principle that the government must treat citizens as individuals, and not as members of racial, ethnic, or religious groups'"—or as members of *any* group, one might add. Were the court to require the university to treat applicants as abstract individuals, our errant class-based equal protection jurisprudence would be headed toward a more principled course.

Shelby County v. Holder

Shelby County raised a very different equal protection issue. Arising from a long and complex history, it posed something of an equal protection puzzle: how to protect both the equal rights of citizens to vote and the equal sovereignty of states—where the power to regulate elections traditionally rests—when some of those states have a history of abusing the voting rights of some of their ctizens. In the end, the puzzle was easily solved by the facts.

To end egregious racially motivated voting restrictions, largely in the South, Congress enacted the Voting Rights Act of 1965. Section 2 of the Act forbids states from enacting any standard, practice, or procedure that would abridge the right to vote on account of race or color. Section 5 requires states to get "preclearance" from federal officials in Washington before making even minor changes in voting procedures. And Section 4(b) provides a "coverage formula" that applies the preclearance requirements to only certain states or political subdivisions, mostly in the South. Thus, in the name of equal protection for voters, the VRA raises serious federalism questions about equal sovereignty regarding the states.

Recognized at the time it was passed as an extraordinary measure and "a drastic departure from basic principles of federalism," the Act's coverage formula and prelearance requirement were initially set to expire after five years. But Congress has reauthorized the VRA several times. And in 2006 it did so for an additional 25 years, piling more requirements on in the process—notwithstanding that much on the ground has changed since 1965.

And therein lies the problem. As Chief Justice John Roberts demonstrated, writing for the Court's majority, the covered jurisdictions today, if anything, have better voting records concerning minorities than the jurisdictions not subject to the requirements. Because section 4 has not been updated in more than 40 years, the Court held it unconstitutional, effectively rendering section 5 unenforceable unless Congress updates the coverage formula (which is not likely at this point in time).

Thus, the equal protection issue here turns out to be straightforward. As the Court held six years ago in *Northwest Austin v. Holder*, the Voting Rights Act "imposes current burdens and must be justified by current needs." Because current needs no longer justify the law's extrordinary measures, the Court held that it could no longer tolerate a situation whereby "one State waits months or years and expends funds to implement a validly enacted law, [while] its neighbor can typically put the same law into effect immediately."

United States v. Windsor

We return now to the more common applications of the equal protection principle, as in *Fisher*, though in a most uncommon context. Except perhaps regarding the related case of *Hollingsworth v. Perry*, no decision was more anxiously awaited this term than *United States v. Windsor*. It was understood by all that the Court might duck *Perry* on standing grounds, as in fact it did. It could have done so in *Windsor* too, but that was less likely, both on the facts of the case and because two appellate courts had already ruled that the 1993 Defense of Marriage Act provision at issue in the case was unconstitutional.

As noted earlier, in finding DOMA's Section 3 unconstitutional Justice Kennedy invoked federalism, due process, and equal protection principles, all wrapped around a core concern with the congressional animus he saw behind the statute. In truth, he could have grounded his argument on federalism alone, for under our federal system, as he went on to show at length, "[b]y history and tradition the definition and regulation of marriage has been treated as being within the authority and realm of the separate States"—indeed, "as a virtually exclusive province of the States." He could have stopped right there with what would have been an argument resting essentially on the Tenth Amendment, because by intruding on the province of the states to define marriage, DOMA "disrupts the federal balance." Instead, finding it "unnecessary" to decide DOMA's constitutionality on federalism grounds, he argued next that whereas the state's decision to recognize same-sex marriages conferred "dignity and status" on this class of persons, DOMA imposes "injury and indignity" on them, depriving them "of an essential part of the liberty protected by the Fifth Amendment." Finding "strong evidence" that the very purpose of DOMA was to stigmatize those in same-sex marriages, Kennedy concluded that so injuring such "politically unpopular" groups "violates basic due process and equal protection principles applicable to the Federal Government" under the Fifth Amendment.

Among the questions Kennedy's opinion has left us, one stands out: Why did he think it necessary to find animus behind DOMA? Perhaps we find the answer here: "In determining whether a law is motivated by an improper animus or purpose, '[d]iscriminations of an unusual character' especially require *careful consideration*. DOMA cannot survive under these principles." (emphasis added) His analysis colored by modern scrutiny theory (in *Turner Broadcasting v. FCC* (1994) he found no fewer than four levels of judicial scrutiny), Kennedy seems to have signaled that "heightened" scrutiny is required when animus is suspected. Whatever his thinking, or the wisdom of charging DOMA's supporters with animus, an analysis grounded on

First Principles, federalism aside, would have been far more straightforward, as outlined above, simply by compelling the federal government to justify denying benefits to same-sex married couples that it was already providing for opposite-sex married couples. Having no reasons sufficient to overcome not only federalism but liberty and equal protection principles, that would have settled the matter, without resort either to motive or to some arbitrary level of judicial scrutiny, a judicial device nowhere to be found in the Constitution.

Still, however "unnecessary" it may have been to decide *Windsor* on federalism grounds, it should not go unnoticed that Kennedy gets to due process and equal protection *through* federalism—through the power of the states, not the federal government, to define marriage. Of particular importance, by so doing he is able to limit the reach of the opinion to those states that have recognized same-sex marriages. Thus, equal protection under the Fifth Amendment requires only that all lawfully married couples *within* a state—opposite-sex and same-sex alike—be treated equally by the federal government. Federal equal protection concerning marriage does *not*—not yet, at least—reach across state borders.

That leaves open the question of how same-sex couples married elsewhere are to be treated if they live now in states that do not recognize same-sex marriages. Apparently that question was settled just after *Windsor* came down when the administration announced that in administering federal programs it would abide by the "place of ceremony" rule, not the "place of residence" rule. It would seem, however, that couples not fully "married" (civil unions, domestic partnerships) may not be so protected. And of course the decision has no bearing on those same-sex couples who wish to marry and would do so but for the refusal of their states to recognize such unions. We come then to the case that might have addressed that matter, *Hollingsworth v. Perry*.

Hollingsworth v. Perry and Beyond

Faced with a Gordian Knot—squaring federalism's differing marital arrangements with the Fifth Amendment's equal protection principle—Justice Kennedy unraveled it for the moment, at least, by employing federalism as his foundational principle: Federalism, coupled with equal protection, comes to the aid of married same-sex couples in states that recognize such unions. But that same principle, federalism, stands in the path of those whose states do not recognize, or outright disallow, same-sex marriage—presently, the majority of our states. For couples in those states, relief will be found, if it is to be found, only under the Fourteenth Amendment.

Unfortunately, but perhaps understandably, the case that might have unraveled the knot completely, *Hollingsworth v. Perry*, did not do so, doubtless because it would have come with a high political price. Given that looming price, the opinion for the Court's unusual majority was written, not surprisingly, by Chief Justice Roberts. A case with surpassing procedural twists, it concerned California's Proposition 8, which amended the state's constitution to define marriage as a union between a man and a woman. After state officials declined to appeal a federal district court decision overturning the measure on due process and equal protection grounds, proponents of the measure stepped in to defend it. But Roberts held that they lacked standing to do so, having suffered no concrete and particularized injury as required under federal standing law—even though the California Supreme Court had ruled that they had sufficient standing under state law to defend the state constitutional amendment. Thus, the district court opinion stands, making same-sex marriage legal in California under a prior state Supreme Court decision.

Justice Kennedy dissented from the Court's standing decision, joined by Justices Thomas, Samuel Alito, and Sonia Sotomayor, noting among much else that the primary purpose of initiatives like Proposition 8 is "to afford the people the ability to propose and to adopt constitutional amendments or statutory provisions that their elected public officials had refused or declined to adopt," and that "this purpose is undermined if the very officials the initiative process seeks to circumvent are the only parties who can defend an enacted initiative when it is challenged in a legal proceeding." Indeed, "the Court insists upon litigation conducted by state officials whose preference is to lose the case," he later added.

Notwithstanding the Constitution's Case or Controversy Clause from which the Court's standing jurisprudence flows, this is no black-letter law. When the Court wants to duck, or step into, a controversy, it can find reasons to do so. Thus, in 1967 in *Loving v. Virginia*, a case not unrelated to *Perry*, the Court ruled anti-miscegenation laws existing at the time in 16 states unconstitutional on due process and equal protection grounds. But 12 years earlier, seeing the resistance its *Brown v. Board of Education* ruling the year before had generated, the Court declined even to hear *Naim v. Naim,* a case on all fours, practically, with *Loving.* All of which raises the question of whether, in cases like *Perry,* federal standing law ought to allow petitioners like these their day in Court, especially since "the State's interest," on which Roberts repeatedly fastened, can hardly be said to be represented here by state officials. Referendum and initiative proceedings, presently available in 27 states, bring to the fore our basic theory of political legitimacy—that the people are the ultimate source of authority. In *Perry,* the "state's interests" just are those of the people, the majority of whom voted for the proposition before the Court.

That still leaves open, of course, the question of whether the people of a state may engage such processes for ends or in ways prohibited by the *federal* Constitution, the supreme law of the land. And on that question here, setting aside the procedural irregularities that many found in the federal district court proceedings, that court got it right, I submit, when it found that Proposition 8 violated the Fourteenth Amendment's liberty and equal protection principles. The decision leads, however, to the more fundamental question raised above in *Fisher:* Why is government involved in marriage at all?

To be sure, the state has an interest in the well being of children. But that's a derivative issue, not the central issue here. Marriage is essentially a contract between two (or, dare I say, more—it's already coming up) people. In a free society parties are or should be at liberty to set whatever contractual terms they wish, provided that the rights of third parties are respected. If two people of the same sex want to call their relationship a "marriage," the government—which belongs to all of us, including those two—must have a compelling reason not to recognize that contract, a reason to treat that couple differently than opposite-sex couples who call their relationship a marriage. Conventional marriage has long taken its rationale and contours from the natural-law tradition, which proscribes certain "unnatural" acts. By contrast, the natural-rights tradition—not entirely, but for the most part—defers not to "society" but to free adult individuals to determine what is "natural," even if that understanding has not always been found among natural rights thinkers.

None of this means, of course, that *any* relationship will count as a marriage: there will always be some requirements, beyond a couple's mere declaration, that will enable us to distinguish between, say, roommates and married couples—and there will always be procedural requirements. Just as our protection of religious freedom doesn't mean than anyone who declares himself a priest or a rabbi will be recognized as one for legal purposes, so too here there will be formal requirements, at least. But as in the area of protected speech, "content-based" or substantive requirements will have to be justified as reflecting more than mere disapproval—justified by the underlying theory of rights or by compelling practical considerations. Only so will individuals be treated equally. Beyond initial recognition, however, there are many other issues that will need to be addressed, especially regarding marital dissolution. For the moment, however, we await a case that will compel the Court to grasp the nettle on this threshold issue as it arises under the Fourteenth Amendment's guarantee of equal protection.

Introduction

*Ilya Shapiro**

This is the 12th volume of the *Cato Supreme Court Review*, the nation's first in-depth critique of the Supreme Court term just ended. We release this journal every year in conjunction with our annual Constitution Day symposium, about two-and-a-half months after the previous term ends and two weeks before the next one begins. We are proud of the speed with which we publish this tome—authors of articles about the last-decided cases have no more than a month to provide us full drafts—and of its accessibility, at least insofar as the Court's opinions allow. This is not a typical law review, after all, whose prolix submissions use more space for pedantic and abstruse footnotes than for article text. Instead, this is a book of articles about law intended for everyone from lawyers and judges to educated laymen and interested citizens.

And we are happy to confess our biases: We approach our subject matter from a classical Madisonian perspective, with a focus on individual liberty, property rights, and federalism, and a vision of a government of delegated, enumerated, and thus limited powers. We also try to maintain a strict separation of law and politics; just because something is good policy doesn't mean it's constitutional, and vice versa. Similarly, certain decisions must necessarily be left to the political process: We aim to be governed by laws, not lawyers, so just as a good lawyer will present all plausibly legal options to his client, a good public official will recognize that the ultimate buck stops with him.

* * *

* Senior fellow in constitutional studies, Cato Institute, and editor-in-chief, *Cato Supreme Court Review*.

Despite the fanfare regarding the Court's heated divisions over certain high-profile cases, the 2012-2013 term saw a high level of unanimity. Indeed, the term saw a relatively low (but in line with recent years) number of dissents, whether that's due to Chief Justice John Roberts's oft-stated desire for the Court to speak more often with one voice, a spate of lower-court intransigence, or something else. Of the 78 cases with decisions on the merits—75 after argument and 3 summary reversals—38 had no dissenters (49 percent, the highest percentage since 2002-2003) and 4 had only one dissenter (5 percent).[1] That means that more than half of the opinions went 8-1 or better, in line with the previous three terms' 55, 61, and 56 percent, respectively. And there were only 52 total dissenting opinions, the lowest in modern history save for those last three years (48, 47, 51). While some commentators accuse the Court of certain biases—most notably of being "pro-business," which alas differs from a pro-market skew—to the extent that's the case, the entire Court is guilty of it, not just the "conservative" coterie.

At the same time, 23 cases went 5-4 (29 percent, the highest percentage since 2008-2009), including the rulings striking down Section 4 of the Voting Rights Act (*Shelby County v. Holder*) and Section 3 of the Defense of Marriage Act (*United States v. Windsor*), and dismissing the Proposition 8 appeal on standing grounds (*Hollingsworth v. Perry*). This means that 78 percent of judgments were either 9-0 or 5-4, significantly higher than the 65 percent average of the previous four terms. In other words, the Court is of one mind on most issues—including significant rulings against outlandish assertions of federal power—but hopelessly split on culture-war and civil-rights issues, as well as certain types of criminal-procedure cases that produce heterodox but consistent divisions.

The Supreme Court reversed or vacated 56 lower-court opinions (72 percent), which is slightly higher than, but in line with, recent years. Following another trend, the total number of opinions (majority, concurring, dissenting) was historically low—169, surpassing only last year's 161, which came from two fewer cases—and the average of 2.17 opinions per case was down from an average of

---

[1] These figures include one 8-0 case and two 7-1 cases. All statistics taken from Kedar Bhatia, October Term 2012 Summary Memo, SCOTUSblog, Jun. 29, 2013, http://www.scotusblog.com/2013/06/october-term-2012-summary-memo.

2.35 over the preceding decade. And due to the low number of 8-1 or 7-1 decisions, only Justices Samuel Alito (twice), Antonin Scalia, and Ruth Bader Ginsburg wrote solo dissents. Notably, neither Chief Justice Roberts nor Justice Elena Kagan have ever written one of those during their entire tenures on the Court (eight and three terms, respectively).

Anthony Kennedy was yet again the justice most often in the majority (71 of 78 cases, or 91 percent), followed by the chief justice (86 percent). Even more significantly, Kennedy was on the winning side in 20 of the 23 5-4 decisions—10 times with the "conservatives," 6 with the "liberals," and 4 in "unconventional" alignments. The second-most winner of 5-4 cases was Justice Clarence Thomas—which may seem surprising, except that he was runner-up to Justice Kennedy each of the previous three years as well. Interestingly, Justices Alito, Kennedy, and Scalia combined to author 13 of the 23 majority opinions in the 5-4 cases, and each justice wrote at least one (which hadn't happened in recent years).

Justice Scalia took over from Justice Ginsburg as the justice most likely to dissent (22 percent of all cases and 42 percent of cases that had dissenters). He thus continued his slide down the list of winning-side justices: going in order from the 2008-2009 term, he has been second, third, fourth, fifth, and, now, dead last. This was the first time he has been in this position during the Roberts Court.

The justice pairings most likely to agree, at least in part, were Justices Ginsburg and Kagan (72 of 75 cases, or 96 percent), almost the same as Justices Sotomayor and Kagan (70 of 73 cases, or 95.9 percent). This is a curious shift from the last few years when the Scalia-Thomas and Roberts-Alito pairs traded off as most likely to agree. And given that the top four agreement pairs, and six of the top eight, consist entirely of Democratic appointees, we could be in an era of significant coherence among the Court's "liberals." Justices Ginsburg and Alito voted together less than anyone else (in only 45 of 77 cases, or 58 percent)—recall that Ginsburg orally read her dissent from two Alito opinions for 5-4 majorities on the final Monday, which apparently displeased Alito[2]—followed very closely by Justices Thomas

---

[2] See Debra Cassens Weiss, Did Alito Roll His Eyes During Ginsburg Dissent?, ABA Journal, Jun. 26, 2013, http://www.abajournal.com/news/article/did_alito_roll_his_eyes_during_ginsburg_dissent.

and Ginsburg (46 of 78, or 59 percent). What's more, three of the four pairings who were least likely to agree included Justice Alito.

The final statistics I have are more whimsical, relating to the number of questions asked at oral argument. Shockingly, Justice Sonia Sotomayor dethroned Justice Scalia as the most frequent Supreme Court talker—though not necessarily the most loquacious; Justice Stephen Breyer tends to ask the longest questions, typically consisting of winding hypotheticals—with an average of 21.6 questions per argument. That was below Scalia's 25.8 average from the last term, but still made Sotomayor the top questioner in 35 percent of cases and put her in the top three a whopping 80 percent of the time. Justice Ginsburg asked the first question most often (in 37 percent of cases), however, followed by Sotomayor (27 percent). Justice Thomas, meanwhile, continued his non-questioning ways—he last issued an interrogatory on February 22, 2006—but did break his silent streak to make a joke, apparently about his alma mater, Yale Law School.[3] Finally, regardless of Justice Sotomayor's exertions, it's safe to say that Justice Scalia remains the funniest justice, generating the most transcript notations of "[laughter]" per argument.[4]

Before turning to the *Review*, I would be remiss if I didn't say a few words about the term's biggest cases, all decided that fateful last week of June.[5] I refer of course to the cases involving racial preferences in college admissions (*Fisher v. UT-Austin*), voting rights (*Shelby County*), and same-sex marriage (*Windsor* and *Perry*).

The casual observer must have been quite confused that last week. First, the Court punted on affirmative action, making it harder to

---

[3] Tom Goldstein, Justice Thomas Speaks, SCOTUSblog, Jan. 14, 2013, http://www.scotusblog.com/2013/01/justice-thomas-speaks.

[4] See, e.g., Bruce Carton, As Usual, Justice Scalia Provokes Most Courtroom Laughter in Supreme Court's Latest Term, Legal Blog Watch, Aug. 14, 2012, http://legalblogwatch.typepad.com/legal_blog_watch/2012/08/as-usual-justice-scalia-provokes-most-laughter-in-supreme-courts-2012-term.html; Adam Liptak, So a Guy Walks Into a Bar, and Scalia Says . . . , N.Y. Times, Dec. 31, 2005, at A1.

[5] Despite the mad dash to the finish, the Court thankfully got all its opinions out without invading July—which was especially fortuitous this year because I was scheduled to (and did) leave on my honeymoon the Saturday after the last scheduled week of opinion releases. Kristin and I had gotten married three weeks earlier but, like most D.C. legal couples, waited till the end of the term to get away. See generally, Ilya Shapiro, The Framers and Love, Cato at Liberty, Jun. 17, 2013, http://www.cato.org/blog/framers-love.

use race in admissions decisions without prohibiting the practice altogether. It then struck down a key part of the Voting Rights Act—and the very next day gutted the Defense of Marriage Act. What is going on? Is the Court liberal or conservative? Is Chief Justice Roberts "playing the long game"[6] or are we living in Justice Kennedy's world?

None of the above. The theme of these cases was captured by President Barack Obama's reaction to the same-sex marriage rulings: "We are all equal under the law." If we're all equal, then we shouldn't be judged by skin color or sexual orientation, and the machinery of democracy shouldn't be gummed up by outdated racial classifications.[7] In other words, the Supreme Court is increasingly embracing the Constitution's structural and rights-based protections for individual freedom and self-governance. Not in every case and not without fits and starts, but on the whole the justices are moving in a libertarian direction.

It's therefore no coincidence that Cato's Center for Constitutional Studies is the only organization to have filed briefs supporting the winning side in each of the three big issues (or that we went 15-3 on the year).[8] Even beyond racial preferences and gay rights, this Court is coming to be defined by what Justice Kennedy has called "equal liberty."

Part of that is Justice Kennedy himself, the swing vote ever since Justice Sandra Day O'Connor retired in 2006. Kennedy was appointed by a Republican president, of course, but his jurisprudence is about as libertarian as we've had on the Court since before the New Deal. How else do you reconcile his votes in hot-button cases ranging from presidential wartime powers to social issues to campaign finance?

Kennedy often frustrates legal scholars, but it's not fair to say that he lacks a coherent legal theory. He's a strong federalist who believes

---

[6] See, e.g., Adam Liptak, Roberts Pulls Supreme Court to the Right, Step by Step, N.Y. Times, Jun. 26, 2013, at A1.

[7] For more on this equal protection theme, see Roger Pilon, Foreword, 2012-2013 Cato Sup. Ct. Rev. i (2013).

[8] I don't count *Perry* in either column. While we ended up with a favorable result—Prop 8 struck down—the Court decided the case on standing grounds, incorrectly in my view, rather than on the constitutional merits. See Ilya Shapiro, A Great Year for Cato at the Supreme Court, Cato at Liberty, Jun. 27, 2013, http://www.cato.org/blog/great-year-cato-supreme-court.

in the inherent dignity of the individual—and that constitutional structures protect that personal liberty. Hence his emotional reading of both the joint dissent in the Obamacare case last year and the majority opinion in the DOMA case now.

But it's more than just Kennedy's vote in 5-4 rulings or any other idiosyncrasies among the justices. Again invoking President Obama's political tropes, to appreciate the Supreme Court dynamic you have to transcend the old ideological divisions and reject the "false choice" between liberal and conservative. Instead, to understand this brave new Court you have to know that it doesn't rule in a vacuum but rather on the laws and government actions that come before it.

Of late, many of the Court's cases involve appeals of restrictions on various freedoms or expansive claims of federal authority. Accordingly, the Court unanimously reversed lower courts on criminal law, environmental regulation, class actions, and more. And the government won fewer than 40 percent of its cases this year—down from a historic norm of 70 percent—including unanimous losses on issues including property rights, securities regulation, tax law, and administrative procedure.

Moreover, most laws have some defect, constitutional or otherwise, and government officials often err in applying them. Prosecutors are overzealous, regulators and bureaucrats overreach, and the Department of Justice pushes the envelope in its legal arguments. The more that these issues are presented to the Court, the more the Court will strike down laws and official actions, thus enhancing its libertarian quotient.

With the term's "big three" cases, the real surprise should be that most people find themselves on opposite sides of the affirmative action (or voting rights) and gay marriage debates. The Constitution is quite clear in its protection of "due process" and "equal protection" of the laws, which means that the government has to treat people fairly and equally. There is thus no justification for a public university to vary admissions standards based on race—much less, as the University of Texas does, to defend preferences for Hispanics by pointing to the need for a "critical mass" of such students, even as it discriminates against Asians, who comprise a smaller part of the student body.

Similarly, while it would be best for the government to get out of the marriage business altogether—and let churches and other private organizations celebrate the institution however they like—if there is to be civil marriage, at the very least the federal government should recognize the lawful marriages that states do.

This year, the Supreme Court vindicated these ideas. We may thus be living the Court's "libertarian moment."

* * *

Turning to the *Review*, the volume begins as always with the previous year's B. Kenneth Simon Lecture in Constitutional Thought, which in 2012 was delivered by former solicitor general Paul Clement and focused on the "constitutional moment" that was the legal challenge to Obamacare. Clement appears frequently before the Court—I joke that I make a living commenting and filing briefs on his docket—and this year was no exception, though he took a rare position opposite Cato to defend DOMA. Last year, however, was his real star turn, when he represented the 26 states suing the federal government in what eventually became *NFIB v. Sebelius*. Clement quickly realized that to win he would have to "run the table" on the five Republican-appointed justices, getting their votes on each of the Commerce Clause, Necessary and Proper Clause, and taxing power arguments. "The good news from the perspective of my clients is that we received 14 out of a possible 15 votes," he comments wryly. While many observers lament the tragedy that Chief Justice Roberts brought on the country by rewriting the law in order to save it, Clement finds a silver lining: Given the five votes against the individual mandate as a mandate, and the seven votes against the coercive expansion of Medicaid, "the long struggle to define the proper balance of power between the federal and state governments—and the judiciary's role in enforcing that balance—will continue."

We move then to the 2012-2013 term, starting with four articles on those hot-button cases that were decided the last week of June. Will Consovoy and Tom McCarthy, partners at Wiley Rein who were among the lawyers who represented Shelby County, Alabama in its challenge to the Voting Rights Act, describe the Court's ruling in the case as a "restoration of constitutional order." By that they mean that throwing out the VRA's outdated "coverage formula" (Section 4(b)) recognizes the reality that, thankfully, America has changed since the systemic racial disenfranchisement of the 1960s justified the constitutional deviation of effectively putting certain states under federal electoral receivership. Moreover, Attorney General Eric Holder's aggressive use of other VRA provisions against jurisdictions that the Justice Department thinks are violating minority voting rights "may prove the points Shelby County was making all along: the emergency necessitating preclearance has passed; traditional litigation remedies can address the vestiges of discrimination that Congress targeted in 2006; and the places where these problems are most prominent are not concentrated in the jurisdictions that used discriminatory tests or devices in 1964, 1968, and 1972."

Next, University of San Diego law professor Gail Heriot, also a member of the U.S. Commission on Civil Rights, writes about *Fisher v. University of Texas at Austin*, the affirmative action case that ended in a bit of a fizzle. We may never know why it took the Supreme Court eight-and-a-half months to come up with a 13-page, near-unanimous ruling, but Heriot puts the case into its proper historical place: "By demanding that in the future a college or university supply 'a reasoned, principled explanation' for its diversity goal and directing courts to use tough-minded strict scrutiny in determining whether its admissions policy is narrowly tailored to achieve that goal, the Court inched the country toward a more sensible vision of the Constitution's requirements in the higher education context." As social scientists increasingly establish that racial preferences don't even benefit the people getting them—because of a phenomenon known as "mismatch"—we may see *Fisher* as their high-water mark.

Our first of two articles on the same-sex marriage cases—really just on the DOMA case, *Windsor*, because the Prop 8 case, *Perry*, ended up being about standing and civil procedure—features Elizabeth Wydra, chief counsel at the Constitutional Accountability Center. Cato and CAC don't always agree on the law, but when we do, it's the most interesting brief in the world (perhaps you've seen the graphic our crack new-media team put together). In any event, here Wydra provides a humanizing background to the case before engaging each of the opinions. "Perhaps most important for advocates of marriage equality," she writes, "the majority's opinion recognizes that the 'States' interest in defining and regulating the marital relation' is 'subject to constitutional guarantees.'" As to the future, I for one agree that Justice Scalia's memorable dissent will prove prophetic: whichever side of the issue you support, the Court's ruling ensures that state bans on gay marriage aren't long for this world.

The other article on *Windsor* comes to us from Duke law professor Ernie Young and Robbins Russell associate Erin Blondel, who coauthored the so-called Federalism Scholars brief (and who will be married the week this volume is released). The brief, which was joined by several law professors whose work has graced these pages, argued that DOMA's Section 3 should fall simply because the federal government has no business defining "marriage." The article is therefore sympathetic to Justice Kennedy's intertwining of federalism, liberty, and equality. Most marriage-equality advocates, Cato included, point to the Fourteenth Amendment—especially its Equal Protection Clause—to advance their cause. As Young and Blondel explain, however, "*Windsor* recognized that federalism *additionally* protects liberty and equality when federal actions threaten those rights."

Moving from federalism to international law, Ken Anderson of American University's Washington College of Law (and the *Volokh Conspiracy* blog) analyzes a case that he originally agreed to cover for last year's *Cato Supreme Court Review*. The Court set *Kiobel v. Royal Dutch Petroleum* for re-argument this term, however, so Anderson had twice the time to cover twice the number of issues. *Kiobel* was a lawsuit brought under the Alien Tort Statute by Nigerians against certain oil companies for alleged complicity with the Nigerian army in various human rights abuses. There were two issues in play: (1) whether the ATS—one of our nation's oldest laws, dating to the first Congress and covering violations of the "law of nations"—recognizes *corporate* liability (as opposed to, say, individual pirates); and (2) whether the ATS can even apply to a suit between foreigners over foreign activities. The Court unanimously answered in the negative on the second question, albeit for two different reasons, and called it a day. Anderson explains the ruling and puts it into its proper context regarding liberty, sovereignty, and civil procedure.

Next we have Dan Epps, a new Climenko Fellow at Harvard Law School, writing on a fascinating criminal procedure case, *Bailey v. United States*. In a 1981 case called *Michigan v. Summers*, the Supreme Court ruled that police can detain the occupants of a premises being searched pursuant to a lawful search warrant. This is an exception to the Fourth Amendment's general prohibition on detentions (not just formal arrests) without probable cause. But how far does this exception extend? In *Bailey*, the Court set a bright line: Police cannot detain people who have left the "immediate vicinity" of the searched area. Epps calls this result correct but "disappointing" because the *Summers* rule itself "is broader than necessary in light of its legitimate justifications." Nevertheless, it's a good thing that the Court "now takes the Fourth Amendment more seriously as a source of determinate legal rules, rather than as an open-minded invitation to declare what is reasonable under all the circumstances of each case."

Ilya Somin of George Mason University Law School, another "Volokh conspirator" and a new member of the *Cato Supreme Court Review* editorial board, then examines the state of the Takings Clause, which has long been like a "poor relation" in the Bill of Rights. This was a good term for property rights, and my nominal doppelganger focuses specifically on the "two steps forward" represented by *Koontz v. St. Johns River Water Management District* and *Arkansas Game & Fish Commission v. United States.* The latter was a unanimous ruling—of course a temporary flooding is subject to the same takings analysis as a permanent flooding or a temporary physical invasion—but *Koontz*, involving the conditions that can be placed on land-use permits, was a 5-4 split along ideological lines. Somin labels that division "a further sign that most liberal jurists are unwilling to support anything more than extremely limited judicial enforcement of constitutional property rights." "In the long run," he laments, "no constitutional right is likely to get robust judicial protection unless there is at least some substantial bipartisan and cross-ideological consensus in favor of it."

Staying on property rights, University of Missouri law professor Josh Hawley covers the term's quirky "raisin case," which got far more media attention than a typical dispute over administrative-law remedies. *Horne v. Department of Agriculture* exemplifies the extent to which all business owners are made to suffer a needless, Rube Goldberg-style litigation process to vindicate their constitutional rights. In this case, the USDA imposed on farmers Marvin and Laura Horne a "marketing order" demanding that they turn over 47 percent of their crop, without compensation, to the Raisin Administrative Committee—a New Deal-era structure that enables the government to control raisin supply and price. A cockamamie scheme, to be sure, but the lawsuit involved whether the Hornes could even challenge the order before transferring their crop. A unanimous Court said, "of course." Hawley explains that "the mere availability of a remedy at law never renders a takings claim *premature* [because] the Takings

Clause is not fundamentally a promise to pay for certain types of property burdens. It is a limit on the government's power to impose those burdens in the first place."

Next we have two articles presenting different perspectives on an area of law that tends to divide libertarians: no, not national security, but intellectual property. This term saw two patent cases that herald the sorts of issues that the Supreme Court is likely to face in coming decades as biotechnology advances. One, *Bowman v. Monsanto*, involved ownership of successive generations of a genetically modified soybean. The Supreme Court rather easily—and unanimously—ruled that a farmer couldn't evade a patent simply by planting and harvesting patented seeds. The other, *Association for Molecular Pathology v. Myriad Genetics*, more controversially involved the patentability of two genes that cause breast cancer—not ownership of the genes in someone's body, as was widely misreported, but the ability to isolate them. The Court was again unanimous here, in a sort of "split the baby" decision, finding that no "naturally occurring" gene could be patented but that complementary DNA ("cDNA") *that is synthesized in a lab* could be.

University of Baltimore law professor Greg Dolin, who also happens to have an M.D., was concerned early in the term about the trend in Court decisions that "have been far less solicitous of patentees than those emanating from the Federal Circuit." For example, "it is precisely because the issue seemed so clear-cut that the decision to hear *Bowman* raised significant worries about the direction that the Supreme Court might take." In *Myriad*, meanwhile, the Court produced "an incoherent opinion instead of a clear exposition of patent law." In the end, however, it "could've been worse."

David Olson of Boston College Law School agrees that the Court "has not clearly stated a uniform statutory interpretation and policy rationale for what should be patentable." Rather than erring on the side of patent protections, however, as would Dolin, Olson suggests a utilitarian analysis: "Instead of trying to decide patentability for cDNA based on whether cDNA is man-made. . . . the Court should ask the simple and central question: will society on net benefit from patents on DNA and cDNA?" Overall, Olson is more upbeat than Dolin and concludes that "the Court's decisions this term should maintain conditions for the encouragement of important genetic science."

My predecessor as editor of this fine publication, the newly tenured DePaul University law professor Mark Moller, makes his triumphant return to these pages with an article on the term's biggest class-action cases. *Amgen v. Connecticut Retirement Plans & Trust Funds* involved the materiality of certain non-disclosures in a securities-fraud lawsuit, while *Comcast v. Behrend* related to the admissibility of expert evidence in an antitrust case—or, rather, whether these issues need be resolved before a class can be certified (which is the whole ballgame in these sorts of cases because of the high cost of civil litigation). Moller views these cases through the lens of the late professor Richard Nagareda's "pro law" framework, which sought to put substantive law onto the procedural bones of the class-action vehicle—such that the goal of the class-certification process becomes finding "common answers" that can drive the remaining litigation. While the Supreme Court ultimately ruled for the plaintiffs in *Amgen* and the defendants in *Comcast*, "every justice signed onto majority opinions that applied some version of the common answers test, confirming that the test is here to stay."

Andrew Grossman of Baker & Hostetler, who co-authored last year's lead article on Obamacare, returns to analyze *City of Arlington v. FCC*, one of the three cases that Cato *lost* this term. *City of Arlington* asked a sort of metaphysical question: Does an administrative agency have jurisdiction (the authority) to decide its own jurisdiction (the scope of that authority)? That may seem like an easy question, but the easy answer—no, that's for Congress to decide, through the legislation that creates and empowers the agency—is unavailable when the statutory text isn't clear regarding whether an agency is properly regulating a given object. The Court, in a split decision, decided to defer to the agencies themselves on this question, just as courts have been doing since the infamous *Chevron* decision in 1984 when evaluating the propriety of agency actions that are non-controversially *within* their jurisdiction. It was a confusing ruling, to say the least. As Grossman puts it, "the Court may, from time to time, engage in misdirection to pull rabbits out of hats, [but] this case was more like pulling a trout out of a pencil-case."

Our final article about the term just past concerns the Court's sole First Amendment case—which is quite a change given that last year we had four articles in this area. My one-time debate opponent, Charles "Rocky" Rhodes of the South Texas College of Law, ably handles *Agency for International Development v. Alliance for Open Society International*, whose mouthful of a title belies the relatively simple issue at its heart: What kinds of conditions can the government attach to federal funds? Here, as part of a program to combat HIV/AIDS, the federal government required its contractors to adopt a policy opposing prostitution. Several funding recipients sued, claiming that this requirement constituted compelled speech that had nothing to do with the purpose of the government program. The Supreme Court agreed. "While the government may impose limits on its grants to ensure that the funds are used appropriately," Rhodes explains, "such limits can't regulate a private entity's speech outside the funded project."

The volume concludes with a look ahead to October Term 2013 by Howard Bashman, who has his own appellate boutique in suburban Philadelphia and authors one of the oldest and most popular "blawgs," *How Appealing*. The Court has already put 47 cases on its docket, perhaps in part due to the justices' desire to front-load oral argument a bit more to avoid the frenetic opinion-writing in the final weeks of June. Here are some highlights: *NLRB v. Noel Canning*, testing the validity of President Obama's recess appointments; *Schuette v. Coalition to Defend Affirmative Action*, regarding a state-constitutional ban on racial preferences in public employment, education, and contracting; *McCutcheon v. FEC*, challenging the aggregate-contribution limits in campaign-finance law; *Kaley v. United States*, on the right to counsel of choice in the context of criminal forfeiture; and *Bond v. United States*, a case on the scope of the treaty power that's making a rare return trip to the high court. Cato has filed briefs in all of those cases, as well as in several other pending certiorari petitions that, if granted, would become high-profile additions. In other words, even if, as Bashman puts it, the new term "does not yet rival the past two terms with regard to the likelihood of capturing the general public's attention"—it feels a bit like an off-year given the absence of Obamacare, gay marriage, and the like—there's still plenty for Court-watchers to watch.

* * *

This is the sixth volume of the *Cato Supreme Court Review* that I have edited, which means that I've now been responsible for half of its volumes. While certain tasks have become easier, others have grown in line with the constitutional issues raised by various government actions. There are thus many people responsible for this endeavor. I first need to thank our authors, without whom there would literally be nothing to edit or read. My gratitude also goes to my colleagues, Trevor Burrus, Bob Levy, Tim Lynch, and Walter Olson, who continue to provide valuable counsel and editing in areas of law with which I'm less familiar. Research assistant Jonathan Blanks makes all of us look good and, most importantly, keeps track of legal associates Lauren Barlow, Julio Colomba, Elisabeth Gusfa, and Gabriel Latner—plus summer associates Zöe O'Herin and Lindsay Short, and legal interns Zachary Politis and Stephen Richer—who in turn performed the more thankless tasks without complaint. Neither the *Review* nor our Constitution Day symposium would be what they are without them.

Finally, thanks to Roger Pilon, the founder of Cato's Center for Constitutional Studies, who I hope is pleased with how this journal has turned out so many years after he conceived it. Roger has advanced liberty and constitutionalism for longer than I've been alive, and I've benefited greatly from the high standard of excellence he's set on those fronts.

I reiterate our hope that this collection of essays will secure and advance the Madisonian first principles of our Constitution, giving renewed voice to the Framers' fervent wish that we have a government of laws and not of men. In so doing, we hope also to do justice to a rich legal tradition in which judges, politicians, and ordinary citizens alike understand that the Constitution reflects and protects the natural rights of life, liberty, and property, and serves as a bulwark against the abuse of government power. In these heady times when the People are beginning to demand an end to unconstitutional government actions and expansions of various kinds, it's more important than ever to remember our proud roots in the Enlightenment tradition.

We hope you enjoy this 12th volume of the *Cato Supreme Court Review*.

A Constitutional Moment?

*Paul D. Clement**

No review of the Supreme Court's October 2011 term would be complete without an extended discussion of the constitutional challenge to the president's health care law. The case dominated the term, and it captured the public's attention like few other Supreme Court cases. This essay traces the arc of the case and assesses what the Court ultimately did with it. While the public discussion has understandably focused on the Court's bottom-line decision to leave the law largely standing, the ruling is important for both its reasoning and its modifications to the legislation that Congress passed. In the long run, however, the decision may be as significant for what the Court did *not* decide. Despite many predictions to the contrary, the Court did not embrace the broad Commerce Clause defense of the individual mandate. As a consequence, the Court's long-running struggle to enforce meaningful outer limits on Congress's power under the Commerce Clause will continue.

The Arc of the Case

The arc of the health care case that took it to the Supreme Court was quite unusual. Many great constitutional cases involving congressional statutes present themselves as major constitutional cases from the very beginning. Take, for example, the constitutional challenge to the McCain-Feingold campaign finance statute, which culminated in the Supreme Court's decision in *McConnell v. FEC*.[1] In that case, the congressional debates were largely constitutional debates, with First Amendment issues front and center. Those First Amendment

* Partner, Bancroft PLLC, and lead counsel for the 26 state plaintiffs in *National Federation of Independent Business v. Sebelius* ("NFIB"). This is an edited version of remarks delivered as the 11th annual B. Kenneth Simon Lecture in Constitutional Thought at the Cato Institute on September 19, 2011.

[1] McConnell v. FEC, 540 U.S. 93 (2003).

issues were taken very seriously from the outset. Indeed, the statute itself recognized the imminence of a First Amendment challenge with a provision for expedited review.

The trajectory of the health care cases was entirely different. While the health care legislation was hotly debated in Congress, it was a political and policy debate, not a constitutional one. Even though legislators challenged the wisdom of the individual mandate, constitutional concerns were not raised until the very end of the debate and were neither central to the debate nor taken particularly seriously.

Moreover, when a number of challengers filed suit, attacking the law as unconstitutional, the suits were nearly universally dismissed as frivolous. They were seen more as a continuation of the policy debate and treated more as political statements than serious constitutional cases with a realistic prospect of success. Even Orin Kerr of the *Volokh Conspiracy*, a relatively sympathetic commentator, gave the suits only a one percent chance of success.[2]

But all of that changed when Judge Henry Hudson issued an opinion striking down the individual mandate as unconstitutional.[3] Then in relatively short order, Judge Roger Vinson did Judge Hudson one better when he struck down the health care law in its entirety.[4] Other challenges were unsuccessful.[5] But then something pernicious started happening: Commentators could not help but notice that the judges striking down the statute as unconstitutional were appointed by Republican presidents while those upholding the law were appointed by Democratic presidents. Much of the coverage of the decisions focused on that disparity, and with a seemingly unprecedented number of people paying attention, such reportage could not help but breed a certain cynicism and a belief that judging is simply politics by other means.

---

[2] Orin Kerr, What Are the Chances That the Courts Will Strike Down the Individual Mandate?, Volokh Conspiracy, Mar. 22, 2010, http://www.volokh.com/2010/03/22/what-are-the-chances-that-the-courts-will-strike-down-the-individual-mandate.

[3] See Virginia v. Sebelius, 728 F. Supp. 2d 768 (E.D. Va. 2010).

[4] Florida v. U.S. Dep't. of Health & Human Servs., 780 F. Supp. 2d 1256 (N.D. Fla. 2011).

[5] See, e.g., Liberty Univ., Inc. v. Geithner, 753 F. Supp. 2d 611 (W.D. Va. 2010); Thomas More Law Ctr. v. Obama, 720 F. Supp. 2d 882 (E.D. Mich. 2010).

Fortunately, the next stage of the trajectory was at the courts of appeals, and the results necessitated a more nuanced narrative. A number of prominent appellate court judges appointed by Republican presidents, such as Laurence Silberman of the D.C. Circuit and Jeffrey Sutton of the Sixth Circuit, voted to uphold the statute. At roughly the same time, Judge Frank Hull, an appointee of President Clinton, was one of two Eleventh Circuit judges to strike down the law in the challenge brought by Florida and a growing number of states. Wholly apart from the merits of the various decisions, this more complicated pattern of judicial decisions had the happy by-product of forcing a more nuanced discussion of the relationship between judicial philosophy and the political party of an appointing president.

Then, something truly remarkable occurred. The Supreme Court decided to grant review of these cases. That much was expected. What was remarkable was not the bare fact that the Court granted review, but the nature and extent of that review. The Court granted the government's petition seeking review of the Eleventh Circuit's decision striking down the individual mandate as unconstitutional. That was all but a foregone conclusion. When a court of appeals invalidates an act of Congress and the solicitor general files a petition, the Supreme Court's review is essentially guaranteed. But the Supreme Court not only granted the government's petition, but also granted separate petitions filed by the states and the private plaintiffs (the National Federation of Independent Business and two individuals) seeking review of the severability question—the question of what would become of the remainder of the statute if the individual mandate were invalidated—and the states' request that the Court consider its challenge to the Medicaid expansion as exceeding the scope of Congress's spending power. The Court's interest in that last issue, in particular, caught commentators by surprise, as the lower courts had dismissed the spending power issue even as they had invalidated the individual mandate.

The Court did not stop there, however. It also accepted the parties' invitation to consider the jurisdictional issue—the federal tax Anti-Injunction Act[6]—that the Fourth Circuit had relied on when it vacated Judge Hudson's decision and dismissed that constitutional

---

[6] 26 U.S.C. § 7421(a).

challenge as unripe.[7] The Court appointed two amici—one to argue for a lack of jurisdiction (essentially to defend the Fourth Circuit's reasoning) and another to defend the Eleventh Circuit's specific severability holding (namely, that if the individual mandate is unconstitutional, the remainder of the statute can remain fully operative). And, most dramatically of all, the Court on its own motion divided the case into four separate arguments—jurisdiction, the mandate, severability, and the Medicaid expansion—and allocated an entire week of argument to the case. The Court initially granted five-and-a-half hours of argument time, which was later expanded to six, to be spread over three days in the second week of its March sitting.

Granting this amount of argument time was unprecedented in the modern era. To put this in perspective, when *McConnell v. FEC* came to the Court, I was involved in the process of formulating the request for argument time. *McConnell* was a sprawling case, involving almost a dozen consolidated challenges, more than a dozen separate constitutional issues, and a lower court opinion that spanned more than a thousand pages. The parties consulted and came up with what they collectively reasoned was the maximum amount of argument time that they could possibly request from the Court: a relatively paltry four hours on a single day. Although one or two commentators still refused to take the constitutional challenge to the health care law seriously, it was crystal clear that the Supreme Court itself was taking the case very seriously indeed.

My personal involvement in the case had a trajectory of its own. I was not present at the creation of these challenges and had no direct role in the district court proceedings. I certainly paid attention when the suit was filed, but was busy with other matters. Thus, when asked about the cases during a National Public Radio program focused on a different topic, my response was tentative. My co-panelist, Walter Dellinger, had studied the cases more closely and had already filed an amicus brief, so he was in a position to predict victory with confidence, suggesting that only Justice Clarence Thomas would accept the challengers' Commerce Clause arguments. Since I had not studied the materials closely, I could only offer a lesson I had learned while defending statutes against constitutional attack during my time in the solicitor general's office: the importance of

[7] Virginia v. Sebelius, 656 F.3d 253 (4th Cir. 2011).

a limiting principle. All nine justices agree that Congress's power under the Commerce Clause is not plenary; thus, if the government asserts a broad conception of Congress's commerce power, it must articulate a clear limiting principle. If Congress can do this, what can it not do?

I became directly involved in the challenge brought by Florida and ultimately 25 other states when the case reached the court of appeals.[8] Even though they were successful in the trial court, the steering committee directing the litigation viewed Supreme Court review as inevitable and so wanted to bring a Supreme Court litigator on board for the appellate briefing and argument. I was less sure that the Eleventh Circuit case was destined for the Supreme Court; there were at least three other circuit court cases that were potential vehicles for Supreme Court review, and some of them were further along in the process of briefing and argument. Still, I was honored to have the chance to represent more than half the states in a case of this magnitude. I argued the case in the Eleventh Circuit. When that Court struck down the individual mandate and then the solicitor general decided to seek Supreme Court, rather than en banc, review of that decision, I knew Supreme Court review was all but guaranteed. Nonetheless, I marveled, along with everyone else, when the Court dedicated a full week to the argument.

The Challengers' Daunting Task

Although the Supreme Court divided the case into four separate arguments, that actually understates the number of issues. In reality, this one case involved six separate issues of surpassing importance. The first day's argument focused on the single issue of jurisdiction concerning the Anti-Injunction Act, a relatively obscure federal statute dating back to the Reconstruction era, which provides that most constitutional challenges to federal taxes must wait until the taxpayer has paid the tax and sought a refund. Fortunately, the Supreme Court unanimously rejected any jurisdictional concerns because Congress had not denominated the mandate as a tax.

The Court dedicated the second day's arguments to what we took to be the heart of the matter, the constitutionality of the individual mandate. But this issue was really three issues in one since

---

[8] Another two states, Virginia and Oklahoma, pursued their own separate challenges.

the government had three independent arguments for the mandate's constitutionality. The government's principal defense—and the issue that dominated discussion of the case both inside and outside the courtroom—depended on the Commerce Clause. But the government also defended the mandate as valid legislation under the Necessary and Proper Clause and as a valid exercise of Congress's taxing power.

Each of these three constitutional arguments provided an independent basis for upholding the statute. Thus, the challengers' task was daunting: they needed to prevail on all three issues. Worse still, past decisions gave strong indications that four justices—Justices Ruth Bader Ginsburg, Stephen Breyer, Sonia Sotomayor, and Elena Kagan—would not be receptive to arguments that the mandate was unconstitutional. Thus, the challenge facing the states and the private plaintiffs was to convince the five other justices who might be amenable to a constitutional challenge on all three issues. In short, the challengers had to run the table and get 15 of a possible 15 votes to prevail.

The good news from the perspective of my clients is that we received 14 out of a possible 15 votes. The bad news is that we needed that 15th vote. Despite repeated suggestions that the challengers' commerce power arguments would appeal only to Justice Thomas, five justices concluded that the mandate was not valid Commerce Clause legislation. The same five justices concluded that the Necessary and Proper Clause did not save the mandate. Nonetheless, the challengers lacked the fifth vote when it came to the taxing power.

The Individual Mandate Was Held Unconstitutional

Although the challengers fell short of a fifth vote on the taxing power question, that does not mean that the constitutionality of the individual mandate was upheld. To the contrary, despite what people read the next day in the newspapers, the Supreme Court found the individual mandate to purchase insurance or pay a penalty unconstitutional. Five justices upheld the statute only by construing the mandate as a tax and upholding it as a valid exercise of the taxing power. But five justices also held that the individual mandate that Congress actually passed could be sustained only under the Commerce Clause or Necessary and Proper Clause. And yet those congressional powers were insufficient, they held, to justify the unprecedented individual mandate. For those skeptical of this reading of the Court's opinion, do not take my word for it. The chief justice's opinion makes this distinction quite clear.

Chief Justice John Roberts emphasized that the government's taxing power argument required the Court to read the statute in a fundamentally different way from its Commerce and Necessary and Proper Clause arguments.

> The Government's tax power argument asks us to view the statute differently than we did in considering its commerce power theory. In making its Commerce Clause argument, the Government defended the mandate as a regulation requiring individuals to purchase health care insurance. The government does not claim that the taxing power allows Congress to issue such a command. Instead, the Government asks us to read the mandate not as ordering individuals to buy insurance, but rather as imposing a tax on those who do not buy the product.[9]

The chief justice then reiterated the point that the taxing power was not just an alternative ground for defending the mandate as written, but rather required a fundamentally different conception and construction of the statute. "Under [the tax] theory, the mandate is not a legal command to buy insurance."[10] Rather, it is "just a tax hike on certain taxpayers who do not have health insurance."[11]

The chief justice also readily admitted that construing the mandate as a tax on the uninsured was not the most straightforward reading of the statute. Instead, "[t]he most straightforward reading of the mandate is that it commands individuals to purchase insurance."[12] Indeed, the belief that the mandate was *not* most naturally read as a tax on the uninsured—as opposed to a mandate to purchase insurance—was integral to the chief justice's opinion in general and to his willingness to address the Commerce Clause and Necessary and Proper Clause in particular. This key point is seen most clearly in his response to Justice Ginsburg's separate opinion. Justice Ginsburg pointedly criticized the chief justice for addressing the Commerce Clause and Necessary and Proper Clause argu-

[9] NFIB v. Sebelius, 132 S. Ct. 2566, 2593 (2012) (opinion of Roberts, C.J.).

[10] *Id.* at 2594.

[11] *Id.*

[12] *Id.* at 2573.

ments at all. She essentially told the chief justice—and here I am only paraphrasing—you like to talk about judicial restraint, but the judicially restrained approach is not to unnecessarily address constitutional issues, so if the mandate is valid under the taxing power, you have no business addressing the other two issues. The chief justice responded directly to this criticism by saying that "the statute reads more naturally as a command to buy insurance than as a tax, and I would uphold it as a command if the Constitution allowed it."[13] In other words, the chief justice viewed his first responsibility as addressing the constitutionality of the statute that Congress actually passed, and only upon finding it impossible to sustain the mandate qua mandate did he find it appropriate to consider whether the statute could be construed in an alternative matter such that it could be sustained under the taxing power.

In the end, the chief justice left little doubt about the difference between the unconstitutional mandate Congress actually enacted and the tax that he sustained. "The federal government does not have the power to order people to buy health insurance."[14] By contrast, "[t]he federal government does have the power to impose a tax on those without health insurance."[15]

The Spending Power Holding: A Sleeper within the Blockbuster

I promised six issues, and the fifth and sixth issues were debated on the third day of arguments. The fifth issue discussed on the morning of the third day was severability, or the consequences for the balance of the statute if the individual mandate were struck down. Although the matter was hotly contested at argument, a majority of the Court never reached the issue because the mandate was recharacterized as a tax, rather than struck *in toto*. Nonetheless, the remarkable fact about the severability issue was that, in the end, four justices were willing to invalidate the statute in its entirety. The argument for total invalidation always seemed to me to be the most difficult aspect of the challengers' argument; thus, the fact that the argument for total invalidation came within a vote of total success is a testament to the centrality of the mandate to the act as a whole.

---

[13] *Id.* at 2600.
[14] *Id.* at 2601.
[15] *Id.*

The sixth issue—whether the Medicaid expansion was a valid exercise of Congress's spending power—was argued on the afternoon of the third day of argument. Although the Court granted a remarkable six hours of argument for the health care case, even that proved insufficient, as the Court kept both advocates at the podium longer than scheduled. The result of that argument was a holding that may prove more important in future cases than anything the Court said about the mandate. In the end, seven justices ruled that Congress exceeded its spending power by conditioning the states continued participation in the entirety of the Medicaid program, including preexisting aspects of the program, on a state's willingness to expand the program to cover substantially larger numbers of the uninsured. The significance of this holding lies largely in the fact that it stands as the first case in which the Court has actually applied the "coercion limit" on the spending power that it had suggested in dicta in earlier cases.

The chief justice's reasoning on the spending power emphasized a key component of the Court's federalism jurisprudence—namely, accountability. "Permitting the Federal Government to force states to implement a federal program would threaten the political accountability key to our federal system."[16] If states are implementing federal programs not based on a voluntary choice for which state citizens can justly hold them accountable, but through the compulsion of the federal government, then state citizens may improperly blame the states for policies that are really the exclusive responsibility of the national government.

The key defect in the Medicaid expansion was Congress's decision to leverage funds for the existing Medicaid program (and states' dependency on those funds) to coerce the states' acceptance of the new funds with the new conditions. "When, for example, such conditions take the form of threats to terminate other significant independent grants, the conditions are properly viewed as a means of pressuring the states to accept policy changes."[17] Congress would have been free to create a separate program that gave states a choice to accept the new funds and the new conditions, but it could not hold the existing program—which Congress itself treated as separate for other

[16] *Id.* at 2602.
[17] *Id.* at 2604.

purposes, such as the degree of federal funding—hostage to this new program such that the consequence of refusing to participate in the new program was the inability to continue to participate in the old one. "What Congress is not free to do is to penalize states that chose not to participate in that new program by taking away their existing Medicaid funding."[18]

In light of the Court's reasoning, the consequence of this spending power defect was to decouple the new and old funding streams and to make clear that states would not forfeit their ability to participate in Medicaid if they refused to expand their programs along the lines envisioned by the new law. The undramatic remedial consequences of the Court's determination have obscured some of the ruling's significance. But there is no mistaking the fact that the Court held this aspect of the law unconstitutional. "We determine . . . that § 1396c is unconstitutional when applied to withdraw existing Medicaid funds from States that decline to comply with the expansion."[19]

Practical Consequences of Court's Partial Invalidation

In the wake of the oral argument, a number of commentators concluded that the entirety of the health care law was in peril. Not only did the Court appear to take the argument about the individual mandate and spending power quite seriously, but the severability argument did not have the feel of an academic debate. Thus, when a majority of the Court upheld the vast majority of the statute, much of the reaction understandably focused on what the Court did not do and did not invalidate. But there is certainly the potential for there to be significant practical consequences of what the Court did do and did invalidate.

The simple fact is that the statute that emerged from the Supreme Court is not the statute that Congress actually passed. Not only has the mandate been converted into a tax, but states now have a choice about whether to participate in the Medicaid expansion. Indeed, both rulings allow choice where Congress imposed a mandate. And choices have consequences. Although it is too early to tell how many individuals will opt to pay a weakly enforced tax rather than purchase health care insurance and how many states will choose not to expand Medicaid, these choices operate in only one direction,

18 *Id.* at 2607.
19 *Id.*

namely, in the direction of leaving fewer individuals with health insurance than Congress envisioned when it enacted the statute. Indeed, the chief justice for his part affirmatively recognized that some individuals would not buy health insurance as a result of his decision. "It may often be a reasonable financial decision to make the payment rather than purchase insurance."[20] And a majority of the states have since indicated that they will not participate in the Medicaid expansion.

Thus, there is no doubting that, relative to what Congress envisioned, millions fewer individuals will be insured in light of the Court's decision, and the statute will not operate as Congress intended. That, in turn, may well cause Congress to reopen the debate over health care, and if the statute is reopened, it is anyone's guess as to what will ensue. In sum, the practical consequences of the Court's decision should not be underestimated.

Jurisprudential Consequences: A Constitutional Moment That Wasn't

Whatever the practical consequences of the Court's decision, the jurisprudential consequences are even more significant. Although the focus has been on the significance of the Court's decision to substantially uphold the statute, the jurisprudential consequences of the Court's refusal to endorse Congress's power to enact the statute as written are at least as significant. If the Court had endorsed the statute as passed, it would have largely signaled the end of the Court's federalism jurisprudence—one of the signal doctrinal achievements of the Rehnquist Court. Thus, in many respects, the significance of the Court's decision lies in the constitutional moment that wasn't and the fact that the Court's federalism jurisprudence remains alive and well.

As Justice Anthony Kennedy has observed, "federalism was the unique contribution of the Framers to political science and political theory. Though on the surface the idea may seem counterintuitive, it was the insight of the Framers that freedom was enhanced by the creation of two governments, not one."[21] The Court's decisions in

---

[20] *Id.* at 2595.

[21] United States v. Lopez, 514 U.S. 549, 575–76 (1995) (Kennedy, J., concurring) (citations omitted).

Lopez and *United States v. Morrison*,[22] invalidating acts of Congress as exceeding Congress's commerce power, and other decisions invoking the Eleventh Amendment to preclude damage actions against the states, were signal achievements of the Rehnquist Court. Yet in the last years of Chief Justice William Rehnquist's tenure, the so-called federalism revolution appeared to be running out of steam, with the late chief justice in dissent in cases upholding congressional power like *Gonzales v. Raich* and *Tennessee v. Lane*.[23]

Nor was it foreordained that the new appointees of President George W. Bush would have the same enthusiasm for federalism as the justices they replaced. While Chief Justice Rehnquist and especially Justice Sandra Day O'Connor cut their teeth in the state courts and in state politics, both Chief Justice Roberts and Justice Samuel Alito had their formative experiences in the executive branch of the federal government. Thus, there was a palpable sense in some circles that the health care case could be the swan song for the federalism revival.

Such considerations certainly produced bold predictions of 8–1 victories for the federal government across the board, particularly when it came to the Commerce Clause challenge. While commentators were willing to concede that Justice Thomas would endorse the challenge, even Justice Antonin Scalia's vote was widely perceived to be "in play." Well after the Supreme Court signaled its own view of the seriousness of the issues by granting unprecedented argument time, commentators were still dismissive of the constitutional case against the statute. Linda Greenhouse's *New York Times* pre-argument commentary provides an example:

> Free of convention, and fresh from reading the main briefs in the case to be argued before the Supreme Court next week, I'm here to tell you: that belief [that both sides have weighty views to present to the Court] is simply wrong. The constitutional challenge to the law's requirement for people to buy health insurance—specifically, the argument that the mandate exceeds Congress's power under the Commerce Clause—is rhetorically powerful but analytically so weak that it dissolves on close inspection. There's just no there there.[24]

[22] United States v. Morrison, 529 U.S. 598 (2000).

[23] Gonzales v. Raich, 545 U.S. 1 (2005); Tennessee v. Lane, 541 U.S. 509 (2004).

[24] Linda Greenhouse, Never Before, N.Y. Times Opinionator Blog, Mar. 21, 2012, http://opinionator.blogs.nytimes.com/2012/03/21/never-before.

My point is not to call out anyone who incorrectly predicted the outcome. After all, literally no one predicted the actual outcome, including the chief justice's taxing power ruling and the 7–2 vote on the spending power. My point rather is to emphasize that there was a substantial body of very reputable opinion that believed that the commerce and spending power challenges were not just narrowly wrong, but entirely frivolous. As the ever-quotable Walter Dellinger told *Politico* on the eve of argument: "You know how they say, 'People were saying it's frivolous, and they're not saying that anymore'? Well, I'm still saying it's frivolous."[25]

Thus, my point is that if that view had prevailed, then we would really have had a constitutional moment on our hands. The long struggle to enforce judicial limits on the Commerce Clause would largely have ended. Five justices declined to let that happen. As Justice Kennedy wrote in his *Lopez* concurrence, "the federal balance is too essential a part of our constitutional structure and plays too vital a role in securing freedom for us to admit inability to intervene when one or the other level of Government has tipped the scales too far."[26]

An Objection and a Conclusion

Allow me to consider an obvious objection to my emphasis on the importance of five justices upholding judicially enforceable limits on the Commerce and Necessary and Proper Clauses. What about the taxing power? Why do limitations on the commerce power matter if Congress can simply turn around and accomplish the same or similar thing via the taxing power? Whatever the merits of the chief justice's taxing power opinion, his decision to embrace the Commerce Clause challenge and uphold the statute only as construed as a tax differs from a straight-up endorsement of the mandate in at least three ways.

First, the difference between the two sources of power matters practically. As noted, the inevitable result of the chief justice's reliance on the tax power, as his opinion expressly recognized, is that some individuals will choose to pay a tax rather than obtain

[25] Josh Gerstein, How the Legal Assault on Obama's Health Law Went Mainstream, Politico, Mar. 25, 2012, available at http://www.politico.com/news/stories/0312/74429.html.

[26] Lopez, 514 U.S. at 578 (Kennedy, J., concurring).

qualifying health insurance.[27] As a result, more individuals will remain uninsured than under the law Congress envisioned. The exact magnitude of this practical difference will become clear only over time, but there will clearly be some practical difference.

Second, there is an important theoretical difference. The taxing power is a less complete and less sweeping power than a comparable ability to impose purchase mandates under the Commerce Clause. If the government's theory of the commerce power—that a purchase mandate has the requisite effect on interstate commerce through the aggregation of the mandated purchases—had prevailed, there would be no logical constraint on Congress's power to enforce the purchase mandate. As the chief justice recognized, even criminal penalties for failing to purchase health insurance would appear to be valid under the government's theory.[28] The taxing power, by contrast, would allow the government to impose tax consequences only for the failure to purchase health insurance.

Third, and perhaps most important, there is a critical structural difference between the two outcomes. Now that five justices have determined that a true individual mandate is not valid under either the Commerce Clause or the Necessary and Proper Clause, and that a mandate can be sustained only as a tax, all of the political checks that make enacting a "tax hike" or imposing a "new tax" difficult should be fully operable in the face of any future effort to enact another individual mandate. The consistent efforts of the president, even after the decision came down, to deny that the mandate was, in fact, a tax underscore the political difficulty and unpopularity of new taxes. To the extent the raison d'être of the mandate was to accomplish certain goals without explicitly raising taxes, a Supreme Court decision holding that a mandate can be upheld only as a tax may create an important political obstacle to future mandates.

In all events, my point in underscoring the differences between the chief justice's taxing power rationale and the government's principal theories for defending the legislation is not to defend the chief justice's rationale or to enter into the debate over whether his opinion should be viewed as a glass half-full or half-empty. Rather, my point is to emphasize that a decision that fully embraced the federal

---

[27] NFIB, 132 S. Ct. at 2601.

[28] See *id*. at 2600.

government's view of Congress's power under the Commerce Clause and the Necessary and Proper Clause would have been a truly significant constitutional moment. It would have signaled an end to one of the principal projects of the Rehnquist Court: reasserting a judicial role in enforcing limits on Congress's commerce power. The fact that five justices rejected the government's effectively plenary view of Congress's power and that seven justices asserted judicially enforceable limits on Congress's spending power means that the long struggle to define the proper balance of power between the federal and state governments—and the judiciary's role in enforcing that balance—will continue. Indeed, with cases concerning the Voting Rights Act, same-sex marriage, and the treaty power before the Court, federalism may take on, if anything, a more significant role in the immediate future.

Shelby County v. Holder:
The Restoration of Constitutional Order

*William S. Consovoy and Thomas R. McCarthy**

The Voting Rights Act of 1965 is possibly the most consequential federal law in our nation's history. Passed in the aftermath of "Bloody Sunday" and pursuant to Congress's authority to enforce the Fifteenth Amendment by "appropriate" legislation, the VRA represented a decisive federal response to the campaign of voting discrimination that had plagued the South since Reconstruction. The law included a plethora of remedies designed to root out systematic efforts to disenfranchise African Americans. Unique among them was Section 5's "preclearance" obligation, which operated against certain states and political subdivisions pursuant to Section 4(b)'s "coverage" formula. Under those provisions, jurisdictions with the worst records of discrimination could not make changes to their voting laws until the Department of Justice—or a special three-judge federal district court in Washington, D.C.—approved them. It took time and effort, but Section 5 was remarkably successful. No one should doubt that preclearance helped transform the South from a bastion of voting discrimination into a place where racial equality is an institutional priority.

At the same time, that undeniable success came at a high cost. Preclearance deviates from our constitutional order in fundamental ways. Under our system of government, states are sovereign in the field of state and local elections. Yet preclearance deprived them of the right to self-government. It is therefore difficult to overstate just how novel preclearance is. For example, the Americans with Disabilities Act prevents state and local courthouses from denying access to the handicapped.[1] But it does not require state and local

---

* The authors are attorneys at Wiley Rein LLP in Washington, D.C. They represented Shelby County, Alabama, in this case.

[1] See Tennessee v. Lane, 541 U.S. 509 (2004).

governments to "preclear" their architectural drawings with DOJ before breaking ground on a new building. Therein lies the difference. It is one thing to ban discrimination in voting. It is another to place an entire region of the country in federal receivership.

In 1966, the Supreme Court upheld Section 5, but only because Congress had shown that the emergency required special measures.[2] The Court made clear that preclearance would otherwise have been inappropriate and that two additional features ensured that this novel law would not permanently upset the division of power between the federal and state governments. First, the formula that Congress used to select those jurisdictions that would be subject to this harsh remedy made sense. It used statutory criteria that followed from the problem that Congress had identified as the chief evil: the use of discriminatory voting tests and devices to keep African Americans from voting. Second, Section 5 was temporary, a measure that would sunset after five years.

Flash forward to 2006. Section 5 is still the law; its substantive reach has expanded over time; Congress is still using the same coverage formula it did in 1965; and the law has just been reenacted for another 25 years. For places like Shelby County, Alabama, then, preclearance would remain in place until 2031 based on tests and devices that had been banned for over 40 years and voting statistics from the 1964 presidential election. But while the Supreme Court warned that Congress's decision in 2006 to reenact the preclearance obligation under that coverage formula raised grave constitutional concerns, it avoided deciding the issue in the first case to raise the question.[3] It was against this backdrop that Shelby County brought its constitutional challenge to Sections 4(b) and 5.

In a 5–4 decision, the Supreme Court ruled that Section 4(b)'s outdated formula was no longer constitutional.[4] Chief Justice John Roberts authored the majority opinion, which was joined by Justices Antonin Scalia, Anthony Kennedy, Clarence Thomas, and Samuel Alito. Without a valid formula, no jurisdiction is subject to preclearance. The majority thus declined to decide whether Section 5 itself exceeded Congress's authority given the improvements that have

---

[2] See South Carolina v. Katzenbach, 383 U.S. 301, 313 (1966).

[3] Nw. Austin Mun. Util. Dist. No. One v. Holder, 557 U.S. 193 (2009) ("NAMUDNO").

[4] Shelby County v. Holder, 133 S. Ct. 2612 (2013).

taken place since 1965. Justice Thomas, who had previously found that Section 5 was no longer constitutional, would have decided that issue once and for all. Justice Ruth Bader Ginsburg, joined by Justices Stephen Breyer, Sonia Sotomayor, and Elena Kagan, dissented. The dissenters would have upheld both challenged sections.

In deciding the case in the way it did, the Supreme Court side-stepped a contentious dispute over the standard that Congress should be held to when exercising Fourteenth or Fifteenth Amendment enforcement authority in the context of voting, afforded Congress the opportunity to go back to the drawing board to design a rational coverage formula, and, most notably, avoided deciding whether preclearance itself remained a constitutional remedy. Unless your definition of "minimalism" is judicial abdication, the Supreme Court's decision invalidating a coverage formula that not even the attorney general could bring himself to defend on its own terms was modest in every relevant sense.

It's now Congress's move. If Congress and the president can find their way to a new coverage formula that can meet the constitutional standard, the battle over Section 5's constitutionality will be joined for a third time since 2006. But perhaps those disappointed with the Supreme Court's decision and interested in pursuing that course should think twice before reinstituting the sweeping preclearance regime reenacted in 2006. "As the *Shelby County* decision shows, when the Court gives the political branches one last chance to remedy a program's constitutional defects, it is probably not bluffing."[5] Congress would be wise to reconsider whether an emergency response to rampant voting discrimination remains justifiable given the transformation our nation has seen since 1965.

In the end, Justice Ginsburg may well be right that "what's past is prologue."[6] But time marches on. President Barack Obama carried Florida, North Carolina, and Virginia. The only African-American senator is a Republican from South Carolina who was appointed by an Indian-American governor. Philadelphia, Mississippi, and Selma, Alabama, have African-American mayors. As Justice Thomas

---

[5] Jeffrey Harris, The Court Meant What It Said in Northwest Austin, SCOTUSBlog, Jun. 25, 2013, http://www.scotusblog.com/2013/06/the-court-meant-what-it-said-in-northwest-austin.

[6] Shelby County, 133 S. Ct. at 2642 (Ginsburg, J., dissenting).

eloquently put it, "Admitting that a prophylactic law as broad as § 5 is no longer constitutionally justified based on current evidence of discrimination is not a sign of defeat. It is an acknowledgment of victory."[7]

I. The Preclearance Regime: 1965–2006

A. *The Voting Rights Act of 1965*

The Fifteenth Amendment guarantees that "[t]he right of citizens of the United States to vote shall not be denied or abridged by the United States or by any State on account of race, color, or previous condition of servitude" and empowers Congress "to enforce this article by appropriate legislation."[8] Following the amendment's ratification, certain states and localities—mostly in the South—initiated a campaign to keep African Americans from voting through violence, intimidation, and discriminatory tests and devices such as literacy tests. In response, Congress passed laws to facilitate case-by-case litigation, and the Supreme Court struck down discriminatory laws and practices time and again. Yet widespread discrimination persisted, and the chances of defeating this campaign of voting interference one case at a time appeared dim. Each time a court struck down a law or practice as violating the Fifteenth Amendment, the state or local government would evade the judicial decree by shifting to a slightly different means of achieving the same discriminatory aim.

By 1965, Congress had seen quite enough and took decisive action. In response to this massive resistance, Congress passed the Voting Rights Act—sweeping legislation designed to root out the racial discrimination in voting that had "infected the electoral process in parts of our country for nearly a century."[9] The VRA created a network of federal remedies that signaled Congress's determination to ensure that African Americans could freely vote. In particular, Section 2 of the VRA created a nationwide judicial remedy against any law or practice enacted "to deny or abridge the right of any citizen of the United States to vote on account of race or color."[10] And Congress

---

[7] NAMUDNO, 557 U.S. at 226 (Thomas, J., concurring in the judgment in part and dissenting in part).

[8] U.S. Const. amend. XV, §§ 1, 2.

[9] Katzenbach, 383 U.S. at 308.

[10] Pub. L. No. 89-110, § 2, 79 Stat. 437 (1965).

later revised that provision to more broadly outlaw any law or practice that "results" in the denial of the right to vote whether or not it was the product of intentional discrimination.[11] Both the United States and private plaintiffs may bring a Section 2 action.

Other remedies operated only against certain jurisdictions with an especially egregious record of discrimination against minority voters. Two remedies in particular imposed on those "covered" jurisdictions were Section 4(a)'s suspension of discriminatory voting tests and devices and Section 5's "preclearance" requirement. Whether a state or political subdivision had a record of abuse serious enough to warrant application of these special measures was determined by a formula set forth in Section 4(b) of the VRA. Under that formula, a state or local jurisdiction became "covered" if it "maintained on November 1, 1964, any test or device" prohibited by Section 4(a) and "less than 50 per centum of the persons of voting age residing therein were registered on November 1, 1964" or "less than 50 per centum of such persons voted in the presidential election of November 1964."[12] Alabama, Alaska, Georgia, Louisiana, Mississippi, South Carolina, Virginia, and parts of Arizona, Idaho, Hawaii, and North Carolina became covered jurisdictions under this formula.[13]

Section 5 was a novel federal remedy. Unlike Section 2's right of action or Section 4(a)'s ban on tests and devices, preclearance did not target specific acts of voting discrimination. "Section 5 . . . was enacted for a different purpose: to prevent covered jurisdictions from circumventing the direct prohibitions imposed by provisions such as §§ 2 and 4(a)."[14] Section 5 accomplished this goal by requiring those "covered" jurisdictions to preclear (with either DOJ or the U.S. District Court for the District of Columbia) new or amended laws involving "any voting qualification or prerequisite to voting, or

---

[11] Pub. L. No. 97-205, § 3, 96 Stat. 134 (1982).

[12] Pub. L. No. 89-110, § 4(b), 79 Stat. at 438 (1965).

[13] Congress permitted a covered jurisdiction to "bail out" of coverage by showing that it had not used a "test or device" in the preceding five years for the purpose or with the effect of denying or abridging the right to vote on account of race, *id.* § 4(a), 79 Stat. at 438, and empowered federal courts in appropriate circumstances to "bail in" a non-covered jurisdiction that violated the Fourteenth or Fifteenth Amendment, *id.* § 3(c), 79 Stat. at 437.

[14] NAMUDNO, 557 U.S. at 218 (Thomas, J., concurring in the judgment in part and dissenting in part).

standard, practice, or procedure with respect to voting different from that in force or effect on November 1, 1964."[15] Section 5 thus went "beyond the prohibition of the Fifteenth Amendment by suspending *all* changes to state election law—however innocuous—until they have been precleared by federal authorities in Washington, D.C."[16] Congress enacted Section 5 for a period of five years.

B. *The Supreme Court Upholds Section 5's Preclearance Requirement under Section 4(b)'s Coverage Formula*

In 1966, the Supreme Court rejected South Carolina's constitutional challenge. In the Court's view, Congress had compiled "reliable evidence of actual voting discrimination in a great majority of the States and political subdivisions affected by the new remedies of the Act."[17] Indeed, the legislative record painstakingly documented the web of discriminatory practices used to deny African Americans the right to vote; statistical evidence verified the widespread impact of voting discrimination throughout the South. As the Court explained, the "registration of voting-age Negroes in Alabama rose only from 14.2% to 19.4% between 1958 and 1964; in Louisiana it barely inched ahead from 31.7% to 31.8% between 1956 and 1965; and in Mississippi it increased only from 4.4% to 6.4% between 1954 and 1964. In each instance, registration of voting-age whites ran roughly 50 percentage points or more ahead of Negro registration."[18] Moreover, "voter turnout levels in covered jurisdictions ha[d] been at least 12% below the national average in the 1964 Presidential election."[19]

The Supreme Court nevertheless recognized that preclearance was an "uncommon exercise of congressional power" and a departure from the normal course of relations between the federal government and the states.[20] Accordingly, the Court's decision to uphold the statute turned on its conclusion that: (1) Congress had compiled overwhelming evidence showing that only a sweeping prior restraint

---

[15] Pub. L. No. 89-110, § 5, 79 Stat. at 439 (1965).

[16] NAMUDNO, 557 U.S. at 202 (emphasis in original).

[17] Katzenbach, 383 U.S. at 329.

[18] *Id.* at 313.

[19] NAMUDNO, 557 U.S. at 222 (Thomas, J., concurring in the judgment in part and dissenting in part).

[20] Katzenbach, 383 U.S. at 328, 334.

like preclearance could successfully combat systematic evasion; and (2) that the formula Congress devised to select the "covered" juris-dictions was "rational in both practice and theory."[21]

As to Section 5, preclearance met the urgent need to put an end to gamesmanship in covered jurisdictions. "Congress knew that some of the States covered by §4(b) of the Act had resorted to the extraor-dinary stratagem of contriving new rules of various kinds for the sole purpose of perpetuating voting discrimination in the face of adverse federal court decrees."[22] It thus "had reason to suppose that these States might try similar maneuvers in the future in order to evade the remedies prescribed for voting discrimination contained in the Act itself."[23] Given the failure of case-by-case litigation, pre-clearance was "an appropriate means of combatting the evil."[24] "[L]egislative measures not otherwise appropriate" were constitutional under those "exceptional conditions" and "unique circumstances."[25]

As to Section 4(b), the coverage formula was rational in "theory" because it used criteria for coverage that bore a logical connection to the chief characteristics that distinguished those states and political subdivisions warranting preclearance from the rest of the country: the use of discriminatory tests and devices and the resulting low voting rates. The formula was rational in "practice" because it ac-curately captured those jurisdictions where voting discrimination was the worst.[26]

C. The 1970, 1975, and 1982 Reenactments

In 1970, Congress reenacted preclearance for five more years and amended the formula to cover any jurisdiction that had maintained a prohibited "test or device" on November 1, 1968, and had voter registration on that date or turnout in the 1968 presidential election of less than 50 percent.[27] The legislation swept in parts of Alaska, Ar-izona, California, Connecticut, Idaho, Maine, Massachusetts, New

---

[21] *Id.* at 330.

[22] *Id.* at 335.

[23] *Id.*

[24] *Id.* at 328.

[25] Katzenbach, 383 U.S. at 334, 335.

[26] *Id.* at 331.

[27] Pub. L. No. 91-285, § 4, 84 Stat. 315 (1970).

Hampshire, New York, and Wyoming. The Supreme Court upheld the reenactment.[28]

In 1975, Congress extended preclearance for another seven years and extended coverage to any jurisdiction that had maintained a prohibited "test or device" on November 1, 1972, and had voter registration on that date or turnout in the 1972 presidential election of less than 50 percent.[29] Alaska, Arizona, Texas, and parts of California, Florida, Michigan, New York, North Carolina, and South Dakota became covered.[30] In upholding this third reenactment, the Supreme Court stressed that it "was necessary to preserve the limited and fragile achievements of the Act and to promote further amelioration of voting discrimination."[31]

In 1982, Congress reenacted the preclearance regime for 25 years.[32] Congress did not amend Section 5 or Section 4(b). It did, however, alter the statute's bail-out provision to, among other things, make a "political subdivision" within a fully covered state eligible.[33] Although this reenactment was not facially challenged,[34] in the following years the Supreme Court twice interpreted Section 5 to limit the law's federalism burden by making it somewhat easier for covered jurisdictions to secure preclearance.[35]

D. The 2006 Reenactment

In 2006, Congress reenacted the VRA for another 25 years.[36] Congress found "the number of African Americans who are registered

---

[28] Georgia v. United States, 411 U.S. 526, 535 (1973).

[29] Pub. L. No. 94-73, § 202, 89 Stat. 401 (1975). Congress also amended the definition of "test or device" to include, among other things, English-only ballots, *id.*, § 203, 89 Stat. at 401–02, and it permanently banned nationwide discriminatory tests and devices, *id.*, § 201, 89 Stat. at 400.

[30] *Id.* § 201, 89 Stat. at 400.

[31] City of Rome v. United States, 446 U.S. 156, 182 (1980) (internal quotes omitted).

[32] Pub. L. No. 97-205, 96 Stat. 131 (1982).

[33] *Id.* § 2(b)(2), 96 Stat. at 131.

[34] See Lopez v. Monterey County, 525 U.S. 266 (1999).

[35] See Reno v. Bossier Parish Sch. Bd., 528 U.S. 320 (2000); Georgia v. Ashcroft, 539 U.S. 461 (2003).

[36] Fannie Lou Hamer, Rosa Parks, and Coretta Scott King Voting Rights Act Reauthorization and Amendments Act of 2006, Pub. L. No. 109-246, 120 Stat. 577 (2006) ("VRARAA").

and who turn out to cast ballots ha[d] increased significantly over the last 40 years, particularly since 1982. In some circumstances, minorities register to vote and cast ballots at levels that surpass those of white voters."[37] Congress also found that "the disparities between African-American and white citizens who are registered to vote ha[d] narrowed considerably in six southern States covered by the temporary provisions . . . and . . . North Carolina" and that "many of the first generation barriers to minority voter registration and voter turnout that were in place prior to the VRA ha[d] been eliminated."[38]

Despite these notable gains, Congress did not update the coverage formula, choosing again to base coverage on election data from 1964, 1968, and 1972. Nor did it ease the preclearance burden. Rather, Congress made the burden even more onerous by amending Section 5 to overrule the Supreme Court decisions that had made it easier for covered jurisdictions to secure preclearance.

Congress purported to justify reenactment on its finding that "vestiges of discrimination in voting continue to exist as demonstrated by second generation barriers constructed to prevent minority voters from fully participating in the electoral process."[39] It further found that evidence of "second generation" barriers could be seen in: (1) racially polarized voting; (2) Section 5 preclearance statistics; (3) "section 2 litigation filed to prevent dilutive techniques from adversely affecting minority voters; (4) enforcement actions filed to protect language minorities; and (5) tens of thousands of Federal observers dispatched to monitor polls in jurisdictions covered by the [VRA]."[40]

E. Congress and DOJ Ignore the Supreme Court's Grave Constitutional Concerns.

The constitutionality of the 2006 reenactment was immediately challenged in *Northwest Austin Municipal Utility District No. 1 v. Holder* ("*NAMUDNO*"). In that case, a small Texas water district claimed that it was eligible for bail out even though it was neither a state nor political subdivision and, if it was not, the law was unconstitutional. The Supreme Court ultimately ruled that the water

---

[37] H.R. Rep. 109-478, at 12 (2006), 2006 U.S.C.C.A.N. 618, 627 (2006).

[38] *Id.*

[39] VRARAA, § 2(b)(2), 120 Stat. at 577.

[40] *Id.* § 2(b)(8), 120 Stat. at 578.

district was in fact eligible for bail out and thus did not reach the constitutional question.

But the Supreme Court made clear that the "preclearance requirements and its coverage formula raise serious constitutional questions" in light of the dramatic changes in the covered jurisdictions since 1965.[41] With eight justices in agreement, the Court explained that "the [VRA] imposes current burdens and must be justified by current needs" and that "a departure from the fundamental principle of equal sovereignty requires a showing that a statute's disparate geographic coverage is sufficiently related to the problem that it targets."[42]

"The evil that § 5 is meant to address may no longer be concentrated in the jurisdictions singled out for preclearance," the Court explained. Moreover, Section 4(b)'s coverage formula "is based on data that is now more than 35 years old, and there is considerable evidence that it fails to account for current political conditions. For example, the racial gap in voter registration and turnout is lower in the States originally covered by § 5 than it is nationwide."[43] The Court added that the law's "federalism concerns are underscored by the argument that the preclearance requirements in one State would be unconstitutional in another. Additional constitutional concerns are raised in saying that this tension between §§ 2 and 5 must persist in covered jurisdictions and not elsewhere."[44]

Justice Thomas would have decided the constitutional question. In his view, "the lack of current evidence of intentional discrimination with respect to voting" meant that Section 5 could "no longer be justified as an appropriate mechanism for enforcement of the Fifteenth Amendment."[45] Justice Thomas recognized that

> Congress passed §5 of the VRA in 1965 because that promise had remained unfulfilled for far too long. But now—more than 40 years later—the violence, intimidation, and subterfuge that led Congress to pass §5 and this Court to

[41] NAMUDNO, 557 U.S. at 204.

[42] *Id.* at 203.

[43] *Id.* (citation omitted).

[44] *Id.*

[45] NAMUDNO, 557 U.S. at 216 (Thomas, J., concurring in the judgment in part and dissenting in part).

uphold it no longer remains. An acknowledgment of §5's unconstitutionality represents a fulfillment of the Fifteenth Amendment's promise of full enfranchisement and honors the success achieved by the VRA.[46]

NAMUDNO effectively put the political branches on notice that a future case challenging the law's constitutionality would have merit and gave Congress and the president the chance to address those serious concerns before that day came. Congress responded by doing absolutely nothing. It held not one hearing, proposed not one bill, and amended not one law.

The Justice Department's response was even more unproductive. Instead of judiciously exercising its statutory authority in order to avoid a constitutional confrontation, DOJ aggressively enforced the law in ways that only served to highlight the problems with the coverage formula. For example, DOJ refused to preclear the Texas and South Carolina voter identification laws even though the Supreme Court previously upheld Indiana's similar law.[47] Likewise, Florida— which needed to obtain preclearance of its laws because 5 of its 62 counties are covered jurisdictions—was forced into preclearance litigation to prove that reducing early voting from 14 days to 8 days is not discriminatory when states such as Connecticut, Pennsylvania, and Rhode Island, have no early voting at all.

Such questionable preclearance denials raised concerns about whether Section 5's mission had strayed from ensuring that minority voters were not disenfranchised to providing DOJ with a convenient and efficient means of imposing its preferred electoral system on covered jurisdictions. By 2010, another constitutional challenge was inevitable.

F. Shelby County's Road to the Supreme Court

1. Shelby County Seeks a Return to Self-Government

Shelby County became a covered jurisdiction not by virtue of any discriminatory conduct on its own part, but because it is located in a fully covered state: Alabama. In fact, Shelby County had never drawn a Section 5 objection to any voting change and had been

---

[46] *Id.* at 229.

[47] See Crawford v. Marion Cnty. Election Bd., 553 U.S. 181 (2008).

involved in almost no voting rights litigation since 1965. Yet it was ineligible for bail out because the City of Calera, a jurisdiction within Shelby County, had drawn one objection from DOJ in 2008. Thus, because Congress chose to retain Section 5 preclearance under Section 4(b)'s coverage formula in 2006, Shelby County faced the prospect of expending significant taxpayer dollars, time, and energy to submit every voting change for preclearance until 2031.

On April 27, 2010, Shelby County filed suit in federal court in Washington, D.C. to resolve the serious constitutional questions left unanswered in *NAMUDNO*. Shelby County sought a judgment declaring Sections 5 and 4(b) of the VRA facially unconstitutional. Shelby County did not seek "bail out" from coverage pursuant to Section 4(a) of the VRA, nor did it seek to have the application of the VRA to Shelby County declared unconstitutional because of facts relating to it alone. Rather, Shelby County argued from the outset that the legislative record assembled by Congress in 2006 contained insufficient justification to require preclearance by any covered jurisdiction.

2. The Attorney General Tries to Avoid a Constitutional Showdown

Because the facial constitutionality of Sections 4(b) and 5 would turn solely on whether the legislative record on which Congress acted in 2006 adequately supported reenactment, Shelby County quickly sought summary judgment.

Instead of addressing Shelby County's challenge on the merits, however, Attorney General Eric Holder pursued a course of delay by seeking discovery on irrelevant issues. Despite conceding that coverage under Section 4(b) subjected Shelby County to the burdens of preclearance, the attorney general sought to discover information concerning the amount of time and resources Shelby County devoted to complying with Section 5. The attorney general also sought discovery as to whether there were reasons, on top of those already pleaded by Shelby County, why it was ineligible for bail out, while suggesting that DOJ might grant Shelby County bail out despite its ineligibility. Last, the attorney general sought discovery as to Shelby County's history of elections and voting, although it was never clear why.

Had the Justice Department's strategy of delay succeeded, it might well have scuttled the case. The discovery sought was so onerous and expensive that it might have forced Shelby County to abandon the case or, at a minimum, delayed resolution for years. Thankfully, the district court saw the attorney general's gambit for what it was and rejected all the requests. As the court explained, all the information that the government sought was either irrelevant or cumulative, and had no bearing on the outcome of Shelby County's facial challenge.[48] Notably, the district court highlighted that the attorney general had conceded in related litigation that a covered jurisdiction has standing to challenge Sections 4(b) and 5.[49]

3. *The District Court Upholds Preclearance but Focuses the Constitutional Debate on Section 4(b)'s Coverage Formula*

After extensive briefing, in which the parties submitted over 1,000 pages of argument, the district court held oral argument. As had become clear during the exchange of briefs, the attorney general had very little to say in defense of the coverage formula. Shelby County thus sought to focus the court's attention on that issue, emphasizing that it was the narrowest and most obvious basis for striking down the preclearance obligation. It was the narrowest because it allowed the court to avoid reaching the question of preclearance more generally. It was the most obvious because the formula was indefensible irrespective of the proper constitutional standard—that is, whether "rational basis" or "congruence and proportionality" applied.

Two days after oral argument, the district court ordered the parties "to submit additional briefing" on "the following question: in considering the reauthorization of Section 5 of the Voting Rights Act in 2006, was it 'rational in both practice and theory,' *South Carolina v. Katzenbach,* . . . for Congress to preserve the existing coverage formula in Section 4(b) of the Act?"[50] The order encouraged the parties "to address each aspect of the question separately—that is, to explain both why Section 4(b) is or is not rational 'in practice' and why Section 4(b) is or is not rational 'in theory.'"[51] Notwithstanding the district court's encouragement, the attorney general declined to separately defend the formula as rational in theory. Instead, he argued that the coverage formula was "reverse-engineered." In other words,

---

[48] Shelby County. v. Holder, 270 F.R.D. 16, 19 (D.D.C. 2010).

[49] *Id.* at 18 n.3.

[50] Shelby County v. Holder, No. 10-cv-00651, Minute Order (Feb. 4, 2011).

[51] *Id.*

the government argued that Congress knew the states it wanted to subject to preclearance and worked backward to construct a formula that would cover them.

In a 151-page opinion, Judge John Bates upheld both Sections 4(b) and 5.[52] The court first ruled that the constitutionality of both sections must be judged under the "congruence and proportionality" standard set forth in *City of Boerne v. Flores*.[53] "*Boerne* merely explicated and refined the one standard of review that has been employed to assess legislation enacted pursuant to *both* the Fourteenth and Fifteenth Amendments."[54] The district court held that, under this standard, "Section 5 remains a 'congruent and proportional remedy' to the 21st century problem of voting discrimination in covered jurisdictions."[55]

The district court also held that "Section 4(b)'s disparate geographic coverage remains 'sufficiently related' to the problem that it targets."[56] First, it covers "those jurisdictions with the worst historical records of voting discrimination," and second, "although the legislative record is primarily focused on the persistence of voting discrimination in covered jurisdictions—rather than on the comparative levels of voting discrimination in covered and non-covered jurisdictions—the record does contain several significant pieces of evidence suggesting that the 21st century problem of voting discrimination remains more prevalent in those jurisdictions that have historically been subject to the preclearance requirement."[57]

4. A Divided D.C. Circuit Panel Sides with the Attorney General but Sharpens the Focus on the Coverage Formula

The D.C. Circuit affirmed.[58] Writing for the majority, Judge David Tatel (joined by Judge Thomas Griffith) concluded that *NAMUDNO* "sets the course for our analysis," thus requiring that Section 5's "'current burdens'" be justified by "'current needs'" and Section

[52] Shelby County v. Holder, 811 F.Supp.2d 424 (D.D.C. 2011).

[53] City of Boerne v. Flores, 521 U.S. 507 (1997).

[54] Shelby County, 811 F. Supp. 2d at 449 (emphasis in original).

[55] *Id.*

[56] *Id.* at 507.

[57] *Id.* at 506, 507.

[58] Shelby County v. Holder, 679 F.3d 848 (D.C. Cir. 2012).

4(b)'s "'disparate geographic coverage [be] sufficiently related to the problem that it targets'" to justify departure from the fundamental principle of "'equal sovereignty.'"[59] The majority further interpreted *NAMUDNO* as "sending a powerful signal" that *Boerne*'s congruence-and-proportionality test is the appropriate constitutional standard.[60]

The majority then considered the nature of the evidentiary record necessary to justify retaining the preclearance obligation for another 25 years. Rejecting Shelby County's argument that preclearance was appropriate only in the face of obstructionist tactics, the majority concluded that Congress need not document "a widespread pattern of electoral gamesmanship showing systematic resistance to the Fifteenth Amendment" to reenact Section 5.[61] The question was not "whether the legislative record reflects the kind of 'ingenious defiance' that existed prior to 1965, but whether Congress has documented sufficiently widespread and persistent racial discrimination in voting in covered jurisdictions to justify its conclusion that Section 2 litigation remains inadequate."[62] The majority concluded that Section 5 passed muster under this standard.

The majority also upheld Section 4(b). It rejected Shelby County's argument that the coverage formula is irrational in theory because it relies on obsolete election data and creates an obvious mismatch between its first-generation triggers and the second-generation evidence in the legislative record. Echoing Attorney General Holder's position, the majority found that the argument "rest[ed] on a misunderstanding of the coverage formula" because "Congress identified the jurisdictions it sought to cover . . . and then worked backward, reverse-engineering a formula to cover those jurisdictions."[63] Indeed, the majority was quite dismissive of Shelby County's rational-in-theory argument, suggesting "Shelby County's real argument is that the statute . . . no longer actually identifies the jurisdictions uniquely interfering with the right Congress is seeking to protect through preclearance."[64]

[59] *Id.* at 857–59 (quoting NAMUDNO, 557 U.S. at 203).

[60] *Id.* at 859.

[61] *Id.* at 863 (quotation omitted).

[62] *Id.* at 864.

[63] *Id.* at 879.

[64] *Id.*

The majority saw that as a "close question."[65] Of the ten fully covered (or almost fully covered) states, five "are about on par with the worst non-covered jurisdictions" and two "had no successful published section 2 cases at all."[66] But relying on data from outside the congressional record, the majority found that several covered states "appear to be engaged in much more unconstitutional discrimination compared to non-covered jurisdictions than the [legislative] data alone suggests."[67] While recognizing that several covered states "appear comparable" to their non-covered peers, the majority reasoned that this was "only because section 5's deterrent and blocking effect screens out discriminatory laws before section 2 litigation becomes necessary."[68] Last, the majority concluded that "bail in" and "bail out" alleviated any remaining concerns with the coverage formula, especially in light of the fact that "the pace of bailout increased" after *NAMUDNO*.[69]

Senior Judge Stephen Williams dissented. Although he viewed Section 5 as problematic, he focused on Section 4(b), concluding that the formula's criteria for coverage were defective "[w]hether . . . viewed in absolute terms (are they adequate in themselves to justify the extraordinary burdens of § 5?) or in relative ones (do they draw a rational line between covered and uncovered jurisdictions?)."[70] Highlighting both the theoretical and practical irrationality of the coverage formula, Judge Williams colorfully noted that while "sometimes a skilled dart-thrower can hit the bull's eye throwing a dart backwards over his shoulder . . . Congress hasn't proven so adept."[71]

He emphasized that *NAMUDNO*'s directive that Section 4(b) must be "sufficiently related to the problem it targets" means that "[t]he greater the burdens imposed by § 5, the more accurate the coverage scheme must be."[72] Judge Williams then discussed the severe burdens of Section 5, finding several aspects of preclearance consti-

---

[65] *Id.*

[66] *Id.* at 879–80.

[67] *Id.* at 880.

[68] *Id.*

[69] *Id.* at 881–82.

[70] *Id.* at 885 (Williams, J., dissenting).

[71] *Id.*

[72] *Id.* (internal quotations omitted).

tutionally troubling. First, Section 5 creates unparalleled federalism problems by "mandat[ing] anticipatory review of state legislative or administrative acts, requiring state and local officials to go hat in hand to [DOJ] officialdom to seek approval of any and all proposed voting changes."[73] Second, Section 5's "broad sweep" applies "without regard to kind or magnitude" of the voting change.[74] And third, Congress's 2006 amendments to the preclearance standard exacerbated Section 5's federalism burden and "not only disregarded but flouted Justice Kennedy's concern" that the statute created serious equal-protection problems.[75]

Given these serious constitutional concerns, Judge Williams explained, "a distinct gap must exist between the current levels of discrimination in the covered and uncovered jurisdictions in order to justify subjecting the former group to § 5's harsh remedy, even if one might find § 5 appropriate for a subset of that group."[76] With regard to the "first generation" barriers on which coverage depends, he concluded that there was no such gap. He instead found a negative correlation "between inclusion in § 4(b)'s coverage formula and low black registration or turnout," emphasizing that "condemnation under § 4(b) is a marker of higher black registration and turnout."[77] He found this to be true for minority elected officials as well: "Covered jurisdictions have far more black officeholders as a proportion of the black population than do uncovered ones."[78]

Judge Williams then addressed the second-generation evidence in the record, explaining that it could not justify the coverage formula either. "The five worst uncovered jurisdictions . . . have worse records than eight of the covered jurisdictions . . . . Of the ten jurisdictions with the greatest number of successful § 2 lawsuits, only four are covered. . . . A formula with an error rate of 50% or more does not seem 'congruent and proportional.'"[79]

---

[73] *Id.*

[74] *Id.* at 886 (Williams, J., dissenting).

[75] *Id.*

[76] *Id.* at 889 (Williams, J., dissenting).

[77] *Id.* at 891 (Williams, J., dissenting).

[78] *Id.* at 892 (Williams, J., dissenting).

[79] *Id.* at 897 (Williams, J., dissenting).

Judge Williams also rejected the purported "blocking" or "deterrent effect" of preclearance as an excuse for the lack of evidence of discrimination peculiar to the covered jurisdictions. In his judgment, "the supposed deterrent effect would justify continued VRA renewals out to the crack of doom. Indeed, [*NAMUDNO's*] insistence that 'current burdens must be justified by current needs' would mean little if § 5's supposed deterrent effect were enough to justify the current scheme."[80] Finally, Judge Williams found that "tacking on a waiver procedure such as bailout" could not save the defective coverage formula because "only 136 of the more than 12,000 covered political subdivisions (*i.e.*, about 1%) have applied for bailout (all successfully)," making it "only the most modest palliative to § 5's burdens."[81]

5. The Supreme Court Accepts the Challenge It Avoided in NAMUDNO

Shelby County's certiorari petition was supported by seven covered states: Alabama, Alaska, Arizona, Georgia, South Carolina, South Dakota, and Texas. The presence of these states on Shelby County's side was significant because it magnified the importance of the case, especially given that no states supported the Texas water district only four years earlier. That fact had been noted at oral argument in *NAMUDNO*.[82]

The attorney general all but acceded to certiorari, acknowledging that Shelby County raised what "is certainly an important question of federal law"[83] and declining to contest that the case presented an appropriate vehicle for resolving the facial constitutionality of Section 5 and Section 4(b). His only argument opposing certiorari was to suggest that the Court defer resolution of these important constitutional questions "until a more fulsome record on bailouts develops in the wake of [*NAMUDNO*]."[84] The Court did not agree.

---

[80] *Id.* at 898 (Williams, J., dissenting).

[81] *Id.* at 901 (Williams, J., dissenting).

[82] Oral Arg. Tr. at 24, NAMUDNO, 129 S. Ct. 2504 (2008) (No. 08-322).

[83] Shelby County v. Holder, No. 12-96, Brief for the Respondents in Opposition at 15 133 S. Ct. 2612 (2013) (No. 12-96).

[84] *Id.* at 33.

II. Section 4(b) of the Voting Rights Act Is Unconstitutional Because Its Coverage Formula Is Irrational in Theory

On June 25, 2013, the Supreme Court invalidated Section 4(b)'s coverage formula as unconstitutional, thus rendering Section 5's preclearance obligation inoperative. Chief Justice Roberts authored the majority opinion, which Justices Scalia, Kennedy, Thomas, and Alito joined in full.

Chief Justice Roberts began the majority's analysis of Sections 4(b) and 5 by highlighting the extraordinary nature of the preclearance obligation. To place this extraordinary remedy in proper context, he reiterated the federalism principles that inhere in our constitutional order. As the chief justice explained, the "federal Government does not . . . have a general right to review and veto state enactments before they go into effect"; the authority to "negative" state laws was considered and rejected at the Constitutional Convention.[85] Rather, the "States retain broad autonomy in structuring their governments and pursuing legislative objectives," which includes "power to regulate elections."[86] "Not only do States retain sovereignty under the Constitution, there is also a 'fundamental principle of equal sovereignty' among the States."[87]

Section 5, accordingly, "sharply departs" from these elemental constitutional principles by "suspend[ing] 'all changes to state election law . . . until they have been precleared by federal authorities in Washington, D.C.'"[88] Indeed, it leaves states powerless to implement laws, sometimes for years, "that they would otherwise have the right to enact and execute on their own."[89] Section 4(b) represents "an equally dramatic departure from the principle that all States enjoy equal sovereignty."[90] It makes nine states (and additional counties) wait "months or years and expend funds to implement a validly enacted law," all while their neighboring states "can typically put

[85] Shelby County, 133 S. Ct. at 2623 (citing 1 Records of the Federal Convention of 1787, pp. 21, 164–68 (M. Farrand ed. 1911); 2 *id.*, at 27–29, 390–92)).

[86] *Id.*

[87] *Id.* (quoting NAMUDNO 557 U.S. at 203).

[88] *Id.* at 2624 (citing NAMUDNO, 557 U.S. at 202).

[89] *Id.*

[90] *Id.* at 2618.

the same law into effect immediately, through the normal legislative process."[91]

Chief Justice Roberts explained that these concerns were not new. Given this drastic departure from our constitutional order, the *Katzenbach* Court had recognized at the outset that preclearance was "stringent" and "potent," an "uncommon exercise of congressional power."[92] So too did that Congress, as it tempered the extraordinary nature of preclearance by authorizing it for only five years. The extraordinary remedy of preclearance was thus held constitutional in *Katzenbach* because it was met by an equally extraordinary record of discriminatory conduct. This "strong medicine" was necessary in 1965 "to address entrenched racial discrimination in voting, 'an insidious and pervasive evil which had been perpetuated in certain parts of our country through unremitting and ingenious defiance of the Constitution.'"[93]

Moreover, Chief Justice Roberts explained that the coverage formula was perfectly rational when enacted in 1965. Linking "the exercise of the unprecedented authority with the problem that warranted it . . . made sense."[94] Section 4(b) had targeted for coverage the jurisdictions that "shared two characteristics: 'the use of tests and devices for voter registration, and a voting rate in the 1964 presidential election at least 12 points below the national average,'"[95] The *Katzenbach* Court had concluded that tying coverage to the use of tests and devices was rational in theory given "their long history as a tool for perpetrating the evil" and that tying coverage to low voting rates was likewise rational in theory "for the obvious reason that widespread disenfranchisement must inevitably affect the number of actual voters."[96] In short, *Katzenbach* upheld the formula as "rational in both practice and theory" because "[i]t accurately reflected those jurisdictions uniquely characterized by voting discrimination

---

[91] *Id.* at 2624.

[92] *Id.*

[93] *Id.* at 2618 (quoting Katzenbach, 383 U.S. at 309).

[94] *Id.* at 2625.

[95] *Id.* (quoting Katzenbach, 383 U.S. at 330).

[96] *Id.* (quoting Katzenbach, 383 U.S. at 330) (internal quotation marks omitted).

on a pervasive scale, linking coverage to the devices used to effectuate discrimination and to the resulting disenfranchisement."[97]

The question for the majority, then, was whether that justification remained valid in 2006. As *NAMUDNO* made clear, there was reason for doubt. "Voter turnout and registration rates now approach parity. Blatantly discriminatory evasions of federal decrees are rare. And minority candidates hold office at unprecedented levels."[98] These conclusions were "not [the Court's] alone. Congress said the same when it reauthorized the Act in 2006."[99] In particular, Congress found that "the number of African-Americans who are registered and who turn out to cast ballots has increased significantly over the last 40 years" and that "[i]n some circumstances, minorities register to vote and cast ballots at levels that surpass those of white voters."[100] To highlight this point, the majority opinion displayed a chart comparing voter registration rates from 1965 to 2004 in the six states originally covered by Section 4(b):[101]

	1965			2004		
	White	Black	Gap	White	Black	Gap
Alabama	69.2	19.3	49.9	73.8	72.9	0.9
Georgia	62.[6]	27.4	35.2	63.5	64.2	−0.7
Louisiana	80.5	31.6	48.9	75.1	71.1	4.0
Mississippi	69.9	6.7	63.2	72.3	76.1	−3.8
South Carolina	75.7	37.3	38.4	74.4	71.1	3.3
Virginia	61.1	38.3	22.8	68.2	57.4	10.8

The chief justice added that Census Bureau data from the most recent election showed further improvements in minority turnout in

---

[97] *Id.* at 2625.

[98] *Id.* (quoting NAMUDNO, 557 U.S. at 202) (internal quotation marks omitted).

[99] *Id.*

[100] *Id.* (quoting H.R. Rep. 109-478, at 12 (2006), 2006 U.S.C.C.A.N. 618, 627 (2006)). That same report concluded that that there had been "'significant increases in the number of African-Americans serving in elected offices,'" in particular, "a 1,000 percent increase since 1965 in the number of African-American elected officials in the six States originally covered by the Voting Rights Act." *Id.* (quoting H.R. Rep. 109-478, at 18 (2006), 2006 U.S.C.C.A.N. 618, 627 (2006)).

[101] Shelby County, 133 S. Ct. at 2626.

the covered states, specifically that "African-American voter turnout exceeded white voter turnout in five of the six States originally covered by § 5, with a gap in the sixth State of less than one half of one percent."[102] Moreover, he noted that the Section 5 objection rate exhibited the same trend. Whereas "in the first decade after enactment of § 5, the Attorney General objected to 14.2 percent of proposed voting changes,"[103] in "the last decade before reenactment, the Attorney General objected to a mere 0.16 percent."[104]

The chief justice credited the VRA for these improvements, as it "has proved immensely successful at redressing racial discrimination and integrating the voting process."[105] To illustrate the point, he highlighted the changes in two towns where voting discrimination had been rampant in the 1960s:

> During the "Freedom Summer" of 1964, in Philadelphia, Mississippi, three men were murdered while working in the area to register African-American voters. On "Bloody Sunday" in 1965, in Selma, Alabama, police beat and used tear gas against hundreds marching in support of African-American enfranchisement. Today both of those towns are governed by African-American mayors.[106]

Given these improvements, the majority lamented the fact that Congress neither "eased the restrictions in § 5 [n]or narrowed the scope of the coverage formula in § 4(b) along the way."[107] Rather, while the nation was making "great strides," Congress made preclearance even more burdensome in 2006 by reenacting the preclearance regime for "another 25 years on top of the previous 40—a far cry from the initial five-year period"—and "expanded the prohibitions in § 5" in the face of Supreme Court decisions attempting to alleviate constitutional concerns with the substantive preclearance standard.[108]

---

[102] *Id.* at 2626 (citing Dept. of Commerce, Census Bureau, Reported Voting and Registration, by Sex, Race and Hispanic Origin, for States (Table 4b)).

[103] *Id.* (citation omitted).

[104] *Id.* (citation omitted).

[105] *Id.*

[106] *Id.*

[107] *Id.*

[108] *Id.*

In Shelby County's view, of course, these were the very reasons why Section 5 is no longer constitutional; and the majority was sympathetic, acknowledging that these "arguments have a good deal of force."[109] But the majority declined to reach that issue because, in its view, a constitutional coverage formula "is an initial prerequisite to a determination that exceptional conditions still exist justifying such an extraordinary departure from the traditional course of relations between the States and the Federal Government."[110] The coverage-formula question needed to be resolved first.

Not surprisingly, the majority found that the coverage formula was unsustainable under *Katzenbach*. Whereas Congress, in 1965, "looked to cause (discriminatory tests) and effect (low voter registration and turnout), and tailored the remedy (preclearance) to those jurisdictions exhibiting both," Congress, in 2006, relied on "a formula based on 40-year-old facts having no logical relation to the present day."[111] That Congress expressly sought to target vote dilution, yet chose to employ a formula tied to ballot access, provided decisive evidence that Section 4(b) was no longer rational in theory.[112] The vote dilution evidence on which Congress relied to reenact Section 5 "played *no role* in shaping the statutory formula" used to base coverage until 2031.[113] In other words, the coverage formula was no longer rational in theory because it was now divorced from the conduct Congress targeted and the legislative record it compiled in support of that statutory aim.

The majority recognized what had been abundantly clear from the litigation's outset: the attorney general could not seriously grapple with the theoretical irrationality of the coverage formula. Instead, the attorney general stuck to the "reverse-engineered" argument. But, as the chief justice explained, that argument "does not even attempt to demonstrate the continued relevance of the formula to the problem it targets."[114] In other words, it was not a theoretical defense of Section 4(b) at all, but an admission that the coverage formula

---

[109] *Id.* at 2625.

[110] *Id.* at 2631 (citations and quotations omitted).

[111] *Id.* at 2629.

[112] *Id.*

[113] *Id.* (emphasis added).

[114] *Id.* at 2628.

could not be defended on its own terms. The majority simply could not accept reasoning under which "there need not be any logical relationship between the criteria in the formula and the reason for coverage; all that is necessary is that the formula happen to capture the jurisdictions Congress wanted to single out."[115] "[I]n the context of a decision as significant as this one—subjecting a disfavored subset of States to 'extraordinary legislation otherwise unfamiliar to our federal system'—that failure to establish even relevance is fatal."[116]

The majority also rejected the government's "fallback argument"—that "because the formula was relevant in 1965, its continued use is permissible so long as any discrimination remains in the States identified in 1965."[117] For good reason. The argument disclaimed any need to defend the coverage formula as "rational in . . . theory,"[118] failed to look to "current political conditions,"[119] and was incompatible with the Fifteenth Amendment purpose to "ensure a better future," not "to punish for the past."[120]

Because it found the coverage formula irrational in theory, the majority did not reach any other issues. However, the majority not so subtly suggested it would have been hard to uphold the formula as rational in practice had it needed to reach that issue. In summarizing the points Judge Williams had made in greater detail, the majority found that "no one can fairly say that" the legislative record "shows anything approaching" the "pervasive," "flagrant," "widespread," and "rampant" discrimination that easily distinguished the covered jurisdictions from the rest of the nation in 1965.[121]

In closing, Chief Justice Roberts acknowledged that "[s]triking down an Act of Congress 'is the gravest and most delicate duty that this Court is called on to perform,'"[122] but explained that Congress had forced the Court's hand. The Court "took care [in *NAMUDNO*] to avoid ruling on the constitutionality of the Voting Rights Act

---

[115] *Id.*

[116] *Id.* (quoting NAMUDNO, 557 U.S. at 211).

[117] *Id.*

[118] Katzenbach, 383 U.S. at 330.

[119] NAMUDNO, 557 U.S. at 203.

[120] Shelby County, 133 S. Ct. at 2629.

[121] *Id.* (citations omitted).

[122] *Id.* at 2631 (quoting Blodgett v. Holden, 275 U.S. 142, 148 (1927) (Holmes, J., concurring)).

when asked to do so, and instead resolved the case then before us on statutory grounds."[123] At that time, he explained, "we expressed our broader concerns about the constitutionality of the Act."[124] Because "Congress could have updated the coverage formula at that time, but did not do so," its "failure to act leaves us today with no choice but to declare § 4(b) unconstitutional."[125]

III. Justice Thomas: No Reason to Delay the Inevitable

Because Justice Thomas had concluded in *NAMUDNO* that Section 5 was unconstitutional, his views on the matter were no secret. He wrote separately only to note that all of the majority's reasons for invalidating Section 4(b) require Section 5's invalidation too.[126] Justice Thomas found it "quite fitting that the Court repeatedly points out that this legislation is 'extraordinary' and 'unprecedented' and recognizes the significant constitutional problems created by Congress' decision to raise 'the bar that covered jurisdictions must clear,' even as 'the conditions justifying that requirement have dramatically improved.'"[127]

Justice Thomas concluded by laying down a marker: "While the Court claims to 'issue no holding on § 5 itself,' its own opinion compellingly demonstrates that Congress has failed to justify 'current burdens' with a record demonstrating 'current needs.' By leaving the inevitable conclusion unstated, the Court needlessly prolongs the demise of that provision."[128]

IV. The Dissent's Passionate Defense of a Statute That the Majority Did Not Strike Down

Justice Ginsburg issued a lengthy and strongly worded dissent that was joined by Justices Breyer, Sotomayor, and Kagan. Yet for all of its tough rhetoric, the dissent is almost entirely unresponsive to the issue actually decided. All the majority held was that Section 4(b)'s coverage formula was no longer rational "in theory" because it

---

[123] *Id.*

[124] *Id.*

[125] *Id.*

[126] *Id.* at 2631–32 (Thomas, J. concurring).

[127] *Id.* at 2632 (Thomas, J. concurring) (quoting *id.* at 2627).

[128] *Id.* (citations omitted).

targeted modern "second generation" barriers with a formula predicated on decades-old "first generation" barriers. Justice Ginsburg ostensibly devotes the final few pages of her dissent to that issue. Tellingly, however, she never really explains why Section 4(b) is rational in theory.

The dissent began by arguing that Shelby County could not bring a facial challenge because of its record of voting discrimination. In other words, because, in the dissent's view, Shelby County would be covered either way, it had no right to challenge the formula as illogical. But that is a difficult argument to mount given that a formula determines coverage and Shelby County was challenging that formula. Surely, a state or political subdivision has standing to challenge the appropriateness of the means chosen to select it for coverage. As the majority put it, the dissent's argument "is like saying that a driver pulled over pursuant to a policy of stopping redheads cannot complain about that policy, if it turns out his license has expired."[129] Either the Congress's formula is legitimate or it is not.

Justice Ginsburg responded that Shelby County "is no 'redhead' caught up in an arbitrary scheme" because Congress studied the issue before selecting it for coverage.[130] But that does not explain or justify why this broken formula was retained. A policy of profiling redheads would be no more defensible if the police department produced a study showing that redheads were statistically more likely to drive on an expired license or had a long-ago history of doing so. If Congress believed that current evidence showed that Shelby County—or any other jurisdiction for that matter—should be subject to preclearance, it should have used a formula based on that evidence. Framing a dispute over the coverage formula's appropriateness as a standing issue just clouds the issue. The Supreme Court is in no position to step into Congress's shoes and make a legislative finding that Shelby County would have been covered no matter what, especially given that Congress was unwilling to make such a finding itself. That is especially true given that Shelby County has *never* drawn a Section 5 objection and had almost no history of voting-rights litigation. Notably, the attorney general had multiple opportunities to challenge Shelby County's standing—and every in-

[129] Shelby County, 133 S. Ct. at 2629.
[130] *Id.* at 2647 n.8 (Ginsburg, J., dissenting).

centive to do so. Instead, he conceded the issue in the district court and declined to press the argument on appeal.

Justice Ginsburg then chided the majority for relying on "equal sovereignty" in deciding the case, arguing that the principle applies only to the admission of states to the Union.[131] As an initial matter, Justices Ginsburg and Breyer had an uphill battle as they joined the *NAMUDNO* decision on which the majority mainly relies for this proposition. Indeed, the majority correctly noted that "the dissent analyzes the question presented as if *NAMUDNO* "never happened."[132] Justice Ginsburg responded that "[a]cknowledging the existence of 'serious constitutional questions,' does not suggest how those questions should be answered."[133] That may be true. But it does not remotely explain how the dissent can claim that precedent does not support the majority's invocation of equal sovereignty when the author joined the relevant decision not four years earlier.

In any event, the dissent makes a mountain out of molehill. If equal sovereignty were to play a decisive role, it would have been in determining whether the formula is rational in practice. That is, the principle would logically bear on the statistical disparity of on-the-ground discrimination needed to justify imposing preclearance on some states but not others. A congressional finding that voting discrimination is three percent worse in New Mexico than in Tennessee, for example, would not be a justifiable basis for departing from the principle of equal sovereignty. But the majority never reached that issue. Equal sovereignty might also bear on whether the "second generation" voting problems Congress identified in 2006 are sufficient to warrant the drastic remedy of preclearance given the burden the law imposes on some states but not others. But the majority never reached that issue either.

The dissent thus spilled considerable ink disputing the validity of a legal principle that was not necessary to the decision. Irrespective of equal sovereignty, the Fifteenth Amendment requires, at a bare minimum, that Section 4(b)'s coverage formula be "appropriate." This formula is inappropriate because it is irrational in theory even under the most generous constitutional standard potentially

---

[131] *Id.* at 2649 (Ginsburg, J., dissenting).

[132] *Id.* at 2630.

[133] *Id.* at 2637 n.3 (Ginsburg, J., dissenting) (citations omitted).

applicable to this statute. No more was required to declare Section 4(b) facially unconstitutional.

The dissent also claimed that the majority threw out preclearance even though "[v]olumes of evidence supported Congress' determination that the prospect of retrogression was real."[134] But a voluminous record cannot save a coverage formula that uses irrational criteria. As the majority explained, "Congress did not use the record it compiled to shape a coverage formula grounded in current conditions."[135] It is untenable to defend Section 4(b)'s criteria for coverage based on the legislative record when "it played no role in shaping the statutory formula" Congress chose.[136] The majority thus did not ignore the legislative record developed in 2006. Congress did.

Justice Ginsburg next wondered why "it should be" that the coverage formula is invalid "[e]ven if the legislative record shows . . . that the formula accurately identifies the jurisdictions with the worst conditions of voting discrimination[.]"[137] But that is an odd question to ask given *Katzenbach*'s command that the coverage formula be "rational in *both practice and theory*."[138] It seems fair to ask, then, whether the dissent believed that *Katzenbach* controlled the dispute. At times, the dissent suggests that *Katzenbach* is not directly applicable because this case involves a *reenactment*. At other times, the dissent criticizes the majority for not following *Katzenbach*. Either way, it is difficult to accept the dissent's charge that the majority's decision to hold Congress in 2006 to the same legislative burden as the Court held Congress in 1965 is an example of judicial immodesty.

The dissent then tried to prove up its premise that as a practical matter the covered jurisdictions are distinguishable from the rest of the country. The majority rightly declined to engage on an issue beyond the scope of its judgment, other than to note that it cannot be disputed that the kind of discrimination that distinguished the South in 1965 no longer exists and that the dissent's reliance on the South's "unique history" is highly problematic.[139] As Justice Thomas

---

134 *Id.* at 2650 (Ginsburg, J., dissenting).

135 *Id.* at 2629.

136 *Id.*

137 *Id.* at 2650 (Ginsburg, J., dissenting).

138 Katzenbach, 383 U.S. at 330 (emphasis added).

139 Shelby County, 133 S. Ct. at 2642 (Ginsburg, J., dissenting).

has explained, "Punishment for long past sins is not a legitimate basis for imposing a forward-looking preventative measure that has already served its purpose."[140]

But the majority could have said far more had it been so inclined. The dissent, for example, relied on the fact that 56 percent of the so-called "successful" Section 2 claims between 1982 and 2006 were in covered jurisdictions. But it is difficult to see this statistic as evidence that the kind of rampant voting discrimination that would make preclearance an appropriate remedy is uniquely present in the jurisdictions selected for coverage. If anything, it shows that Section 2 is an effective remedy. Regardless, the Section 2 data lose any persuasive value once they are disaggregated state by state. No fewer than 12 non-covered states had more "successful" Section 2 lawsuits than two covered states—Alaska and Arizona—neither of which had any. The Section 2 data do not suggest that the coverage formula is rational in practice. They demonstrate the opposite.

The nearest the dissent came to grappling with the formula's theoretical irrationality was its suggestion that the government's reverse-engineering argument has merit. In Justice Ginsburg's view, so long as Congress determined that "the jurisdictions captured by the coverage formula still belonged under the preclearance regime . . . there was no need to alter the formula."[141] As noted above, however, that answer is not responsive to the requirement set forth in *Katzenbach* that the formula's criteria rationally relate to the problem Congress is targeting. In 1965, Congress was targeting jurisdictions that used tests and devices to depress minority voting, and it constructed a formula to target that problem. In 2006, Congress chose a new target—second-generation barriers—but used the old triggers.

Indeed, the dissent admitted that the formula's use of voting tests that have been banned for decades as a coverage trigger is problematic. But other than pronouncements about the VRA's "grand aim" and the emergence of "second-generation barriers . . . as attempted *substitutes* for the first-generation barriers,"[142] Justice Ginsburg never explains why it is appropriate to rely on the latter to target the former.

---

[140] NAMUDNO, 557 U.S. at 226 (Thomas, J., concurring in the judgment in part and dissenting in part).

[141] Shelby County, 133 S. Ct. at 2651 (Ginsburg, J., dissenting).

[142] *Id.* (emphasis in original).

The fundamental defect of the government's reverse-engineering argument that the dissent was incapable of curing is its reliance on the irrelevancy of the statute's criteria for coverage to sustain a formula that must be rational in theory.

In a final effort to salvage the coverage formula, the dissent pointed to "bail out" and "bail in" as solving any problems with Section 4(b). Again, these aspects of the VRA have nothing to do with whether the formula is rational in theory. At most, these statutory mechanisms for letting some jurisdictions out of preclearance and bringing others into the system might bear on whether the formula is rational in practice. That is, the judiciary might tolerate some imperfections in the coverage map so long as the jurisdictions that have been mistakenly captured have a means of freeing themselves and those wrongly left off the list can be subjected to preclearance if they are found to have violated the Fourteenth or Fifteenth Amendment. But this has nothing to do with whether coverage triggers continue to bear a logical and rational relationship to current conditions.

Had the Court needed to reach this issue, moreover, it would have had good reason to be skeptical of bail out's ability to save Section 4(b). First, history shows that it helps only at the margins and cannot solve the massive problems with this formula. Only about 1 percent of the more than 12,000 covered jurisdictions bailed out prior to the statute's reenactment in 2006. Second, bail out today is fundamentally different from bail out in 1965. As originally envisioned, bail out was intended to liberate those jurisdictions that should never have been covered in the first place. Since 1982, however, it is a kind of parole statute. Bail out lets jurisdictions that can show to DOJ's satisfaction that they are no longer troublemakers out of jail with 10 years of supervised release. Hence, bail out is no longer responsive to the formula's over-inclusiveness. Unlike the 1965 bail-out provision, which allowed jurisdictions to show that they were wrongly convicted, the 2006 version assumes their guilt and requires evidence of rehabilitation to secure release. Reliance on bail in is even less persuasive. Bail in operates nationwide and is tied to judicial findings of Fourteenth and Fifteenth Amendment violations. If anything, the availability of bail in highlights the flaws inherent in Section 5.

In sum, the dissent simply had no answer to the majority's conclusion that Section 4(b)'s coverage formula is irrational in theory. The dissent offers a host of reasons why Congress should no longer have to defend the formula as rational in theory notwithstanding *Katzenbach*, why those leading the charge for reenactment might have assumed that the outdated formula would be upheld, and why the coverage formula is rational in practice. Whether or not those arguments have merit—we think not—they are no substitute for an argument on why *Katzenbach*'s requirement that the formula be rational in theory has been met or why that requirement has lost legal pertinence.

It therefore makes sense that the dissent would devote most of its opinion to why Section 5 remains constitutional. When you have little to say, change the subject. Because the issue was beyond the scope of the majority's holding, however, it turned into a one-sided conversation. Yet it would be wrong to assume that the majority's failure to decide that question amounted to implicit concurrence in the dissent's view. Congress and the president should learn from the *NAMUDNO* experience and take the Court's concerns seriously before attempting to reinstall this same preclearance regime under a revised coverage formula.

This is not to say that the dissent might not attract a fifth vote to its view if the Court is squarely confronted with Section 5's constitutionality in a future case. Indeed, it would be wrong to hazard a guess as to what might happen. But given the secondary evidence of discrimination that Congress relied on in 2006, the massive improvements in the covered jurisdictions since 1965, and Section 2's ability to respond to the "vestiges" of discrimination that concerned Congress in 2006, the dissent's suggestion that it is somehow "implausible" to reach the conclusion that Section 5 is unconstitutional seems like a stretch. Preclearance continues to raise serious constitutional questions that will need to be answered if the issue again reaches the Supreme Court.

V. Where to from Here?

By invalidating Section 4(b), the Court rendered Section 5 inoperable. Henceforth, no state or political subdivision must preclear its voting laws. But the Court was careful to point out that it was not issuing a decision as to Section 5 and that "Congress may draft another formula based on current conditions."[143] If Congress and the president can meet that challenge, the Section 5 preclearance regime

---

[143] *Id.* at 2631.

will be revived. But that may be easier said than done. Designing a formula to target those regions of the country where racially polarized voting and vote dilution—Congress's principal concerns in 2006—might prove difficult as those and other second-generation barriers are not as amenable to description by formula as voting tests and devices and low registration and voting rates.

Congress would also need to ensure that the formula is rational in practice. Given that the second-generation barriers are not concentrated in jurisdictions covered under the old formula, Congress presumably would need to bring new jurisdictions into the preclearance regime and set others free. That may prove politically troublesome. The stigma of coverage and the burden that preclearance imposes on state and local governments make it unlikely that any jurisdiction would willingly subject itself to preclearance—let alone one that has never before been subject to that obligation. Moreover, DOJ's promise to aggressively utilize the litigation-based remedies of VRA Sections 2 and 3 to bring challenges against jurisdictions it believes are interfering with minority voting rights may prove the points Shelby County was making all along: the emergency necessitating preclearance has passed; traditional litigation remedies can address the vestiges of discrimination that Congress targeted in 2006; and the places where these problems are most prominent are not concentrated in the jurisdictions that used discriminatory tests or devices in 1964, 1968, and 1972.

But if Congress overcomes these hurdles, questions as to Section 5's constitutionality still remain. The Supreme Court has twice now expressed grave doubts about Congress's ability to show that the conditions justifying unprecedented interference with the basic right of self-government persist today. Though the Court has shown restraint in declining to reach that issue when narrower grounds could resolve the dispute, it would be wrong to conclude that the Court would hesitate to do so if the issue needs deciding. The question now is whether Congress and the president want to provoke that confrontation.

Fisher v. University of Texas: The Court (Belatedly) Attempts to Invoke Reason and Principle

*Gail Heriot**

Oracles can be . . . well . . . Delphic, and the great judicial oracle in Washington is no exception. The cryptic opinion in *Fisher v. University of Texas*[1]—the first decision on affirmative action in higher education in a decade—is a good example. Predicting what it will mean for the future is not easy.

Nevertheless, for supporters of race neutrality, there may be reason for modest optimism. When compared with the range of realistic alternatives, *Fisher*'s actual outcome may be ever-so-slightly encouraging. The Court could have issued a "good for this case only" ticket to Abigail Fisher that would have had no real precedential value. Instead, the Court's 7–1 majority chose to clarify the applicable standard in a way that ratchets up the pressure on colleges and universities—and sent Abigail Fisher's case back to the U.S. Court of Appeals for the Fifth Circuit for adjudication based on that more demanding standard.[2] By requiring that in the future a college or university supply "a reasoned, principled explanation" for its diversity goal and directing courts to use tough-minded "strict scrutiny" in determining whether its admissions policy is narrowly tailored to achieve that goal, the Court inched the country toward a more sensible vision of the Constitution's requirements in the higher education context. The peculiarly deferential attitude toward colleges and universities found in *Grutter v. Bollinger*,[3] the University of Michigan case

*Professor of law at the University of San Diego, and member of the U.S. Commission on Civil Rights.

[1] 133 S. Ct. 2411 (2013).

[2] *Id*. at 2416.

[3] 539 U.S. 306 (2003).

from a decade ago, has not yet reached the judicial attic—where it belongs—but it may be on its way.

Still, no one should get carried away by optimism. The fundamental problem is that complete success was never among the alternatives in the *Fisher* case. Even an opinion flatly prohibiting racial preferences in admissions would have been only a step along the road to removing race from consideration in college and university admissions. Making progress down that road is nevertheless imperative.

This essay begins with some policy background on the affirmative action debate, followed by a description of the relevant legal precedents going into *Fisher* litigation, then an explanation of the *Fisher* opinion, and finally some concluding thoughts. *Fisher* itself is a very short and thin opinion—alas we won't know for decades why it took the Court more than eight months to issue a 13-page opinion—so most of the action is outside the four corners of the case.

Why It Matters

There are many reasons to oppose race-preferential admissions policies. Perhaps the most fundamental is this: As Justice Clarence Thomas discussed in his *Fisher* concurrence, for all the good intentions of those who originated these policies, they apparently don't work.[4] If the mounting empirical evidence is correct, we now have fewer African-American physicians, scientists, and engineers than we would have had using race-neutral methods. We have fewer college professors and lawyers too. Whatever affirmative action's legal and constitutional status, it has backfired on its own terms.[5]

That is not what college and university administrators, many of whom have dedicated their lives to promoting affirmative action, want to hear. But as UCLA law professor Richard Sander and legal journalist Stuart Taylor Jr. discuss in their 2012 book, *Mismatch: How Affirmative Action Hurts Students It's Intended to Help, and Why*

---

[4] Fisher, 133 S. Ct. at 2422–32 (Thomas, J., concurring). The research behind this assertion was brought to the Court's attention by two amicus curiae briefs, including mine. See Amicus Curiae Brief of Gail Heriot et al., in Support of Petitioner Fisher, 133 S. Ct. 2411 (2013) (No. 11-345); Amicus Curiae Brief of Richard Sander et al., in Support of Petitioner Fisher, 133 S. Ct. 2411 (2013) (No. 11-345).

[5] See Gail Heriot, The Sad Irony of Affirmative Action, 14 Nat'l Aff. 78 (2013).

Universities Won't Admit It, it is getting increasingly difficult for these administrators to view themselves as being on the side of the angels.

Sadly, even if a few schools were willing to admit the backfire, it would be difficult for them to do much about it individually. They are caught in a collective-action problem. If just one selective school goes cold turkey on race-preferential admissions, it will enroll few (and in some cases no) members of under-represented minorities. Such a school is unlikely to be willing to go it alone. Even if it wanted to, its federally appointed accrediting agency probably would refuse accreditation.[6] That's why a judicious push from the Court may be necessary to get the process of winding down race preferences started.[7]

Here's the crux of the problem: One consequence of widespread race-preferential policies is that minority students tend to enroll in colleges and universities where their entering academic credentials put them toward the bottom of the class. While academically gifted under-represented minority students are hardly an endangered species, there are not enough to satisfy the demand of top schools. When the most prestigious schools relax their admissions policies in order to admit more minority students, they start a chain reaction, resulting in a substantial credentials gap at nearly all selective schools. The problem that this credentials gap creates is sometimes referred to as "mismatch."

Fisher itself helps illustrate this. According to data released by the University of Texas, the mean SAT scores (out of 2400) and mean high school grade-point averages (GPAs, on a 4.0 scale) varied widely by race for the regular admittees of the entering class of 2009. This particular set of data does not include those accepted through the so-called Top Ten Percent program, which guarantees admission to all students graduating in the top ten percent (since changed to eight percent) of Texas high schools:[8]

---

[6] For an example of the strong pressure that nonacademic accreditors place on sometimes-unwilling schools to increase diversity, see Gail Heriot, The ABA's "Diversity" Diktat, Wall St. J., Apr. 28, 2008.

[7] See Gail Heriot, The Politics of Admissions in California, 14 Acad. Questions 29 (2001) (noting that after the implementation of California's Proposition 209 racial diversity at some University of California campuses increased while it decreased at others).

[8] Univ. of Texas Office of Admissions, Implementation and Results of Texas Automatic Admissions Law (HB 588) at the University of Texas, Sec. 1: Demographic Analysis of Entering Freshmen, Fall 2010, at 14. For a description of the university's Top Ten Percent program, see *infra* note 53 and accompanying text.

Group	Combined SAT	High School GPA
Asians	1991	3.07
Whites	1914	3.04
Hispanics	1794	2.83
African Americans	1524	2.57

These are, of course, averages. Some students have credentials well above (or well below) the average for their group. For perspective, it is worth noting that the SAT scores for the average Asian student in the above chart were in the 93rd percentile of 2009 SAT-takers nationwide; meanwhile, the average African-American student was in the 52nd percentile.

All this has the predictable effect of lowering the college or professional school grades the average non-Asian minority student earns.[9] And the reason is simple: While some students will outperform their entering credentials, just as some students will under-perform theirs, most students perform in the general range that their entering credentials suggest.[10] This point is so fundamental that admissions officers should be required to recite it aloud at the beginning and end of each workday.

The strongest evidence on why the credentials gap is bad comes from science and engineering. Contrary to what some expect, college-bound African-American and Hispanic students are just as likely to be interested in majoring in science and engineering as

[9] The average African-American first-year law student has a grade-point average in the bottom 10 percent of his or her class. And while undergraduate GPAs for affirmative action beneficiaries aren't quite as disappointing, that is in part because affirmative action beneficiaries tend to shy away from subjects like science and engineering, which are graded on a tougher curve than other subjects. See Richard Sander, A Systemic Analysis of Affirmative Action in Law Schools, 57 Stan. L. Rev. 367, 427–28 (2004); Peter Arcidiacono, Esteban Aucejo & Ken Spenner, What Happens After Enrollment? An Analysis of the Time Path of Racial Differences in GPA and Major Choice, 1 IZA J. Lab. Econ. 5 (2012).

[10] No serious supporter of race-preferential admissions denies this. In their highly influential defense of affirmative action, The Shape of the River: Long-Term Consequences of Considering Race in College and University Admissions 72 (1998), former Ivy League university presidents William G. Bowen and Derek Bok candidly admitted that low college grades for affirmative action beneficiaries present a "sobering picture." For a discussion of how the data presented in *The Shape of the River* actually supports the mismatch theory and not affirmative action policies, see Heriot, The Sad Irony of Affirmative Action, *supra* note 5, at 88–91.

white students. Indeed, empirical research shows that they are a little more so.[11] But these are more-difficult-than-average majors. Many students abandon them. Significantly, African-American and Hispanic students jump ship at much higher rates than whites. A recent study at Duke University, for example, found that approximately 54 percent of black males switched out of science and engineering majors, whereas only 6 percent of white males did.[12]

It is not surprising that students with lower entering academic credentials disproportionately give up on their ambition to get a science or engineering degree more often than those with higher academic credentials. What some do find unexpected is this: Three in-depth studies have demonstrated that *part of the effect is relative*. An aspiring science or engineering major who attends a school where her entering academic credentials put her in the middle or the top of her class is more likely to persevere and ultimately succeed than an *otherwise identical student* attending a more elite school where those same credentials place her toward the bottom of the class. Put differently, affirmative action is a hindrance, not a help, for preference beneficiaries who aspire to earn a degree in science and engineering.[13]

[11] See, e.g., Alexander Astin & Helen Astin, Undergraduate Science Education: The Impact of Different College Environments on the Educational Pipeline in the Sciences 3–9, Table 3.5 (1992).

[12] Arcidiacono et al., *supra* note 9. These authors also dispelled the common belief that affirmative action beneficiaries "catch up" after their freshman year with their better-credentialed classmates. What happens instead is that many transfer to majors where the academic competition is less intense and where students are graded on a more lenient curve. Their GPAs increased, but their standing relative to their peer group did not. Some argue that what are really needed are more role models for minority students who aspire to be physicians, engineers, lawyers, professors, and so on. But here it is worth noting that the credentials-gap effect is by no means confined to affirmative action beneficiaries. White students who receive legacy preferences have the same experience, earning lower grades than white non-legacies at the end of their first year. Although the gap narrows over time, this is only because legacy students also shift away from science and toward the humanities. It is exceedingly unlikely that anti-legacy bias, lack of legacy role models, or any other argument commonly advanced to explain racial disparities in science explains legacies' drift toward softer majors. They are thus likely to be the wrong explanations for under-represented minorities.

[13] Rogers Elliott, A. Christopher Strenta, Russell Adair, Michael Matier & Jannah Scott, The Role of Ethnicity in Choosing and Leaving Science in Highly Selective Institutions, 37 Res. Higher Educ. 681 (1996); Frederick Smyth & John McArdle, Ethnic and Gender Differences in Science Graduation at Selective Colleges with Implications for Admission Policy and College Choice, 45 Res. Higher Educ. 353 (2004); Richard

Each of these three studies used a different database and a different methodology. Yet all came to that same conclusion, and the effect they found was substantial. One of them—by University of Virginia psychologists Frederick Smyth and John McArdle (now at the University of Southern California)—found that among a sample of under-represented minority students at 23 universities who intended to major in science, mathematics, or engineering, 45 percent more of the women and 35 percent more of the men would have succeeded in attaining their goal if they had attended a school where their entering credentials had been about average.[14] To my knowledge, no one has attempted to rebut any of these studies, much less all three of them.

Similar research had found that the same problem is reducing the number of African-American college students who decide to attend graduate school and become college professors. It is no secret that students who get good grades like school better than students whose performance is not so stellar. Given that, a nationwide policy of race-preferential admissions policies—which cannot help but produce disappointing grades for a disproportionate number of under-represented minority students—was always likely to dampen their enthusiasm for an academic career. The only serious question was how strong the effect would be. In *Increasing Faculty Diversity: The Occupational Choices of High-Achieving Minority Students*, Stephen Cole and Elinor Barber found it was substantial. The authors, whose 2003 book has been unrebutted, noted that among their sample of African-American students with high SAT scores, only 4 percent of those with college GPAs at or near 2.6 wanted to become college professors. Among those with college GPAs at or near 4.0, however, the number was over 20 percent.[15] Naturally, those with higher grades

---

Sander & Roger Bolus, Do Credentials Gaps in College Reduce the Number of Minority Science Graduates?, Working Paper (Draft July 2009) ("[S]tudents with credentials more than one standard deviation below their science peers at college are about half as likely to end up with science bachelor degrees, compared with similar students attending schools where their credentials are much closer to, or above, the mean credentials of their peers.").

[14] Smyth & McArdle, *supra* note 13, at 373.

[15] Stephen Cole & Elinor Barber, Increasing Faculty Diversity: The Occupational Choices of High-Achieving Minority Students (2003). For an account of tensions between the authors and their funders at the Mellon Foundation that arose on account of these conclusions, see Robin Wilson, The Unintended Consequences of Affirmative Action, The Chronicle of Higher Education, Jan. 31, 2003.

were disproportionately attending schools where they did not need a preference in order to be admitted.

Finally, research into law students by UCLA law professor Richard Sander has produced similar results: More African-American students would graduate and pass the bar examination if they attended law schools at which their entering credentials put them in the broad middle or upper portion of the class.[16]

Some have argued that, owing to shortcomings in the available data, Sander's findings should not be taken as the last word on law school affirmative action.[17] In 2007, the U.S. Commission on Civil Rights agreed that while Sander's research was important and impressive, more research would be useful before his conclusions could be accepted as final.[18] But the story didn't end there. Sander assembled an ideologically diverse team of researchers to continue the research on a different database. But some of the same people who originally argued that more research was necessary then argued successfully that Sander's team should not be permitted access to data that would allow them to supplement the research.[19] For some, defending race-preferential admissions is not about doing what is best for minority students.

Like an out-of-touch emperor dismissing bad news from the battlefront, higher education has ignored this literature for more than a decade. The troops must carry on, regardless of the casualties—or so the emperor has declared. The U.S. Commission on Civil Rights issued two reports on the mismatch topic and distributed them to college and university presidents, provosts, deans, and admissions officers. The response has been silence.

Ordinarily, one would not expect the Court to weigh in on research of this kind. But by permitting state universities to engage in

[16] Richard Sander, A Systemic Analysis of Affirmative Action in Law Schools, 57 Stan. L. Rev. 367 (2004). See also Richard Sander & Jane Bambauer, The Secret of My Success: How Status, Eliteness and School Performance Shape Legal Careers, 9 J. Empirical Legal Stud. 893 (2012) (in predicting income of law school graduates, getting good grades mattered more than getting into a top law school, once entering credentials are controlled for).

[17] See, e.g., Ian Ayres & Richard Brooks, Does Affirmative Action Reduce the Number of Black Lawyers?, 57 Stan. L. Rev. 1807 (2005).

[18] U.S. Comm'n on Civil Rights, Affirmative Action in Law Schools (2007).

[19] See Richard Sander & Stuart Taylor, Jr., Mismatch: How Affirmative Action Hurts Students It's Intended to Help, and Why Universities Won't Admit It 233–44 (2012).

racial discrimination in admissions, the Court, in *Grutter*, implicitly took the position that affirmative action has beneficial effects that justify deviating from the usual overwhelming presumption against such practices.[20] The least it can do now is provide colleges and universities with an obligation to take a hard look at the data.

With *Fisher*, the Court has arguably done exactly that. It is difficult to see how a college or university can give "a reasoned, principled explanation" for its goal of reaping the educational benefits of diversity (which is the only goal the case law approves) or prove that its race-preferential admissions policy is "narrowly tailored" to achieve that goal without addressing this research.[21] Although the Commission on Civil Rights could not force colleges and universities to grapple with this issue, maybe the *Fisher* decision can.

Pre-*Fisher* Decisions: *Bakke*, *Gratz* and *Grutter*

Not everyone agrees with my assessment that advocates of race neutrality have reason for modest optimism. On the day *Fisher* was announced, Columbia University President Lee Bollinger opined with characteristic certainty that the University of Texas would have no trouble on remand showing that its policy complies with the law.[22] Of course, Bollinger is a longtime promoter of race-preferential admissions, but some advocates of race neutrality also view the case as a win for him and his allies.[23]

They could turn out to be right. But it is important to note that in the days and weeks that have followed the release of previous

---

[20] The Court's citation to Kenneth and Mamie Clark's famous doll experiments in Brown v. Bd. of Educ., 347 U.S. 483 (1954), has been justifiably criticized by legal scholars who rightly argue that school segregation would have been unconstitutional even if the experiment had come out the other way. There is a principle involved—the principle of non-discrimination. One could similarly argue that it shouldn't matter whether race-preferential admissions are harmful or not; they're unconstitutional anyway. But it is difficult to argue that a special constitutional exception to the principle of non-discrimination should be made to permit them in the face of extensive evidence that they cause more harm than good.

[21] Fisher, 133 S. Ct. at 2419.

[22] See PBS NewsHour (June 24, 2013).

[23] See, e.g., David Bernstein, Fisher is a Significant Loss for Opponents of Affirmative Action Preferences, The Volokh Conspiracy, Jun. 25, 2013, http://www.volokh.com/2013/06/25/fisher-is-a-significant-loss-for-opponents-of-affirmative-action-preferences.

Supreme Court opinions on race-preferential admissions policies, misinterpretations and mispredictions tended to dominate the commentary. It is going to take a little while to see how this story unfolds. In the meantime, colleges and universities should prepare for more than one contingency.

Consider, for example, the famously fractured decision in *Regents of the University of California v. Bakke* (1978).[24] Immediately after that 4–1–4 decision was issued, many affirmative action supporters viewed it as a major loss. But in retrospect it seems screamingly obvious that they had won big.

In *Bakke*, the University of California at Davis Medical School had been reserving a specific number of seats in its class for under-represented minority members.[25] As a result, it wound up admitting minority applicants whose entering academic credentials were dramatically lower than those of their fellow admittees.[26] Four members of the Court—Chief Justice Warren Burger and Justices William Rehnquist, John Paul Stevens, and Potter Stewart—took the position that Title VI's plain language prohibited discrimination against whites as well as blacks.[27] Another four—Justices Harry Blackmun, William Brennan, Thurgood Marshall, and Byron White—concluded that Title VI's prohibition was only intended to prohibit race discrimination that would be unconstitutional if practiced by a state actor.[28] On the issue

[24] 438 U.S. 265 (1978).

[25] *Id.* at 272–76.

[26] In 1973, the average MCAT scores for regular admittees and special admittees at UC-Davis were as follows:

	Regular	Special
Science	83rd percentile	35th percentile
Verbal	81st percentile	46th percentile
Quantitative	76th percentile	24th percentile
General Information	69th percentile	33rd percentile

Similarly, overall undergraduate GPAs in 1973 averaged 3.49 for regular admittees and 2.88 for special admittees. The science undergraduate GPAs—usually considered the most important aspect of a medical school applicant's undergraduate record—average 3.51 for regular admittees and 2.62 for special admittees in 1973. *Id.* at 277 n.7.

[27] 438 U.S. 265, 408 (Stevens, J., concurring in the judgment in part and dissenting in part). Title VI states, "No person . . . shall, on the ground of race, . . . be subjected to discrimination under any program or activity receiving Federal financial assistance." Civil Rights Act of 1964, title VI, sec. 601, codified at 42 U.S.C. sec. 2000d.

[28] *Id.* at 324 (Brennan, J., White, J., Marshall, J., Blackmun, J., concurring in the judgment in part and dissenting in part).

of constitutionality, these four justices stated that "where there is reason to believe" that minority under-representation "is a product of past racial discrimination," race-preferential admissions policies are permissible as a method of helping to place minority members in their rightful position.[29] They therefore took the position that the medical school's policy was constitutional.

The tie-breaking vote was thus Justice Lewis Powell's. One by one, he rejected the various justifications advanced by the regents for the medical school's discriminatory policies—including the need to "reduc[e] the historic deficit of traditionally disfavored minorities . . . in the medical profession" and the need to "increas[e] the number of physicians who will practice in [underserved] communities."[30] Most memorably, he objected to the argument that past societal discrimination can justify compensatory discrimination by a state university. "No one denies the regrettable fact that there has been societal discrimination in this country against various racial and ethnic groups," he wrote. But the notion that "but for this discrimination by society at large, Bakke 'would have failed to qualify for admission,' because Negro applicants . . . would have made better scores" requires "a speculative leap"—a leap he was not willing to take.[31]

Justice Powell was particularly troubled by the expansiveness of the argument that affirmative action can be justified as compensation for past societal discrimination. He opined that "if it may be concluded on this record that each of the minority groups preferred by [the medical school's] special program is entitled to the benefit of the presumption, it would seem difficult to determine that any of the dozens of minority groups that have suffered 'societal discrimination' cannot also claim it, in any area of social intercourse."[32] Mormons, for example, have been the victims of violence at the hands of state militias.[33] Could that entitle them to demand tax credits? Would anything be left of equal protection if state actors were permitted to make whatever compensatory adjustments they deem appropriate?

[29] Id. at 366.

[30] Id. at 306 (opinion of Powell, J.).

[31] Id. at 297 n.36.

[32] Id.

[33] See Missouri Executive Order No. 44 (October 27, 1838) ("The Mormons must be treated as enemies, and must be exterminated or driven from the state if necessary for the public peace—their outrages are beyond all description.").

But Justice Powell left the door open what he probably thought was just a crack. After rejecting most of the regents' justifications, he examined their final Hail Mary: The educational benefits to all students of a diverse student body. Unlike the other reasons they advanced, the diversity justification purported to be for the direct benefit of all students and not a redistribution of benefits from some to others.[34] Here Powell was receptive.

That did not, however, dispose of the case for Justice Powell. He was still of the opinion that Allan Bakke must be admitted to the medical school. His concern was that the school had reserved a particular number of seats for targeted racial minorities. He reasoned that the educational benefits of diversity come not just from race but from many kinds of diversity, from political ideology to musical talent. For a school to reserve 16 seats for targeted races—and none for students who might contribute to diversity in other ways—seemed incongruous. Without knowing how many under-represented minority members would be admitted in a particular year without preferential treatment it would be hard to know whether those 16 seats were necessary to foster racial diversity. It would also be hard to know what other kinds of diversity might have to be sacrificed in order to fill those 16 seats based on race.[35]

After the *Bakke* decision, some affirmative action advocates fixed upon a bottom line that went against them—that Bakke himself must be admitted to the medical school. And they also voiced their frustrations with Powell's rejection of the non-diversity justifications offered for the medical school's policy. For them, Justice Powell left the wrong door ajar. As far as they were concerned, the purpose of race-preferential admissions policies was to confer a benefit on under-represented minority students in particular, not to enhance the general educational experience. For a variety of related reasons, they wanted more minority college graduates, more minority

[34] Additionally, Powell apparently was impressed by the fact that Harvard University had been seeking geographical diversity in its students since the 1920s. See 438 U.S. at 321 (appendix to opinion of Powell, J.). He was apparently unaware that this policy was part of an effort to ensure that the number of Jewish students, who were concentrated in the New York City area, would not become "too high." See generally Marcia Graham Synnott, The Half-Opened Door: Discrimination and Admissions at Harvard, Yale, and Princeton, 1900–1970 (1979).

[35] 438 U.S. at 315–20 (opinion of Powell, J.).

professionals, and more minority successes generally, not more robust classroom debate. At best, Justice Powell's opinion seemed to
hijack the policies that they had helped formulate.[36]

But it did not take long for this early reaction to fade and for colleges and universities to see how easily they could accomplish their
goals simply by adopting the rhetoric of "diversity." It didn't matter
whether they believed in it.[37]

Sometimes the change in rhetoric was accomplished only awk-
wardly, as in the following conversation, the gist of which I over-
heard at my own university in the 1990s:

> MY ASSISTANT: Could you tell me what time the affirmative
> action committee meets with the provost?
>
> PROVOST'S ASSISTANT: We don't have an affirmative action
> committee.
>
> MY ASSISTANT: We don't? That's funny because . . . .
>
> PROVOST'S ASSISTANT: It's a diversity committee, not an
> affirmative action committee. There's an important difference
> and I've been told not to mix them up.
>
> MY ASSISTANT: OK, then could you tell me when the diversity
> committee is meeting with the provost?
>
> PROVOST'S ASSISTANT: Ten o'clock.

[36] See Alan Dershowitz, Affirmative Action and the Harvard College Diversity-
Discretion Model: Paradigm or Pretext, 1 Cardozo L. Rev. 379, 407 (1979).

[37] Slowly, the pendulum has swung in other ways too. Not only is *Bakke* no longer
considered a loss by advocates of race-preferential admissions, but Powell himself
is now lionized as a defender of civil rights. But while Powell was a learned and
compassionate man, his defense of civil rights in other contexts was not exactly
leonine. As a Richmond school board chairman and a member of the Virginia Board of
Education during the crucial years following the Supreme Court's decision in *Brown v.
Board of Education*, the gentlemanly Powell did not distinguish himself as an advocate
of desegregation "with all deliberate speed." See Jerome Karabel, The Chosen: The
Hidden History of Admission and Exclusion at Harvard, Yale and Princeton 496
(2005) (quoting John C. Jeffries Jr., Justice Lewis F. Powell Jr. 2, 234, 172 (2001)). In
contrast, California Supreme Court Justice Stanley Mosk, who authored the state court
opinion holding that race-preferential admissions policies were unconstitutional, had
been an advocate for civil rights throughout his legal and political career. Despite this
record, many progressives never forgave him for his stand in *Bakke*—even in death.
See Stanley Mosk, 88, Long a California Supreme Court Justice, N.Y. Times, Jun. 21,
2001, at C13.

Translation: Justice Powell has taken the position that diversity is the only legitimate justification among those commonly advanced for racial preferences. Our university would be well advised to do everything possible to fit its program within the safe harbor he created. That means remedying past discrimination is out and diversity is in—at least rhetorically. Get with the program.[38]

In theory, at least, it would have been possible to bring an action proving that a university's "diversity policy" was pretextual and not actually based on a concern for diversity's educational benefits. As Columbia law professor Kent Greenawalt, a skeptic of race-preferential admissions, declared soon after *Bakke*, "I have yet to find a professional academic who believes the primary motivation for preferential admission has been to promote diversity in the student body for the better education of all the students."[39] But in the more practical world of public-interest litigation, it would have been overwhelmingly expensive and pointless. Even if a lawsuit could be won, a defendant university would likely obtain new leadership and assert that the new leadership is motivated by diversity in its admissions policy.

Twenty-five years later, when the Court announced its decisions in the twin cases of *Gratz v. Bollinger*[40] and *Grutter v. Bollinger*, some of the early media assessments were again off-target. Since Jennifer Gratz was victorious in the former and the University of Michigan was the victor in the latter, some suggested that the result was essentially a tie. By this time, however, even moderately well-informed college and university administrators knew the actual score. They understood that by tracking Powell's rationale in *Bakke*, the Court

[38] For a discussion of how the concept of "diversity" took off from Powell's opinion on admissions in *Bakke* and has spread into other areas, see Peter Wood, Diversity: The Invention of a Concept (2003).

[39] Kent Greenawalt, The Unresolved Problems of Reverse Discrimination, 67 Cal. L. Rev. 87, 122 (1979). Similarly, Harvard law professor Alan Dershowitz wrote: "The raison d'etre for race-specific affirmative action programs has simply never been diversity for the sake of education. The checkered history of 'diversity' demonstrates that it was designed largely as a cover to achieve other legally, morally, and politically controversial goals. In recent years, it has been invoked—especially by professional schools—as a clever post facto justification for increasing the number of minority students in the student body." Dershowitz, *supra* note 36, at 407.

[40] 539 U.S. 244 (2003).

had hit the ball out of the park on their behalf in *Grutter*. They also understood that their loss in *Gratz* was trivial.

Gratz concerned at most a cosmetic matter, similar to the issue that gave Mr. Bakke his "good for this case only" victory. In *Bakke*, Powell was concerned that the medical school had set aside a specific number of seats in the class for minority students only. In *Gratz*, now-Chief Justice Rehnquist, writing for the six-member majority, could not abide the fact that the University of Michigan had assigned a specific number of points—exactly 20—to African-American, Hispanic, or American-Indian applicants. This advantage was worth an entire letter grade in high school GPA. In other words, an African-American applicant with a high-school record of straight Bs (GPA of 3.0) would be treated the same as an Asian-American student with a high school record of straight As (GPA of 4.0), all other things being equal.[41]

Curiously, it was apparently not the size of the preference that disturbed the Court. Extremely large preferences were given to minority applicants at the University of Michigan Law School in *Grutter* too. Indeed, Judge Danny Boggs in his Sixth Circuit dissent in *Grutter* referred to their "staggering magnitude."[42] There was something about assigning a particular number of points that offended at least Justices Sandra Day O'Connor and Stephen Breyer (the two whose votes switched from *Grutter* to *Gratz* to form the conflicting results). Was the point system somehow inconsistent with the diversity rationale? Or was it just too in-your-face? Either way, it was enough to swing a narrow (and jurisprudentially unimportant) win for Ms. Gratz.

Grutter on the other hand decided the issue that mattered: whether a state university can, consistently with the Constitution, give preferential treatment to African-American, Hispanic, and American-Indian applicants, thereby disadvantaging white and Asian-American applicants. Here, in one sense, the five-member majority opinion broke little in the way of new ground. Powell's controlling opinion in *Bakke* had endorsed the diversity rationale as a legitimate justification for race preferences, even very large race preferences. *Grutter* advanced the ball only by putting, for the first time, the Court's full imprimatur behind Justice Powell's logic.

[41] Brief for Petitioners at 25, Gratz v. Bollinger, 539 U.S. 244 (2003) (No. 02-516).
[42] Grutter v. Bollinger, 288 F.3d 732, 776 (6th Cir. 2003) (Boggs, J., dissenting).

But in another sense, *Grutter* was a shocker. Contained within the opinion was a passage that should have raised concerns even among adamant supporters of race-preferential admissions policies: It introduced the concept of deference to colleges and universities into the calculation.

As lawyers know, courts ordinarily apply the highest level of scrutiny to state action that involves race discrimination, a standard known as "strict scrutiny." It has been described as "a searching *judicial* inquiry."[43] As Powell put it in *Bakke*, when government decisions "touch upon an individual's race . . . he is entitled to a *judicial* determination that the burden he is asked to bear on that basis is precisely tailored to serve a compelling governmental interest."[44]

Yet in *Grutter*, the majority purported to defer to the "educational judgment" of the University of Michigan Law School. Rather than conduct a "searching judicial inquiry" into the matter, the Court deferred in some undefined way to the law school.[45] But the concept of deference to the judgment of a college or university is wholly foreign to strict scrutiny. One cannot both defer to the judgment of discriminators and strictly scrutinize their actions. The two are opposites. Deference necessarily eviscerates strict scrutiny, leaving only its tough-talking rhetorical shell. Indeed, as Justice Thomas has pointed out, during the Jim Crow era, many Southern school districts insisted, probably sincerely, that all students learn better in segregated settings.[46] If deference had been accorded these schools, *Brown v. Board of Education* itself would have come out differently.

After *Grutter*, well-informed state actors no longer had to assume that racially discriminatory state action was overwhelmingly likely to be found unconstitutional—at least not in higher education and maybe not in other contexts. Since *Grutter*, one Pennsylvania school experimented with the idea of homerooms segregated by race and sex.[47] It is unthinkable that they would have even considered this if *Grutter* had not thrown wide the door that *Bakke* cracked open.

---

[43] E.g., City of Richmond v. J.A. Croson Co., 488 U.S. 469, 493 (1989) (emphasis added).

[44] Bakke, 438 U.S. at 299 (opinion of Powell, J.) (emphasis added).

[45] See Grutter, 539 U.S. at 328–29.

[46] Fisher, 133 S. Ct. at 2422 (Thomas, J., concurring).

[47] See, e.g., Monika Plocienniczak, Pennsylvania School Experiments with "Segregation," CNN (Jan. 28, 2011).

Grutter-deference ensured that lawsuits against race-preferential admissions policies would be rare—a least for a while. Lawsuits are expensive. Lawsuits against state colleges and universities are especially expensive. For the shoestring operations that ordinarily bring public-interest litigation of this kind, spending that kind of money requires reasonable confidence in victory. It also requires reasonable confidence that the victory will have a significant impact on admissions policies in the future.[48] For the purposes of long-term strategy, "good for this day only" victories, like those in *Bakke* and *Gratz*, might as well be losses. Adding to any potential plaintiff's worries, the Court announced that "good faith on the part of a university is presumed absent a showing to the contrary."[49] Lawsuits arguing that a university's concern for the educational benefits of diversity was pretextual were definitely not being encouraged. The country had other concerns at the time—the wars in Afghanistan and Iraq, terrorism, then the Great Recession. Colleges and universities were going to be left to their own devices.

But seemingly invulnerable institutions sometimes get careless. As a result, issues worthy of litigation do come along. After 2003, many colleges and universities expanded their race-preferential admissions policies, secure in their belief that *Grutter*-deference would

---

[48] Moreover, quite apart from the financing, all one has to do is spend a minute or two on Google to understand why students do not line up to become plaintiffs in these cases: The Internet is littered with grotesque personal attacks on Ms. Fisher and also on Ms. Gratz and Barbara Grutter. See, e.g., James Taranto, The Woman Who Fought Racial Preference, Wall St. J., Jun. 29, 2013, at A15 (reporting violent threats against Gratz).

[49] 539 U.S. at 329 (internal quotations omitted). What makes this somewhat embarrassing is the wealth of admissions from academics that the educational benefits of diversity are not the motivation for race-preferential admissions. While *Grutter* was under consideration by the Court, Harvard law professor Randall Kennedy wrote: "Let's be honest: Many who defend affirmative action for the sake of 'diversity' are actually motivated by a concern that is considerably more compelling. They are not so much animated by a commitment to what is, after all, only a contingent, pedagogical hypothesis. Rather, they are animated by a commitment to social justice. They would rightly defend affirmative action even if social science demonstrated uncontrovertibly that diversity (or its absence) has no effect (or even a negative effect) on the learning environment." Randall Kennedy, Affirmative Reaction, The American Prospect, Mar. 1, 2003. See generally Brian Fitzpatrick, The Diversity Lie, 27 Harv. J.L. & Pub. Pol'y 285 (2003) (giving other examples and pointing out incompatibilities between diversity in theory and race-preferential admissions in practice).

protect them.[50] The University of Texas, however, did so clumsily. During the pre-*Grutter* period, when it was operating under a court order not to give race preferences, it bragged that it had been able to diversify its student body without them. Later, when it re-adopted preferences pursuant to *Grutter*, it was rather difficult to argue that the reinstituted preferences were needed. The university already claimed it had achieved that purpose. Instead, it became obvious that the university had a different goal in mind—moving as close as it could to the demographics of the state of Texas—not bringing in a "critical mass" of minority students in order to obtain for its students the educational benefits of diversity. Such a purpose had been rejected as unconstitutional in *Grutter*.

The Buildup to *Fisher*

In 1996, seven years before *Grutter* and *Gratz*, the U.S. Court of Appeals for the Fifth Circuit decided *Hopwood v. Texas*.[51] In *Hopwood*, the Fifth Circuit, anticipating that the Supreme Court would not adopt Justice Powell's *Bakke* opinion, held that Texas's race-preferential admissions policy violated the Fourteenth Amendment's Equal Protection Clause. This policy was no different from many other admissions policies. Selective colleges and universities in the Fifth Circuit were thus obliged to end their practice of according preferential treatment to members of under-represented races in admissions.

To comply with *Hopwood*, the University of Texas altered its admissions policies to drop direct consideration of race and instead added the consideration of a Personal Achievement Index. The PAI took into account various "special circumstances," such as the socio-economic status of the student's family, languages other than English spoken at home, and whether the student was reared in a single-parent home. PAI scores were combined with Academic Index scores,

---

[50] See, e.g., Althea Nagai, Racial and Ethnic Preferences in Undergraduate Admission at the University of Michigan, Center for Equal Opportunity, Oct. 17, 2006, available at http://www.ceousa.org/content/blogcategory/78/100 (empirical study finding that the University of Michigan actually increased the average preference level for African Americans after *Gratz*).

[51] 78 F.3d 932 (5th Cir. 1996).

which consisted of high school rank and standardized-test scores to determine whether a student would be admitted.[52]

In 1997, the Texas legislature took things a step further and adopted what is sometimes called "the 10 Percent Solution."[53] Under this statute, students with grades in the top 10 percent of each Texas high school were automatically admitted, regardless of their SAT scores or other academic credentials. This approach has generally been unpopular with faculty, on the ground that it weakens the academic qualifications of the class as a whole. A student who graduates in the top 10 percent of an uncompetitive high school with weak SAT scores will often not perform as well academically as a student who graduates only in the top 20 percent of a more competitive high school with stronger SAT scores. On the other hand, the 10 Percent Solution did guarantee more racial diversity than the university's previous policy would have in the absence of explicit race preferences.

In 1996, the last year in which race was directly considered at the University of Texas, the freshman class had been 18.6 percent African American and Hispanic. In 1999, with the combination of the 10 Percent Solution and the "AI + PAI" methods of selecting students, the university announced that "enrollment levels of African American and Hispanic freshmen . . . returned to those of 1996, the year before the *Hopwood* decision." Indeed, it celebrated the fact that "minority students earned higher grade point averages [in 1999] than in 1996 and ha[d] higher retention rates."[54]

By 2003, the University of Texas was bringing in higher numbers of African-American, Hispanic, and Asian-American students than it had in the old days of considering race directly, causing the school

---

[52] Brief for Petitioner at 3, Fisher v. Univ. of Texas at Austin, 133 S. Ct. 2411 (2013) (No. 11-345) ("Abigail Fisher Brief").

[53] Tex. Educ. Code Ann. § 51.803 (West 1997). As Justice Ruth Bader Ginsburg suggests in her dissent, the legal status of the 10 Percent Solution is itself open to question; if its purpose is to increase the number of minority students, it is arguably racially discriminatory too. Fisher, 133 S. Ct. at 2432 (Ginsburg, J., dissenting). On the other hand, policies like the 10 Percent Solution have garnered the support of race-neutrality supporters like former University of California Regent Ward Connerly. *Fisher* did not address this issue, but it is worth pointing out, however, that whatever its legal status, it usually will create fewer *race-specific* mismatch problems, since its beneficiaries—students who would not have gotten in under a policy focusing on standardized test scores—are of all races and ethnicities.

[54] Abigail Fisher Brief, *supra* note 52, at 4.

to declare that it had "effectively compensated for the loss of affir- mative action." In 2004, the entering class was 21.4 percent African American or Hispanic and 17.9 percent Asian American.

But *Grutter* overruled *Hopwood*. After that, other Fifth Circuit se- lective schools were free to resume their old, race-preferential poli- cies. But in Austin things were different. The 10 Percent Solution was statutory, and hence any internal change in policy would have to be in addition to that law. Nevertheless, within hours of the *Grut- ter* decision, the University of Texas announced that it would be re- introducing the direct consideration of race into its admissions pol- icy. After studying the matter for a while, it adopted a policy under which African Americans and Hispanics would receive credit for their race in their PAI calculation.[55]

By 2007, the university's freshman class was 19.7 percent Hispanic, 19.7 percent Asian American, and 5.8 percent African American.[56] The effect of the direct consideration of race, however, seems to have been small. In 2004, the last year in which race was not considered directly, 15.2 percent of the non-top 10 percent enrollees were Afri- can-American or Hispanic. In 2008, when race was considered di- rectly in calculating PAIs, this number increased to 17.9 percent. By far, most minority students—and most students generally—come in through the 10 Percent Solution. If one makes the assumption that the increase from 15.2 percent to 17.9 percent was wholly a result of direct consideration of race—a dubious assumption—race would have been the deciding factor in only 33 cases, or 0.5 percent of the seats in the entering class of 2008.[57]

Abigail Fisher applied for admission to that entering class of 2008. Al- though a fine student, she did not quite make the top 10 percent of her suburban Houston high school. Her SAT scores were not high enough

[55] Although most students at the University of Texas are admitted through the 10 Percent Solution, PAI scores matter for all students, since AI + PAI scores are used to determine eligibility for particular programs of study. Abigail Fisher Brief, *supra* note 52, at 8.

[56] Abigail Fisher Brief, *supra* note 52, at 11.

[57] *Id.* at 9–10. In *Parents Involved in Community Schools v. Seattle School District No. 1*, the Supreme Court held a school-integration plan that had an effect on only a tiny number of student attendance assignments unconstitutional in part because the racially-discriminatory aspects of the plan had insufficient effect on diversity to justify them. 551 U.S. 701 (2007).

to make up the difference—at least when competing against students who were given priority on account of their race. She ended up going out of state to Louisiana State University but brought a lawsuit against the University of Texas and its officers in federal court, citing the Fourteenth Amendment, 42 U.S.C. Sections 1981 and 1983, and Title VI of the Civil Rights Act of 1964.

Fisher argued that the University of Texas had gone beyond *Grutter* and the Constitution in several ways. For example, she contended that rather than seek a "critical mass" of minority students in order to facilitate a rich and varied discussion of issues, Texas was seeking as far as practicable to approximate state demographics in its entering class. The university countered that it was trying to attain diversity not just in the entering class as a whole, but in each and every major, program and classroom, and that doing so requires high numbers of minority students. Fisher then responded that *Grutter* authorizes only critical mass in the class as a whole and that an open-ended license to discriminate until "critical mass" is established in every nook and cranny of the university is too open-ended to be constitutional. Moreover, she argued that the university itself had already admitted that it had achieved the optimal degree of racial diversity using the 10 Percent Solution, and that race discrimination to obtain higher numbers of under-represented minorities proved that the admissions policy could not be narrowly tailored to serve that interest.

The district court would have none of Fisher's arguments. On cross-motions for summary judgment on liability, Judge Sam Sparks granted the university's motion, stating that "as long as *Grutter* remains good law, [the University of Texas's] current admissions program remains constitutional."[58] The Fifth Circuit panel affirmed. Judge Patrick Higginbotham, writing for the court, agreed that *Grutter* controlled the case and that *Grutter*-deference generally protected the decisions made by the University of Texas in the formulation of its admissions policy.[59]

Judge Emilio Garza agreed, but wrote separately to let it be known that he did not consider this a happy result:

---

[58] Fisher v. Univ. of Texas, 645 F. Supp. 2d 587, 613 (W.D. Tex. 2009). The proceedings had already been bifurcated into liability and remedy phases.

[59] Fisher v. Univ. of Texas, 631 F.3d 213, 216–17 (5th Cir. 2011), en banc reh'g denied, 644 F.3d 301 (5th Cir. 2011).

Whenever a serious piece of judicial writing strays from fundamental principles of constitutional law, there is usually a portion of such writing where those principles are articulated, but not followed. So it goes in *Grutter*, where a majority of the Court acknowledged strict scrutiny as the appropriate level of review for race-based preferences in university admissions, but applied a different level of scrutiny markedly less demanding. To be specific, race now matters in university admissions, where, if strict scrutiny were properly applied, it should not.[60]

A petition for en banc review produced seven votes in favor and nine against, as well as an opinion by Chief Judge Edith Jones dissenting from the failure to grant an en banc hearing.[61] The University of Texas had won its case, but not without inspiring several distinguished jurists to raise grave concern over *Grutter*-deference.

On February 21, 2012, the Court granted Abigail Fisher a writ of certiorari.

The Long-Awaited Decision

Fisher was argued on October 10, 2012. The decision was not announced until June 24, 2013, and Justice Anthony Kennedy's opinion for the Court is only 13 pages long. Only Justice Thomas's very readable concurrence elaborates at any length.

Eight and a half months is a long time for such a puny Court opinion. This long wait has caused some observers to wonder if there is a backstory—perhaps an earlier draft of the opinion that never saw the light of day. But if there was, we will probably never hear about it, or at least not until all the justices currently serving are dead (as is the standard practice for the release of justices' papers). The opinion that counts is the one the Court issued, which was joined by seven justices.[62]

---

[60] *Id.* at 247 (Garza, J., specially concurring).

[61] Fisher v. Univ. of Texas, 644 F.3d 301, 304 (5th Cir. 2011) (en banc) (Jones, C.J., dissenting).

[62] The opinion was joined by Chief Justice John Roberts as well as Justices Antonin Scalia, Thomas, Breyer, Samuel Alito, and Sonia Sotomayor. Only Justice Ginsburg dissented. Scalia and Thomas each submitted concurring opinions as well. Justice Elena Kagan recused herself because she had worked on the case while she was solicitor general.

The Court did not sweep away *Grutter v. Bollinger* and hold that race-preferential admissions policies are unconstitutional—as advocates of race-neutral admissions had hoped for and advocates of race-preferential policies had come to fear. Some of the latter have argued that this enhances the precedential value of *Grutter*: The more often a Court applies it, the more difficult it is to overrule. [63]

Such an argument might carry weight if the Court had applied *Grutter* without further comment. But, as Justice Kennedy takes great pains to point out, the Court simply accepted *Bakke, Grutter,* and *Gratz* "as given for the purposes of deciding this case."[64] Justice Scalia elaborated briefly on this point in his one-paragraph concurring opinion: "The petitioner in this case did not ask us to overrule *Grutter*'s holding that a 'compelling interest' in the educational benefits of diversity can justify racial preferences in university admissions."[65] Scalia further states that he adheres to the view he expressed in *Grutter* that the "'Constitution proscribes government discrimination on the basis of race, and state-provided education is no exception.'"[66]

Rather than entrench the *Grutter* decision, *Fisher* thus conspicuously reserves the issue of *Grutter*'s viability.[67] The fact that Justices Scalia and Thomas, both strong advocates of the position that the Constitution mandates race neutrality, concurred in the Court's opinion is evidence that they believe there is a significant chance that the *Fisher* case will be resolved in favor of Ms. Fisher on remand

[63] See, e.g., PBS NewsHour (June 24, 2013) (remarks of Columbia University President Lee Bollinger).

[64] Fisher, 133 S. Ct. at 2417.

[65] *Id.* at 2422 (Scalia, J., concurring).

[66] *Id.* (Scalia, J., concurring) (quoting Grutter v. Bollinger, 539 U.S. 306, 349 (2003) (Scalia, J., concurring in part and dissenting in part)).

[67] Fisher *did* request in her brief for the Court to "overrule *Grutter* to the extent needed to bring clarity to the law and restore the integrity of strict scrutiny review in the higher education setting." Abigail Fisher Brief, *supra* note 52, at 53. At oral argument, however, petitioner's counsel stated in response to a question by Justice Breyer, "[W]e are not trying to change the Court's disposition of the issue in *Grutter*. Could there be . . . a compelling interest in . . . using race to establish a diverse class." Oral Argument at 8, Fisher v. Univ. of Texas at Austin, 133 S. Ct. 2411 (2013) (No. 11-345). But a statement of what the petitioner is "trying to change" is not the same thing as a waiver of an argument explicitly made and discussed in the briefs. What is clear is that petitioner had throughout the litigation emphasized the argument that the University of Texas's admissions policy violated even *Grutter*.

under the newly clarified standard and that, if not, the issue of *Grutter*'s viability can be brought up again on a second trip to the Court.

Another road not taken would have been to hold flatly that preferential treatment may not be used to drive the numbers of under-represented minorities as high as 20 percent (although race-neutral methods could of course be used in a way that results in such an enrollment): Whatever the *Grutter* Court meant by "critical mass," it did not mean 20 percent. But such a ruling would have been awkward, because both *Bakke* and *Gratz* had condemned rigid quantification. The Court was thus unlikely to want to set a quota-like ceiling on race-preferential admissions, especially given that it would have had precious little useful precedential effect. Texas is a majority-minority state. If a university in a state with more typical demographics were to attempt to approximate its demographics in its freshman class, its goal for under-represented minorities would likely be lower than 20 percent. It would be hard to distinguish such an effort from an attempt to enroll a "critical mass" of under-represented minority students for diversity purposes. Such a ruling would have been a victory for Fisher, but it would not have sparked greater introspection on the part of colleges and universities across the nation—something that the Court's actual opinion has some potential to do.[68]

So what road did the Court take? Rather than render a final judgment on the case, it took the opportunity to clarify the applicable standard in broad terms. In particular, it addressed the most controversial part of *Grutter*—deference to the academic judgment of colleges and universities—and made its limitations clearer.

Strict scrutiny has been the centerpiece of equal-protection doctrine for the better part of a century. It makes clear that laws that discriminate on the basis of race (and of certain other "suspect classifications," such as religion and national origin) will be subjected

[68] The Court could have taken it upon itself to apply its newly clarified *Grutter* standard to the record and decide the cross-motions for summary judgment too. Instead, it stated that "fairness to the litigants and the courts that heard the case requires that it be remanded so that the admissions process can be considered and judged under a correct analysis." It therefore remanded to the Fifth Circuit—explicitly *not* the district court—for a decision on the already-existing record. Fisher, 133 S. Ct. at 2421 ("Whether this record . . . is sufficient is a question for the Court of Appeals in the first instance"). In *Adarand Constructors, Inc. v. Peña*, the Court also remanded to the lower court to apply the strict scrutiny standard it had held applicable to the case. 515 U.S. 200 (1995).

to the utmost scrutiny and upheld only in rare circumstances. The test is usually rendered as having two parts: A state must be able to show that a racially discriminatory law (1) serves a compelling governmental interest, not just a legitimate or important governmental interest; and (2) is narrowly tailored to serve that interest.

Up until the last couple of decades or so, the conventional wisdom was that the strict scrutiny test was virtually insurmountable, and that the only racially discriminatory actions by a state that would be upheld would be those that were so obviously necessary (for example, temporarily segregating prisoners by race during a prison yard race riot) that no one would be foolish enough to litigate them. As Stanford law professor Gerald Gunther famously put it, the Court's strict scrutiny doctrine was "'strict' in theory and fatal in fact."[69] After *Grutter*, however, it threatened to become a flaccid thing, at least when applied to college and universities.

Grutter was unclear about whether its controversial deference was intended to apply to every aspect of the strict scrutiny test or only to certain aspects of it. In granting summary judgment to the University of Texas, the Fifth Circuit panel interpreted it to be all-encompassing. Interestingly, at the time of the *Grutter* decision, Justice Kennedy seemed to lean toward a broad interpretation too. "The Court confuses deference to a university's definition of its educational objective," he wrote, "with deference to the implementation of this goal."[70]

Ten years later, Kennedy, faced with the task of making sense of *Grutter*'s ill-advised deferential posture, was less inclined to interpret it in a way he believed would create mischief. Instead, he attempted to outline as sensible an approach to questions of race-preferential admissions as possible while staying within the letter and perhaps even the spirit of *Grutter*.

He began by pointing out what *Grutter* actually said on the subject of deference, which was that a university's "educational judgment that such diversity is essential to its educational mission is one to which we defer." He then made two points: First, only "some"

---

[69] Gerald Gunther, Foreword: In Search of Evolving Doctrine on a Changing Court: A Model for a Newer Equal Protection, 86 Harv. L. Rev. 1, 8 (1972). In later years, the Court went out of its way on more than one occasion to deny this. See Adarand Constructors, Inc. v. Peña, 515 U.S. 200, 237 (1995).

[70] 539 U.S. 306, 388 (2003) (Kennedy, J., dissenting).

deference is due on this issue, "not complete" judicial deference.[71] Second, there must be a great deal more than a university's mere assertion that in the educational judgment of its faculty a diverse student body is essential to its educational mission. "A court, of course, should ensure that there is a reasoned, principled explanation for the academic decision."[72]

Next, Justice Kennedy made it clear that *Grutter*-deference applies only to the "compelling governmental interest" portion of the strict scrutiny test. As to narrow tailoring, strict scrutiny applies in full force, which presumably requires a "reasoned, principled explanation" from the defendant and more. He wrote:

> Once the University has established that its goal of diversity is consistent with strict scrutiny, however, there must still be a further judicial determination that the admissions process meets strict scrutiny in its implementation. The University must prove that the means chosen by the University to attain diversity are narrowly tailored on that goal. *On this point, the University receives no deference.*[73]

Kennedy's interpretation of *Grutter* does not contradict any specific language in that opinion. But if the justices signing on to the near-unanimous *Fisher* opinion had only been *Grutter* dissenters, critics, fairly or unfairly, would likely have called it a sleight of hand. Fortunately for the majority, however, Justice Stephen Breyer, who had been part of the *Grutter* majority, was on board, as was Justice Sonia Sotomayor—herself famously a recipient of an affirmative action preference. The only other remaining member of the *Grutter* majority, Justice Ruth Bader Ginsburg, dissented in *Fisher*, but did not argue that the Court's opinion misrepresents the holding in *Grutter*.[74]

As a result, we have now a two-track strict scrutiny test for campus diversity policies. For compelling governmental interest, "some deference" is appropriate, though the college or university must be prepared with "a reasoned, principled explanation" for its choice. For narrow tailoring, the full force of strict scrutiny is appropriate,

---

[71] Fisher, 133 S. Ct. at 2419.

[72] *Id.*

[73] *Id.* at 2414 (emphasis added).

[74] Justices Sandra Day O'Connor, David Souter, and John Paul Stevens, the other members of the *Grutter* majority, have since retired.

presumably including "reasoned, principled explanations" for many choices.

Double standards, however, tend to be unstable. Up until the *Fisher* decision, there was no need to patrol the boundary between the "compelling governmental interest" and the "narrow tailoring" portion of the strict scrutiny test. Indeed, many careful lawyers would have scoffed at the notion that a distinct boundary was possible. Consider, for example, how the need to patrol the boundary would have affected the now-discredited *Korematsu v. United States*.[75] There, the Court allowed clear discrimination on the basis of national origin when it upheld an evacuation order of "all persons of Japanese ancestry" (including many natural-born American citizens) from large portions of the United States—an order that resulted in many persons of Japanese ancestry being placed in internment camps for the duration of World War II. Was the supposed compelling interest national security? Or was it the need to remove nationals of enemy nations and their children or grandchildren from the country's vulnerable West Coast so as to prevent espionage and to put them in places where they could do little or no harm? If the latter, the actions of the United States were clearly narrowly tailored and the analysis shifts to whether the governmental interest was truly compelling. If the former, the governmental interest is clearly compelling, and the analysis must center on whether the government's actions are narrowly tailored to serve that purpose. Up until *Fisher*, it didn't matter which part of the test was being analyzed. Now it does.

How the boundary will be drawn in *Fisher* (and future cases) may depend on what the judges who apply the dual standard thinks about race-preferential admissions. In the hands of a judge who is sympathetic to the position of the University of Texas as a matter of policy, as much of the analysis as possible may be pushed into the "compelling governmental interest" part of the test. In the hands of a judge who favors race neutrality, however, the bulk of the analysis may be pushed into "narrow tailoring." It is worth noting, however, that *Fisher* refers simply to "the educational benefits that flow from student body diversity" as the relevant compelling interest.[76] It is

---

[75] 323 U.S. 214 (1944).

[76] Fisher, 133 S. Ct. at 2419 (quoting *Grutter*, 539 U.S. at 330) (internal quotation marks omitted).

also worth noting that if the *Fisher* case makes it back to the Supreme Court in the near future, it is likely to face five justices—Scalia, Kennedy, Thomas, and Alito, and Chief Justice John Roberts—who have a history of skepticism toward race-preferential admissions policies.

So what will be the upshot of the *Fisher* decision? No one has a crystal ball, of course. But colleges and universities have to think about these issues now. If they wait until they are in court to decide how to fashion their policies, they will likely find the task impossible.

I very much doubt that the way colleges and universities have justified their individual policies in the recent past will continue to work. Many schools have operated under the assumption that they can justify their policy in isolation—that all they need to do is show their application and yield rates and thus prove that without preferences they would have fewer under-represented minorities than they regard as minimally necessary. But it is not just the fact of a race-preferential admissions policy that must be defended now, but also the details of the particular policy and its effects on educational outcomes. Just as different forms of diversity must be balanced against each other, different pedagogical problems must be considered against each other. More specifically, the pedagogical advantages of racial diversity must be balanced against the pedagogical disadvantages of gaps in academic credentials.

This evaluation will probably not be easy to do without meticulous work. The Court will be asking questions: If you are really concerned about capturing the educational benefits of diversity, why do you need to admit students whose academic credentials put them two standards below the mean? Why can't you cut it off one-and-three-quarters standard deviations lower than the mean? What is the graduation rate of students in that category? How often do they succeed in their initial major? Are the race preferences at your flagship campus so large that they decrease the level of diversity at your other campuses? If your flagship campus rejected engineering-interested minority students who would need preference to be admitted and instead accepted them to one of your other campuses, would that increase racial diversity in your graduate engineering school in the future since the chances of their success (and thus the chances that they will go on to graduate school) are greater at one of your other campuses? The list of potential questions is very long.

The bottom line, however, is that if capturing the educational benefits of diversity is the goal, the academic judgments that must be made in fashioning an actual policy are numerous and never-ending. Those judgments cannot be simple-minded sentimental ones and they definitely cannot be political in nature. Reason and principle must prevail.

If *Fisher* does nothing else, it should force colleges and universities to confront the research on mismatch in a detached and scientific manner.[77] That means using ideologically diverse teams of qualified, independent investigators—persons whose job and prestige are not dependent on maintaining the status quo. It means adequately funding and supporting the investigation with access to data. It means following standard scientific procedures by making the data available to qualified researchers who wish to critique the work.

A college that undertakes such research and concludes in good faith that the mismatch research is wrong may well be given the benefit of the doubt. That much of *Grutter*-deference may remain intact post-*Fisher*. But as long as colleges and universities continue to discriminate on the basis of race, they will be called upon to confront new research that tends to show that their policy should be modified or eliminated.

Meanwhile, a legislator who pressures a state college to "improve its diversity numbers" on pain of a budget cut may be setting that school up for a lawsuit. Caving to such pressure may be the practical thing to do in view of the importance of funding. But it is not a principled basis for an academic decision. It is politics.[78] The same goes

---

[77] See *supra* notes 4–21 and accompanying text. The research discussed there was hardly a bolt from the blue. Divorced from the affirmative-action context, the conclusion that preferential treatment in admissions can be against the beneficiary's interest would be ordinary and unobjectionable. See James Davis, The Campus as a Frog Pond: An Application of the Theory of Relative Deprivation to Career Decisions of College Men, 72 Am. J. Soc. 17, 30–31 (1966). Writing before affirmative action, Davis found that college grades were more strongly correlated with the decision to enter a high-prestige career than was the selectivity of the institution. Davis therefore offered the following advice: "Counselors and parents might well consider the drawbacks as well as the advantages of sending a boy to a 'fine' college, if, when doing so, it is fairly certain he will end up in the bottom ranks of his graduating class."

[78] More than 23 percent of medical school and 15 percent of law school admissions officers report pressure to engage in race-preferential admissions from state governmental entities. See Susan Welch & John Gruhl, Affirmative Action and Minority Enrollments in Medical and Law Schools 80, Table 3.3 (1998).

for other funding sources—from the federal government to private foundations to wealthy alumni. If a college or university is adjusting its policies in order to qualify for funding, its decision is hard to justify as an academic one and it is not based on principle. Funding sources would thus do well to avoid creating opportunities for lawsuits against their intended beneficiaries.

A fortiori, caving to pressure from student groups cannot form any part of a "reasoned, principled explanation" for an academic decision.[79] The more agitation that goes on at a particular campus for diversity, the more difficult it will be for that institution to prove that its policy is the product of a reasoned, principled inquiry into matters of pedagogy.[80]

Predictions Are Hard to Make, Especially about the Future

I began by saying that while predictions are difficult to make, I am somewhat optimistic that *Fisher* will have a beneficial effect on the debate over race-preferential admissions. If the Court is steadfast in its insistence on reasoned and principled explanations, and if it does indeed strictly scrutinize race-preferential admissions policies to ensure that they are narrowly tailored to fit authorized goals, *Fisher* may force attention on the downsides of racial preferences.

Nevertheless, I am under no illusion that a mass abandonment of race-preferential admissions policies is imminent. This will take time. There is something in the human soul that doesn't like to hear that the project it has been working on for 40 years has done more harm than good. At every college and university in the country,

---

[79] Fisher, 133 S. Ct. at 2419.

[80] For example, two years ago at the University of Wisconsin, a student mob egged on by the vice provost for diversity and climate, overpowered hotel staff to interrupt a press conference at which the speaker was critical of race-based admissions. See Peter Wood, Mobbing for Preferences, Chronicle of Higher Education, Sept. 22, 2011. See also Ben LeFebvre, Wham BAMN: Group Stirs Controversy in Fight for Civil Rights, Metro Times, Jan. 11, 2006. The organization whose tactics are discussed in the Lefebvre article—the Coalition to Defend Affirmative Action, Integration and Immigrant Rights by Any Means Necessary (known as"BAMN")—will be before the Court next term in Schuette v. Coalition to Defend Affirmative Action, 652 F.3d 607 (6th Cir. 2012) (en banc), cert. granted, 133 S. Ct. 1633 (Mar. 25, 2013) (No. 12-682), a case concerning the constitutionality of the Michigan Civil Rights Initiative.

there are many who are irrevocably in the category of true believer.[81] Moreover, since some accrediting agencies act essentially as diversity cartel enforcers, it is difficult for schools where preference-skeptics dominate to eliminate or even decrease preferential treatment.[82]

But for those who see mismatch as the most troubling aspect of race-preferential admissions, this is not an all-or-nothing game. The smaller the credentials gap between preference beneficiaries and the other students, the smaller the likelihood of harm.[83] Puritans may insist that only total victory can be called victory, but I am not a Puritan.

To achieve even modest success along these lines, however, colleges and universities must believe that there is at least a possibility they will wind up in court if they do not take steps to protect themselves. Given that litigation is expensive and the fact-intensive litigation that the Court seems to anticipate is very expensive, one can be certain that there will not be hundreds of lawsuits or even dozens.

---

[81] Sudden change may be difficult for other reasons too. State colleges and universities have evolved along lines that they may well not have in the absence of affirmative action preferences: Gaining admittance outside the affirmative action track has become more difficult than it was in the 1960s. It is entirely possible that if race preferences had been held to be generally illegal in *Bakke*, the fragile political coalition that supported the "super-competitive/racially diverse" model would never have emerged and the nation's most elite state universities would be somewhat less competitive. As it stands, the individual school may find it difficult to eliminate race-preferential admissions without making other changes to its admissions structure. Whether there is sufficient political support for the super-competitive model of state universities in the absence of race preferences remains to be seen.

[82] See Margaret Jackson, University of Colorado Heals Diversity Gap, Denver Post (April 21, 2012) ("The university has made a concerted effort to improve diversity among its students since its accrediting body . . . cited the school for 'non-compliance' in 2010, when just 106 of 614 students were minorities"); Gail Heriot, The ABA's "Diversity" Diktat, Wall St. J., Apr. 28, 2008, at A19. See Susan Welch & John Gruhl, Affirmative Action and Minority Enrollments in Medical and Law Schools 80, Table 3.3 (1998) (when asked whether they felt pressure from any source to engage in preferences, 24 percent of medical schools and 31 percent of law schools volunteered that they felt pressure from accrediting agencies). If courts or other authorities were to make clear that accrediting agencies will not be deferred to and that a school that allows itself to be pressured this way is not making an academic judgment but a political one, that would open up colleges and universities to use their own discretion. I predict that the diversity of approaches that would ensue would surprise many on both sides of the debate.

[83] It may also be true that the more colleges and universities avoid credentials gaps for students who plan to major in science and engineering, the smaller the harm.

There will be some. Public-interest litigators will likely target their lawsuits carefully. In the short run, at least, if *Fisher* has the effect of reducing the level of preferential treatment received by under-represented minority students, it will be in part because word has gotten around—not just to colleges and universities, but to students—that the evidence of its failure is persuasive.

In sum, the Court has made an effort to invoke reason and principle in the debate over race-preferential admissions policies. Advocates of race neutrality would have preferred it if the particular principle the Court invoked had been . . . race neutrality. Until it does so, there is unlikely to be sweeping change. But even incremental change is welcome.

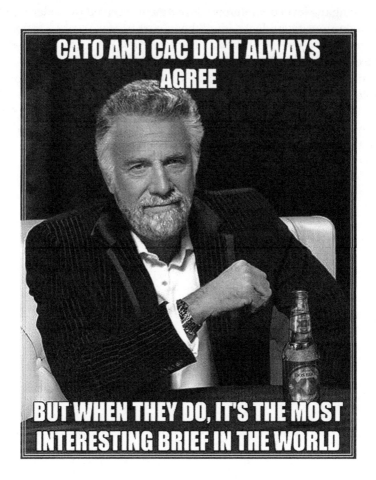

Reading the Opinions—and the Tea Leaves—in *United States v. Windsor*

By Elizabeth B. Wydra*

The Supreme Court issued a groundbreaking ruling on the final day of its 2012–2013 term, when, in *United States v. Windsor*, a five-justice majority struck down Section 3 of the Defense of Marriage Act—which excluded legally married same-sex couples from more than 1,000 federal benefits—as a violation of the Fifth Amendment.[1] The DOMA decision was issued exactly 10 years to the day after the Court recognized a constitutional right of privacy in the intimate relations of gay men and lesbians in *Lawrence v. Texas*,[2] a ruling repeatedly cited by the *Windsor* majority in upholding the constitutional rights of married same-sex couples to equal dignity and treatment.

The Court also issued a ruling in *Hollingsworth v. Perry*, dismissing the case for lack of jurisdiction after finding that the proponents of Proposition 8, which changed California's constitution to define marriage as between a man and a woman, did not have standing to defend it on appeal.[3] *Perry* was a victory for advocates of marriage equality in that the Court's dismissal allowed to stand the district court's order striking down Prop 8 as unconstitutional under the Fourteenth Amendment, but neither the majority nor the dissent weighed in on the ultimate question of whether the Constitution bars states from excluding same-sex couples from the institution of marriage. Accordingly, the opinions in *Windsor* provide the most fertile hunting ground for clues as to the future of marriage equality in

---

* Chief counsel, Constitutional Accountability Center; counsel of record for briefs submitted on behalf of CAC and the Cato Institute in *Hollingsworth v. Perry* and *United States v. Windsor*.

[1] 133 S. Ct. 2675 (2013).

[2] 539 U.S. 558 (2003).

[3] 133 S. Ct. 2652 (2013).

the high court. This article will focus on reading the opinions—and the tea leaves—of the *Windsor* case.[4]

I. Case Background

Most Supreme Court cases do not have at their core a cinematic, "almost mesmerizingly romantic" love story.[5] But the journey that ended with Edith Windsor declaring herself "joyous" at having won everything she "asked and hoped for"[6] in her challenge to the DOMA provision that defined marriage for purposes of federal law as "only a legal union between one man and one woman as husband and wife"[7] is a moving tale of love, loss, and history-making.

Edith "Edie" Windsor and her late spouse, Dr. Thea Spyer, fell in love in the early 1960s.[8] In pre-Stonewall New York City, after a failed marriage to a man, Ms. Windsor in desperation called an old friend and said, "If you know where the lesbians go please take me."[9] That night, in a Greenwich Village restaurant, Edie met Thea, and the two danced all night until Edie got a hole in her stocking.[10] In 1967, they moved in together and became engaged. Spyer, a clinical psychologist, proposed to Windsor with a diamond brooch instead of a ring, to avoid questions from Windsor's colleagues at IBM about the identity of her "fiancé." Despite having attained the highest technical

[4] There were, of course, also substantial and interesting questions regarding standing and jurisdiction in both *Windsor* and *Perry*, but these issues will not be addressed by this article.

[5] Amy Davidson, Will the Supreme Court Recognize Edith Windsor?, New Yorker, Mar. 21, 2013, http://www.newyorker.com/online/blogs/closeread/2013/03/edith-windsor-doma-supreme-court-ginsburg-scalia.html. In fact, a film has been made about the couple's story. Edie and Thea: A Very Long Engagement (2009), trailer available at http://www.youtube.com/watch?v=lL83Yl4-9Vc.

[6] Matthew Perlman, et al., Edith Windsor, Center of Supreme Court's DOMA Ruling, Wins "Everything We Asked and Hoped for," N.Y. Daily News, Jun. 26, 2013, available at http://www.nydailynews.com/new-york/edith-windsor-wins-hoped-article-1.1383602.

[7] Defense of Marriage Act, 110 Stat. 2419, Section 3 (1996) (amending the Dictionary Act, 1 U.S.C. § 7).

[8] Brief on the Merits for Respondent Edith Schlain Windsor at 1, United States v. Windsor, 133 S. Ct. 2675 (No. 12-307) ("Windsor Brief").

[9] Adam Gabbatt, Edith Windsor and Thea Spyer: "A Love Affair That Just Kept On and On and On," Guardian, Jun. 26, 2013, available at http://www.theguardian.com/world/2013/jun/26/edith-windsor-thea-spyer-doma.

[10] *Id.*

rank as a computer programmer at IBM, Windsor did not feel able to disclose her full identity at work.[11]

Spyer was diagnosed with multiple sclerosis in 1977, eventually suffering paralysis, and Windsor quit her job to care for Spyer.[12] With Spyer's health continuing to decline, the couple flew to Canada in May 2007 to get married.[13] (In 1993, the couple had registered as domestic partners when New York City law changed to recognize civil unions.[14]) Just as the first night they met, Windsor and Spyer danced together at their wedding, with Windsor on the arm of her wife's wheelchair.[15] Windsor has said that people asked her about the couple's decision to get married, "'What could be different? You've lived together for over 40 years—what could be different about marriage?' . . . And it turned out that marriage could be different."[16]

Both in their late 70s, Windsor and Spyer spent their last two years together as a married couple. In February 2009, Spyer died, leaving her estate to her spouse.[17] Because of DOMA, however, Windsor was not recognized as Spyer's spouse under federal law and thus could not qualify for the marital exemption from the federal estate tax, which excludes from taxation "any interest in property which passes or has passed from the decedent to his surviving spouse."[18] Windsor thus paid $363,053 in estate taxes and filed a refund suit in the U.S. District Court for the Southern District of New York—the federal trial court in Manhattan—alleging that DOMA violated the Constitution's guarantee of equal treatment under the law. Windsor prevailed in the district court as well as in the U.S. Court of Appeals for the Second Circuit.[19]

---

[11] *Id.* Windsor Brief at 2–3.

[12] Richard Wolf, Gay Marriage Case: A Long Time Coming for Edie Windsor, USA Today, Dec. 8, 2012, available at http://www.usatoday.com/story/news/nation/2012/12/07/edie-windsor-gay-marriage-supreme-court/1737387.

[13] Windsor, 133 S. Ct. at 2683.

[14] *Id.*

[15] Wolf, *supra* note 12.

[16] *Id.*

[17] Windsor, 133 S. Ct. at 2683.

[18] 26 U.S.C. § 2056(a) (1997).

[19] Windsor v. United States, 833 F.Supp.2d 394 (S.D.N.Y. 2012), aff'd 699 F.3d 169 (2d Cir. 2012).

II. The Statute

In 1996, Congress enacted the Defense of Marriage Act, with two operative sections: Section 2, which purports to authorize states to refuse to recognize lawful same-sex marriages performed in other states,[20] and Section 3, which provided:

> In determining the meaning of any Act of Congress, or of any ruling, regulation, or interpretation of the various administrative bureaus and agencies of the United States, the word "marriage" means only a legal union between one man and one woman as husband and wife, and the word "spouse" refers only to a person of the opposite sex who is a husband or a wife.[21]

Section 3, challenged in the *Windsor* case, did not prohibit states from recognizing same-sex couples' marriages, but it did control more than 1,000 federal laws that relate to marital or spousal status,[22] including "laws pertaining to Social Security, housing, taxes, criminal sanctions, copyright, and veterans' benefits."[23] Couples like Windsor and Spyer found themselves in marriages that were recognized by the state in which they lived, but rejected by the federal government. Because of DOMA's Section 3, legally married same-sex couples could not file joint federal tax returns. They were denied some privileges of intellectual property. Federal employees could not share health insurance and other medical benefits with a same-sex spouse, and gay and lesbian couples were denied the protections of the Family and Medical Leave Act. Section 3 even denied a surviving gay or lesbian spouse notification of his or her military spouse's death in the line of duty, and prevented married same-sex couples from being buried together in veterans' cemeteries.[24] As the *Windsor* Court explained, "by its great reach, DOMA touches many aspects of married and family life, from the mundane to the profound."[25]

---

[20] 28 U.S.C. § 1738C (1996).

[21] 1 U.S.C. § 7 (1996).

[22] Windsor, 133 S.Ct. at 2688.

[23] Windsor, 133 S. Ct. at 2688, 2694.

[24] Windsor Brief, at 6–7; see also Windsor, 133 S. Ct. at 2694.

[25] Windsor, 133 S. Ct. at 2694.

In passing DOMA, the report from the House of Representatives concluded that "it is both appropriate and necessary for Congress to do what it can to defend the institution of traditional heterosexual marriage. . . . The effort to redefine marriage to extend to homosexual couples is a truly radical proposal that would fundamentally alter the institution of marriage."[26] The House Report explained that DOMA expresses "both moral disapproval of homosexuality, and a moral conviction that heterosexuality better comports with traditional (especially Judeo-Christian) morality."[27]

III. The Opinions

A. The Majority Opinion

The majority opinion in *Windsor*, authored by Justice Anthony Kennedy and joined by Justices Ruth Bader Ginsburg, Stephen Breyer, Sonia Sotomayor, and Elena Kagan, does not mince words: "DOMA writes inequality into the entire United States Code."[28] The "principal effect" of the statute "is to identify a subset of state-sanctioned marriages and make them unequal. . . . DOMA undermines both the public and private significance of state-sanctioned same-sex marriages; for it tells those couples, and all the world, that their otherwise valid marriages are unworthy of federal recognition."[29] According to the *Windsor* majority, DOMA's intent to interfere "with the equal dignity of same-sex marriages" was "its essence."[30] Because the "Constitution's guarantee of equality 'must at the very least mean that a bare congressional desire to harm a politically unpopular group cannot' justify disparate treatment of that group," the statute was struck down as violating "basic due process and equal protection principles applicable to the Federal Government."[31]

In analyzing the majority opinion and its conclusion, it helps to ask several key questions. First, and most important, does the conclusion square with the Constitution's text and history? What does it portend for advocates both for and against recognition of same-sex

[26] H.R. Rep. No. 104-664, at 12–13 (1996).

[27] *Id.* at 16; see Windsor, 133 S. Ct. at 2693.

[28] Windsor, 133 S. Ct. at 2694.

[29] *Id.*

[30] *Id.* at 2693 (citation omitted).

[31] *Id.*

couples' marital status in the states? Does the majority opinion recognize that gay men and lesbians have a constitutional right to marry the person of their own choosing?

1. The Windsor *Ruling and the Constitution's Text and History*

Although Justice Antonin Scalia accused the majority of employing "legalistic argle-bargle" in his dissent,[32] the majority's conclusion is supported by constitutional text and history.[33] The Due Process Clause of the Fifth Amendment (which was the operative constitutional provision in *Windsor* because DOMA is a federal enactment) and the Equal Protection Clause of the Fourteenth Amendment (which was passed in the wake of the Civil War to protect against state and local government action) guarantee to all persons the equal protection of the laws. While, of course, the text of the Fifth Amendment "is not as explicit a guarantee of equal treatment as the Fourteenth Amendment," the Court has repeatedly held that "the Constitution imposes upon federal, state, and local governmental actors the same obligation to respect the personal right to equal protection of the laws."[34] Indeed, the *Windsor* majority explicitly braided together the Fifth Amendment guarantee of liberty with the Fourteenth Amendment's express protection of equality, noting that "[w]hile the Fifth Amendment itself withdraws from Government the power to degrade or demean in the way [DOMA] does, the equal protection guarantee of the Fourteenth Amendment makes that Fifth Amendment right all the more specific and all the better understood and preserved."[35]

The text of the Equal Protection Clause of the Fourteenth Amendment is sweeping and universal: "No State shall . . . deny to *any person*

---

[32] Windsor, 133 S. Ct. at 2709 (Scalia, J., dissenting).

[33] See Brief of the Cato Institute and Constitutional Accountability Center as Amici Curiae in Support of Respondents, United States v. Windsor, 133 S. Ct. 2675 (No. 12-307) ("Cato-CAC Brief in Windsor").

[34] Adarand Constructors, Inc. v. Pena, 515 U.S. 200, 213, 231–32 (1995); see also Lyng v. Castillo, 477 U.S. 635, 636 n.2 (1986) ("The federal sovereign, like the States, must govern impartially. The concept of equal justice under law is served by the Fifth Amendment's guarantee of due process, as well as by the Equal Protection Clause of the Fourteenth Amendment.") (quoting Hampton v. Mow Sun Wong, 426 U. S. 88, 100 (1976)); Weinberger v. Wiesenfeld, 420 U.S. 636, 638 n.2 (1976) ("This Court's approach to Fifth Amendment equal protection claims has always been precisely the same as to equal protection claims under the Fourteenth Amendment.").

[35] Windsor, 133 S. Ct. at 2695.

within its jurisdiction the equal protection of the laws."[36] While the amendment was written and ratified in the aftermath of the Civil War and the end of slavery, and "in some initial drafts [it] was written to prohibit discrimination against 'persons because of race, color or previous condition of servitude,' the Amendment submitted for consideration and later ratified contained more comprehensive terms."[37] It protects *all* persons. It secures the same rights and same protection under the law for all men and women, of any race, whether young or old, citizen or alien, gay or straight.[38] No person, under the Fourteenth Amendment's text, may be consigned to the status of a pariah, "a stranger to [the State's] laws."[39] The Fourteenth Amendment's sweeping guarantee of equal legal protection means, first and foremost, equality under the law and equality of rights for all persons. Under the plain text, this sweeping guarantee applies to gay men and lesbians, as the *Windsor* majority assumes.

The original meaning of the Equal Protection Clause confirms what the text makes clear: that equality of rights and equality under the law apply broadly to any and all persons within the United States. History shows that the original meaning of the Equal Protection Clause secures to all persons "'the protection of equal laws,'"[40] prohibiting arbitrary and invidious discrimination and securing equal rights for all classes and groups of persons. The Fourteenth Amendment's framers' own explanations of the Equal Protection Clause during congressional debates, press coverage of the proposal

---

[36] U.S. Const. amend. XIV, § 1 (emphasis added).

[37] J.E.B. v. Alabama ex rel. T.B., 511 U.S. 127, 151 (1994) (Kennedy, J., concurring).

[38] See Yick Wo. v. Hopkins, 118 U.S. 356, 369 (1886) ("These provisions are universal in their application, to all persons within the territorial jurisdiction, without regard to any differences of race, color, or of nationality."); Civil Rights Cases, 109 U.S. 3, 31 (1883) ("The fourteenth amendment extends its protection to races and classes, and prohibits any state legislation which has the effect of denying to any race or class, or to any individual, the equal protection of the laws."). See generally Brief of the Cato Institute and Constitutional Accountability Center as Amici Curiae in Support of Respondents at 4–10, Hollingsworth v. Perry, 133 S. Ct. 2652 (2013) (No. 12-144) ("Cato-CAC Brief in Perry").

[39] Romer v. Evans, 517 U.S. 620, 635 (1996).

[40] *Id.* at 634 (quoting Skinner v. Oklahoma ex rel. Williamson, 316 U.S. 535, 541 (1942)).

and ratification process, and the Supreme Court's earliest decisions interpreting the clause all affirm this basic understanding.[41]

Introducing the amendment in the Senate, Jacob Howard explained that the Equal Protection Clause "establishes equality before the law, and . . . gives to the humblest, the poorest, and most despised . . . the same rights and the same protection before the law as it gives to the most powerful, the most wealthy, or the most haughty."[42] The guarantee of equal protection, he went on, "abolishes all class legislation in the States and does away with the injustice of subjecting one caste of persons to a code not applicable to another. . . . It protects the black man in his fundamental rights as a citizen with the same shield which it throws over the white man."[43] Senator Howard's reading of the Fourteenth Amendment—never once controverted during the debates and widely reported "in major newspapers across the country"[44]—demonstrated that "[t]he Equal Protection Clause was intended to work nothing less than the abolition of all caste-based and invidious class-based legislation,"[45] ensuring "the law's neutrality where the rights of persons are at stake."[46] Emphasizing this point in an article published shortly after Congress sent the Fourteenth Amendment to the states for ratification, the *Cincinnati Commercial* explained that the Fourteenth Amendment wrote into the Constitution "the great Democratic principle of equality before the law," invalidating all "legislation hostile to any class."[47] "With this section engrafted upon the Constitution, it will be impossible for any Legislature to enact special codes for one class of its citizens."[48] Press coverage emphasized that the amendment "put in the fundamental law the declaration that all citizens were entitled to equal rights in this Republic,"[49] placing all "throughout the land upon the same footing of equality before the law, in order to prevent unequal

---

[41] See Cato-CAC Brief in Perry, at 10–14.

[42] Cong. Globe, 39th Cong., 1st Sess. 2766 (1866).

[43] *Id.* See also *id.* at 2961 (Sen. Poland) (noting that the Equal Protection Clause aimed to "uproot and destroy . . . partial State legislation").

[44] McDonald v. City of Chicago, 130 S. Ct. 3020, 3074 (2010) (Thomas, J., concurring).

[45] Plyler v. Doe, 457 U.S. 202, 213 (1982).

[46] Romer, 517 U.S. at 623.

[47] Cincinnati Commercial, Jun. 21, 1866, at 4.

[48] *Id.*

[49] Chicago Tribune, Aug. 2, 1866, at 2.

legislation."[50] The original meaning of equality, as it was written into the Constitution, was neutrality under the law for all persons—it was broad and inclusive, and there is no reason to exclude gay men and lesbians from this promise of equality.

The *Windsor* majority opinion is in line with the constitutional text and history of the Fourteenth Amendment, which provides the rubric or analog under which the Supreme Court has applied an equal protection component of the Fifth Amendment. Echoing Justice Kennedy's opinion in *Romer*, which invalidated a "status-based enactment" that denied equal rights to gay men and lesbians, "not to further a proper legislative end but to make them unequal to everyone else,"[51] the *Windsor* majority struck down DOMA Section 3 because the "avowed purpose and practical effect of the law here in question are to impose a disadvantage, a separate status, and so a stigma"[52] on married same-sex couples. Noting that DOMA placed "same-sex couples in an unstable position of being in a second-tier marriage," the majority concludes that this "differentiation demeans the couple, whose moral and sexual choices the Constitution protects, [citing *Lawrence*], and whose relationship the State has sought to dignify," and "humiliates tens of thousands of children now being raised by same-sex couples."[53]

2. The Windsor *Ruling and the Future of State Marriage Laws*

The majority's conclusion that Section 3 of DOMA violates constitutional guarantees of equal protection and due process, coupled with an apparent compassion for the real and dignitary harm discriminatory marriage laws visit upon gay and lesbian couples and their families, is encouraging to many advocates of marriage equality. But Justice Kennedy's opinion gives hope to advocates on both sides of the issue.

For those who wish to maintain state laws excluding gay and lesbian couples from the institution of marriage, the threads of federalism running through the majority opinion might be cause for optimism. Justice Kennedy repeatedly refers to the democratic workings

---

[50] Cincinnati Commercial, Aug. 20, 1866, at 2.

[51] Romer, 517 U.S. at 635.

[52] Windsor, 133 S. Ct. at 2693.

[53] *Id.* at 2694.

of state law in recognizing marriage equality. Describing the history of marriage law in New York, he specifically highlights the "statewide deliberative process that enabled its citizens to discuss and weigh arguments for and against same-sex marriage."[54] The majority opinion gestures to the inherent dignity of gay and lesbian couples' relationships, noting that "[p]rivate, consensual sexual intimacy between two adult persons of the same sex may not be punished by the State, and it can form 'but one element in a personal bond that is more enduring'"[55]—but the opinion appears to rely on New York's decision "to give further protection and dignity to that bond,"[56] rather than any inherent right of the couple to have their bond recognized. The majority characterizes New York's marriage-equality law as a reflection of "the community's considered perspective on the historical roots of the institution of marriage and its evolving understanding of the meaning of equality,"[57] which could be at odds with an argument that same-sex couples have a right, not subject to the whims of a democratic majority, to have their bond recognized by state marriage laws.

But a close reading of the majority opinion suggests that it is not really about federalism (regardless of what Chief Justice John Roberts and Justice Samuel Alito say in their dissents, discussed below). First, the majority rejects the argument that the federal government has no power whatsoever to "make determinations that bear on marital rights and privileges."[58] The Court cites several examples of "congressional statutes which affect marriages and family status" when relevant to other federal policies and goals, noting that "when the Federal Government acts in the exercise of its own proper authority, it has a wide choice of the mechanisms and means to adopt."[59] Congress may constitutionally intrude, in at least some contexts, on the state's traditional regulation of marriage.

Second, to the extent DOMA's intrusion into the state realm of marriage regulation is relevant to the majority's analysis, it is to

---

[54] *Id.* at 2689.

[55] *Id.* at 2692 (quoting Lawrence, 539 U.S. 557, 567).

[56] *Id.* at 2692.

[57] *Id.* at 2692–93.

[58] *Id.* at 2690.

[59] *Id.*

demonstrate "DOMA's unusual deviation from the usual tradition of recognizing and accepting state definitions of marriage."[60] As Justice Kennedy previously wrote in *Romer*, "[d]iscriminations of an unusual character especially suggest careful consideration to determine whether they are obnoxious to the constitutional provision."[61] Making it clear that the ruling is not about federalism, the *Windsor* majority states that "it is unnecessary to decide whether [DOMA's] federal intrusion on state power is a violation of the Constitution because it disrupts the federal balance."[62]

Perhaps most important for advocates of marriage equality, the majority's opinion recognizes that the "States' interest in defining and regulating the marital relation" is "subject to constitutional guarantees."[63] Citing *Loving v. Virginia*, the case that struck down bans on interracial marriage as unconstitutional, Justice Kennedy affirms that "State laws defining and regulating marriage, of course, must respect the constitutional rights of persons."[64]

Moreover, the point that "marriage between a man and a woman no doubt had been thought of by most people as essential to the very definition of that term"[65] is not likely to be the end of the inquiry for the justices in the *Windsor* majority. Inequality rooted in "tradition" is as much a blot on the Constitution's guarantee of equal protection as novel forms of discrimination. As Justice Kennedy wrote in *Lawrence*, "the fact that the governing majority . . . has traditionally viewed a particular practice as immoral is not a sufficient reason for upholding a law prohibiting the practice."[66] The infamous *Plessy v. Ferguson* upheld the constitutionality of segregation based on "the

---

[60] *Id.* at 2693.

[61] Romer, 517 U.S. at 633 (quoting Louisville Gas & Elec. Co. v. Coleman, 277 U.S. 32, 37–38 (1928)); see also Free Enterprise Fund v. Public Co. Accounting Oversight Bd., 130 S. Ct. 3138, 3159 (2010) (observing that sometimes "the most telling indication of [a] severe constitutional problem . . . is the lack of historical precedent" for Congress's actions) (quoting Judge Kavanuagh's dissent, Free Enterprise Fund v. Public Co. Accounting Oversight Bd., 537 F.3d 667, 669 (2008).

[62] Windsor, 133 S. Ct. at 2692

[63] *Id.*

[64] *Id.* at 2691 (citing Loving v. Virginia, 388 U.S. 1 (1967)).

[65] *Id.* at 2689.

[66] Lawrence, 539 U.S. at 577 (quoting Bowers v. Hardwick, 478 U.S. 186, 216 (1986) (Stevens, J., dissenting)).

established usages, customs, and traditions of the people," [67] whereas *Lawrence* explained that "neither history nor tradition"[68] could save an otherwise unconstitutional law.

If pressed, Justice Kennedy would likely have a difficult time justifying state authority to discriminate against gay and lesbian couples when it comes to marriage. As the *Windsor* majority opinion notes, states do enjoy traditional authority to regulate marriage, but this authority must be used in compliance with the Constitution. Indeed, the Constitution consciously modifies traditional or usual governmental regulatory authority to ensure that it is not used for impermissible ends. It was commonly understood at the time the Fourteenth Amendment was ratified that the Equal Protection Clause "was intended to promote equality in the States, and to take from the States the power to make class legislation and to create inequality among their people."[69] The Court's precedents, the most relevant of which were authored by Justice Kennedy, firmly establish that the Equal Protection Clause requires "neutrality where the rights of persons are at stake," forbidding states from "singling out a certain class of citizens for disfavored legal status or general hardships."[70] Under precedents such as *Romer*, settled equal protection principles apply with full force to legislation and state constitutional amendments that discriminate based on sex and sexual orientation. No matter how committed to federalism Justice Kennedy (and any other members of the Court) may be, under the Equal Protection Clause, states may not deny to gay men or lesbians rights basic to "ordinary civic life in a free society,"[71] just "to make them unequal to everyone else."[72]

3. The Windsor *Ruling and a Right to Marriage Equality*

All of this begs the question to which everyone reading *Windsor* is searching for an answer: do gay men and lesbians have a constitutional right to marry the person of their own choosing? The *Windsor* ruling does not decide this question, as the majority makes sure to

---

[67] 163 U.S. 537, 550–51 (1896).

[68] 539 U.S. at 577–78 (quoting Bowers, 478 U.S. at 216 (Stevens, J., dissenting)).

[69] Cong. Globe, 42nd Cong., 2nd Sess. 847 (1872) (Sen. Morton).

[70] Romer, 517 U.S. at 623, 633.

[71] *Id.* at 631.

[72] *Id.* at 635.

disclaim.[73] But the opinion, the Constitution's text and history, and other precedents suggest an answer.

Justice Kennedy's previous gay rights rulings have recognized that, for same-sex and heterosexual couples alike, the "State cannot demean their existence or control their destiny."[74] In *Lawrence*, the Court affirmed that "our laws and traditions afford constitutional protection to personal decisions relating to marriage" because of "the respect the Constitution demands for the autonomy of the person in making these choices."[75] "Persons in a homosexual relationship may seek autonomy for these purposes, just as heterosexual persons do."[76]

The Constitution protects a right for gay and lesbian couples to marry against state infringement, as evidenced by the text and original meaning of the Fourteenth Amendment, which would be the operative constitutional provision in any challenge to state marriage laws. The framers of the Fourteenth Amendment recognized the right to marry as a basic civil right of all persons, "one of the vital personal rights essential to the orderly pursuit of happiness."[77] These rights were intended to apply equally to all persons.[78] The equality of rights secured by the Fourteenth Amendment's Equal Protection Clause thus includes the equal right to marry the person of one's choice, "sheltered by the Fourteenth Amendment against the State's unwarranted usurpation, disregard, or disrespect."[79]

The amendment's framers recognized the right to marry the person of one's choosing as a crucial component of freedom and liberty—a right that had long been denied under the institution of slavery. Slaves did not have the right to marry, and slaves in loving relationships outside the protection of the law were time and again separated when one slave was sold to a distant buyer.[80] As Sena-

---

[73] Windsor, 133 S. Ct. at 2696.

[74] Lawrence, 539 U.S. at 578.

[75] *Id.* at 574.

[76] *Id.*

[77] Loving, 388 U.S. at 12 (discussing how the Fourteenth Amendment's Due Process Clause protects substantive, fundamental rights such as marriage).

[78] See generally Cato-CAC Brief in Perry.

[79] M.L.B. v. S.L.J., 519 U.S. 102, 116 (1996).

[80] See Herbert G. Gutman, The Black Family in Slavery and Freedom, 1750–1925, at 318 (1976) ("[O]ne in six (or seven) slave marriages were ended by force or sale").

tor Jacob Howard explained, a slave "had not the right to become a husband or father in the eye of the law, he had no child, he was not at liberty to indulge the natural affections of the human heart for children, for wife, or even for friend."[81]

Indeed, few rights were more precious to the newly freed slaves than the right to marry. With the abolition of slavery, "ex-slaves themselves pressed for ceremonies and legal registrations that at once celebrated the new security of black family life and brought their most intimate ties into conformity with the standards of freedom."[82] "[M]ass wedding ceremonies involving as many as seventy couples at a time became a common sight in the postwar South."[83] The right to marry "by the authority and protection of Law," confirmed that the newly freed slaves, finally, were "beginning to be regarded and treated as human beings."[84]

Justice Kennedy's opinions on the rights of gay men and lesbians appear to understand that, just as the rights to marry and create a family were basic elements of liberty that had been wrongly withheld from African Americans, discriminating against someone because of whom he or she loves, desires, and wishes to form a family with, denies gay men and lesbians "their dignity as free persons."[85] Although Kennedy's *Windsor* opinion provides a disclaimer at the end that the "opinion and its holding are confined to those lawful marriages"[86] already recognized by the states—and not, presumably, to same-sex couples who would like to marry but are prevented from doing so by discriminatory state laws—the language preceding that caveat, along with the Constitution's text and history, and other Supreme Court precedent suggest that the Court might be amenable to recognizing that gay and lesbian couples have a constitutional right to marry.

---

[81] Cong. Globe, 39th Cong., 1st Sess. 504 (1866).

[82] II Freedom: A Documentary History of Emancipation, 1861–1867, at 660 (I. Berlin et al. eds. 1982).

[83] Leon F. Litwack, Been in the Storm So Long: The Aftermath of Slavery 240 (1979).

[84] II Freedom, *supra* note 82, at 604.

[85] Lawrence, 539 U.S. at 567.

[86] Windsor, 133 S. Ct. at 2696.

B. The Dissenting Opinions

Despite the majority's disclaimer about the reach of its ruling, the implications of the *Windsor* opinion are hotly contested by the dissenting justices. Each of the three dissents takes the majority opinion to mean something quite different.

Chief Justice Roberts, perhaps unsurprisingly given his penchant for judicial minimalism, attempts to portray Justice Kennedy's opinion as very narrow, with no implication whatsoever for "the distinct question whether the States, in the exercise of their 'historic and essential authority to define the marital relation,' may continue to utilize the traditional definition of marriage."[87] The chief justice sees the majority's defense of constitutional equal protection and due process rights as nothing more than a federalism ruling, declaring "it is undeniable that [the majority's] judgment is based on federalism."[88] Although he tries to spin the majority's ruling as accepting that state definitions can constitutionally vary from state to state,[89] the opinion's language is in fact much more ambiguous, as discussed above.

Rather than pretending that the majority had accepted a federalism argument, Justice Alito penned a separate dissent to make the argument himself that the Constitution does not enshrine marriage equality, but rather "leaves the choice to the people, acting through their elected representatives."[90] According to Justice Alito, there is no constitutional right to marry a person of the same sex.[91] And the equal protection framework "is ill suited for use in evaluating the constitutionality of laws based on the traditional understanding of marriage."[92] (Of course, the Court applied the Equal Protection and Due Process Clauses to the claim for marriage rights in *Loving v. Virginia*—against a defense that Virginia's law prohibiting couples of different races from marrying was "traditional" and had roots back to the colonial period—but Alito does not cite that precedent even once in his dissent.) In the end, even as he remains skeptical that

[87] *Id*. at 2696 (2013) (Roberts, C.J., dissenting) (quoting majority op. at 2692).

[88] *Id*.

[89] *Id*. at 2697.

[90] *Id*. at 2711 (2013) (Alito, J., dissenting). See also *id*. at 2720 ("I hope that the Court will ultimately permit the people of each State to decide this question for themselves.").

[91] *Id*. at 2716.

[92] *Id*.

federalism is in fact at the core of the majority opinion, Justice Alito is willing to go along with Chief Justice Roberts's gloss on the majority's ruling, declaring that "[t]o the extent that the Court takes the position that the question of same-sex marriage should be resolved primarily at the state level, I wholeheartedly agree."[93]

Justice Scalia, however, won't be "fool[ed] . . . into thinking that this is a federalism opinion."[94] Cutting right to the chase, he argues that the majority discusses the states' traditional power to regulate marriage because it "needs some rhetorical basis to support its pretense that today's prohibition of laws excluding same-sex marriage is confined to the Federal Government (leaving the second, state-law shoe to be dropped later, maybe next Term)."[95]

Justice Scalia doesn't view the majority's opinion as a true equal protection ruling either, since the majority does not settle upon a tier of scrutiny for review—that is, "whether, under the Equal Protection Clause, laws restricting marriage to a man and a woman are reviewed for more than mere rationality."[96] But he should not be terribly surprised that the majority opinion does not rehearse the standard tiers-of-scrutiny inquiry: Justice Kennedy, particularly in his *Romer* opinion, has followed a line of reasoning in equal protection jurisprudence, associated with Justice John Paul Stevens, that emphasizes the clause's text and its broad protection rather than formalistic tiers of scrutiny.[97] As Justice Stevens explained: "There is only one Equal Protection Clause. It requires every State to govern impartially. It does not direct the courts to apply one standard of review in some cases and a different standard in other cases."[98] Although *Romer* technically applied rational basis review, the *Romer* Court did not find that it needed to apply any form of heightened

---

[93] *Id.* at 2720.

[94] *Id.* at 2705 (Scalia, J., dissenting).

[95] *Id.* at 2705.

[96] *Id.* at 2706.

[97] See David H. Gans, Perfecting the Declaration: The Text and History of the Equal Protection Clause of the Fourteenth Amendment, at 40, available at http://theusconstitution.org/think-tank/narrative/perfecting-declaration-text-and-history-equal-protection-clause-fourteenth.

[98] Craig v. Boren, 429 U.S. 190, 211–12 (1976) (Stevens, J., concurring).

scrutiny because Colorado's law discriminating against gay men and lesbians violated the most basic precepts of equal protection.[99]

Unable to place the *Windsor* majority's opinion into a doctrinal box, Justice Scalia concludes that "[t]he sum of all the Court's nonspecific hand-waving is that [DOMA] is invalid (maybe on equal-protection grounds, maybe on substantive-due-process grounds, and perhaps with some amorphous federalism component playing a role) because it is motivated by a 'bare desire to harm' couples in same-sex marriages."[100] As he has asserted previously—and vigorously—in his *Lawrence* dissent,[101] Justice Scalia believes that the Constitution allows "the government to enforce traditional moral and sexual norms."[102] So the fact that DOMA reflected moral disapproval of gay and lesbian relationships is of no consequence to Justice Scalia. Even so, he finds "there are many perfectly valid—indeed, downright boring—justifying rationales for this legislation," for example, avoidance of choice-of-law issues.[103]

What Justice Scalia really thinks is going on in the majority's opinion is the laying of a foundation for a ruling striking down state denials of marital status to same-sex couples:

> It takes real cheek for today's majority to assure us, as it is going out the door, that a constitutional requirement to give formal recognition to same-sex marriage is not at issue here— when what has preceded that assurance is a lecture on how superior the majority's moral judgment in favor of same-sex marriage is to the Congress's hateful moral judgment against it.[104]

He claims that the majority's view of state marriage laws that discriminate against gay and lesbian couples is "beyond mistaking."[105] To demonstrate, Justice Scalia's dissent takes several passages from the majority opinion about DOMA's unconstitutional effect and pur-

---

[99] See Gans, *supra* note 97, at 37–39.

[100] Windsor, 133 S. Ct. at 2707 (Scalia, J., dissenting) (quoting the majority op., at 2693).

[101] Lawrence, 539 U.S. at 599 (Scalia, J., dissenting).

[102] Windsor, 133 S. Ct. at 2707 (Scalia, J., dissenting).

[103] *Id.*

[104] *Id.* at 2709.

[105] *Id.*

pose with respect to state-sanctioned marriages of same-sex couples and substitutes "state law" for DOMA, and "constitutionally protected sexual relationships, see *Lawrence*," for state-sanctioned marriages.[106] He believes it is just a matter of "waiting for the other shoe" to drop.[107]

IV. What Comes Next?

Justice Scalia did not have to wait very long to hear "the other shoe" drop. On July 22, 2013, less than a month after the Supreme Court's ruling, a federal district court in Ohio relied on *Windsor* to conclude that the state of Ohio violates the Equal Protection Clause by refusing to recognize the marriages of same-sex couples lawfully solemnized in other states.[108] Explaining that Ohio has traditionally recognized valid out-of-state marriages even if Ohio law does not authorize such marriages—for example, marriages between first cousins or minors—Judge Timothy Black held that Ohio violated the Equal Protection Clause by refusing to recognize the same-sex plaintiffs' lawful Maryland marriage.[109] Judge Black acknowledged that "the holding in *Windsor* is ostensibly limited to a finding that the federal government cannot refuse to recognize state laws authorizing same sex marriage," but said that, "just as Justice Scalia predicted in his animated dissent, by virtue of the present lawsuit, 'the state-law shoe' has now dropped in Ohio."[110]

The Ohio ruling, whether it holds up on appeal or not, is interesting because it gives a clue as to how courts will interpret *Windsor*. Rather than viewing it as a ruling about federalism, the Ohio court explained that "[i]n *Windsor*, the Supreme Court applied the principle of equal protection."[111] Applying this same principle, the court determined that Ohio unconstitutionally created "two tiers of couples" by discriminating against same-sex married couples, and

---

[106] *Id.*

[107] *Id.* at 2710.

[108] Obergefell v. Kasich, Case No. 1:13-cv-501 (S.D. Ohio, July 22, 2013) (Order Granting Plaintiffs' Motion for a Temporary Restraining Order).

[109] *Id.*

[110] *Id.* at 2.

[111] *Id.* at 6.

concluded that "[t]his lack of equal protection of law is fatal."[112] The district court explained that the "purpose served by [Ohio's law] treating same-sex married couples differently than opposite-sex married couples is the same improper purpose that failed in *Windsor* and *Romer*: 'to impose inequality' and to make gay citizens unequal under the law."[113]

Although the Ohio ruling is slightly narrower than the ultimate question of whether states may prohibit same-sex couples from marrying under their own laws—the Ohio case, like *Windsor*, is about a government treating same-sex couples' lawful marriages differently from the way it treats opposite-sex couples' lawful marriages—lawsuits pressing the more fundamental claim are moving forward in at least 10 states,[114] and it is likely this issue will find its way back before the Supreme Court.

But some Americans—on both sides of the issue—would rather see the marriage-equality debate settled through democratic processes, not the courts. As Justice Scalia recounts in his *Windsor* dissent, the political process has handed wins and losses to both sides of the fight.[115] He argues that "[f]ew public controversies touch an institution so central to the lives of so many, and few inspire such attendant passion by good people on all sides. . . . There have been plebiscites, legislation, persuasion, and loud voices—in other words, democracy."[116] Justice Scalia's preferred method of resolution is to "let the People decide."[117]

Some marriage-equality supporters appear to agree to a certain extent, at least urging caution as lawsuits proceed.[118] There is concern that a new wave of lawsuits could lead to a backlash[119] and, as more states pass laws recognizing same-sex unions, some

---

[112] *Id.* at 8.

[113] *Id.* at 11.

[114] See, e.g., Harris v. McDonnell, Case No. 5:13-cv-00077-MFU (W.D. Va.) (filed Aug. 1, 2013), available at http://www.aclu.org/files/assets/complaintwithfilinginfo.pdf.

[115] Windsor, 133 S. Ct. at 2710–11 (Scalia, J., dissenting).

[116] *Id.* at 2710.

[117] *Id.* at 2711.

[118] Lila Shapiro, Marriage Equality Lawsuits After DOMA Arise in South, Midwest, As Gay Right Groups Urge Caution, Huffington Post, Jul. 31, 2013, http://www.huffingtonpost.com/2013/07/31/marriage-lawsuits-doma_n_3679005.html.

[119] *Id.*

marriage-equality supporters have essentially said, "don't mess with progress."[120] Regardless of whether it is sound political strategy to focus on legislatively establishing marriage equality in as many states as possible before heading back to the Supreme Court, however, the fact is that the Constitution simply does not "let the People decide" when it comes to fundamental rights and liberties.

While the Constitution creates a vibrant system of federalism, with states free to experiment with diverse policies that best fit their communities' needs and preferences, it also places certain rights and freedoms beyond the reach of state experimentation. This restriction is why Justice Scalia's paean to the American "system of government that permits us to rule *ourselves*"[121] falls flat in this context. "We the People" have decided that we will not put our most cherished rights and liberties up to a vote. Indeed, many provisions of the Bill of Rights—such as the guarantees of freedom of speech and religion, and the prohibition against warrantless searches—were specifically intended to protect the politically unpopular. The Constitution stands for the proposition that some rights aren't left to the whims of a democratic majority. Equality before the law is one of those rights.

That said, by the time the Supreme Court turns again to the constitutionality of discriminatory marriage laws, the legal landscape could be substantially changed. Sexual intimacy between same-sex partners was deemed a crime in about a dozen states only 10 years ago, whereas today 13 states and the District of Columbia recognize the right of same-sex couples to marry. It is likely that, as Lambda Legal, one of the most prominent legal advocates for gay rights, has suggested, the "path to victory" for marriage equality "will be achieved by a combination of lawsuits, legislation, ballot measures and engagement with others."[122] But if the country's history with racially discriminatory marriage laws is any guide, the Supreme Court will eventually need to step in to ensure the Constitution's promise of equality for all.

---

[120] Emily Bazelon, "Backlash Whiplash," Slate, May 14, 2013, http://www.slate.com/articles/news_and_politics/jurisprudence/2013/05/justice_ginsburg_and_roe_v_wade_caution_for_gay_marriage.html.

[121] Windsor, 133 S. Ct. at 2710 (Scalia, J., dissenting) (emphasis in original).

[122] Jon W. Davidson, Marriage Equality for All: Getting from Here to There, Lamda Legal Blog, Jul. 11, 2013, http://www.lambdalegal.org/blog/marriage-equality-for-all-getting-from-here-to-there.

In 1967, 16 states still had laws on the books that prohibited couples of different races from marrying. In the previous 15 years, 14 states had repealed similar laws prohibiting interracial marriage, reflecting progress achieved through the democratic process. But the Supreme Court did not sit back and wait to see if the remaining holdout states would follow suit when a couple, Mildred and Richard Loving, asked the court to strike down Virginia's ban on interracial marriage. Instead, the Court in *Loving* applied the Constitution's guarantees of equality and liberty to strike down Virginia's discriminatory marriage law as unconstitutional.[123] The Court's opinion noted that marriage is something traditionally left to the states. It observed that there was a long history of limiting marriage to persons of the same race—Virginia's law had roots in the colonial period. It acknowledged that the drafters of the Fourteenth Amendment may not have specifically or expressly intended it to strike down laws prohibiting couples of different races from marrying. It also noted that some states had recently established more equitable marriage laws of their own accord. And yet the Supreme Court still struck down Virginia's discriminatory marriage law because it was unconstitutional. The same will likely happen eventually with respect to state marriage laws that discriminate against gay and lesbian couples. Such a ruling will, like *Loving*, be consistent with, and indeed is required by, the Constitution's text and history.

At a certain point, a community's "evolving understanding of the meaning of equality,"[124] as the *Windsor* majority puts it, will need to be squared with the meaning of equality and liberty promised by the Constitution. When a state has failed to get itself in line with constitutional requirements, it is entirely appropriate for the courts to step in. While our national charter is, in part, focused on empowering the People in a republican government, it is also dedicated to protecting the rights of often unpopular minorities "against even responsive, representative, majority government."[125] Justice Scalia chides the *Windsor* majority in his dissent for not issuing "[a] reminder that disagreement over something so fundamental as marriage can still be

---

[123] See Loving, 388 U.S. at 12.

[124] Windsor, 133 S. Ct. at 2698.

[125] Akhil Reed Amar, The Bill of Rights: Creation and Reconstruction 215 (1998).

politically legitimate."[126] But the Constitution tells us in no uncertain terms that equality is not to be apportioned based on popularity or political convenience. And, as the Ohio district court highlighted in striking down that state's law discriminating against same-sex couples' valid out-of-state marriages, "the public interest is promoted by the robust enforcement of constitutional rights"[127]—perhaps even when some of us initially don't like it.

When the right case comes before the Supreme Court, it should not shy away from applying the Constitution's guarantee of equality under the law to guarantee gay men and lesbians the same marriage rights as everyone else.

---

[126] Windsor, 133 S. Ct. at 2711 (Scalia, J., dissenting).

[127] Obergefell, *supra* note 108, slip op. at 14 (quotation omitted) (quoting Am. Freedom Def. Initiative v. Suburban 15 Mobility for Reg. Transp., 698 F.3d 885, 896 (6th Cir. 2012)).

Federalism, Liberty, and Equality in *United States v. Windsor*

*Ernest A. Young and Erin C. Blondel**

In *United States v. Windsor*,[1] the Supreme Court struck down Section 3 of the federal Defense of Marriage Act (DOMA), which defined marriage as exclusively between a man and a woman for purposes of federal law.[2] On the same day, the Court decided *Hollingsworth v. Perry*,[3] which involved California's Proposition 8—a state provision, added by voter initiative to the California constitution, likewise prohibiting the recognition of same-sex marriage. One question in these marriage cases was whether these two provisions should stand or fall together based on equal protection principles applicable to all levels of government in our system, or whether it made any difference that DOMA was a *federal* law. As it happened, *Perry* went away on standing grounds.[4] But Justice Anthony Kennedy's majority opinion in *Windsor* left little doubt that federalism principles were

*Young is the Alston & Bird Professor at Duke Law School. Blondel is an associate at Robbins, Russell, Englert, Orseck, Untereiner & Sauber LLP. The authors were coauthors of the Brief of Federalism Scholars as Amici Curiae in Support of Respondent in United States v. Windsor, 133 S. Ct. 2675 (2013) (No. 12-307), available at http://scholarship.law.duke.edu/faculty_scholarship/2858. We are particularly grateful to our colleagues in that endeavor, Jonathan Adler, Lynn Baker, Randy Barnett, Dale Carpenter, Carina Cuellar, Roy Englert, and Ilya Somin, for their many helpful insights and staunch support, and to Bob Levy, Ilya Shapiro, and Gregg Strauss for comments on this essay. This commentary draws upon the amicus brief, but at least to some extent it reflects our own views that our co-signatories may or may not share. They deserve credit for the good parts but should not be blamed for any mistakes.

[1] 133 S. Ct. 2675 (2013).

[2] Pub. L. 104-199, 110 Stat. 2419 (Sep. 21, 1996) (codified at 1 U.S.C. § 7).

[3] 133 S. Ct. 2652 (2013).

[4] See *id.* at 2659. The standing holding in *Perry* raises an important federalism question of its own concerning the extent to which state law may create interests sufficient to support standing in the federal courts. One of us has ventured some preliminary thoughts about that issue elsewhere. See Ernest A. Young, In Praise of Judge Fletcher—and of General Standing Principles, Ala. L. Rev. (forthcoming Fall 2013).

crucial to the result. DOMA was unconstitutional not simply because it treated gay and straight couples unequally but because it intruded on the states' sovereign authority to define marriage for themselves.

The extent to which federalism should affect these cases was controversial before the Court's decision,[5] and the extent to which it actually *did* matter to the decision remains controversial in its wake.[6] Chief Justice John Roberts's dissent (written in damage-control mode) argued that federalism was crucial to the majority's decision, leaving the Court free to go the other way should a *state* prohibition on same-sex marriage come before it.[7] Justice Antonin Scalia's dissent (written in outrage mode) dismissed Justice Kennedy's invocation of federalism as mere window-dressing, designed to make the majority's embrace of same-sex marriage more palatable to a skeptical public.[8] Only time will tell who was right, of course. But we think that controversy over whether equal protection or federalism is the "best" or "truest" ground for invalidating DOMA misses the fundamental ways these two broad constitutional principles are pervasively intertwined.

Most constitutional lawyers acknowledge (although it often slips their minds) that the Constitution's structural features—federalism and separation of powers—along with its rights and equality provisions secure the liberty of the people.[9] Less well understood is that rights and structure intersect at the doctrinal level as well. The

[5] Compare George F. Will, DOMA Is an Abuse of Federalism, Wash. Post, Mar. 20, 2013, available at http://articles.washingtonpost.com/2013-03-20/opinions/3787 0263_1_doma-defense-of-marriage-act-general-police-power, with Linda Greenhouse, Trojan Horse, N.Y. Times Opinionator Blog, Apr. 3, 2013, http://opinionator.blogs.nytimes.com/2013/04/03/Trojan-horse.

[6] E.g., Michael McConnell, Debating the Court's Gay Marriage Decisions, The New Republic, Jun. 26, 2013, available at http://www.newrepublic.com/article/113646/supreme-court-strikes-down-doma-dismisses-prop-8-debate ("Justice Kennedy has sought to find a formula that enables him to invalidate the denial of same-sex marriage at the national level without doing so in every state. Federalism would have provided such a path, but he did not take it."); Sandy Levinson, A Brief Comment on Justice Kennedy's Opinion in Windsor, Balkinization, Jun. 26, 2013, http://balkin.blogspot.com/2013/06/a-brief-comment-on-justice-kennedys.html (writing off *Windsor's* federalism arguments as "some blather about traditional state sovereignty and marriage").

[7] 133 S. Ct. at 2696–97 (Roberts, C.J., dissenting).

[8] *Id.* at 2705 (Scalia, J., dissenting).

[9] See, e.g., Bond v. United States, 131 S. Ct. 2355 (2011).

Court's opinion in *Windsor* beautifully illustrates that intersection. Federalism principles played a critical role in defining the contours of the equality right at stake, limiting which governmental interests could weigh against that right, and influencing the level of deference that the Court owed to how Congress had weighed those rights and interests. Rather than choosing between federalism and rights-based approaches to the case, *Windsor* demonstrated how federalism can become an integral part of the rights calculus.

It is already fashionable for *Windsor's* admirers and detractors to dismiss Justice Kennedy's opinion as "muddled" or "incoherent."[10] This essay takes the radical view that the opinion's reasoning is not only coherent but brilliant—the best explanation yet of how federalism and equality doctrine intersect.[11] Part I describes the controversy over same-sex marriage and the litigation challenging DOMA. Part II discusses the doctrinal interconnection between federalism and equality in Justice Kennedy's opinion. These doctrinal links are not the only, nor even the most important, connections between constitutional structure and equality. But we think that *Windsor* dealt a blow not only to barriers to same-sex marriage but also to the doctrinal silos that have long constrained our constitutional thinking.

I. DOMA and the Debate over Same-Sex Marriage

Federalism has structured our national conversation about same-sex marriage. Beginning in the 1990s, some states put the issue on the national agenda by experimenting with same-sex marriage. Congress enacted DOMA in 1996 to contain those experiments, both by

---

[10] See, e.g., Levinson, *supra* note 6 (noting "the intellectual awkwardness of [Kennedy's] opinion" and comparing it to "a camel (i.e., a horse designed by a committee)"); Andrew Sullivan, The Method in Kennedy's Muddle, The Dish, Jun. 27, 2013, http://dish.andrewsullivan.com/2013/06/27/the-method-in-kennedys-muddle/; McConnell, *supra* note 6 ("[T]he DOMA decision is a logical mishmash, portending more litigation and more instability."); Tara Helfman, A Ruling Without Reason, Commentary, Jun. 26, 2013, http://www.commentarymagazine.com/2013/06/26/a-ruling-without-reason ("In a 26-page opinion brimming with constitutional catch phrases but containing no coherent rationale, the Court delivered an outcome that many find politically favorable but that no serious reader could possibly find legally sound.").

[11] Although we like to think Justice Kennedy might have built on our brief, see Federalism Scholars, *supra* note *, his opinion contains much that we only wish we'd thought of first.

ensuring that federal law and unwilling states need not recognize same-sex marriages and by raising the costs for states that might try same-sex marriage in the future. We strongly suspect that not only the states' traditional primacy over marriage but also the Court's revival of constitutional limits on Congress's enumerated powers during the same period[12] contributed to Congress's decision not to go further and simply ban same-sex marriage across the board. One of federalism's primary functions is to create institutional space for fundamental disagreements about visions of the good life.[13]

Similarly, when DOMA and state same-sex-marriage bans were challenged in court, the federal courts' own federalist-style organization allowed different federal courts of appeals to experiment with different visions of how federalism and equality interact. Given how the same-sex marriage issue percolated up to the Supreme Court, *Windsor's* strong reliance on federalism should have surprised no one.

A. *The Stunning Evolution of Public Opinion and American Law*

Congress passed (with President Bill Clinton's approval) DOMA in 1996[14] when the possibility that states might permit same-sex marriage was only dawning on most Americans. Three years earlier the Hawaii Supreme Court had all but held that same-sex couples had a right to marry;[15] many expected that Hawaii's courts ultimately would recognize that right (they did). Most Americans first reacted skeptically: in 1996 27 percent of Americans supported same-sex marriage, while 68 percent opposed it.[16] Their laws reflected that: by 2000 about 40 states (including Hawaii) banned same-sex marriage by statute or constitutional amendment.[17]

---

[12] See, e.g., United States v. Lopez, 514 U.S. 549 (1995).

[13] See, e.g., Lynn A. Baker & Ernest A. Young, Federalism and the Double Standard of Judicial Review, 51 Duke L. J. 75, 136–40 (2001).

[14] Pub. L. No. 104-199, 110 Stat. 2419.

[15] Baehr v. Lewin, 852 P.2d 44 (Haw. 1993).

[16] Marriage, Gallup.com, http://www.gallup.com/poll/117328/marriage.aspx (last visited July 29, 2013). All statistics about same-sex-marriage opinions in this essay can be found here.

[17] Same Sex Marriage Laws, Nat'l Conf. of State Legislatures, http://www.ncsl.org/issues-research/human-services/same-sex-marriage-laws.aspx#2 (last visited July 29, 2013).

Other states, however, began experimenting with same-sex marriage. From 2003 through 2009, the supreme courts of Massachusetts, Iowa, California, and Connecticut held, under their state constitutions, that same-sex couples had a right to marry.[18] Starting in 2009, several state legislatures permitted same-sex marriage; and in 2012 voters began approving same-sex marriage in referenda.[19]

As of this writing, 13 states and the District of Columbia permit same-sex marriage, and similar legislation pends elsewhere. Twelve states and the District of Columbia permit civil unions or domestic partnerships that confer some or all rights that married couples enjoy.[20] About 35 states have adopted statutes or constitutional amendments prohibiting same-sex marriage.[21] Fifty-four percent of Americans favor a right to same-sex marriage; 43 percent oppose it.

B. *Same-Sex Marriage in the Federal District and Circuit Courts*

Perry and *Windsor* emerged from that ongoing evolution in public opinion and American law.

Windsor was one of two cases in which a lower federal court struck down DOMA's Section 3 on Fifth Amendment equal protection grounds. Edith Windsor and Thea Spyer, partners since 1963, married in Ontario, Canada, in 2007 and returned home to New York City.[22] New York state law recognized their marriage,[23] but when Spyer died two years later, DOMA prohibited Windsor from claiming the marital exemption to the federal estate tax. Windsor paid $363,053 in estate taxes, then requested and eventually sued for a refund.[24] Nancy Gill

---

[18] Kerrigan v. Comm'r of Pub. Health, 957 A.2d 407 (Conn. 2008); Varnum v. Brien, 763 N.W.2d 862 (Iowa 2009).

[19] See Research Guides: Same-Sex Marriage Laws, The Ohio State University Moritz College of Law, http://moritzlaw.osu.edu/library/samesexmarriagelaws.php (last visited July 29, 2013).

[20] *Id.*

[21] Same Sex Marriage Laws, *supra* note 17. These categories are not exclusive. Many states that permit same-sex marriage also allow civil unions or domestic partnerships, and some states that prohibit same-sex *marriage* nonetheless allow same-sex civil unions or domestic partnerships. See *id.*

[22] Windsor v. United States, 833 F. Supp. 2d 394, 397 (S.D.N.Y. 2012).

[23] At the time, most New York courts recognized out-of-state same-sex marriages; the state's legislature legalized same-sex marriage in 2011. Windsor, 133 S. Ct. at 2689.

[24] Windsor, 833 F. Supp. 2d at 397.

and other plaintiffs brought the second case in Massachusetts when they were denied federal benefits (in Gill's case, the right to add her same-sex spouse to her federal health insurance) because of DOMA.[25] The Commonwealth of Massachusetts filed a companion suit, *Massachusetts v. Department of Health & Human Services (DHHS)*, claiming that DOMA violated the Tenth Amendment and the Spending Clause.[26]

Unlike *DHHS* and *Windsor*, the *Perry* plaintiffs were not married under state law but argued that, under the Fourteenth Amendment's Equal Protection Clause, they were entitled to marry their same-sex partners. The California Supreme Court had held in 2008 that limiting marriage to opposite-sex couples violated the state's equal protection clause,[27] but voters overruled that decision through a ballot initiative, Proposition 8, amending the California constitution to permit only opposite-sex marriage.[28] Between the California court's decision and Proposition 8's effective date, the state issued marriage licenses to over 18,000 same-sex couples.[29] Two same-sex couples who sought but were denied marriage licenses after Proposition 8 became effective sued the state to challenge the new law.

In all three cases, at different points during litigation, executive officials refused to defend the constitutionality of DOMA and Proposition 8. The Obama administration concluded that gays and lesbians are a suspect class, laws burdening them are subject to intermediate scrutiny, and DOMA failed that standard. California's attorney general conceded that Proposition 8 was unconstitutional; the other state defendants simply refused to defend it. Others intervened, however, to defend the enactments. The U.S. House of Representatives' Bipartisan Legal Advisory Group (BLAG) voted to defend DOMA and intervened in *DHHS* and *Windsor*. Proposition 8's proponents, led by then-state-senator Dennis Hollingsworth, similarly intervened in *Perry*.

DHHS, *Windsor*, and *Perry* presented a spectrum of constitutional arguments. Most fundamentally, the Supreme Court's prior decisions

---

[25] Gill v. Office of Personnel Mgmt., 699 F. Supp. 2d 374, 379–83 (D. Mass 2010).

[26] 698 F. Supp. 2d 234 (D. Mass. 2010). These cases were consolidated on appeal. Massachusetts v. Dep't of Health & Human Services (DHHS), 682 F.3d 1 (1st Cir. 2012).

[27] In re Marriage Cases, 183 P.3d 384 (Cal. 2008).

[28] Perry v. Brown, 671 F.3d 1052, 167–68 (9th Cir. 2012).

[29] *Id.* at 1067–68.

addressing laws aimed at gay relationships, *Romer v. Evans*[30] and *Lawrence v. Texas*,[31] (probably deliberately) obscured the constitutional framework for analyzing such laws. What level of scrutiny applied, even what provision of the Constitution governed (equal protection or substantive due process) remained unsettled.[32]

Windsor and *DHHS* raised the additional question of how to treat *federal* laws addressing same-sex relationships. The Court had never addressed a statute burdening those relationships under the Fifth Amendment. And in *DHHS* litigants objected that the federal government had no business defining marriage at all.

But the biggest question was whether the Supreme Court was ready to flatly strike down gay-marriage bans. *DHHS* and *Windsor* left room for courts to rule on uniquely federal grounds and leave undisturbed state laws and amendments banning gay marriage. *Perry*, which directly challenged a state constitutional amendment approved by California voters under the U.S. Constitution, left less room for middle ground—though the Obama administration and the U.S. Court of Appeals for the Ninth Circuit tried to find it.[33]

BLAG offered a number of justifications for DOMA that, it said, at least met rational basis's generous standard: DOMA preserved each sovereign's (including the federal government's) ability to define marriage for itself; it ensured national uniformity of benefits; it preserved past legislative judgments and protected the public fisc; Congress wanted to proceed with caution before recognizing a new marriage form; and the federal government wanted to support traditional families and encourage parents to rear their biological offspring.[34] The

---

[30] 517 U.S. 620 (1996).

[31] 539 U.S. 558 (2003).

[32] Whatever the virtues of this approach as a matter of judicial statesmanship, it infuriated a generation of law students, who could not tell what to put in their outlines.

[33] The Obama administration proposed an "eight state solution" under which same-sex marriage bans would be unconstitutional only in states that permitted civil unions or domestic partnerships with the same rights, but not the same title, as married couples. Brief of the United States as Amicus Curiae in Hollingsworth v. Perry, 133 S. Ct. 2652 (2013) (No. 12-144). This position laid an egg at the Supreme Court. See, e.g., Erin Fuchs, The Supreme Court Was Highly Skeptical of Obama's Weird Gay Marriage Argument, Business Insider, Mar. 28, 2013. The Ninth Circuit's solution is discussed below.

[34] Merits Brief of Bipartisan Legal Advisory Group at 28–49, United States v. Windsor, 133 S. Ct. 2675 (2013) (No. 12-307).

House report accompanying DOMA asserted that the statute defended and nurtured traditional, heterosexual marriage; defended traditional morality; and preserved the public fisc.[35]

After the respective district courts invalidated DOMA and Proposition 8, the U.S. Courts of Appeals for the First, Second, and Ninth Circuits affirmed, each on different grounds.

The First Circuit applied "a closer than usual review"[36] (dubbed by BLAG's counsel "rational basis plus"[37]) for two reasons. First, the court identified an open secret in Supreme Court jurisprudence: when statutes disadvantage unpopular minorities, the Court sometimes has professed to apply rational-basis review while conducting a more searching inquiry than it would for, say, a tax law. Second, the Supreme Court has shown less deference to legislative judgment when statutes undermine federalism and state sovereignty, such as in *United States v. Lopez*.[38] DOMA raised both concerns—it uniquely burdened same-sex couples and intruded in an area of traditional state authority. Thus, the First Circuit applied somewhat more searching scrutiny to BLAG's proffered justifications and found them inadequate. The court rejected the Tenth Amendment and Spending Clause arguments, however.

The Second Circuit took a more traditional path. The court held that intermediate scrutiny applies to denials of same-sex marriage because gays and lesbians are a discrete minority and have historically suffered persecution. The court then analyzed the rationales offered to justify DOMA and ruled that they did not survive intermediate scrutiny. But it agreed with the First Circuit that the states' primary authority over marriage was "a reason to look upon Section 3 of DOMA with a cold eye."[39]

Finally, the Ninth Circuit held that Proposition 8 violated the Fourteenth Amendment because it withdrew a right to marry that state law had conferred on gay couples.[40] Once the California Su-

---

[35] Massachusetts v. Dep't of Health & Human Servs. (DHHS), 682 F.3d 1, 14 (1st Cir. 2012). The report also said DOMA respected state sovereignty, obviously referring to Section 2 rather than Section 3. *Id.*

[36] DHHS, 682 F.3d at 8.

[37] Windsor v. United States, 699 F.3d 169, 180 (2d Cir. 2012).

[38] DHHS, 682 F.3d at 10–13.

[39] Windsor, 699 F.3d at 181–86.

[40] Perry v. Brown, 671 F.3d 1052, 1076–92 (9th Cir. 2012).

preme Court ruled that the state constitution required allowing gay marriage, California voters could not rescind that right without a legitimate reason. These different approaches by the First, Second, and Ninth Circuits left the Court with a variety of models for viewing the relationship between state power and equality.

C. DOMA in the Supreme Court

In the fall of 2012, the U.S. Supreme Court granted certiorari in *Hollingsworth v. Perry* and *United States v. Windsor.*[41] The Court heard both cases back to back in March and decided both on June 26, 2013. *Perry* had presented the cleanest, up-or-down constitutional challenge to same-sex-marriage bans. The Supreme Court dodged, dismissing the case on standing grounds.[42] But the Court held that *Windsor* was justiciable and struck down DOMA's Section 3 on narrower, but still significant, grounds. Justice Kennedy wrote the majority opinion; Chief Justice Roberts and Justices Scalia, Clarence Thomas, and Samuel Alito dissented.

Like his opinions in *Romer* and *Lawrence*, Justice Kennedy's *Windsor* opinion left much of the legal framework he was applying implicit. But a framework is there, and the First Circuit's decision in *Gill* provides a useful reference point.

As the First Circuit did, the *Windsor* majority identified two related concerns: (1) states had chosen to recognize these marriages as they did opposite-sex marriages, and (2) the federal government, through DOMA, singled out some state-created marriages for disapproval. The majority also, like the First Circuit, essentially applied rational-basis-plus scrutiny. The Court conspicuously failed to adopt (or even mention) intermediate scrutiny. But it did not apply deferential rational-basis scrutiny either. It held, citing *Romer*, that DOMA's "'[d]iscriminations of an unusual character' especially require careful consideration."[43]

---

[41] United States v. Windsor, 133 S. Ct. 2675 (2012); Hollingsworth v. Perry, 133 S. Ct. 786 (2012). The Court held the petition in *DHHS* but ultimately denied certiorari, 133 S. Ct. 2887 (2013), presumably because Justice Kagan was recused. See Lyle Denniston, Kagan, DOMA, and Recusal, SCOTUSblog, Nov. 2, 2012, http://www.scotusblog.com/?p=154714.

[42] Hollingsworth v. Perry, 133 S. Ct. 786 (2013).

[43] Windsor, 133 S. Ct. at 2691–93.

The majority began with federalism. Traditionally, states have virtually exclusively governed family law, subject to constitutional limits. Though the federal government has power to decide who gets federal benefits, sometimes differently than state law would, the government has never before treated married couples within the same state differently. It has accepted state marital determinations and then decided who gets federal benefits.[44]

Though the majority declined to rule that DOMA exceeded the federal government's powers, the states' decision to include same-sex couples in state-created marriages was nonetheless critical. That judgment is a "far-reaching legal acknowledgment of the intimate relationship between two people, a relationship deemed by the State worthy of dignity in the community equal with all other marriages."[45] DOMA, however, rejects "the usual tradition of recognizing and accepting state definitions of marriage" and "deprive[s] same-sex couples of the benefits and responsibilities that come with the federal recognition of their marriages."[46]

Thus, once states decided to classify same-sex couples as married, the federal government decided to "use[] this state-defined class for the opposite purpose—to impose restrictions and disabilities."[47] The Court described those disabilities in philosophical and practical terms. DOMA's "avowed purpose and practical effect," as BLAG openly admitted, was "to impose a disadvantage, a separate status, and so a stigma" on state-recognized same-sex marriages.[48] As a result, "DOMA forces same-sex couples to live as married for the purpose of state law but unmarried for the purpose of federal law," which "diminish[es] the stability and predictability of basic personal relations" and "tells those couples, and all the world, that their otherwise valid marriages are unworthy of federal recognition."[49]

The majority also cataloged ways that DOMA, practically speaking, treated same-sex marriages as second class. Same-sex couples were deprived of federal benefits and protections in healthcare,

[44] *Id.*
[45] *Id.* at 2692.
[46] *Id.* at 2693.
[47] *Id.* at 2692.
[48] *Id.* at 2693.
[49] *Id.* at 2694.

bankruptcy, and taxation. Ethics rules and special protection did not apply to federal officials' same-sex spouses. Parenting was more expensive for same-sex couples. Altogether, "DOMA divests married same-sex couples of the duties and responsibilities that are an essential part of married life."[50]

Put simply, "[w]hat the State of New York treats as alike the federal law deems unlike by a law designed to injure the same class the State seeks to protect."[51] "By doing so [DOMA] violates basic due process and equal protection principles applicable to the Federal Government."[52]

II. The Doctrinal Intersections of Federalism and Rights

After discussing the states' preeminent role in defining marriage, the *Windsor* majority wrote that "[d]espite these considerations, it is unnecessary to decide whether this federal intrusion on state power is a violation of the Constitution because it disrupts the federal balance."[53] Early commentators have read that line as conceding that the case wasn't really about federalism—that the Court's extended account of federalism was, as Justice Scalia put it, merely a "rhetorical basis to support its pretense that today's prohibition of laws excluding same-sex marriage is confined to the Federal Government."[54] This interpretation gives short shrift to Justice Kennedy's statement immediately following that "[t]he State's power in defining the marital relation is of central relevance in this case quite apart from principles of federalism."[55] The remainder of our essay explores what he possibly could have meant.

A. *The Enumerated Powers Argument That Wasn't*

The "principles of federalism" that Justice Kennedy decided the case "quite apart from" were traditional arguments about limits on the federal government's enumerated powers.[56] It is not surprising

50 *Id.* at 2695.

51 *Id.* at 2692.

52 *Id.* at 2693.

53 *Id.* at 2692.

54*Id.* at 2705 (Scalia, J., dissenting); see, e.g., Helfman, *supra* note 10.

55 133 S. Ct. at 2692.

56 *Id.*

that the Court did not analyze the case from that perspective, given that no court of appeals had relied on such an argument and the Court had granted certiorari only on the plaintiffs' equal protection challenge. The Court did have an enumerated-powers argument before it, however, in the amicus brief filed by several federalism scholars.[57] Although the Court did not rely on that ground, developing that argument can make a useful foil for the federalism argument that the Court *did* adopt.

Of course, no specific enumerated federal power to define marriage exists. Nor does DOMA fit under the Commerce Clause: although weddings are often highly commercial (ask anyone who's paid for one), marriage itself is generally not a commercial activity.[58] One can imagine federal marriage legislation under Section 5 of the Fourteenth Amendment. But the Section 5 argument is asymmetrical; it is very hard to say that it is unconstitutional for a state to *recognize* same-sex marriage, so there is no constitutional violation for DOMA to prevent or remedy by withdrawing recognition.[59]

The best arguments thus would have to maintain that defining marriage to exclude same-sex couples is "necessary and proper" to Congress's exercise of its other enumerated powers to regulate commerce or spend federal money. That position is intuitively powerful, especially given the Court's precedents recognizing broad federal power and adopting a deferential standard of review for necessary and proper cases.[60] They don't, in other words, call it the "Sweeping Clause" for nothing.[61] But the Court has suggested in recent years that the Necessary and Proper Clause is no longer a blank check allowing Congress to evade the limits on its specifically enumerated powers. In *National Federation of Independent Business v. Sebelius*,[62] five justices rejected a Necessary and Proper Clause argument for upholding the

---

[57] Federalism Scholars, *supra* note *, at 11–25.

[58] But see RussianBrides.com, http://www.russianbrides.com/mail-order-brides.htm (demonstrating that particularly when it comes to sex, there's a commercial version of almost everything).

[59] Cf. City of Boerne v. Flores, 521 U.S. 507 (1997).

[60] E.g., McCulloch v. Maryland, 17 U.S. (4 Wheat.) 316 (1819).

[61] See Gary Lawson & Patricia B. Granger, The "Proper" Scope of Federal Power: A Jurisdictional Interpretation of the Sweeping Clause, 43 Duke L. J. 267, 270 n.10 (1993).

[62] See 132 S. Ct. 2566, 2591–93 (2012) (plurality opinion of Roberts, C.J.); *id.* at 2644–47 (Scalia, Kennedy, Thomas, and Alito, JJ., dissenting).

individual health insurance mandate, and some of the Court's other recent Necessary and Proper Clause opinions have cautioned against reading the clause too broadly.[63]

The Court's underdeveloped case law appears to impose three distinct requirements for valid legislation under the Necessary and Proper Clause. First, such legislation must be "incidental" to the exercise of an enumerated power.[64] Congress may employ unenumerated *means* so long as they are necessary and proper to the accomplishment of an enumerated *end*.[65] But it does not allow pursuing unenumerated *ends* or using unenumerated *means* for their own sake.[66] As Chief Justice John Marshall warned in *McCulloch v. Maryland*, "should Congress, under the pretext of executing its powers, pass laws for the accomplishment of objects not intrusted to the government; it would become the painful duty of this tribunal . . . to say, that such an act was not the law of the land."[67] Distinguishing incidental and primary purposes will often be hard. But sometimes Congress is not particularly subtle. It seems safe to say that a law entitled "The Defense of Marriage Act" regulates marriage *for its own sake*—not as an incidental way to make some other federal regulatory scheme more effective. And Paul Clement's brief defending DOMA was candid enough to argue in precisely those terms.[68]

Second, also traceable to *McCulloch*, the unenumerated means must be "plainly adapted" to Congress's enumerated end.[69] That means

[63] E.g., United States v. Comstock, 130 S. Ct. 1949 (2010); *id.* at 1970 (Alito, J., concurring in the judgment) ("[T]he term 'necessary' . . . requires an 'appropriate' link between a power conferred by the Constitution and the law enacted by Congress. . . . And it is an obligation of this Court to enforce compliance with that limitation.") (citing McCulloch, 17 U.S. (4 Wheat.) at 415). See generally Ilya Somin, Taking Stock of *Comstock*: The Necessary and Proper Clause and the Limits of Federal Power, 2009-2010 Cato Sup. Ct. Rev. 239 (2010).

[64] See NFIB, 132 S. Ct. at 2591 (stating that the Necessary and Proper Clause "vests Congress with authority to enact provisions 'incidental to the [enumerated] power, and conducive to its beneficial exercise'") (quoting McCulloch, 17 U.S. (4 Wheat.) at 418).

[65] See generally Comstock, 130 S. Ct. at 1956; David Engdahl, The Spending Power, 44 Duke L. J. 1, 18–24 (1994).

[66] See, e.g., McCulloch, 17 U.S. (4 Wheat.) at 411 (stressing that creating a corporation is "never used for its own sake, but for the purpose of effecting something else").

[67] *Id.* at 423.

[68] See *supra* note 34 and accompanying text.

[69] See 17 U.S. (4 Wheat.) at 421 ("Let the end be legitimate, let it be within the scope of the constitution, and all means which are appropriate, which are plainly adapted

the means and ends must fit, and the Court's analysis is tradition-ally deferential.[70] But although *McCulloch* is often credited as origi-nating the rational-basis standard, Justice Kennedy recently went out of his way to insist that the hyper-deferential post-1937 version of rational-basis review, employed in substantive due process and equal protection cases not involving fundamental rights or suspect classifications, does not apply to the Necessary and Proper Clause.[71] Rather, "[t]he rational basis [required] . . . is a demonstrated link in fact, based on empirical demonstration."[72]

Demonstrating that link for DOMA would be difficult. The act de-fines marriage to exclude same-sex couples in more than 1,100 differ-ent federal statutes. A provision that applies shotgun-style to more than 1,100 federal laws is "plainly adapted" to none. Congress was not trying to improve the tax code or the immigration laws, for ex-ample. Although those exercises of Congress's enumerated powers do sometimes require the federal government to determine which state-sanctioned marriages it will recognize for specific federal pur-poses, DOMA was not enacted for any such purpose.

Finally, unenumerated means must be not only "necessary" to achieving some enumerated end but also "proper."[73] In the Founding era, that meant that laws "must be consistent with principles of sepa-ration of powers, principles of federalism, and individual rights."[74]

to that end, which are not prohibited, but consist with the letter and spirit of the constitution, are constitutional.").

[70] But see NFIB, 132 S. Ct. at 2579 (cautioning that "deference in matters of policy cannot, however, become abdication in matters of law").

[71] See Comstock, 130 S. Ct. at 1966 ("This Court has not held that the *Lee Optical* test, asking if 'it might be thought that the particular legislative measure was a rational way to correct' an evil, is the proper test in this context. Rather, under the Necessary and Proper Clause, application of a 'rational basis' test should be at least as exacting as it has been in the Commerce Clause cases, if not more so.") (Kennedy, J., concurring in the judgment) (citing Williamson v. Lee Optical, Inc., 348 U.S. 483, 487–88 (1955)). We need not remind the gentle reader that Justice Kennedy might as well have a numeral "5" tattooed on his forehead for these purposes.

[72] *Id.* (attributing this standard to "the Commerce Clause cases").

[73] See, e.g., Printz v. United States, 521 U.S. 898, 923–24 (1997); see also Comstock, 130 S. Ct. at 1967–68 (Kennedy, J., concurring in the judgment) ("It is of fundamental importance to consider whether essential attributes of state sovereignty are compromised by the assertion of federal power under the Necessary and Proper Clause.").

[74] Lawson & Granger, *supra* note 61, at 297.

But that formulation—if it is to be more than tautological—is hard to unpack. In *NFIB*, the chief justice suggested that the individual health insurance mandate was improper because it extended federal power in a way that had no obvious stopping point.[75]

For DOMA, the strongest argument is that Congress had appropriated a power that is reserved exclusively to the states. And Congress's intrusion on that power interfered with the states' own exercise of their powers over marriage. First, it required state officials to disregard state law when administering federal programs. State officials administering veterans' cemeteries, for example, had to exclude veterans' same-sex spouses in spite of state law. Second, DOMA interfered with implementing and enforcing state law itself and imposed substantial costs on the states. For example, it made spousal-support orders between same-sex couples unenforceable in bankruptcy and precluded using garnishment procedures ordinarily available for monies in federal hands (such as income-tax refunds, or federal wages and benefits payments). It prevented state income tax regimes from "piggybacking" on federal forms, rules, and enforcement. And it increased the taxes that states as employers pay when they extend health insurance to same-sex spouses.[76] These effects reflect DOMA's fundamental purpose, which was to discourage states from adopting a definition of marriage that departed from Congress's preferences.[77]

Some have suggested, however, that Congress *always* has the power to define terms in its enactments.[78] Because this essay is primarily

---

[75] 132 S. Ct. at 2588 (opinion of Roberts, C.J.); accord *id.* at 2646 (joint dissent); see also Jonathan Adler, Judicial Minimalism, the Mandate, and Mr. Roberts, in The Health Care Case: The Supreme Court's Decision and Its Implications (Nathaniel Persily, Gillian E. Metzger & Trevor W. Morrison eds., 2013).

[76] See Brief of Federalism Scholars, *supra* note *, at 32–35.

[77] See 133 S. Ct. at 2693 (DOMA's purpose "is to discourage enactment of state same-sex marriage laws . . . . The congressional goal was 'to put a thumb on the scales and influence a state's decision as to how to shape its own marriage laws.'" (quoting Massachusetts, 682 F.3d at 12–13)). One might analyze many of these burdens as conditions on the federal monies and other benefits that states accept in order to participate in federal programs. From that perspective, however, DOMA probably could not validly apply to any programs that states elected to participate in prior to DOMA's effective date. See, e.g., NFIB, 132 S. Ct. at 2603–06 (striking down retroactive conditions on Medicaid participation).

[78] See, e.g., Nicholas Quinn Rosenkranz, Congress Has Power to Define the Terms of Its Own Statutes, Volokh Conspiracy, Mar. 6, 2013, http://www.volokh.

about the arguments the Court *did* address in *Windsor*, one of us has analyzed this argument for a broad federal "definition power" in a separate essay.[79] Briefly, there are three basic answers. First, federal definitions for terms like "marriage" are hardly inevitable or essential. Federal law has traditionally taken state law as it found it with respect to marriage and other basics of family law. Under DOMA, federal law *continued* to take state marriage law as it found it—except for refusing to recognize state-sanctioned same-sex marriages. Second, *everything* Congress does must be tied to an enumerated power. When Congress offers definitions for statutory terms, it is using the Necessary and Proper Clause power, and its definitions—like everything else done under that power—still must be incidental, plainly adapted, and proper. Calling Congress's action a "definition" changes nothing.

The third objection ties the Necessary and Proper Clause arguments to the equal protection analysis, which the rest of this essay focuses on. Even if Congress can define its terms, Congress's enumerated powers limit the range of *interests* that Congress may assert in support of those definitions when they are challenged under the Constitution's rights and equality provisions. Congress might define "marriage" so that its statutes are intelligible, but it cannot assert an interest in maintaining the traditional institution of marriage in

---

com/2013/03/06/congress-has-power-to-define-the-terms-of-its-own-statutes; Nicholas Quinn Rosenkranz, There Is No Federalism Objection to Section Three of the Defense of Marriage Act, Volokh Conspiracy, Mar. 24, 2013, http://www.volokh. com/2013/03/24/there-is-no-federalism-objection-to-section-three-of-the-defense-of-marriage-act; see also Ed Whelan, Badly Confused Amicus Brief on Federalism in DOMA Case, Nat'l Rev. Online, Mar. 5, 2013, http://www.nationalreview.com/bench-memos/342256/badly-confused-amicus-brief-federalism-doma-case-ed-whelan (offering a more ad hominem version of the same argument).

[79] See Ernest A. Young, DOMA and the Limits of Congress's Power to Define Its Terms, Case Western Res. L. Rev. (forthcoming Spring 2014). For shorter responses, see Ernie Young, DOMA and Federalism: What Are the Limits of Congress's Power to Define Terms in Federal Statutes? A Reply to Whelan and Rosenkranz, Volokh Conspiracy, Mar. 7, 2013, http://www.volokh.com/2013/03/07/doma-and-federalism-what-are-the-limits-of-congresss-power-to-define-terms-in-federal-statutes-a-reply-to-whelan-and-rosenkranz; Randy Barnett, The Chief Justice's Excellent Hypothetical: Under Our System of Federalism, Can You Be Both Married and Unmarried at the Same Time?, Volokh Conspiracy, Mar. 28, 2013, http://www.volokh.com/2013/03/28/the-chief-justices-excellent-hypothetical-under-our-system-of-federalism-can-you-be-both-married-and-unmarried-at-the-same-time; Jonathan H. Adler, A Final Response to Ed on DOMA, Nat'l Rev. Online, Apr. 1, 2013, http://www.nationalreview.com/bench-memos/344376/final-response-ed-doma-jonathan-h-adler.

response to an equal protection challenge. That is because maintaining that institution is not itself within any of Congress's enumerated powers. What Congress cannot do, in other words, is exactly what BLAG did in the *Windsor* litigation: assert that it has the same interest as a state to define who can and cannot be married.

B. Federalism and Equal Protection

The Court did not, of course, reach these enumerated powers arguments in *Windsor*. It decided the case on equal protection grounds, prompting not only Justice Scalia but also numerous commentators to discount the holding's federalism element. That reaction, in our view, fundamentally misunderstands the majority opinion. Structural principles like federalism and separation of powers exist to protect individual liberty.[80] We generally think of this protection in a macro sense: federalism, like separation of powers, helps form a system of checks and balances that makes it more difficult for either level of government to act tyrannically and provides institutional outlets for divergent views. But federalism also operates in a *micro* sense, shaping individual-rights doctrine. Justice Kennedy's *Windsor* opinion is, in fact, the best illustration we have of how structural analysis can—and should—inform individual rights.

Edith Windsor's equal protection challenge to DOMA necessarily included several elements. Unlawful discrimination occurs with respect to some right or interest, and the courts had to define that interest with some precision. BLAG offered particular governmental interests to justify DOMA, and the courts had to assess those interests. Finally, the courts had to determine the "fit" between the government's interests and Congress's means, which required deciding how much deference, if any, to show Congress's judgment of that fit. Justice Kennedy's opinion demonstrates that federalism played a key role at each step of this analysis.

1. Defining the Right

It seems natural to think of *Windsor* and *Hollingsworth* as cases about whether gay and straight people have equal rights to marry.

---

[80] See, e.g., New York v. United States, 505 U.S. 144, 181 (1992) ("[T]he Constitution divides authority between federal and state governments for the protection of individuals.").

That is not quite correct. *Hollingsworth*, which challenged California's prohibition of same-sex marriage, did raise that question. In *Windsor*, however, even BLAG did not argue that Edith Windsor and Thea Spyer were not lawfully married. All parties recognized that state law settled that point. The question was whether the federal government, through DOMA, could constitutionally refuse to recognize that marriage. Hence, the solicitor general framed the question presented as: "Whether Section 3 of DOMA violates the Fifth Amendment's guarantee of equal protection of the laws as applied to persons of the same sex who are legally married under the laws of their State."[81]

The last phrase is critical: Edith Windsor and Thea Spyer were "legally married under the laws of their State." They did not assert that justice or fairness entitled them to marry; they insisted that their state's law had conferred marital status upon them and that Congress could not treat some people with that status differently from others without denying equal protection of the laws. That struck a chord with the *Windsor* majority, which emphasized that "the State's decision to give this class of persons the right to marry conferred upon them a dignity and status of immense import. When the State used its historic and essential authority to define the marital relation in this way, its role and its power in making the decision enhanced the recognition, dignity, and protection of the class in their own community."[82]

The Court's focus on the *state's* determination that Windsor and Spyer could marry rather brilliantly dissolved what, in our view, has always been the dilemma at the heart of debates about same-sex marriage. At least since *Loving v. Virginia*, marriage has been recognized as a fundamental right.[83] It is hornbook law that governmental

---

[81] Petition for a Writ of Certiorari Before Judgment in United States v. Windsor, at I, 133 S. Ct. 2675 (2013) (No. 12-307), available at http://sblog.s3.amazonaws.com/wp-content/uploads/2012/10/12-307-Petition.pdf.

[82] 133 S. Ct. at 2692. See also Randy Barnett, Federalism Marries Liberty in the DOMA Decision, Volokh Conspiracy, Jun. 26, 2013, at http://www.volokh.com/2013/06/26/federalism-marries-liberty-in-the-doma-decision (emphasizing this aspect of *Windsor*).

[83] 388 U.S. 1 (1967) (holding that anti-miscegenation laws violate the Equal Protection Clause).

classifications that burden or unequally allocate a fundamental right are subject to strict (and usually fatal) scrutiny.

But strict scrutiny requires the government to discriminate among *similarly situated* people. Opponents of same-sex marriage contend that marriage just *is*—and has always been—an institution involving one man and one woman; hence, gay and straight couples cannot be similarly situated. Proponents, of course, disagree. It is not easy to resolve that debate without relying on one's moral priors.[84]

The *Windsor* majority, however, focused on the fact that the great state of New York had already resolved—and as a matter for federalism, was *entitled* to resolve—that question through its own democratic processes. State law defined the class of similarly situated persons for purposes of Windsor's equal protection claim.[85] As Justice Kennedy explained:

> The class to which DOMA directs its restrictions and restraints are those persons who are joined in same-sex marriages made lawful by the State. DOMA singles out a class of persons deemed by a State entitled to recognition and protection to enhance their own liberty. It imposes a disability on the class by refusing to acknowledge a status the State finds to be dignified and proper.[86]

That approach made Justice Scalia's *sturm und drang* about democratic deliberation singularly inappropriate: the Court did not impose its own view of whether same-sex marriages should be recognized; it accepted New York's.[87]

It is worth remembering that state law provides the predicate for federal constitutional claims all the time. Property interests, for example, are generally a function of state law; hence, claims under the Takings and Due Process Clauses, as well as the Fourth Amendment,

---

[84] That is not to say that there is no right answer, either as a legal or a moral matter. Our point is simply that the question is a difficult one.

[85] See 133 S. Ct. at 2694 ("DOMA contrives to deprive some couples married under the laws of their State, but not other couples, of both rights and responsibilities.").

[86] *Id.* at 2695–96.

[87] Compare, e.g., *id.* at 2711 (Scalia, J., dissenting) ("We might have covered ourselves with honor today, by promising all sides of this debate that it was theirs to settle and that we would respect their resolution. We might have let the People decide."), with Marriage Equality Act, 2011 N.Y. Laws 749 (codified at N.Y. Dom. Rel. Law Ann. §§ 10-a, 10-b, 13) (2011) (deciding).

often turn on whether the government has invaded an interest defined by state law.[88] Contracts Clause claims likewise require first establishing a valid contract under state law.[89] In all these contexts, federalism provides a positivist alternative to some Platonic notion of "property" or "contract"—or "marriage." The Constitution gives states authority to define those terms, and federal law takes state law as it finds it.[90]

There are, of course, exceptions. State law definitions may not violate the federal Constitution. Virginia's power to define marriage did not save its anti-miscegenation law, which violated the Equal Protection Clause by discriminating on the basis of race.[91] State prohibitions on same-sex marriage, such as Proposition 8, might also violate that provision. But that is a harder question than whether *Congress* may refuse to recognize marriages that a state has already sanctioned. Like property and contracts, state law defined and elevated Edith Windsor and Thea Spyer's marriage.

The close connection between the state's power to define marriage and the dignity of individuals is not simply theoretical—it is also highly practical and emotional. As the Federalism Scholars' brief argued, "DOMA creates significant uncertainty with [the] private realm. It forces same-sex couples to live a divided life, married for state purposes but unmarried for federal ones."[92] Or, as Justice Ruth Bader Ginsburg famously put it at oral argument, DOMA transforms

[88] See, e.g., Lucas v. S.C. Coastal Council, 505 U.S. 1003, 1030 (1992) (noting "our traditional resort to 'existing rules or understandings that stem from an independent source such as state law' to define the range of interests that qualify for protection as 'property' under the Fifth and Fourteenth Amendments") (takings claim) (quoting Board of Regents of State Colleges v. Roth, 408 U.S. 564, 577 (1972) (due process claim)); United States v. Jones, 132 S. Ct. 945, 951 (2012) (holding that warrantless GPS surveillance violates the Fourth Amendment where it would amount to a trespass upon individual property interests).

[89] See, e.g., Indiana ex rel. Anderson v. Brand, 303 U.S. 95 (1938).

[90] See generally Richard H. Fallon, Jr., John F. Manning, Daniel J. Meltzer, & David L. Shapiro, Hart and Wechsler's The Federal Courts and the Federal System 459 (6th ed. 2009) ("Federal law is generally interstitial in its nature. . . . Congress acts . . . against the background of the total *corpus juris* of the states in much the way that a state legislature acts against the background of the common law, assumed to govern unless changed by legislation."). We would add, of course, that Congress can only change the state law background by legislation if it acts within its enumerated powers.

[91] See Loving, 388 U.S. at 11–12.

[92] Brief of Federalism Scholars, *supra* note *, at 36.

a "full marriage" into a "skim-milk marriage."[93] Same-sex married couples—like *all* married couples—justifiably rely on the solidity and permanence of state law's recognition of their relationships. DOMA's intrusion on those relationships threatens their well-being and undermines their dignity. As Edith Windsor said after Thea died, "In the midst of my grief, I realized that the federal government was treating us as strangers."[94]

Invalidating DOMA hardly ensures that state law will recognize all same-sex relationships. But ensuring that people can rely on state law to settle their family relationships without Congress interfering promotes notice, reliance, and political accountability.[95] As Justice Kennedy put it, "DOMA rejects the long-established precept that the incidents, benefits, and obligations of marriage are uniform for all married couples within each State, though they may vary, subject to constitutional guarantees, from one State to the next."[96] Whether or not Edith Windsor and Thea Spyer had a right to have New York recognize their marriage, once it did so they were entitled to rely on that decision.

2. The Government's Interests

Federalism also constrained the interests that could justify DOMA by tightening the Court's standard of review and prompting the Court to reject Congress's primary interest outright. The Court simply ignored several of the interests that BLAG asserted, including an interest in maintaining a nationally uniform definition of marriage for purposes of federal law and protecting the federal fisc.[97] The most plausible reason for the Court's silence was that it did not think these interests had much to do with Congress's *actual* purpose. Rather, the Court said, "The history of DOMA's enactment and its

[93] Transcript of Oral Argument at 71, U.S. v. Windsor, 133 S. Ct. 2675 (2013) (No. 12-307).

[94] Amy Davidson, The Skim Milk in Edith Windsor's Marriage, The New Yorker, Mar. 28, 2013, http://www.newyorker.com/online/blogs/comment/2013/03/edith-windsors-victory-doma.html.

[95] See Brief of Federalism Scholars, *supra* note *, at 36 (arguing that "DOMA blurs lines of political accountability for this intrusion, particularly when state officials must administer federal rules that do not respect marriage rights under state law").

[96] 133 S. Ct. at 2692.

[97] See BLAG Brief, *supra* note 34, at 28–49 (discussing these interests).

own text demonstrate that interference with the equal dignity of same-sex marriages, a dignity conferred by the States in the exercise of their sovereign power, was more than an incidental effect of the federal statute. It was its essence."[98]

Under traditional rational basis review, however, courts generally do not hold the legislature to its actual purpose as long as some possible basis justifies the law.[99] But the Court has not always been so deferential, even in cases purporting to apply rational basis review.[100] In *Romer v. Evans*[101]—also a case about gay rights, also written by Justice Kennedy—the Court applied what some have called "active rational basis" review or "rational basis with bite."[102] *Romer* diverged from traditional rational basis review in two ways. First, it addressed only the government interests actually asserted by Colorado in defense of its law; it did not, as it traditionally does in rational basis cases, unleash its imagination (or its law clerks) to think up better ones.[103] Second, it somewhat tightened the "fit" required between the government's interests and means.

Justice Kennedy's *Windsor* opinion followed the same pattern. It considered only DOMA's *actual* purpose, which it found to be "to

---

[98] 133 S. Ct. at 2693.

[99] See, e.g., FCC v. Beach Commc'ns, Inc., 508 U.S. 307, 314–15 (1993).

[100] See, e.g., City of Cleburne v. Cleburne Living Ctr., Inc., 473 U.S. 432, 458 (1985) (Marshall, J., dissenting) (suggesting that "perhaps the method employed must . . . be called 'second order' rational-basis review"); Massachusetts v. U.S. Dept. of Health & Human Servs., 682 F.3d 1, 10–11 (1st Cir. 2012) (Boudin, J.); United States v. Then, 56 F.3d 464, 468 (2d Cir. 1995) (Calabresi, J., concurring) (noting "that the usually deferential 'rational basis' test has been applied with greater rigor in some contexts").

[101] 517 U.S. 620 (1996).

[102] See, e.g., Kevin G. Walsh, Comment, Throwing Stones: Rational Basis Review Triumphs over Homophobia, 27 Seton Hall L. Rev. 1064 (1997) (noting speculation that *Romer* "contains a tier . . . of 'active' rational basis review"); Jeremy B. Smith, Comment, The Flaws of Rational Basis with Bite: Why the Supreme Court Should Acknowledge Its Application of Heightened Scrutiny to Classifications Based on Sexual Orientation, 73 Fordham L. Rev. 2769 (2005).

[103] That would not have been hard to do. Colorado's Amendment 2 prohibited anyone from raising a discrimination claim based on sexual orientation. That was far too broad for the state's asserted rationale, which was to "respect . . . other citizens' freedom of association." 517 U.S. at 635. But the state *could* have argued that expanding the category of discrimination claims always raises compliance costs and enforcement costs, and that reducing such costs is a legitimate government interest. If the Court had addressed that interest, it would surely have had overtly to embrace a higher level of scrutiny in order to strike down the law.

impose a disadvantage, a separate status, and so a stigma upon all who enter into same-sex marriages made lawful by the unquestioned authority of the States."[104] As he noted, "The stated purpose of the law was to promote an 'interest in protecting the traditional moral teachings reflected in heterosexual-only marriage laws.' . . . Were there any doubt of this far-reaching purpose, the title of the Act confirms it: The Defense of Marriage."[105] The Court also, as we discuss in Section 3 below, required a somewhat closer fit between means and ends than it often does in pure rational-basis cases.

The question, then, is what prompted the Court to tighten its review in *Windsor*? Early commentators have emphasized Justice Kennedy's comments about the dignity of same-sex couples and their families: "[DOMA's] differentiation demeans the couple, whose moral and sexual choices the Constitution protects . . . . And it humiliates tens of thousands of children now being raised by same-sex couples."[106] But each time that Kennedy mentioned dignity, he emphasized that this was a "relationship [that] *the State* has sought to dignify."[107] Each of the burdens that he cited deprived same-sex couples of *state-law* rights and responsibilities.[108] "DOMA singles out a class of persons deemed by a State entitled to recognition and protection to enhance their own liberty. It imposes a disability on the class by refusing to acknowledge a status the State finds to be dignified and proper."[109]

It was not just that DOMA was mean, in other words. Its meanness arose because it sought to put asunder a union that New York has already recognized. That was "strong evidence of a law having

---

[104] 133 S. Ct. at 2693.

[105] *Id.* (quoting H.R. Rep. No. 104-664, at 12–13 (1996)).

[106] 133 S. Ct. at 2694; see also *id.* at 2695 ("DOMA instructs all federal officials, and indeed all persons with whom same-sex couples interact, including their own children, that their marriage is less worthy than the marriages of others.").

[107] *Id.* at 2694 (emphasis added); see also *id.* at 2696 ("The federal statute is invalid, for no legitimate purpose overcomes the purpose and effect to disparage and to injure *those whom the State, by its marriage laws, sought to protect* in personhood and dignity." (emphasis added)).

[108] The same can be said of the Court's invocations of "animus" as an illegitimate basis for a law. See *id.* at 2693 (citing Romer, 517 U.S. at 633). Justice Kennedy introduced that discussion by stressing that "DOMA seeks to injure the very class New York seeks to protect." *Id.*

[109] *Id.* at 2695–96.

the purpose and effect of *disapproval* of that class [of same-sex couples married under state law]."[110] Singling out a particular class for disapproval was an important trigger of "active rationality" review in *Romer*.[111] But it was DOMA's displacement of the state-law norms that raised the fear of class legislation.[112] Writing for the First Circuit in *DHHS*, Judge Michael Boudin reached the same conclusion more directly: "Given that DOMA intrudes broadly into an area of traditional state regulation, a closer examination of the justifications that would prevent DOMA from violating equal protection . . . is uniquely reinforced by federalism concerns."[113]

Federalism thus helps explain why the Court limited its review to DOMA's *actual* purpose. It equally explains how the Court assessed the legitimacy of that governmental interest. BLAG's merits brief in *Windsor* opened with the striking—and unprecedented—claim that "the federal government has the same latitude as the states to adopt its own definition of marriage for federal-law purposes."[114] Although the brief rested this assertion on "[b]edrock principles of federalism,"[115] the relevant section lacked a single citation to precedent or other authority.[116] There was a reason for that omission.

One can put the federalism objection to this interest either of two ways. The milder is to say that this is simply an interest that Congress

[110] *Id.* at 2693 (emphasis added).

[111] See, e.g., 517 U.S. at 623 (citing Justice Harlan's admonition that "the Constitution 'neither knows nor tolerates classes among citizens'") (quoting Plessy v. Ferguson, 163 U.S. 537, 559 (1896); *id.* at 627 ("Homosexuals, by state decree, are put in a solitary class with respect to transactions and relations in both the private and governmental spheres."); *id.* at 633 (emphasizing "the principle that government . . . remain[s] open on impartial terms to all who seek its assistance" and observing that "[r]espect for this principle explains why laws singling out a certain class of citizens for disfavored legal status . . . are rare"); *id.* at 635 ("We must conclude that Amendment 2 classifies homosexuals not to further a proper legislative end but to make them unequal to everyone else. This Colorado cannot do."); see generally Jack Balkin, Windsor and the Constitutional Prohibition against Class Legislation, Balkinization, Jun. 26, 2013, at http://balkin.blogspot.com/2013/06/windsor-and-constitutional-prohibition.html.

[112] See also 133 S. Ct. at 2696 (Roberts, C.J., dissenting) ("The majority sees a more sinister motive, pointing out that the Federal Government has generally (though not uniformly) deferred to state definitions of marriage in the past.").

[113] DHHS, 682 F.3d at 13.

[114] BLAG Brief, *supra* note 34, at 19.

[115] *Id.*

[116] See *id.* at 30–33.

does not have because it falls outside Congress's enumerated powers.[117] As John Marshall wrote in *McCulloch*, for an "end [to] be legitimate," it must be "within the scope of the constitution."[118] One important and often-forgotten implication of this statement is that while there are "necessary and proper" *means* to enumerated ends, there are no "necessary and proper"—but unenumerated—federal *ends* or interests.[119] Otherwise, the Supremacy Clause would cause Congress's purpose to discourage same-sex marriage to preempt *state* laws recognizing same-sex marriage because they would "stand[] as an obstacle to the accomplishment and execution of the full purposes and objectives of Congress."[120] No one thinks DOMA had that effect.

Justice Kennedy described BLAG's argument even more starkly, as "candid[ly]" acknowledging a "congressional purpose to influence or interfere with state sovereign choices about who may be married."[121] The objection is not just that the federal government lacked an interest in defining marriage, but that its attempt to do so anyway interfered with the *states'* choices. If Congress had constitutional power to define marriage, however, then that interference would be fine. In *Gonzales v. Raich*, for example, because the Supreme Court concluded that Congress *did* have power to prohibit marijuana consumption, California's contrary choice was constitutionally irrelevant.[122] But in *Windsor*, Justice Kennedy seems to have viewed Congress's interference as violating the principle he identified in *Comstock*, that "essential attributes of state sovereignty [may not be] compromised by the assertion of federal power under the Necessary and Proper Clause."[123]

---

[117] See, e.g., Windsor, 699 F.3d at 187 (reasoning that "because the decision of whether same-sex couples can marry is left to the states, DOMA does not, strictly speaking, 'preserve' the institution of marriage as one between a man and a woman").

[118] 17 U.S. (4 Wheat.) at 421.

[119] See, e.g., Engdahl, *supra* note 65, at 18–20.

[120] Hines v. Davidowitz, 312 U.S. 52, 67 (1941); see also Catherine M. Sharkey, Against Freewheeling, Extratextual Obstacle Preemption: Is Justice Thomas the Lone Principled Federalist?, 5 N.Y.U. J. L. & Lib. 63, 66 (2010) (describing obstacle preemption as "an expansive route whereby state law tort claims are ousted not by express statutory text, but rather on account of their implied conflict with the purposes and objectives of the federal regulatory scheme").

[121] 133 S. Ct. at 2693.

[122] 545 U.S. 1, 29–31 (2005).

[123] See *supra* note 73.

That is why BLAG's argument did not count as a legitimate federal interest.

Finally, we consider an additional interest that the government asserted but that the Court ignored. In the same sentence that it insisted Congress has a coequal authority to define marriage for itself, BLAG also said that Congress "has a unique interest in treating citizens across the nation the same."[124] One might question how strong this interest in uniformity really is,[125] but it lacks the bad odor of an effort simply to harm a particular class of citizens. Nonetheless, the Court ignored it—which necessarily entailed a judgment, implicit or not, that it was not a legitimate federal interest in this context. Why not? The Court must have concluded that Congress simply lacks authority to make judgments about who is married; it has no constitutional option other than to take state law as Congress finds it, in all its variegated glory.[126]

3. Deference as to Fit

The Court decided *Windsor* primarily on the ground that DOMA lacked any legitimate federal interest.[127] But the Court also had something to say about fit, complaining that "DOMA frustrates [New York's] objective through a system-wide enactment with no identified connection to any particular area of federal law."[128] Likewise, the Court dismissed any possibility that DOMA might be a revenue measure:

---

[124] BLAG Brief, *supra* note 34, at 19.

[125] See, e.g., United States v. Kimbell Foods, Inc., 440 U.S. 715, 730 (1979) (rejecting "generalized pleas for uniformity as substitutes for concrete evidence that adopting state law would adversely affect administration of the federal programs"); Amanda Frost, Overvaluing Uniformity, 94 Va. L. Rev. 1567 (2008).

[126] The Second Circuit explicitly rejected BLAG's uniformity argument on federalism grounds. See 699 F.3d at 186 ("Because DOMA is an unprecedented breach of longstanding deference to federalism that singles out same-sex marriage as the only inconsistency (among many) in state law that requires a federal rule to achieve uniformity, the rationale premised on uniformity is not an exceedingly persuasive justification for DOMA.").

[127] See 133 S. Ct. at 2695 ("[T]he principal purpose and the necessary effect of this law are to demean those persons who are in a lawful same-sex marriage. This requires the Court to hold . . . that DOMA is unconstitutional as a deprivation of the liberty of the person protected by the Fifth Amendment of the Constitution.").

[128] *Id.* at 2694.

The particular case at hand concerns the estate tax, but DOMA is more than a simple determination of what should or should not be allowed on an estate tax refund. Among the over 1,000 statutes and numerous federal regulations that DOMA controls are laws pertaining to Social Security, housing, taxes, criminal sanctions, copyright, and veterans' benefits.[129]

And the Court's catalog of nonsensical results under DOMA—for example, DOMA permitted gifts to the same-sex spouses of senators and other officials that otherwise would be illegal under federal ethics laws[130]—apparently rejected the notion that DOMA was sufficiently related to any legitimate end the government might assert.

Ordinary rational basis review generally permits laws to be significantly over- or underinclusive.[131] DOMA's shortcomings in this regard were extreme: applying to more than 1,100 federal laws at once, it was rationally related to none.[132] Nonetheless, it is hard to avoid the impression that the Court ratcheted up the level of scrutiny. Judge Boudin's opinion for the First Circuit was more explicit, concluding that "[i]f we are right in thinking that disparate impact on minority interests and federalism concerns both require somewhat more in this case than almost automatic deference to Congress's will, this statute fails that test."[133]

It is critical to remember, however, that "ordinary" rational basis review is not itself part of the Constitution. It is a doctrinal test that the Supreme Court has developed for specific reasons—in particular, to defer to democratically elected legislatures that presumably have superior institutional capability to decide social and economic issues. Those underlying justifications for judicial deference have

---

[129] *Id.*

[130] *Id.* at 2695.

[131] See, e.g., Williamson v. Lee Optical of Okla., Inc., 348 U.S. 483, 489 (1955).

[132] Cf. DHHS, 682 F.3d at 13 (noting that "only one day of hearings was held on DOMA . . . and none of the testimony concerned DOMA's effects on the numerous federal programs at issue").

[133] *Id.* at 15. The First Circuit explicitly "[did] not rely upon the charge that DOMA's hidden but dominant purpose was hostility to homosexuality." *Id.* at 16. Its analysis turned instead on its conclusion that "Supreme Court decisions in the last fifty years call for closer scrutiny of government action touching upon minority group interests and of federal action in areas of traditional state concern." *Id.*

complex implications, however, in a case like *Windsor*. Not one but *two* legislatures are in play: Congress and New York's. It is hardly obvious why Congress is more worthy of deference than the New York legislature—both institutions, after all, have similar democratic pedigrees and institutional competences.[134]

To the extent that the Court required a somewhat closer-than-usual fit between means and ends in *Windsor*, it may have concluded that Congress was not the appropriate institution entitled to deference when it comes to marriage. Justice Kennedy's repeated reference to the states' primacy in this area suggested that Congress does not enjoy the same strong presumption of constitutionality when it interferes with state law as when legislating on traditional federal subjects within its enumerated powers. We do not suggest that that was the *only* reason for a lesser degree of deference. Like *Romer*, *Windsor* leaves the strong impression that same-sex couples share many of the indicia that make racial and gender classifications suspect, even if the Court seems reluctant to say so outright. Nonetheless, we think that, in this context, respect for federalism played a crucial role in dissuading the Court from deferring to Congress.

Conclusion

At a time when the Constitution lacked a Bill of Rights, much less an Equal Protection Clause, James Madison invoked both federalism and separation of powers as forming a "double security" protecting "the rights of the people."[135] The Court echoed that language two years ago: "The federal system rests on what might at first seem a counterintuitive insight, that 'freedom is enhanced by the creation of two governments, not one'"; hence, "'federalism secures to citizens the liberties that derive from the diffusion of sovereign power.'"[136] *Windsor* illustrates this dynamic, perhaps better than any case in recent memory. Edith Windsor prevailed because the state of New York had established her right to marriage equality in state law, and Congress lacked legitimate authority to interfere with that right.

---

[134] If anything, one can argue that a state legislature is closer to the people. See, e.g., Michael W. McConnell, Federalism: Evaluating the Founders' Design, 54 U. Chi. L. Rev. 1484, 1509 (1987).

[135] The Federalist No. 51, at 320 (James Madison) (Clinton Rossiter ed., 1961).

[136] Bond, 131 S. Ct. at 2364 (2011) (quoting Alden v. Maine, 527 U.S. 706, 758 (1999); New York v. United States, 505 U.S. 144, 181 (1992)).

This close relationship between federalism, liberty, and equality has often eluded even seasoned observers. Writing in the *New York Times*, Court-watcher Linda Greenhouse attacked the notion of a federalism-based resolution in *Windsor*. "Federalism tends to emerge from under the rocks in times of constitutional ferment," Greenhouse said, and she asserted that "striking down DOMA on federalism grounds is a truly bad idea, and the campaign for marriage equality would be worse off for it."[137] To reach that conclusion, however, one would have to believe that if Justice Kennedy had not been distracted by federalism, the Court would have issued a strong rights-based decision mandating same-sex marriage across the board. The argument and decision in *Perry* suggest—somewhat to the surprise of many observers, including us—that such a resolution was simply not in the cards in 2013.

It is true that, as the chief justice argued in dissent, DOMA's federalism problems could distinguish *Windsor* in subsequent suits challenging state-law same-sex-marriage bans.[138] And "while '[t]he State's power in defining the marital relation is of central relevance' to the majority's decision to strike down DOMA here, . . . that power will come into play on the other side of the board in future cases about the constitutionality of state marriage definitions."[139] But we have a hard time seeing how state sovereignty will weigh particularly heavily in favor of state same-sex marriage bans. That value is embodied in the rational-basis test that applies to equal protection challenges not implicating a suspect or quasi-suspect class, and the states will probably be allowed to assert continuity with traditional moral teaching on marriage as a legitimate interest in a way that Congress, in *Windsor*, was not. The odds of striking down traditional state marriage laws under ordinary rational-basis review were never good, however.

---

[137] Greenhouse, *supra* note 5. Greenhouse also impugned the motives of the conservative and libertarian scholars who filed the federalism brief against DOMA. See *id*. (intoning "[b]eware of conservatives bearing gifts" and comparing our argument to Virginia's racist defense of its anti-miscegenation laws). We have not seen any post-decision columns from her lamenting DOMA's demise or explaining how the gay-rights movement is worse off.

[138] 133 S. Ct. at 2696 (Roberts, C.J., dissenting).

[139] *Id*. at 2697.

But federalism does not justify rejecting any of the various forms of heightened scrutiny proposed for discrimination against homosexuals.[140] Our Constitution imposes national checks on state abuses, just as it counts on the states to check national ones. Hence, in myriad cases involving state laws challenged under heightened scrutiny pursuant to principles of equal protection, free speech, or due process, federalism generally has not been a significant impediment. Many of those cases—involving public education,[141] tort liability,[142] and regulation of the medical profession[143]—also implicated well-established, traditional state functions. As Greenhouse pointed out, federalism was not an obstacle to the assault on Virginia's prohibition of interracial marriage in *Loving v. Virginia*.[144] And rightly so. As the Court has frequently pointed out, the Fourteenth Amendment was always intended and understood as an incursion into and constraint on state sovereignty.[145]

Windsor recognized that federalism *additionally* protects liberty and equality when federal action threatens those rights. As Madison insisted, that protection was part of the Constitution's first-line strategy for ensuring individual freedom. Although we cannot develop the argument here,[146] we believe that the remarkable success of the gay-rights movement owes a great deal to our federal system. As Justice Kennedy recognized in another recent case, "Federalism . . . allows States to respond, through the enactment of positive law, to the initiative of those who seek a voice in shaping the destiny of their own times without having to rely solely upon the political processes that control a remote central power."[147] The movement for marriage equality has surely benefited from the opportunity to implement same-sex-marriage in sympathetic states and to demonstrate to a

[140] See, e.g., Letter from the Attorney General to Congress on Litigation Involving the Defense of Marriage Act, Feb. 23, 2011, available at http://www.justice.gov/opa/pr/2011/February/11-ag-223.html (arguing for heightened equal protection scrutiny).

[141] Brown v. Bd. of Educ., 347 U.S. 483 (1954).

[142] New York Times Co. v. Sullivan, 376 U.S. 254 (1964).

[143] Roe v. Wade, 410 U.S. 113 (1973).

[144] See Greenhouse, *supra* note 5.

[145] See, e.g., Fitzpatrick v. Bitzer, 427 U.S. 445 (1976).

[146] See Ernest A. Young, Exit, Voice, and Loyalty as Federalism Strategies: Lessons from the Same-Sex Marriage Debate, U. Colo. L. Rev. (forthcoming Spring 2014).

[147] Bond, 131 S. Ct. at 2364.

watching nation that the institution is not so threatening as some moral traditionalists might have feared.[148] Whether or not the Court ever strikes down state-law same-sex-marriage bans under the Equal Protection Clause, *Windsor* removed a significant impediment to that broader liberalization process in DOMA. In so doing, the Court reminded us how our federalism can profoundly enhance liberty.

---

[148] See generally Dale Carpenter, The Federal Marriage Amendment: Unnecessary, Anti-Federalist, and Anti-Democratic, 570 Cato Inst. Policy Analysis, at 10–12 (Apr. 2006), available at http://www.cato.org/publications/policy-analysis/federal-marriage-amendment-unnecessary-antifederalist-antidemocratic (articulating how federalism has been beneficial to democratic debate over same-sex marriage).

Kiobel v. Royal Dutch Petroleum: The Alien Tort Statute's Jurisdictional Universalism in Retreat

*Kenneth Anderson**

I. Introduction

A case (unusually) spanning two Supreme Court terms, *Kiobel v. Royal Dutch Petroleum*[1] offered the Court an opportunity to provide much-needed guidance on the proper scope of the Alien Tort Statute.[2] The ATS, a long-obscure provision of the first Judiciary Act of 1789, was forgotten shortly after it was passed until it was revived in the 1980s by activist lawyers seeking a vehicle for all manner of lawsuits against an ever-expanding list of private actors, based on claims of violations of international law. As plaintiffs in the last decade have undertaken ATS suits against corporations, the stakes have grown precipitously and the battles have become more sharply contested.

This essay begins by setting *Kiobel* and the ATS in the legal and policy context of transnational legal disputes. Behind the legal questions of jurisdiction are more abstract questions of liberty and sovereign popular government—what issues of political and moral principle are at stake in these disputes? Following this context-setting, I turn to the *Kiobel* case itself, setting its facts alongside the text of the ATS and summarizing its unusual procedural history at the Court. I then turn to the history of the statute, its long desuetude and modern revival, and give a brief history of the kinds of claims made under the ATS by the time of the *Kiobel* decision. In doing so, I bring out the legal and political controversies that gradually swirled around the ATS—both narrowly doctrinal legal controversies on one hand and deeply

* Professor of Law, Washington College of Law at American University.
[1] Kiobel v. Royal Dutch Petroleum Co., 133 S. Ct. 1659 (2013).
[2] 28 U.S.C. § 1350.

contested political questions on the other, raising at bottom the legal legitimacy of U.S. courts' claims to reach extraterritorially so far and deep under the authority of "international law."

At the heart of the modern ATS, I suggest, is its peculiar textual commingling of international and domestic law predicates. At the level of political theory, I go on to ask whether the ATS in its modern incarnation is best understood not truly as "international law" but instead as what might be called the "law of the hegemon," imposed by a dominant global power in an act of will. I speculate that the Court's retreat from the attempt to carry out universal jurisdiction through distinctively American legal mechanisms represents a tacit judgment that American hegemony, in a world of competitive and rising new global and regional powers, does not have the reach it once had.

The Court made a surprising pivot in *Kiobel*. It took the case in order to settle whether corporations could be liable in ATS suits, but it instead decided to settle the more fundamental question of when American courts have jurisdiction over foreign defendants, whether individual or otherwise. I examine in detail the two main *Kiobel* opinions—the majority opinion by Chief Justice John Roberts and the minority concurrence (agreeing in result, but not reasoning) by Justice Stephen Breyer. I conclude by observing that other laws—and not the ATS alone—raise problems of cross-border and extraterritorial jurisdiction, and offer some speculation on what questions remain after *Kiobel* and whether the decision will indeed act as a practical limit on ATS litigation.

II. Liberty, Self-Governance, and the Problem of Universal Jurisdiction

The ATS and *Kiobel* embody a large, thorny problem in a global economy governed by particular national legal systems—whose courts shall have jurisdiction to hear what kinds of claims against which kinds of actors? One traditional approach to jurisdiction seeks to assign disputes to the "right" national legal system and directs other national systems to refrain from hearing cases more suitably heard elsewhere. At the opposite pole is so-called universal jurisdiction, in which (at least for certain offenses of high seriousness) any national legal system can assert jurisdiction over an alleged wrongdoer and dispute, at least if a "home" legal system has not provided an adequate remedy for a wrong.

If its literal, surface language is read without further inquiry, the ATS—all in a single sentence in the first Judiciary Act of 1789—provides an extremely unusual hybrid of these two approaches. It seemingly asserts the jurisdiction of U.S. courts over apparently any violation of the law of nations, and without stated territorial limitation. This is to create a sort of quasi-universal jurisdiction for international law violations. And yet it does so only via an action in tort, and it makes that action available *only* to alien plaintiffs, not to U.S. citizens. Judges, lawyers, academics—the Court itself—have wondered at this peculiarity. Does an obscure 1789 statute really bestow the gift of an unlimited credit card, as it were, on contemporary and global human rights claims? As a historical matter, could this possibly have been the intent of Congress in the infant republic?

A dearth of historical background or legislative history specific to the statute's enactment has made this question difficult to answer. In any case, for it to matter, one has to believe that judges interpreting the statute today would be swayed by the historical context in which its language was written. At least until recently, the ATS has grown up as an ahistorical construction, as judges have interpreted the raw language in light of contemporary concerns. In its first consideration of the ATS a decade ago, *Sosa v. Alvarez-Machain*, the Court did introduce a historical element, but left it still mostly within judges' prudential discretion.[3] At the same time, historical inquiry into how the ATS fit into the context of its own time, and into the traditional understandings of jurisdiction that then held sway, has continued. The new historical inquiry tends to reveal a mostly commonsense meaning to the ATS as a law drafted to remedy particular diplomatic and political difficulties of a sort that would presumably have concerned the First Congress. It is not rooted in some drastic departure from traditional jurisdictional categories in which the appropriate scope of judicial power relates closely to the territory on which the allegedly tortious behavior took place.

Although not without its own disputes, the new historical scholarship is thus generally unfavorable to the ahistorical universal-jurisdiction construction of the ATS elaborated in U.S. courts over the last two decades. This is so if for no other reason than that the ahistorical construction could not purport to explain—even merely

---

[3] Sosa v. Alvarez-Machain, 542 U.S. 692 (2004).

as a plausible hypothesis—why Congress in 1789 would ever have enacted the ATS. Calling it "mysterious" and "obscure"—two common appellations describing the ATS—or saying with a shrug, "Well, it did," are not enough. Yet an important question has been, even as this new historical work has developed, whether courts would back off on their own from the ahistorical, universalist judicial constructions of jurisdiction widely in place today. By this point, judicial constructions have made the ATS a legal vehicle for tort suits by alien plaintiffs against entirely alien defendants over alleged actions taking place entirely outside U.S. territory.

The accumulation of precedent in favor of ahistorical universal-jurisdiction readings of the ATS essentially ensured that only the Supreme Court could settle these issues of fundamental interpretation. The Court's earlier venture into the field, *Sosa*, had failed to do so. In *Sosa*, the Court did invoke the language of traditional jurisdiction as a factor in judicial caution, but it declined to draw clear lines of a jurisprudential sort. Instead, it prudentially chose to prune the formal legal categories of causes of action that would be available under the ATS. That still left a framework of universal jurisdiction over a contested set of claims. *Kiobel*, by contrast, returns to historical analysis of the traditional bases on which a court might exercise cross-border jurisdiction. It thus appears to signal a genuine retreat from capacious universal-jurisdiction concepts and, perhaps just as important, a reinvigoration of traditional doctrines of national jurisdiction by courts across borders in a global political economy. Traditional grounds of jurisdiction over cross-border claims might be interpreted narrowly or broadly—and *Kiobel*'s several opinions offer both—but the intellectual locus of argument has now shifted firmly away from assertions of universal jurisdiction based on a literal reading of the words of the ATS.

This shift back toward traditional bases of jurisdiction in civil claims that run cross-border or extraterritorially matters quite a lot in considerations of liberty—particularly economic freedom—under conditions of administrative, regulatory states. The concern at the global level is that unfettered, universal tort regimes such as the ATS undermine the concept that morally legitimates sovereignty as far as the United States goes—popular sovereignty, the sovereignty of the people over a government answerable to them. Popular sovereignty for the people of the United States can only work, as a general moral principle, if it is limited to the will of that people and respects the will of others in the world. Traditionally, this is done by tying "peoples" to "places," thus yielding a basic jurisdictional principle in which both the sovereignty and the limits of national courts are established and legitimized by the sovereign peoples with which they correspond. In this conception of the role of courts and their anti-majoritarian character in a system of sovereign self-government, jurisdiction is a moral and political concept, and not merely a technical legal one. This is because the traditional bases of jurisdiction—over sovereign territory and over a sovereign's nationals, particularly—ensure both that those subjected to the justice of a national sovereign's courts have some legitimate connection to its rule and that those same subjects are not subjected to the rule of others with whom they have no connection.

Courts and judges, that is, are not simply about "justice" in the abstract; they are also about a particular institutional role in a system of self-governance and, hence, liberty. Universal jurisdiction threatens sovereignty and, in the case of the United States and other countries governed by a rule of law that runs to the people, threatens the rule of law and the liberty of its people to govern themselves. Chief Justice Roberts quotes Justice Joseph Story's opinion in *The La Jeune Eugenie*: "No nation has ever yet pretended to be the *custos morum* [guardians of morals] of the whole world."[4] It's not on account of mere judicial prudence that national courts should decline to be the moral custodians of the world, but instead a matter of fundamental legitimacy for the concept of self-governance that, in the American conception, arises from the people and the pooling of their liberties to govern themselves.

In practice, to be sure, we know fully that there are instances of genocide, crimes against humanity, slavery, and a handful of other crimes that nearly all of us are willing to put into a special category —those whose perpetrators have made themselves *hostis humani generis*, enemies of all mankind. The problem with all universal-jurisdiction arrangements, insofar as they purport also to accept the basic principles of sovereign self-governance as a feature of liberty, is how to keep this genuine if narrow moral and legal category in check.

---

[4] Kiobel, 133 S. Ct. at 1668 (citing United States v. The La Jeune Eugenie, 26 F. Cas. 832, 847 (C.C.D. Mass. 1822)).

How do you keep the door open only to the most egregious and obvious claims, and only against those who are directly responsible? One way is to treat the predicate acts as crimes prosecutable only by public authority, not as matters of private pursuit through actions seeking civil liability for money damages. A second is to limit the targets of such legal actions to morally culpable agents—that is, to individual defendants. It is noteworthy that the jurisprudence of the ATS does neither of these things—quite the contrary—and *Kiobel*, however useful its contribution, fails to address either of those crucial issues. The International Criminal Court, by contrast, does both of those—and even it, or at least its successive prosecutors, is arguably showing a remarkable internal dynamic toward expansion. While universal jurisdiction for certain truly awful things is not truly in dispute, there is no getting around the internal drive of schemes of universal jurisdiction to become a one-way ratchet of expansion.

Thus we see the importance of the ATS in the grander narrative of liberty and self-governing polities. President Abraham Lincoln once defined sovereignty, which we sometimes call self-government, as a "political community, without a political superior."[5] The ATS's universalist reach is incompatible with that, for ourselves and for others. Yet it would be morally wrong, not to say churlish, to rest upon abstractions of political theory and ignore the liberties of those whose interests are often sought to be vindicated through ATS suits. The ATS's original human rights case, *Filártiga v. Peña-Irala*, arose against a former foreign official living illegally in the United States who was quite plausibly alleged to have been involved in torture and forced disappearance.[6] While there is an excellent case to be made that such a case, even with plaintiffs and defendant both physically resident in the United States, was essentially committed to the foreign policy and political branches of the U.S. government rather than the courts, torture and murder also present questions of liberty.

But the more recent cases that have emerged for large monetary claims are only notionally about genocide, crimes against humanity, slavery, and so on. In actual, practical fact, the most sympathetic of them are about labor conditions in faraway places, child labor, wages, the safety of factories in places like Bangladesh, and environmental

---

[5] Abraham Lincoln, Message to Congress, Special Session, July 4, 1861.

[6] Filártiga v. Peña-Irala, 630 F.2d 876 (2d Cir. N.Y. 1980).

damage. These raise questions of individual liberty and self-governance in the global economy, too, at least morally. Yet the ATS and similar devices for using the U.S. courts post hoc to regulate labor or environmental conditions in the global manufacturing or commodities supply chain—and not even necessarily when done by U.S. entities, but by anyone anywhere—cannot possibly succeed, even if one thought it the moral course to pursue them. These are important goals, but they will have to be pursued in other ways.

III. The ATS Considered as a Statute and *Kiobel*'s Roots in *Sosa*

The ATS reads in its entirety:

> The district courts shall have original jurisdiction of any civil action by an alien for a tort only, committed in violation of the law of nations or a treaty of the United States.[7]

Apart from two appearances in late 18th-century cases, another in a Supreme Court opinion from 1908, and an opinion from 1960 in the U.S. Court of Appeals for the Second Circuit,[8] the ATS was dormant and unknown until resurrected by human rights lawyers in the 1970s and '80s as a vehicle for pursuing human rights violators. Concerns about ATS overreach have been a constant from that day to this. Seeming clarifications like *Sosa* left enough basics unsettled to provide encouragement to litigants and judges who were inclined toward capacious views of the ATS or of the law of nations (nowadays often defined as a matter of "customary international law").

Indeed, the most profound effect of *Sosa* was quite possibly the opposite of what the Court may have intended. *Sosa* said that claims under the statute had to allege misconduct universally acknowledged as serious under international law. The result was to ratchet up the rhetorical nature of claimed violations—plaintiffs *had* to charge defendants with extreme misconduct to keep an ATS claim going. In that case, however, everything becomes—well, *genocide* or something similar. What might have been thought to be serious and yet, for all

---

[7] 28 U.S.C. § 1350 (2013).

[8] See Moxon v. The Fanny, 17 F. Cas. 942 (No. 9,895) (D.C. Pa. 1793); Bolchos v. Darrel, 3 F.Cas. 810 (No. 1,607) (D.S.C. 1795); O'Reilly de Camara v. Brooke, 209 U.S. 45 (1908); Khedivial Line, S.A.E. v. Seafarers' Int'l Union, 278 F.2d 49, 51–52 (2d Cir. 1960) (per curiam).

that, "ordinary," labor or environmental misconduct was suddenly re-described using the language of genocide, crimes against humanity, war crimes, slavery, and a few others. The most serious international crimes were cheapened into a rote pleading in order to get into federal court.

Beyond *Sosa*'s failure as a prudential heuristic for the lower courts, it did not answer—indeed it specifically reserved, in a famous footnote—a crucial question: could *corporate* entities, with their deep pockets, be sued along with individuals? The Court's restraint on this point ensured that it would have to revisit the question. Between *Sosa* and *Kiobel*, ATS litigation shifted sharply from individual to corporate defendants, and from claims of *direct* participation or responsibility in human rights violations to claims of corporate "aiding and abetting" of such violations by governments and others. In an increasingly globalized and interlinked economic environment, many different behaviors can be construed as "aiding and abetting."

The claims advanced in *Kiobel* exemplified this trend. The plaintiffs were Nigerian nationals alleging that during the 1990s, various corporations, including defendant Royal Dutch Petroleum (Shell, a non-U.S. corporation), aided and abetted the Nigerian government in human rights and environmental abuses constituting violations of the law of nations. Shell denied the factual allegations as well as their adequacy as factual predicates to support such extreme charges as genocide and crimes against humanity (particularly as arising from alleged environmental harms). As a legal matter, it also contested whether the law of nations admitted of corporate liability and whether either the law of nations or the *Sosa* standard recognized aiding and abetting as a distinct category of violation. Because of the costs threatened by a discovery process for acts taking place in remote parts of Nigeria 15 or so years ago, among other reasons, the district court ruled that while in its view—as a matter of law—corporate liability and aiding and abetting liability could go forward, it would certify these questions for direct appeal to the Second Circuit.

The Second Circuit's decision in *Kiobel* created a sensation within the ATS legal community because the majority (in a 2-1 vote) held in sweeping terms that only individuals and not corporations could properly be ATS defendants.[9] The dissent was an equally sweeping

[9] *Kiobel*, 133 S. Ct. at 1668.

cri de coeur on behalf of universal jurisdiction and the global rule of law. The Second Circuit decision created a sharp circuit split—one that mirrored in important ways the majority and the dissent in the Second Circuit panel—and the Supreme Court agreed to hear the case.

Kiobel is procedurally unusual in that it was accepted for argument by the Supreme Court in 2011 on the circuit-split question: whether the ATS reached corporations as defendants. At oral argument, however, the justices repeatedly pressed counsel on a quite different and legally prior issue—advanced especially by several of the (many) amicus briefs submitted to the Court[10]—whether the ATS even had legal purchase on a case like *Kiobel*, which had no U.S. domestic links of person or place and thus no traditional base of jurisdiction whatsoever. It was a case in which plaintiffs, defendants, and the territory where alleged misconduct had occurred were all foreign—what the vernacular of ATS litigation has come to call a "foreign-cubed" case.[11]

During oral argument, the justices were drawn into these questions of territorial jurisdiction. Since they had not been part of the original questions set for the parties (strikingly, they were drawn largely from the amicus briefs, and it is not too much to say that the amicus briefs redefined the question for the Court), after oral argument the Court set additional argument for the following term on the following question:

> Whether and under what circumstances the Alien Tort Statute, 28 U.S.C. § 1350, allows courts to recognize a cause of action for violations of the law of nations occurring within the territory of a sovereign other than the United States.[12]

Additional argument took place on October 1, 2012, and the Court handed down its decision on April 17, 2013. As to the holding, it was unanimous (9-0) in favor of defendant Shell. On the reasoning of the

---

[10] The Cato Institute submitted amicus briefs in both rounds of Supreme Court argument in support of defendant Shell; the author of this article likewise signed (successive) amicus briefs submitted by a group of legal scholars, also in support of defendant.

[11] Transcript of Oral Arg., Kiobel v. Royal Dutch Petroleum. Co., 133 S. Ct. 1659 (2013) (No. 10-1491).

[12] Kiobel v. Royal Dutch Petroleum Co., 132 S. Ct. 1738 (2012) (No. 10-1491) (Order for Reargument).

holding, however, the Court split 5-4: a majority opinion (authored by Chief Justice Roberts, joined by Justices Antonin Scalia, Anthony Kennedy, Clarence Thomas, and Samuel Alito) and a minority concurrence (authored by Justice Breyer, joined by Justices Ruth Bader Ginsburg, Sonia Sotomayor, and Elena Kagan), with two additional short concurrences (one by Kennedy; and one by Thomas, joined by Alito). The opinions address themselves solely to the question for additional argument—the territorial reach of the ATS—and the question of the initial argument, corporate liability under the ATS, thus remains unanswered.[13]

IV. *Filártiga* and the Modern Reboot of the ATS

Talk of jurisdiction can seem abstract. It could be argued: isn't the modern ATS a way of helping to rectify some very real harms at little real cost to Americans' liberty? The cases at issue are against corporations, mostly large multinational corporations with ready access to lawyers. Some allegations routinely made in ATS filings are undoubtedly mere filler, but many others do cite serious abuses, whether actual violations of the "law of nations" or not.[14] And what of abuses by American corporations, which would be reachable even under more traditional jurisdictional bases? Apart from the expenditure of some judicial resources—which might be an important practical issue, but

---

[13] In a somewhat related case, arising not under the ATS but under the 1992 Torture Victim Protection Act (TVPA), Mohamad v. Palestinian Auth., 132 S. Ct. 1702 (2012) (accepted for review by the Court in 2011; argued in 2012 in tandem with the first round of *Kiobel* argument), the Court ruled, in an opinion by Justice Sotomayor, that the TVPA did not apply to organizations, including the defendant Palestinian Authority. The opinion affirmed the holding of the D.C. Circuit and relied on the language of the statute referring to "individuals," which it interpreted to mean actual human beings. The TVPA decision was unanimous and appears to have little of the controversy attached to the ATS cases.

[14] Chinese corporations operating mines in African countries such as Zambia have had many well-documented abuses, often of a very serious nature, including the shooting and wounding of 11 local Zambian workers by Chinese managers of a coal mine in that country. See Chibaula D. Silwamba, Zambia Charges Chinese in Mine Shootings, CNN.com, Oct. 20, 2010, http://www.cnn.com/2010/world/africa/10/19/zambia.chinese.mine.shooting/index.html; see also Human Rights Watch, "You'll Be Fired if You Refuse": Labor Abuses in Zambia's Chinese State-Owned Copper Mines, 2011, available at http://www.hrw.org/sites/default/files/reports/zambia1111ForWebUpload.pdf.

not one of principle—what do other Americans have to lose from a broadly interpreted ATS?

Something like this line of reasoning seems to have animated the courts in their early embrace of the ATS in the late 1970s and '80s. Certainly, that was my personal experience as a human rights lawyer in the 1980s.[15] Volunteering and then working professionally for human rights organizations, my anecdotal perception was that opinions within the New York City human rights advocacy community shifted and overlapped around two general currents. The first was that the ATS was a great avenue for bringing U.S. courts to bear, by creating a form of universal jurisdiction for human rights cases on an expanding writ of what "human rights" could be read to mean. The second, cutting the other direction (and a strand of opinion that essentially disappeared after 1990), was that ATS litigation, like most human rights litigation in U.S. courts, was a distraction from the avenues that strategically mattered. What mattered was pressure on the executive through Congress and the media, in order to influence the United States' bilateral relations with other countries. Human rights litigation, however valued by lawyers, was very often an expensive diversion of resources toward judicial victories that, even when they happened, left no lasting mark. The world, of course, has changed. These views were not entirely inconsistent at the time—a matter of strategic judgment and resource allocation—but they cut in different directions.

Another factor advancing broad readings of the ATS was that at that point originalism had not yet become respectable in academic circles—not that human rights lawyers would likely have paid it much heed in any case. Instead the statute offered plain language with its own austere power and beauty; a relic from the time-before-time that nonetheless served as a key to unlock the door in the present to everything that one might imagine under the rubric of the law of nations. The language was unencumbered ("blessedly so," one leading human rights lawyer in the early 1980s remarked to me) by

[15] I started volunteering for Human Rights Watch—then Helsinki Watch and Americas Watch Committees—through the Harvard Law School Human Rights Program in 1983, and later went to work for Human Rights Watch as the first director of its Arms Division. I also worked for the International Human Rights Law Group, and later became general counsel to the Open Society Institute.

any 18th-century legislative history, or 19th- and 20th-century lines of cases, that might undercut its abstract purity in the 20th.

It was against that backdrop that the Second Circuit opened today's ATS era with its pathbreaking opinion in *Filártiga*. Reversing the district court's dismissal of the claim on traditional jurisdictional grounds, the appeals court reached to the language of the ATS to hold that (1) because torture was a violation of "the law of nations"; and (2) because the plaintiffs were aliens (citizens of Paraguay whose son, they contended, had been kidnapped and tortured to death by Paraguayan police agents responsible to defendant Peña-Irala); therefore (3) the district courts had "original jurisdiction" of "any civil action" in "tort" in the suit.[16] True, the case for U.S. court jurisdiction was enabled, or at least strengthened, by the fact that at the time of the suit, both plaintiffs and the defendant were physically present in the United States (defendant Peña-Irala was arrested and deported for having overstayed his visa). Moreover, attempts to pursue a case in Paraguayan courts had gone nowhere. In that sense, traditional jurisdictional considerations of some contact with the United States as a forum, and some comity-like consideration such as exhaustion of local remedies (insofar as a meaningful exercise), had been met.

Those considerations aside, however, the suit still consisted of a U.S. tort action by one alien against another alien for acts occurring entirely in a foreign place at a time years earlier at which the defendant had been a senior police official of a foreign sovereign; the sovereign government of Paraguay, of course, could not be hauled into U.S. district court. Yet Judge Irving Kaufman had no difficulty in laying out for the court (in sweeping language that Justice Breyer rather pointedly quotes): "[F]or purposes of civil liability, the torturer has become—like the pirate and slave trader before him—*hostis humani generis*, an enemy of all mankind."[17]

Judge Kaufman's opinion raised much applause and a few skeptical eyebrows, the latter especially when the judge wrote an article for the *New York Times Magazine* a few months later, largely endorsing a sweepingly universal and expansionist vision of the human rights role of U.S. federal courts in the world. The obligation of the federal courts to identify

[16] Filártiga, 630 F.2d at 878.
[17] *Id.* at 890.

egregious violations of international law is in many ways analogous to the courts' traditional role in redressing deprivations of civil liberties that occur at home. . . . The articulation of settled norms of international law by the Federal courts, much like their adherence to constitutional precepts, is an expression of this nation's commitment to the preservation of fundamental elements of human dignity throughout the world.[18]

This is stirring stuff, and in the heady early days of the ATS, it did not seem far-fetched. After all, if one looked to the statute (quite apart from any weight attached to the physical presence of plaintiff and defendant in the United States, which—take note—Justice Breyer specifically registers in his *Kiobel* concurrence), the literal words of the ATS require for U.S. jurisdictional purposes no more than an alien plaintiff and alleged conduct sufficiently well-pled to constitute a violation of the law of nations or a treaty of the United States. By some historical fortuity, in other words, this ancient statute almost miraculously offered a U.S.-law-specific way to take jurisdiction over certain universally condemned acts, such as piracy. Maybe this was not true universal jurisdiction as international lawyers would recognize it, but it was something similar and maybe even better, because affording something lacking in international law as such—civil liability.

It remained less than clear whether the ATS established, on its own, any actual causes of action, or instead functioned as a jurisdiction-granting statute that depended on other statutory vehicles to give it substantive claims to adjudicate. That issue arose in a case four years after *Filártiga*—*Tel-Oren v. Libyan Arab Republic*[19]—and occasioned a famous colloquy between D.C. Circuit Judges Harry Edwards and Robert Bork in their respective concurrences. Judge Bork argued that the ATS was a purely jurisdictional statute, and without something further, it conferred jurisdiction but gave plaintiffs no grounds on which to sue. His core contention was that neither treaties nor customary international law (the "law of nations" in the ATS) create individual, private rights of action in U.S. courts, unless self-executing or otherwise enabled by implementing legislation; and the ATS's

[18] Irving R. Kaufman, A Legal Remedy for International Torture?, N.Y. Times Mag., Nov. 9, 1980, at 44.

[19] 726 F.2d 774 (D.C. Cir. 1984) (per curiam).

reference to the law of nations or treaties of the United States did not suffice to create them.[20]

Judge Edwards agreed that neither customary international law nor treaties directly created private causes of action, but took the view that the ATS established something in U.S. domestic law that was more than mere jurisdiction. It transfused, so to speak, some amount of substance from international law into domestic law, through its reference to international law, and once part of domestic law, that was sufficient to create a substantive cause of action as a matter of domestic law.[21] I spell out this debate in *Tel-Oren*, partly because the two sides are analytically clear and distinct, and partly because—although lower courts created a body of precedent allowing substantive ATS claims, contra Judge Bork—the question posed was not finally decided until *Sosa*, 15 years later.

V. International Law or "Faux-International Law," Manufactured through the ATS?

How does *Sosa* answer the *Tel-Oren* debate? Solely jurisdictional or not? Private rights of action or not? Chief Justice Roberts explains in *Kiobel* that the statute

> provides district courts with jurisdiction to hear certain claims, but does not expressly provide any causes of action. We held in *Sosa v. Alvarez-Machain*, however, that the First Congress did not intend the provision to be "stillborn." The grant of jurisdiction is instead "best read as having been enacted on the understanding that the common law would provide a cause of action for [a] modest number of international law violations." We thus held that federal courts may "recognize private claims [for such violations] under federal common law."[22]

The Supreme Court had taken *Sosa* in part to provide some limits to the kinds of claims that were being recognized in the district courts and courts of appeal; hence Roberts's reference to a "modest number" of causes of action.[23] During the two decades preceding *Sosa*,

---

[20] *Id.* at 822–23 (Bork, J., concurring).

[21] *Id.* at 786 et seq. (Edwards, J., concurring).

[22] Kiobel, 133 S. Ct. at 1663 (2013) (citations omitted).

[23] *Id.*

the human rights community had brought a considerable number of ATS cases in the district courts. Many of them were uncontested—the defendants did not appear—resulting in default judgments. Others were what we might call "lightly contested": defendants without substantial legal resources against comparatively well-funded, increasingly specialized human rights lawyers for the plaintiffs.

These suits were against individuals, typically former officials of some obviously abusive regime; the individuals and their assets were often either unavailable or judgment-proof. So, for a long time, the practical effect of ATS suits was largely symbolic. District court judges sometimes used them as occasion for pronouncements about the universality of human rights norms, and the growing roster of often uncontested or lightly contested claims encouraged broader views of the litigable content of "the law of nations."

Even though these cases largely had not been litigated in meaningful ways, they created an accumulation of plaintiff-favorable holdings over time, as district court rulings cited each other in an increasingly thick web of seeming precedent, amid ever-stronger and more confident statements about the content of international law. The irony is that even as the federal courts moved to embrace "international law" as something they would enforce, they did so opining as distinctly American courts in distinctly American ways taking distinctly American views of the content of that "international law."

In principle, American courts could ascertain the content of "international law" as readily as they could check up on the Internal Revenue Code. In practice, however, judges become familiar with such bodies of law by way of the arguments of lawyers practicing before them. And these uncontested or lightly contested cases sometimes—oftentimes—left less-than-expert federal court judges hearing a well-informed view of international law only from one side, that of the human rights advocacy lawyers.

As the number and sweep of the claims in ATS suits grew, one group watched with especially mixed feelings: foreign international law experts (whether from the academy, international organizations, or foreign ministries). On one hand, these respectable outsiders to American jurisprudence—America's closest allies and friends, especially, but also economic and trading partners—mostly favored the outcomes from the standpoint of substantive human rights. On the other hand, they could not help feeling some dismay at the sweeping moralism and frequently inexpert pronouncements of the courts in the then-sole superpower. This was true both as to the *content* that American courts discerned in international law, and even more as to the *sources of authority* to which American judges turned in ascertaining and citing the content of international law: namely, *each other*.

As an example of distinctively American content, consider the strangely domesticated variety of international law articulated in *Sosa*, in which the Court refused to countenance causes of action founded on "violations of any international law norm with less definite content and acceptance than the historical paradigms familiar" when the ATS was enacted in 1789. No doubt the Court had good reasons of caution and prudence to draw such a line, but it seems almost to imply that its special version of international law would be considered to have stopped dead in its tracks in Blackstone's day, not just in its content but in its mechanisms of elaboration. Such an implication would strike most observers in other countries as a fantastically radical rewrite of actually existing international law.[24]

On the question of sources of authority, meanwhile, the court was simply more comfortable and familiar citing sister federal courts than to parse the pronouncements of tribunals halfway around the world. How could it be otherwise? That is as it *should* be in a system whose domestic legitimacy depends upon fidelity to legal authority derived from within that system. The American legal system is embedded in a constitutional republic in which the rule of law derives from the sovereignty of the people, through *their* constitution—that is, from *within*. The most persuasive and binding precedent for a U.S. court will therefore be an opinion of the Supreme Court, or the appellate court above itself; failing that, another appellate court, or another district court. And the procedural rules of the game—the rules of civil procedure, evidence, and so on—are necessarily those of the federal courts, too. These are federal courts elaborating, as Chief Justice Roberts says, "federal common law" whose content happens to be "international law"—in some sense. But the qualifiers—the scare quotes, or "in some sense"—are inevitable here. If this project was international law, where was the role of the *rest* of the world in creating it?

---

[24] Sosa v. Alvarez-Machain, 542 U.S. 692, 732 (2004).

Actual international law, the law of nations and treaties, does not operate this way. It has its own structure of authority, even if the nature of that authority is highly contested and is not likely ever to have the comfortable hierarchy of law in a settled domestic system. Those many disputes aside, it can be said with fair certainty that whatever the structure of authority—the "doctrine of sources"—in international law, it is not going to consist of the district and appellate courts of the United States citing each other.

So a deep question remains: is the ATS generating "international law"? Is ATS litigation a form of "state practice" in the evolution of customary international law, the state practice of a powerful state whose views (whether presented to the world through pronouncements of the State Department or by judges of the federal courts) will always matter? Does ATS jurisprudence constitute "international law" that happens to be proffered through the mechanism of American courts, as Judge Kaufman (author of *Filártiga*) and so many other early supporters believed? Or, instead, is it a sort of "faux-international law": distinctly American law styling itself "international" and "universal," but really just another exercise of American hubris and extraterritorial overreach?

Seen from the outside, the "international law" of the ATS is turned in upon itself, a nearly perfect narcissism, its gaze fixed on American law, processes, procedures, sources of authority, and precedent. And if we were to see the continued forging of a new body of "international law" exclusively in U.S. courts, might not such a body of law someday be turned against America's own friends and trading partners and their interests? So long as the targets were the Ferdinand and Imelda Marcoses of the world, fleeing the Philippines for Hawaii, the friends of international law in many countries could embrace the substantive outcomes and largely refrain from lawyerly critique. Eventually, however, the targets were to become—we know where this is going, so no plot spoiler here—not Marcos (or the Lockerbie bombers, Manuel Noriega, nor any other classic villains of the 1980s and '90s), but corporations like Royal Dutch Petroleum.

VI. Does "Faux-International Law" Matter or Are These Merely Forms of Words?

Increasingly, everyone seems aware of the "faux-international law" problem, and increasingly desirous of not appearing, well, *imperial* (or hegemonic, a word I will turn to later) in the course of American court pronouncements on the law of nations. We might ask, though, whether anything more is at stake than words. Why not concern ourselves instead with the law's functional role?

I don't think it can work this way—not in the long run. Although its functional role might start in American courts, it reaches out universally and globally. I say this as someone who is an unapologetic American sovereigntist, a believer in American hegemony as the fundamental guarantor of basic order on the planet. I find myself somewhere between shock and awe at, well, the chutzpah, especially in the claim that it is still somehow international law. Beyond that, however, I think it unsustainable. And I'm strongly inclined—without any good evidence—to believe that the Court in *Kiobel* not only agrees with this, but is seeking, majority and minority alike, to undo the damage to the legitimacy of American legal interests done by the fiction that the ATS is about international law.

Through ATS, the United States has been exercising radically extraterritorial jurisdiction over occurrences in other countries. The sole source of legitimacy for doing so would be the claim that we are simply enforcing international law as recognized more or less universally in all nations. If not—if we are instead imposing distinctively American outcomes on these foreign disputes in a way that overrides the outcomes that the national legal systems involved would have generated—then foreign parties and their sovereigns have no reason to regard extraterritorial ATS litigation as anything other than bullying (but also preening) by a powerful state through its courts. And by now we have arrived at this point. Foreign parties don't regard the ATS as legitimate or as implementing genuine international law, and won't ever—not our close friends and allies, let alone China or Russia. Even the Canadians resent it.

And then we tell them that they will undergo the American tort system.

I should mention in my experience over the years of observing ATS cases, that judges do not share this view. They don't see it as any legal fiction here; they believe that they *are* pronouncing on international law. They sometimes take great pride in it, as carrying out universal moral obligations. Perhaps that is shifting, and perhaps it will shift particularly following *Kiobel*, with its strong reassertion that the ATS is about extraterritoriality and federal common law, not universal jurisdiction and international law. But a year or two after *Sosa* was handed down, I was present as an expert witness at the Agent Orange ATS case before the Honorable—the inimitable—Jack Weinstein (district judge for the Eastern District of New York).[25] Judge Weinstein opened the oral argument by saying that, in some sense, the court sat as an international court, pronouncing on international law. I don't think many present at argument would disagree that he said this with a great deal of pride. He went on to repeat much the same language in his opinion.[26]

It fell to a very young Justice Department lawyer, offering the government's statement of interest, to say with some trepidation—I paraphrase, and Judge Weinstein took this with all good humor—with all due respect, your Honor, this is not an international tribunal, but a federal district court convened under the authority of the Constitution and laws of the United States.

VII. The Corporate Turn in ATS Suits

In any case, none of this might have mattered. The ATS might have remained an American legal twist on universal jurisdiction, dealing with symbolically important cases but not taking on targets with the incentives and the resources to push back. It might have been seen as precisely what hegemons possessed of an interest in moral justice, legal technicalities aside, are supposed to do; the academics can carp and cry over international law in the law reviews. Besides, the United States was not completely alone in this legal innovation: Belgium, Spain, and several other countries also had some national form of quasi-universal jurisdiction, with a variety of restraints (shifting over time) on their national courts' exercise of jurisdiction, but nonetheless going beyond the traditional bases of jurisdiction. Part of the pressure exerted by these European national courts was through the ability of courts of one country within the European Union to be able to issue arrest warrants generally respected by other countries throughout the EU—as, for example, Chile's General Augosto Pinochet discovered when he was held in Britain in 1998.

---

[25] In re Agent Orange Product Liability Litigation, 373 F. Supp. 2d 7 (E.D.N.Y. 2005).

[26] *Id.* at 17 ("In judging international human rights claims against domestic corporations or others, courts in the United States with jurisdiction act as quasi international tribunals.").

But these were generally criminal proceedings and limited to individual persons. The United States, by contrast, offers liability in civil tort asserted as a domestic law remedy. To some, the ATS has also seemed oddly morally off-base by seeming to proffer tort rather than criminal law as the appropriate legal response to such offenses as genocide or crimes against humanity. Surely only a criminal prosecution would morally do, at least in the first instance? The response is, to be sure, that victims will take what they can get; the ATS may not be a perfect fit in bringing victims justice, but it's still better than nothing. And, in practical litigation terms, an ATS lawsuit offers a far easier burden of proof for the plaintiffs to meet—the civil action standard of "preponderance of the evidence" rather than the criminal standard of "beyond a reasonable doubt."

So runs the argument. But it is worth taking a closer look at the deep disconnect between the international and American conceptions here. Although the list of violations of international law that can be committed by private parties, as opposed to states, has expanded greatly in the modern era, it is still a short list. By and large, international law is still a law of states, with very limited applicability to private parties. The prohibitions aimed at private parties consist of *criminal* acts, for which wrongdoers are held *individually* criminally liable. There is currently no concept in international law of civil liability, or tort liability, of private parties—even bearing in mind that international law is a matter of plausible, pragmatic interpretation rather than certainty in many things, international law experts generally would, I believe, assent to these two assertions. One reason this can be asserted is that, institutionally, the international order offers no institutional locus for either civil liability or entity liability. To take one of the most obvious examples, the International Criminal Court has neither, and not for want of direct discussion during the ICC's establishment. This might conceivably change in the future, and there are certainly many people pressing to change it, but to date that is the situation.

The casual turn toward aiming ATS tort actions against corporations with deep, deep pockets—after all, the statute nowhere said that only individuals can be sued—was another departure from the general pattern of existing international law. So was the marked emphasis on "aiding and abetting" as a basis of liability; what this means in international law (that is, international law "out there") remained a matter of some considerable debate, even as American law eagerly raced ahead. And as mentioned above, the *Sosa* move in invoking Blackstone and the law as it stood in 1789 entirely unhinged the ATS from international law as practiced in the world at large.

A word more on the notion of freezing offenses mostly as they stood in 1789: When I say that no one but the U.S. Supreme Court would think of stopping where we stood then, I do not mean merely that the concepts of genocide and crimes against humanity are absent from the Founding account of the "law of nations" yet could not possibly be omitted from an account of that law today. Nor do I mean that the rest of the world has evolved various newer ideas in international law and must be listened to if we are to mean the "law of nations." I mean, specifically, that no modern *American* would stop with 1789, even aside from the issues of genocide and crimes against humanity, because no modern American would defend a list that failed to include slavery, as Blackstone's did.

Not only was slavery not part of Blackstone's canon of unlawful acts for which individuals could be made answerable under the law of nations; it was part of the lawful American domestic order under what, by a reaching analogy, we might think of as the "federal common law" of 1789. So everyone recognized that some modern norms would have to be accepted. *Sosa* attempted to handle this by formulating a rule that new, modern norms would be admitted only if they exhibited a specificity and acceptance equivalent to norms accepted in Blackstone's day.

The *Sosa* effort to fashion a standard was elegant, in its own way, and arguably correct in the abstract. As a practical instruction to judges hearing cases, however, it was discretionary and unpredictable, as well as encouraging pleading as an extreme sport, in which an ordinarily serious dispute about labor conditions, environmental standards, or health and safety, would be re-couched as accusations of genocide, crimes against humanity, slavery and forced labor, and so on. Some corporations might prefer to cut their losses and do as little damage to their reputations as possible; others, in my experience as an expert witness, took genuine umbrage at the accusations—often the most serious crimes in the international canon—and dug in to defend themselves.

The stakes were higher still because U.S. tort processes would be employed: American-style discovery, a presumption of the American rule that each side pays its own costs, and all the other appurtenances of American civil litigation that have caused many foreign corporations to wonder whether they should even enter the U.S. market and thus become subject to this tort regime. The ATS meant that they could be sued in tort in any case, even without any other connection to the United States, a presence in the United States, or any of the standard bases of jurisdiction. Fear of the costs of discovery was, as always, a powerful inducement to settle—and even more so in cases that might involve plantations in Liberia, maquiladoras in Guatemala, or a Chinese corporation's treatment of workers in Asia or Africa. Multinational corporations of all nationalities were becoming concerned. They did not see that *Sosa* acted as much of a brake if the practical question was whether one could get the case dismissed on summary judgment, without going to discovery.

Foreign governments likewise were unhappy. In one of the most famous examples, they raised concerns that corporations that did business in apartheid-era South Africa might find arrangements struck in good faith with the South African government undermined by litigation under the ATS in the United States. The South African government had negotiated with the corporations that had been present in South Africa with many concerns in mind—getting paid something, while not driving business out of the country and losing jobs and economic activity over the long term. Was it really right for a U.S. court to unwind those arrangements on its own say-so through the ATS, when the corporations' home governments had raised no objection at the time? Moreover, foreign governments—including those of America's closest friends and allies, such as Canada, Britain, and the Netherlands—increasingly began to be concerned with the effects of ATS litigation on their own corporations.

Defenders of the ATS pointed out that U.S. judges had been accorded prudential discretion (which they often used) to curtail litigation under the statute in deference to national interests in foreign relations, comity with other nations, and the prerogatives of other branches of government. But it all remained maddeningly discretionary and unpredictable, from the standpoint of foreign governments and defendants alike—and all the more unfair and insupportable because it was untethered to actual international law processes in which their countries could participate.

Particularly after the financial collapse of 2008, another consideration also gained prominence: whatever sense the ATS made, it made as a "law of the hegemon"—an expression of the might of a superpower that could impose its will on everyone else and that was, for good measure, the home country of many, even most, of the world's leading multinational enterprises. By the late 2000s, however, the hegemon's place in the world was starting to look somewhat dicey. The centrality of the United States to the world economy had markedly declined, with major new economic powerhouses arising in China, India, Brazil, and elsewhere. The United States was in at least relative—if not absolute—decline. Yet here was its legal system continuing to assert the hubris of the superpower, as if it were still 1990.

VIII. The First *Kiobel* Argument and Corporate Liability

It long seemed to many observers that the Supreme Court would have to settle the corporate liability question. The opportune case arrived in the form of the Second Circuit's sweeping rejection of corporate liability in its *Kiobel* decision in 2010. The circuit split was stark, and perhaps that made it more attractive as a vehicle for Supreme Court review.

The argument over corporate liability in ATS cases comes down to the relationship between the international law predicate of the statute and the domestic remedy also embedded in the statute. The argument that corporations cannot be defendants in ATS suits runs as follows: Corporations, unlike individuals or states, are not possible subjects of liability under existing international law and so cannot violate it. They lack the capacity to do so. International law might have been formulated differently, and might still one day, but today, corporations lack the legal capacity to violate international law. Since they cannot violate it, there is no violation, with respect to them, of the law of nations or a treaty of the United States. If there is no violation of international law by a party, there is no basis for a civil action against it by an alien, in tort, under the ATS. A violation requires a violator who is legally capable of being the violator; otherwise one has a harmful act but not a violation of international law. The argument against corporate liability in essence says that there isn't a violation of international law, at least as it regards the corporation, and so there is no basis for an ATS suit.

The argument for corporate liability might attack two different points of this argument. First, it disputes the premise that there is no liability for corporations in international law. Despite some contrary academic opinion, however, it is probably reasonably accepted that international law up until now does not create liability for entities such as corporations.

Accepting the premise, then, the second point of attack is to deny that it matters who or what violated international law; it is enough that there is a violation for the ATS suit to go forward. Liability can be found against a party based not on the fact that it violated international law—the fact of a violation as such, without specific attribution as to the culprit—but on the basis that on U.S. tort law principles, the defendant would be liable. U.S. domestic tort law permits corporate liability, and having satisfied the requirement of an international violation—without regard to whether there is an actor in the international-law sense—the legal regime turns into ordinary American tort law, in which a corporation can be held liable. In a sort of cosmopolitan bait-and-switch, liability in domestic tort law can be assigned for a violation that has not been held to have a violator for purposes of the very international law that describes the substantive offense.

The two are severable, on this argument, and once having found actions that satisfy the international law predicate, then it is normal and accepted that a national court apply its own standards of procedure, liability, and remedy, which, in this case, involves identifying the liable actor under domestic law and imposing tort liability. This was the argument that predominated for corporate liability in the first round of *Kiobel* argument. How it would have come out is unknown, though it is likely to be addressed at some future point. It bears observing, however, that even in the corporate liability round of *Kiobel* argument, the conceptual debate has shifted radically from where it began back in the *Filártiga* era.

If the *Filártiga* era saw the ATS as part of a movement to create universal jurisdiction around certain norms of international law, the plaintiffs' best argument for corporate liability is a signal retreat from that. It is not an argument from international law; on the contrary, faced with the difficulty that its target is likely *not* a subject of international law to date, the move by plaintiffs is to retreat to emphasize the ordinary *domestic* nature of the ATS. It deemphasizes the idea of universal jurisdiction of serious international law norms, emphasizing instead that liability is created, and the liable party identified, by operation of domestic law. The legal theory thus constitutes an extraterritorial application of a domestic law that merely contingently refers to the law of nations and treaties of the United States and the existence of some behavior that violates it, irrespective of the liability status of the actor in international law.

This is a remarkable change for the ideological trajectory of the ATS and its use. More than that, it is a remarkable change in the fortunes of the idea of universal jurisdiction in national courts. There are other international law drivers of change as well. The founding of the International Criminal Court, for example, establishes an international forum beyond national courts and takes pressure off them to offer universal access for serious human rights violations, principally. But the debate over corporate liability sets the stage for the second round of argument in *Kiobel*. The situation in the Court leading from the first argument to the second is mostly, and correctly, seen as a concern about foreign-cubed ATS suits seeming to have no connection to the United States. It is as if to say, even before talking about corporate liability and who can be a defendant, why is this case even here? Why U.S. courts at all? Or, as Justice Alito put it in the first oral argument:

> The first statement—the first sentence in your brief in the statement of the case is really striking: "This case was filed . . . by twelve Nigerian plaintiffs who alleged . . . that Respondents aided and abetted the human rights violations committed against them by the Abacha dictatorship . . . in Nigeria between 1992 and 1995." What does a case like that— what business does a case like that have in the courts of the United States?[27]

What business, indeed? Other justices, notably Justice Kennedy and Chief Justice Roberts, pressed the same question, and hence the second round of argument the following term.

---

[27] Transcript of Oral Arg. at 11, Kiobel v. Royal Dutch Petroleum. Co., 133 S. Ct. 1659 (2013) (No. 10-1491).

IX. The Second *Kiobel* Argument, Jurisdictional Bases, and Chief Justice Roberts's Application of the Presumption against Extraterritoriality

The *Kiobel* result was 9-0, but the reasoning split 5-4, with two additional short concurrences. Chief Justice Roberts's opinion describes *Sosa's* holding and notes that it did not address the jurisdictionally prior question raised in *Kiobel*: whether the ATS may properly "reach conduct occurring primarily in the territory of a foreign sovereign." He describes the ATS as a statute that might be read to have extraterritorial reach; indeed, all of its universal-jurisdiction practice is bound to precisely that feature.

But in that case, the ATS must be tested against a presumption in U.S. practice—the presumption against extraterritoriality. In this regard, the *Kiobel* court emphasizes the importance of the presumption against extraterritoriality that it recently confirmed in *Morrison v. National Australia Bank*.[28] *Morrison* was a securities law case, and its concerns ran not to universal criminal norms of human rights but to ordinary international financial and securities transactions and the intersecting laws of different states governing them. In that regard, the Roberts opinion reaffirms that the presumption against extraterritoriality is not simply about cross-border economic or regulatory law but extends across other apparently unrelated subjects, such as international human rights law, as well. Alternatively, however, and far from insignificantly, one might see the application of *Morrison* to ATS cases involving corporate defendants as an implicit recognition of the economic reality of most of these ATS claims—they are not truly about gross human rights violations, genocide, slavery, or crimes against humanity at all, but instead quite ordinary (even if serious) disputes over labor and environmental issues as part of international business enterprises. Thus *Morrison*, as an economic law case, is particularly appropriate. Reliance upon *Morrison* can be seen as an implicit observation that the gap between the terms of pleading and the realities of corporate behaviors—even when they constitute genuine labor and environmental abuse deserving of a remedy or preventive regulation by the proper authority—could not be greater. The legal doctrine underpinning the assertion of *Morrison's* presumption against extraterritoriality in the case of the ATS, however,

---

[28] Morrison v. Nat'l Australia Bank Ltd., 130 S. Ct. 2869 (2010).

is that the ATS is about extraterritoriality and is thus to be located somewhere within the *traditional bases of jurisdiction*, rather than the special, international-law-driven category of *universal jurisdiction* (and all the conceptual difficulties and problems of keeping it cabined that this concept brings). It is a two-stage shift logically, though Chief Justice Roberts's opinion does not put it this way: first, a return to earth, as it were, in abandoning pretensions to international-law-driven universal jurisdiction and, second, in returning to the traditional categories of jurisdiction, landing on territoriality as the basis. Having landed on territory as the core criterion for ATS jurisdiction, Roberts then offers the presumption against extraterritoriality in such a way as to make territoriality something of a straitjacket that confines expansive claims of ATS jurisdiction or causes of action. A novel or judicially creative cause of action under the law of nations won't help a plaintiff if it won't apply beyond U.S. territory.

The presumption is explained, quoting *Morrison*, as being a judicially created canon of interpretation providing that "when a statute gives no clear indication of an extraterritorial application, it has none."[29] The opinion refers to the weighty concerns of the judiciary keeping itself out of the executive's role in foreign affairs and adds, quoting from *Microsoft Corp. v. AT&T Corp.*, that the presumption reflects the fact that "United States law governs domestically but does not rule the world."[30] Like *Morrison*, *Microsoft* is also a case about economic matters. The emphasis on the application of these economic law cases to what are supposed to be the deepest matters of human rights law suggests that the Court seeks to put the ATS back on the ordinary footing of other statutes, rather than tacitly treating it differently because of its long intertwining with human rights moralism. It also argues for a historically based, commonsensical understanding of the behaviors with which the First Congress would be concerned—behaviors that, with the exception of piracy and an inconsistent 1795 opinion by Attorney General William Bradford,[31] would all take place on U.S. territory. The *Kiobel* majority plainly thinks that the ATS has been misconstrued by the courts for many years—though without significant pushback from the Court—and that in light of

---

[29] Kiobel, 133 S. Ct. at 1664 (quoting Morrison, 130 S. Ct. at 2878).

[30] *Id.* (quoting Microsoft Corp. v. AT&T Corp., 550 U.S. 437, 454 (2007)).

[31] Att'y Gen. William Bradford, Breach of Neutrality, 1 Op. Atty. Gen. 57 (1795).

historical research on its, in retrospect, not really so mysterious objectives, it should be returned to application on U.S. territory.

Finally, the emphasis on contemporary cases drawn from cross-border commerce, such as *Morrison* and *Microsoft*, offered to buttress the presumption against extraterritoriality, might subtly imply a view, *sotto voce*, that these corporate ATS cases are, in practical terms, what this essay has already described: efforts to cobble together a de facto scheme of cross-border liability-driven corporate regulation. By applying the presumption against extraterritoriality, Chief Justice Roberts tries to ensure that any such future scheme will be based on clear congressional provision.

This in effect pushes the ball back into Congress's court. If Congress wants to do as it did in the Torture Victim Protection Act and create detailed, specific conditions for extraterritorial reach, it can do so with regard to the ATS. But the courts will not do so. Moreover, the presumption operates along with the other requirements of *Sosa* as to permissible causes of action; though it is clear that most of the bite will come from the presumption. The chief justice passes lightly over an objection that Justice Breyer raises in his concurring opinion; the presumption against extraterritoriality is not thought to address a jurisdictional statute. The answer to this, for Roberts, is that the part of the ATS raising extraterritorial concerns is the part of the ATS that goes beyond conferring jurisdiction—the part, in other words, that *Sosa* said was necessary in order that it not be "stillborn." As to the doctrine of "transitory torts"—which the plaintiffs emphasized in their arguments—the majority says that the ATS has to be treated like U.S. domestic law with regards to its causes of action:

> The question under *Sosa* is not whether a federal court has jurisdiction to entertain a cause of action provided by foreign or even international law. The question is instead whether the court has authority to recognize a cause of action under U.S. law to enforce a norm of international law.[32]

The chief justice's opinion is modest and leaves an escape hatch. The presumption against extraterritoriality is, after all, only a presumption, and might in some particular case be overcome; Justice Kennedy, too, emphasizes that the door is not completely shut in his

[32] Kiobel, 133 S. Ct. at 1661.

brief concurrence. What might overcome the presumption, however, is not established plainly. More striking than the opinion's escape hatch is its implicit acknowledgment that its apparently sharply limiting rule, drawn from the presumption against extraterritoriality, is not enough to close the door to unwarranted ATS claims and requires a supplement. The opinion closes by adding that even where "claims touch and concern the territory of the United States, they must do so with sufficient force to displace the presumption."[33] Which is to say that after having announced an apparently tough rule aimed at preventing the ATS from going abroad in search of monsters to destroy, the Roberts opinion recognizes that a territorially based rule is not actually enough to achieve its intended limits in the modern, interlinked world. The practical reality is that so very many things might be said to touch or concern U.S. territory—an Internet message being passed through U.S. servers, for example, or the mere presence of an office in New York.

Thus, the presumption against extraterritoriality is not by itself sufficient to place out of reach all the activities that the majority intends to preclude. It has to be supplemented with an additional rule about territory itself: that a territorial claim of jurisdiction must be . . . well, the opinion does not say exactly, but it clearly means something more than mere or incidental. So the opinion concludes by toughening the substance of territoriality, observing that corporations "are often present in many countries, and it would reach too far to say that mere corporate presence suffices."[34] One might be forgiven for thinking that, in fashioning new, genuinely meaningful fetters on the ATS, it is this final toughening of the meaning of territoriality, rather than the presumption against extraterritoriality, that over time will do most of the work for the *Kiobel* majority. Justice Alito's concurrence, joined by Justice Thomas, doesn't even trust this additional toughening requirement and bolsters "touch and concern" by saying that claims will be barred unless the *domestic* conduct of a defendant "is sufficient to violate an international law norm that satisfies *Sosa*'s requirements of definiteness and acceptance among civilized nations."[35]

[33] *Id.* at 1669.

[34] *Id.*

[35] *Id.* at 1671 (Alito, J., concurring).

X. Justice Breyer's Concurrence and Its Holistic Approach to Jurisdiction

Justice Breyer's concurrence is a dissent by any other name—but not quite. It wants to have its cake and eat it too; it wants to have the "right" human rights cases available for redress under the ATS without letting it be used to cobble together a de facto civil liability regime for routine matters.

The most cosmopolitan of the justices, Justice Breyer would likely have been thought—back at the time of *Sosa*, for example, by me at least—to be the most receptive to establishing what were then termed "global government networks" of regulators or judges of different states, coming together at the informal administrative (rather than legislative or formal institutional) level, to establish coordination among participants in the network. Such an administrative solution might manage problems of coordination that political bodies such as the United Nations or the political leadership of national states would not manage successfully. It is easy to imagine that Justice Breyer, in the late 1990s or early 2000s, might have been drawn to the use of the ATS precisely in order to achieve a measure of civil-liability control over multinational corporations in the global supply chain or the global financial system. Not the United States courts as *custos morum* of the whole world, and less still an endorsement of the "law of the hegemon"—but a global network of judges doing something very much like that. He said as much in several speeches and appeared to embrace a genuinely technocratic vision of judging, the legitimacy of court systems, and the "horizontal" legitimacy of judges around the world as administrative mechanisms for harmonizing efforts to further the regulatory efficiency of the global system, at least in such matters as the economy, on the one hand, and human rights, on the other, and given its fragmented nature.

It is hard to see much of this technocratic cosmopolitanism in Breyer's *Kiobel* opinion, however. The world has changed with the rise of new, competitive, economically jostling great powers. On the contrary, even if he is obviously concerned to hold greater flexibility and discretion in reserve to apply the ATS in situations that are genuinely *hostis humani generis*—not dressed-up labor or environmental disputes—his opinion is no less committed than the chief justice's to relocating the proper jurisdictional basis for the ATS in the traditional categories. It is not an offer to join the federal courts together with court systems worldwide to create a de facto, horizontally coordinated regime for regulating global corporations. It is, however, an offer to harmonize this aspect of U.S. jurisdictional rules with those of America's allies and friends who provided proposals for the United States based in genuinely international law, rather than what I have called in this essay "faux-international law."

Breyer affirmatively quotes the Restatement (Third) of Foreign Relations for these traditional international law categories and says, in effect, that the ATS ought to be limited to them, but also ought to be able to make use of all of them.[36] He criticizes the formal limitations of Roberts's narrow reliance on territoriality, in part by observing that piracy is a problem for the majority's approach, for example, because although piracy takes place on the high seas, the actual acts of piracy take place on ships, which are part of the flag territory. Considered more broadly, Justice Breyer's point is that, when all is said and done, the issue of limits for the ATS is whether there are sufficient contacts in any sense—territory, persons, causes, effects—close or substantial enough to satisfy a traditional, yet holistic, test. He sums this up as a three-part test of jurisdiction under the ATS:

> (1) the alleged tort occurs on American soil, (2) the defendant is an American national, or (3) the defendant's conduct substantially and adversely affects an important American national interest, and that includes a distinct interest in preventing the United States from becoming a safe harbor (free of civil as well as criminal liability) for a torturer or other common enemy of mankind.[37]

Breyer's approach, as he himself notes, is roughly the same as that taken by America's friends and allies in their amicus briefs to the Court. They do not see themselves as limited under the traditional grounds of international law to narrowly territorial approaches, as the Roberts opinion does. He purports to stake out approximately the same ground for the United States as our friends and allies stake out for themselves, and this involves a holistic approach to jurisdiction.

[36] Id. at 1671 (Breyer, J., concurring).

[37] Id. (Breyer, J., concurring).

The issues lie with the third alternative. The Breyer concurrence seems to make it rather easy on itself, in the sense of preserving all the freedom and discretion that the ATS already has, by defining important national interests to include American values, and defining a distinct interest in ensuring that the United States not become a safe harbor for genuinely bad people. This maneuver returns to the core concerns of the ATS cases of the 1980s and appears to implicate both persons present in the United States—Marcos, for example, or Peña-Irala, the Paraguayan police official—or their property, such as bank accounts or assets that, Breyer says, ought not to enjoy a safe harbor from criminal or civil liability.

Whether Justice Breyer means this in some distinctly "territorial" sense—the physical presence of persons or assets—he does not say. His opinion cites the ringing language of *Filártiga* as to the common enemies of mankind. But in his discussion of the case and its relevance to his third test, he places emphasis on rejecting precisely the element that Judge Kaufman thought was what made the ATS special—its raison d'être—the ATS as eliminating the need for any territorial, personal, or contacts-based notion of jurisdiction beyond the claims of human rights as such. On the contrary, Justice Breyer's approach emphasizes the obligation not to serve as a safe harbor for very bad people (in human rights law terms) or their assets—while specifically making note that the defendant in *Filártiga* had found physical safe harbor in the United States, and stating that because the "defendant's alleged conduct violated a well-established international law norm, and the suit vindicated our Nation's interest in not providing a safe harbor, free of damages claims, for those defendants who commit such conduct."[38] He makes the same observation of Ferdinand Marcos as well.

There are two points to make about Breyer's third alternative. One is that if he is serious about denying safe harbor—allowing an ATS suit—based upon physical presence of the person, it is not clear that the Roberts approach would not treat the presumption as inapplicable in that case as well. In other words, when a "bad person" is (or perhaps was) in the United States, territoriality might well be satisfied for Chief Justice Roberts, at least in some situations. Second, however, Breyer's test has to raise concerns that it is merely a path to

[38] *Id.* at 1675 (Breyer, J., concurring).

the same old problematic discretion to find jurisdiction, merely using new language, yet reaching the same results. For example, might a defendant's assets be deemed to have found "safe harbor" in the United States—and thus a possible claim under the ATS—because they pass through the Federal Reserve Wire Network ("Fedwire") for bank clearance, or some equally ephemeral contact?

The problem for Justice Breyer, as for Chief Justice Roberts, is that they cannot find a stable line between seeing the ATS as being genuinely about the common enemies of mankind—the "real deal," as it were—and the desire of many in the advocacy community to see the ATS as a mechanism for regulating transnational corporate enterprises in their ordinary functions. These activists see the ATS as effectively playing a regulatory role, particularly regarding labor and environmental issues—far indeed from genocide and crimes against humanity—and creating a de facto regime of international civil liability that the nations of the world have thus far somehow neglected to establish. The lesson from lower-court litigation is similar but with certain key distinctions: given a discretionary tool, district court judges seem mostly to want to create a global yet distinctly American tort regime—while forcing key claims into international-criminal-law categories of the most serious sorts imaginable.

Hence, the abiding question for Justice Breyer's third alternative: does it simply recapitulate the problem of squishiness that made *Sosa* unworkable? It is easy to read Breyer's third test so as to fit practically anything into the guise of national interests and a capacious notion of safe harbor. It is hard not to think that it permits judges who want the ATS to expand to expand it, and judges who want the ATS to contract to contract it—or, in other words, *Sosa* redux. And yet we must give Justice Breyer's *result* its due and acknowledge that he seems clearly to want to reframe the ATS debate away from universality and cosmopolitan justice. After all is said and done, the Breyer opinion concurs with the majority's result and denies that the contacts in *Kiobel* are sufficient to engage the ATS. That has to count for something.

XI. Conclusion

In a better world than ours, I suppose, Justice Breyer's approach is intellectually the more compelling one. It harmonizes with others in the world that we care about, and it returns the ATS to something much more recognizable as international law. It is doctrinally more correct than the majority, as far as the bases of jurisdiction recognized in international and foreign relations law. Its assertion of American values as important, cognizable interests in the ATS need not be, in principle at least, a loophole through which to drive any and all results. And its emphasis on not providing safe harbor to very bad people and their assets has considerable merit.

Moreover, it bears observing one last time that both the Breyer and Roberts opinions are firmly rooted in a retreat to traditional cross-border jurisdictional principles in the correct perception that universal jurisdiction for civil liability in national courts is not a workable concept. And that in any case, what American jurisprudence called universal jurisdiction under the ATS was simply extraordinary—to others in the world—extraterritorial reach under a uniquely American statute. The claims to be carrying out the universal claims of international law rang hollow and illegitimate. Either the majority or the minority approach is an improvement over where ATS jurisprudence has gone, given the failure of *Sosa* to provide a clear rule, and especially since ATS litigation decisively took the "corporate" turn. The questions have not yet been fully answered—starting, peculiarly, with corporate liability and "aiding and abetting" liability, on which the Court might have been expected to pronounce, given that these were the issues originally granted certiorari and given that they were briefed and argued. American corporations have a strong interest in a clear Supreme Court ruling that corporations cannot properly be defendants in ATS cases.

At the end of the day, however, we don't live in a better world; we live in the world of the American tort system. Certainly I do not believe that the Breyer approach offers enough practical protection against gradual expansion of claims and the erosion of levees that Breyer would claim have been sturdily erected. It simply preserves and assigns too much to discretion in the lower courts. The Roberts approach is less intellectually compelling, vastly cruder, sometimes inconsistent—and far more grounded in the reality of bringing to heel a form of law long since gone feral. The Breyer approach is intellectually perfectionist but likely ineffective; the Roberts approach is far from intellectually perfect, but its crude limits are likely to provide more effective signals of lines not to be crossed.

ATS litigation is thus transformed by *Kiobel*, but the ATS is by no means dead. Even if disputes are now framed as arguments over extraterritoriality rather than universal jurisdiction, alternative theories of jurisdiction and liability are already emerging.[39] For that matter, state courts and state law have begun to provide an alternative outlet for litigation under the rubric of "transnational torts."[40] Moreover, days after the Court handed down the *Kiobel* decision, it accepted review in *Bauman v. DaimlerChrysler*—a 2011 Ninth Circuit case holding that Daimler AG, a German parent company with no operations or employees in the United States, could be sued under the ATS for human rights abuses allegedly committed by an Argentine subsidiary aiding and abetting the Argentine government during its "dirty war" of the 1970s, solely on the theory that the parent company had sufficient contacts with California through its U.S.-distribution subsidiary to support personal jurisdiction.[41]

It might seem obvious that *Kiobel* ought to moot that decision, but the questions are not the same as an acknowledged "foreign-cubed" case because at issue is whether and what contacts are sufficient to establish personal jurisdiction. *Bauman* is really an attempt by the plaintiffs to turn a foreign-cubed case into one by which agency theory provides a path to finding personal jurisdiction—and thus is no longer entirely "foreign" or premised purely on "universal" considerations. In other words, the case is an attempt to sidestep the formal doctrine of legal separation of corporate entities; it asserts a view that multinational corporate enterprises are to be treated as essentially one economic entity. This is, indeed, a plausible view of their globally unitary economic substance, but by arguing for economic substance over legal form, it renders impossible any real legal principle for why any particular national court should or should not hear a case.

---

[39] For an excellent summary of this debate, see *Opinio Juris*'s online symposium on the ATS after *Kiobel*. An Hertogen, Kiobel Insta-Symposium Insta-Roundup, Opinio Juris, Apr. 18, 2013, http://opiniojuris.org/2013/04/18/kiobel-insta-symposium-insta-roundup (collecting all contributions).

[40] See Roger Alford, Kiobel Insta-Symposium: The Death of the ATS and the Rise of Transnational Tort Litigation," Opinio Juris, Apr. 17, 2013, http://opiniojuris.org/2013/04/17/kiobel-instthe-death-of-the-ats-and-the-rise-of-transnational-tort-litigation.

[41] DaimlerChrysler AG v. Bauman, 133 S. Ct. 1995 (2013) (No. 11-965) (granting cert. petition).

Chief Justice Roberts's requirement of "touch and concern" will likely start to be fleshed out in *Bauman*—as too will the next permutation of Justice Breyer's *Kiobel* approach. And perhaps the first thing we will discover in *Bauman* is that "touch and concern" is, in fact, a more holistic consideration of jurisdiction, beyond territory as such, to draw upon personal jurisdiction and "contacts" in a holistic way (holistic, that is, whether used to go forward or to dismiss). Such a result would lead—particularly with Justice Kennedy's (almost inevitable) warning in his short *Kiobel* concurrence that he won't be bound by a mechanical rule and anticipates many unanticipated permutations down the ATS road—to a somewhat ironic question as to whether the *Kiobel* majority's "touch and concern" will turn out to invite just as much discretion among the lower courts as *Sosa* did and Justice Breyer's national-interest balancing test threatens to do.

Still, as former State Department legal adviser John Bellinger has observed of the Court's decision to review *Bauman*, many believe that

> the Court would not have accepted the case unless it plans to reverse the Ninth Circuit. Conservative justices are loathe to miss an opportunity to try to curb the Ninth Circuit's consistent efforts to be a world court, and the more liberal justices may have wanted to demonstrate (as Justice Breyer argued in his concurrence in *Kiobel*) that the extraterritorial reach of the Alien Tort Statute can be limited by other jurisdictional restrictions.[42]

But the jurisdictional restrictions Bellinger refers to, on all sides of the Court, are drawn from the standard, traditional bases of jurisdiction. To be sure, the proper invocation of jurisdiction in transnational economic affairs might arise as an issue in many more avenues of legal dispute than simply the ATS. Whatever the legal avenue, however, our world is becoming one in which economic activity reaches across many borders, with many degrees of business involvement, presence, and activity. It is also a world in which the number of political and economic powers with a robust sense of their sovereign rights and a protective attitude toward their domestic corporations

---

[42] John Bellinger, Justice Department Urges Supreme Court to Reverse Ninth Circuit in Bauman v. DaimlerChrysler, Lawfare, Jul. 12, 2013, http://www.lawfareblog.com/2013/07/justice-department-urges-supreme-court-to-reverse-ninth-circuit-in-bauman-v-daimlerchrysler.

is increasing, not decreasing. Battles over the proper assertion of jurisdiction in a globalized world are likely only to get hotter. Yet that is in part precisely because the standard bases of jurisdiction, with all their complexities of doctrine in the United States and elsewhere, are now squarely at issue.[43] Universal jurisdiction, being essentially political rather than legal, was always legally simpler by comparison.

---

[43] As this article goes to press, the Second Circuit has issued a new ruling in a long-running ATS case, dismissing all substantive claims as barred by the Supreme Court's decision in *Kiobel*. Balintulo v. Daimler AG, No. 09-2778-cv(L), 2013 WL 4437057 (2d Cir. Aug. 21, 2013). In an opinion written by Judge José Cabranes (who also wrote the Second Circuit opinion in *Kiobel*), the court described *Kiobel* as holding that "federal courts may not, under the ATS, recognize common-law causes of action for conduct occurring in the territory of another sovereign" and, moreover, that it was not relevant whether the defendant was a U.S. or foreign corporation. *Id.* at *1. While agreeing with the Second Circuit's outcome, I am uncertain that the Supreme Court—and in particular Justice Kennedy—would endorse such a broad reading of *Kiobel*'s majority opinion. *Balintulo* illustrates at a minimum, however, that the argument over jurisdiction under the ATS is likely to shift from the presumption against extraterritoriality as such to an argument over what Chief Justice Roberts's opinion meant by "touch and concern." How much "touching" and "concerning" is enough?

Bailey v. United States: Another Win for that "Doggone Fourth Amendment"

*Daniel Epps**

More than 30 years ago, *Michigan v. Summers* established a bright-line rule that police, when executing a search warrant for contraband at a home, may detain occupants of the residence for the duration of the search.[1] That rule is a categorical exception to the Fourth Amendment's general prohibition on detentions—or "seizures" of the person—that are not based on probable cause. This year, in *Bailey v. United States*, the Supreme Court refused to extend the *Summers* rule further, holding that police have no categorical power to detain occupants who have left the immediate vicinity of the premises being searched.[2]

Bailey got the bottom-line result right. The probable-cause requirement is a well-established component of the reasonableness mandated by the Fourth Amendment. The government could point to no legitimate interest that would justify a limited exception from that requirement without swallowing it entirely. By declining to extend the *Summers* rule in *Bailey*, the Court reaffirmed the probable-cause requirement and made clear that it cannot be discarded simply because it poses inconvenience to police efforts to investigate crime.

Bailey is in one sense disappointing: Both the majority and Justice Antonin Scalia (who filed a separate concurrence) declined to criticize the *Summers* rule itself, which is broader than necessary in light of its legitimate justifications—even though both appeared to recognize the flaws in *Summers*'s reasoning. More important, however, is what *Bailey* demonstrates about the current state of search-and-seizure doctrine as a whole. The Court has in recent years become

* Climenko Fellow and Lecturer on Law, Harvard Law School. Thanks to Danielle D'Onfro, Garrett Epps, and Matt Owen for helpful feedback.

[1] 452 U.S. 692, 702 (1981).

[2] 133 S. Ct. 1031 (2013).

more careful in its analysis of Fourth Amendment issues, requiring a tighter fit between exceptions to rules like the probable-cause requirement and their justifications. It now takes the Fourth Amendment more seriously as a source of determinate legal rules, rather than as an open-ended invitation to declare what is reasonable under all the circumstances of each case. Those who believe that the Fourth Amendment should impose meaningful constraints on police action should see that as a good development. It guards against the risk that judges will effectively render Fourth Amendment protections meaningless by discarding them whenever they become inconvenient for police.

Legal Background

The Fourth Amendment provides that "[t]he right of the people to be secure in their persons, houses, papers, and effects, against unreasonable searches and seizures, shall not be violated, and no Warrants shall issue, but upon probable cause." The Supreme Court has made clear that the ban on "unreasonable . . . seizures" means that, as a general matter, police may not forcibly detain a person without probable cause to believe that he has committed or is committing a crime.[3] That rule "has roots that are deep in our history."[4] Under English common law, peace officers could make warrantless arrests only when they had "reasonable grounds to believe" the arrestee had committed a felony, and that rule has been incorporated into Fourth Amendment doctrine.[5]

Despite its historical pedigree, however, the probable-cause requirement—like most other Fourth Amendment rules[6]—has significant exceptions. Most notably, *Terry v. Ohio*[7] and its progeny provide

---

[3] See, e.g., Dunaway v. New York, 442 U.S. 200 (1979); United States v. Watson, 423 U.S. 411, 416–19 (1976); see also Devenpeck v. Alford, 543 U.S. 146, 152 (2004).

[4] Henry v. United States, 361 U.S. 98, 100 (1959).

[5] See, e.g., Wayne R. LaFave, Search and Seizure: A Treatise on the Fourth Amendment § 5.1(b), at 15 (2012). There is some historical disagreement over whether warrantless *misdemeanor* arrests were permissible only for breaches of the peace. See Atwater v. City of Lago Vista, 532 U.S. 318 (2001).

[6] See, e.g., Phyllis T. Bookspan, Reworking the Warrant Requirement: Resuscitating the Fourth Amendment, 44 Vand. L. Rev. 473, 481 (1991) ("Today, the warrant requirement is notable more for its exceptions than its enforcement.").

[7] 392 U.S. 1 (1968).

that when police have "reasonable, articulable suspicion" of criminal activity, they may briefly detain an individual for the purpose of questioning the individual.[8] The Court's stated rationale for such exceptions to the "general rule requiring probable cause" is that some seizures are "so substantially less intrusive than arrests" that they may be justified under a "balancing test" where strong law-enforcement interests are present.[9]

At issue in *Bailey* was the scope of one such exception: the rule, established in *Michigan v. Summers*, that police may detain "an occupant of premises being searched for contraband pursuant to a valid warrant" during the search.[10] In *Summers*, the police had a warrant to search a home for drugs. As they approached the home, they found the home's owner, George Summers, descending the front steps, and immediately detained him. After finding narcotics in the basement, police arrested Summers. Summers had heroin on his person and was charged with drug possession as a result. Because police would not have had the chance immediately to arrest Summers had they not detained him during the search, the validity of the search of Summers's person depended on the validity of the original detention. Given that the detention was surely a seizure, and given that it was clear that police lacked probable cause to arrest Summers at the time he was initially detained, the Court found it necessary to consider whether a special exception to the normal probable-cause requirement was justified.

In an opinion by Justice John Paul Stevens, and over the dissent of Justice Potter Stewart (joined by Justices William Brennan and Thurgood Marshall), the Court concluded that such an exception was appropriate as a categorical matter.[11] Justice Stevens reached that conclusion after assessing the interests at stake and conducting a balancing test.

On the one hand, the Court concluded that detention incident to a search warrant was only a minimal intrusion on the liberty and privacy of the detained person.[12] First, it was of "prime importance"

[8] See Illinois v. Wardlow, 528 U.S. 119, 123 (2000); see also, e.g., Florida v. Royer, 460 U.S. 491, 498–99 (1983).

[9] Dunaway, 442 U.S. at 210.

[10] 452 U.S. 692, 702 (1981).

[11] *Id.* at 705.

[12] *Id.* at 701–02.

that police had obtained a warrant to search for contraband.[13] A "neutral and detached magistrate had found probable cause to believe that the law was being violated in [the residence] and had authorized a substantial invasion of the privacy of the persons who resided there"; Summers's detention was "admittedly a significant restraint on his liberty," but it "was surely less intrusive than the search itself."[14] Second, the Court reasoned that a detention during a search "is not likely to be exploited by the officer or unduly prolonged in order to gain more information, because the information the officers seek normally will be obtained through the search and not through the detention."[15] And finally, the Court determined that a detention in the detainee's "own residence . . . could add only minimally to the public stigma associated with the search itself and would involve neither the inconvenience nor the indignity associated with a compelled visit to the police station."[16]

The *Summers* Court identified three "legitimate law enforcement interest[s]" weighing heavily in favor of permitting detention.[17] First and "most obvious" was the "interest in preventing flight in the event that incriminating evidence is found."[18] Second was the interest in "minimizing the risk of harm to the officers"; because "the execution of a warrant to search for narcotics is the kind of transaction that may give rise to sudden violence or frantic efforts to conceal or destroy evidence," the Court reasoned that "[t]he risk of harm to both the police and the occupants is minimized if the officers routinely exercise unquestioned command of the situation."[19] Finally, the Court thought that allowing detention would facilitate "the orderly completion of the search," because occupants' "self-interest may induce them to open locked doors or locked containers to avoid the use of force that is not only damaging to property but may also delay the completion of the task at hand."[20]

---

[13] *Id.* at 701.

[14] *Id.*

[15] *Id.*

[16] *Id.* at 702.

[17] *Id.*

[18] *Id.*

[19] *Id.* at 703.

[20] *Id.* at 702–03.

In addition, the Court stressed that the "connection of an occupant to th[e] home" being searched pursuant to a warrant gave rise to legitimate "suspicion of criminal activity," thereby providing "an objective justification for the detention."[21] Weighing all the relevant considerations, the Court held that "a warrant to search for contraband founded on probable cause implicitly carries with it the limited authority to detain the occupants of the premises while a proper search is conducted."[22]

Summers was short on the specifics of permissible detention. Justice Potter Stewart, in dissent, warned that the majority's rule would permit "a detention of several hours" allowing police to "make the person a prisoner in his own home for a potentially very long period of time."[23] That prediction proved true when, more than two decades later, the Court clarified the reach of the *Summers* rule in *Muehler v. Mena*.[24] There, the Court held that "[i]nherent in *Summers'* authorization to detain an occupant of the place to be searched is the authority to use reasonable force to effectuate the detention."[25] Applying that rule, the Court concluded that it was permissible for police to keep a home's occupant in handcuffs for several hours during the course of a search (although the Court left open the possibility that the detention could have been unreasonable if it extended longer than the duration of the search).[26] Several years later, in *Los Angeles County v. Rettele*, the Court ruled that police searching a home pursuant to a warrant have the authority, under *Summers*, to hold the home's occupants at gunpoint while securing the premises.[27]

Summers was also unclear about precisely which "occupants" it allowed police to detain. The Court's opinion used the term loosely. Did it mean to refer only to residents, or did it mean anyone who was currently occupying the premises at the time of the search? The opinion can be read both ways. A number of the Court's arguments appear premised on the fact that Summers was detained at

---

[21] *Id.* at 703–04.

[22] *Id.* at 705 (footnote omitted).

[23] Summers, 452 U.S. at 711 (Stewart, J., dissenting).

[24] 544 U.S. 93 (2005).

[25] *Id.* at 98–99.

[26] *Id.* at 100–02.

[27] 550 U.S. 609, 613–16 (2007).

his own home,[28] but some of the opinion's offered rationales for the detention—such as minimizing harm to officers—do not necessarily turn on whether the detained person actually lives at the home being searched. There is some disagreement on this question.[29] It is unlikely, however, that *Summers* detentions could remain limited to owners in practice. Police will not necessarily know whether someone is an owner or a mere visitor at the time of detention.[30]

A related, but distinct, area of uncertainty—and here's where we come to the issue in *Bailey*—is whether someone can be an "occupant" under *Summers* after he has left the premises. Here, too, *Summers* is ambiguous. The term "occupant" can be plausibly read as meaning someone who is presently "occupying" the residence; and the Court noted that its rule allowed police to require an occupant "to remain" in his home during a search.[31] But it also could refer to someone who simply *lives* at the residence. Supporting that reading is the fact that Summers himself was seized not while he was inside his home, but rather while he was in the process of leaving. Indeed, the Court explicitly observed that it did not "view the fact that [Summers] was leaving his house when the officers arrived to be of constitutional significance."[32]

Lower courts predictably divided on this question. A number held that police could choose to detain a departing occupant so long as they did so "as soon as practicable" after his departure.[33] Others concluded that the power to detain under *Summers* did not extend

---

[28] See, e.g., Summers, 452 U.S. at 702 ("[B]ecause the detention in this case was in respondent's own residence, it could add only minimally to the public stigma associated with the search itself . . . .").

[29] See Amir Hatem Ali, Note, Following the Bright Line of *Michigan v. Summers*: A Cause for Concern for Advocates of Bright-Line Fourth Amendment Rules, 45 Harv. C.R.-C.L. L. Rev. 483, 497–500 (2010) (noting disagreement in lower courts); LaFave, *supra* note 5, § 4.9(e) at pp. 924–26 & nn.142–44 (same).

[30] In *Bailey* itself, police detained Bailey's passenger even though he claimed to be a friend whom Bailey was driving home. 133 S. Ct. at 1036. And police did not end Bailey's detention once he denied living at the apartment being searched. *Id.*

[31] Summers, 452 U.S. at 705; see also Brief for Petitioner at 18–19, Bailey v. United States, 133 S. Ct. 1031 (2013) (No. 11-770).

[32] Summers, 452 U.S. at 702 n.16.

[33] See, e.g., United States v. Montieth, 662 F.3d 660 (4th Cir. 2011) (collecting cases).

beyond the premises themselves.[34] *Bailey* presented an ideal vehicle for the resolution of the split.

Case Background

Like so many other Fourth Amendment cases in recent decades, *Bailey* arose out of a narcotics investigation. Police received a tip from an informant who claimed that "a heavy set black male with short hair known as Polo" was selling drugs out of a basement apartment in Wyandanch, New York.[35] Police obtained a warrant to search for a handgun. While the search team was preparing to execute the warrant, detectives observed two men leaving the residence, both of whom fit the vague description of "Polo." The men got in a vehicle and drove away; after they had traveled for several hundred feet, the detectives began pursuing them while other officers began the search.

Once the two men were approximately one mile away from the home, the detectives pulled the vehicle over, ordered the men out, frisked them, and handcuffed them. One of the men, Chunon Bailey, initially admitted to residing at the basement apartment. When told that he was being detained incident to a search warrant for that residence, Bailey said "I don't live there. Anything you find there ain't mine, and I'm not cooperating with your investigation."[36] One of the keys that was found on Bailey's person turned out to open the basement apartment.

Bailey was subsequently charged with federal gun and drug offenses; at trial, he sought to suppress his incriminatory statements and the apartment key, arguing that his seizure was unreasonable and not authorized by *Summers*.[37] The district court denied the motion, and the Second Circuit affirmed. In an opinion by Judge José Cabranes, the court concluded that "the very interests at stake in *Summers* . . . permit detention of an occupant nearby, but outside of, the premises" being searched.[38] According to the Second Circuit, refusing to extend *Summers* to detentions like Bailey's "would put police officers executing a warrant in an impossible position: when

---

[34] See, e.g., Commonwealth v. Charros, 824 N.E.2d 809 (Mass. 2005).

[35] Bailey, 133 S. Ct. at 1036 (internal quotation marks omitted).

[36] Id.

[37] Id.

[38] United States v. Bailey, 652 F.3d 197, 205 (2d Cir. 2011).

they observe a person of interest leaving a residence for which they have a search warrant, they would be required either to detain him immediately (risking officer safety and the destruction of evidence) or to permit him to leave the scene (risking the inability to detain him if incriminating evidence was discovered)."[39]

The Second Circuit did not, however, see the *Summers* power as limitless; it cautioned that "*Summers* is not a license for law enforcement to detain 'occupants' of premises subject to a search warrant anywhere they may be found incident to that search."[40] Instead, in the court's view, *Summers* established "a duty based on both geographic and temporal proximity; police must identify an individual *in the process of leaving* the premises subject to search and detain him *as soon as practicable* during the execution of the search."[41] "Because the officers acted as soon as reasonably practicable in detaining Bailey once he drove off the premises subject to search . . . his detention during the valid search of the house did not violate the Fourth Amendment."[42]

The Supreme Court granted Bailey's petition for certiorari. At the merits stage, Bailey placed great emphasis on the Court's recent decision in *Arizona v. Gant*.[43] *Gant* was not directly on point as a legal matter; the case concerned police authority to search incident to an arrest, rather than the power, at issue in *Bailey*, to detain incident to a search.

The specific issue in *Gant* was when police can search vehicles incident to an arrest of the driver. Typically, police cannot search a vehicle absent probable cause to believe that it contains contraband (or the driver's consent).[44] But the Court's decision in *New York v. Belton*[45] had been understood as creating a blanket exception to that rule, under which police were permitted to search a vehicle incident to arrest whenever the driver was arrested. The *Belton* rule was ostensibly founded upon the rationales of officer safety and preservation

---

[39] *Id.*

[40] *Id.* at 208.

[41] *Id.* at 206.

[42] *Id.* at 207.

[43] 556 U.S. 332 (2009).

[44] See United States v. Ross, 456 U.S. 798, 808–09 (1982); Carroll v. United States, 267 U.S. 132, 155–56 (1925).

[45] 453 U.S. 454 (1981).

of evidence,[46] but neither seemed applicable to situations in which the police search a vehicle while the arrested driver is handcuffed and locked in the back of a squad car. For that reason, *Belton* became subject to serious criticism.[47] In *Gant*, a narrow majority of the Court (Justice Stevens, joined by Justices Scalia, David Souter, Clarence Thomas, and Ruth Bader Ginsburg) effectively overruled the case, holding that a search of an automobile incident to arrest is permissible "only if the arrestee is within reaching distance of the passenger compartment at the time of the search or it is reasonable to believe the vehicle contains evidence of the offense of arrest."[48]

Seeking to build a similar coalition, Bailey invoked *Gant* at every turn. Just as *Gant* recognized that the *Belton* rule could not be "untether[ed]" from its underlying justifications (preservation of evidence and safety of officers), so too should the Court refuse to extend *Summers* beyond the "immediate vicinity" of a home, where its rationales no longer apply, Bailey argued.[49] Thus, although *Gant* did not deal with the precise issue in *Bailey*, it nonetheless provided a helpful analogy.

The government, for its part, did not take the bait; its brief never cited *Gant*. Instead, the government challenged the premise of Bailey's argument: Although Bailey had cast the *Summers* rule as Fourth Amendment doctrine's only categorical rule "that supports the detention of an individual, solely for ordinary law-enforcement purposes, without any degree of individualized suspicion,"[50] the government stressed language in *Summers* suggesting that the existence of a search warrant gave police "an identifiable and individualized basis to detain" a departing occupant of a home to be searched.[51] The government strongly contested Bailey's argument that the "legitimate

[46] The *Belton* rule was derived from the general search-incident-to-arrest exception to the warrant requirement recognized in *Chimel v. California*, 395 U.S. 752 (1969), which was premised on those two rationales, see *id.* at 763.

[47] See, e.g., Thornton v. United States, 541 U.S. 615, 626–29 (2004) (Scalia, J., concurring in the judgment).

[48] Gant, 556 U.S. at 351.

[49] Brief for Petitioner, *supra* note 31, at 21 (quoting Gant, 556 U.S. at 343) (brackets omitted).

[50] *Id.* at 15.

[51] Brief for the United States at 24, Bailey v. United States, 133 S. Ct. 1031 (2013) (No. 11-770) (emphasis omitted).

law enforcement interest[s]" recognized by *Summers* were inapplicable beyond the "immediate vicinity" of the premises being searched; it gave special emphasis to the safety rationale, warning that departing occupants could return to the scene of a search and assault the officers present.[52]

At oral argument, Bailey appeared to have the wind at his back. Several justices appeared skeptical of the government's position. Justice Anthony Kennedy wondered why the government's arguments would not justify detention of any person with a connection to the premises being searched, even if not nearby when the search began.[53] Chief Justice John Roberts questioned whether *Summers* was right to suggest that "you can detain the people because they might want to give the officers assistance. Well, if they want to give them assistance, they don't have to be detained."[54] Nothing better summed up the day the government was having, however, than Justice Scalia's response to one of the government's arguments about law-enforcement interests: "All law enforcement would be a lot easier if we didn't have the doggone Fourth Amendment. I mean, the Fourth Amendment is an impediment to law enforcement. Of course it is. There—there's no doubt about that."[55] No one in attendance that day left the courtroom with any doubt about Justice Scalia's view of the case.

The Decision

Predictably, in light of the oral argument, the Supreme Court reversed. The Court rejected the Second Circuit's "as soon as reasonably practicable" rule and instead held that authority to detain under *Summers* extends no further than "the immediate vicinity of the premises to be searched."[56] The vote was 6–3. Justice Kennedy wrote for the majority, joined by Chief Justice Roberts and Justices Scalia, Ginsburg, Sonia Sotomayor, and Elena Kagan; Justice Stephen Breyer dissented, joined by Justices Thomas and Samuel Alito.[57]

---

[52] See *id*. at 35–42.

[53] See, e.g., Transcript of Oral Argument at 50, Bailey v. United States, 133 S. Ct. 1031 (2013) (No. 11-770).

[54] *Id*. at 48.

[55] *Id*. at 57.

[56] Bailey, 133 S. Ct. at 1041.

[57] Interestingly, despite Bailey's efforts to analogize the case to *Gant*, not all of the justices saw the two cases as similar. Chief Justice Roberts and Justice Kennedy both

Justice Kennedy's majority opinion reached its holding after analyzing each of the interests identified by *Summers* and concluding that none of them applied with the same force to individuals who have left the premises being searched. Regarding safety to officers, the Court acknowledged the possibility that, as the government had warned,[58] a home's occupant might return to the premises while a search was ongoing.[59] The Court's response, however, was that "[o]fficers can and do mitigate that risk, however, by taking routine precautions, for instance by erecting barricades or posting someone on the perimeter or at the door."[60] Moreover, the government's argument proved too much; "[t]he risk . . . that someone could return home during the execution of a search warrant is not limited to occupants who depart shortly before the start of a search."[61]

The Court quickly dispensed with the Second Circuit's argument that Bailey's proposed rule would put police in an "impossible position."[62] As the Court saw it:

> Although the danger of alerting occupants who remain inside may be of real concern in some instances . . . this safety rationale rests on the false premise that a detention must take place. If the officers find that it would be dangerous to detain a departing individual in front of a residence, they are not required to stop him.[63]

Here, Justice Kennedy's opinion channeled Justice Scalia's concurrence in the judgment in *Thornton v. United States*,[64] a pre-*Gant* case in which cracks in the *Belton* rule began to show. Responding to the argument that "since the officer could have conducted the search at the time of arrest (when the suspect was still near the car), he should

---

dissented in *Gant*, but sided with Bailey; Justice Thomas joined the *Gant* majority but dissented in *Bailey*.

[58] See Brief for the United States, *supra* note 51, at 35–42.

[59] Bailey, 133 S. Ct. at 1039.

[60] *Id.*

[61] *Id.*

[62] United States v. Bailey, 652 F.3d 197, 205 (2d Cir. 2011).

[63] Bailey, 133 S. Ct. at 1031.

[64] 541 U.S. 615 (2004).

not be penalized for having taken the sensible precaution of securing the suspect in the squad car first,"[65] Justice Scalia explained:

> The weakness of this argument is that it assumes that, one way or another, the search must take place. But conducting a . . . search is not the Government's right; it is an exception—justified by necessity—to a rule that would otherwise render the search unlawful. If sensible police procedures require that suspects be handcuffed and put in squad cars, then police should handcuff suspects, put them in squad cars, and not conduct the search.[66]

Justice Kennedy did not cite this concurrence; having dissented in *Gant,* Justice Kennedy may be disinclined to endorse the reasoning that led to that decision. But the concurrence's echoes are unmistakable.

The majority then explained that the interest in "the orderly completion of the search" is tied to "the vicinity of the premises to be searched."[67] "If occupants are permitted to wander around the premises," they could actively interfere with the search; but "[t]hose risks are not presented by an occupant who departs beforehand."[68] As for *Summers*'s suggestion that detained occupants could be persuaded to open locked containers, "it would have no limiting principle were it to be applied to persons beyond the premises of the search."[69]

Next was the interest in preventing flight. This interest, one might think, would be *stronger* under facts like those in *Bailey* than where the occupant is found at the premises. If the need to prevent flight justifies detaining those who are still present when the search commences, it surely should justify detaining those who have recently left (and thus are possibly fleeing) the premises. For this reason, Justice Kennedy's majority opinion found it necessary essentially to redefine the flight interest out of existence. Taking the lead from Bailey,[70] the Court explained that the prevention-of-flight interest

[65] *Id.* at 627 (Scalia, J., concurring in the judgment).

[66] *Id.*

[67] Bailey, 133 S. Ct. at 1040.

[68] *Id.*

[69] *Id.*

[70] See Brief for Petitioner, *supra* note 31, at 17–18 ("[*Summers*] did not suggest that, standing alone, the interest in preventing flight would serve as a sufficient basis for a

was subordinate to the other two interests recognized in *Summers*: It "serves to preserve the integrity of the search by controlling those persons who are on the scene," but it "does not independently justify detention of an occupant beyond the immediate vicinity of the premises to be searched."[71]

Having concluded that *Summers's* law-enforcement interests were weaker when applied to detentions of recent occupants, the Court turned to the interests of the detained individual. Detentions outside the home involve "an additional level of intrusiveness," because such public detentions often involve "the additional indignity of a compelled transfer back to the premises, giving all the appearances of an arrest."[72] In light of its assessment of the balance of interests, the Court concluded that "[a] spatial constraint defined by the immediate vicinity of the premises" was a necessary limitation on the *Summers* rule.[73] Because Bailey's detention occurred nowhere near the premises, the Court declined to elaborate on how courts should define "immediate vicinity," suggesting only that "[i]n closer cases courts can consider a number of factors . . . including the lawful limits of the premises, whether the occupant was within the line of sight of his dwelling, the ease of reentry from the occupant's location, and other relevant factors."[74]

Justice Scalia, joined by Justices Sotomayor and Kagan, filed a concurring opinion. He found the case easy: "[*Summers*] applies only to seizures of 'occupants'—that is, persons within 'the immediate vicinity of the premises to be searched.' Bailey was seized a mile away. Ergo, *Summers* cannot sanction Bailey's detention. It really is that simple."[75] He criticized the Second Circuit and the dissenting justices for seeking to "replace [*Summers's*] straightforward, binary inquiry with open-ended balancing."[76] While seeming to defend the *Summers* rule, however, he acknowledged that the Court's opinion in

---

detention. . . . Instead, the interest in preventing flight is better understood as overlapping with, and thereby reinforcing, the other interests supporting the *Summers* rule.").

[71] Bailey, 133 S. Ct. at 1040–41.

[72] *Id.*

[73] *Id.* at 1042.

[74] *Id.*

[75] *Id.* at 1043 (Scalia, J., concurring) (citation omitted).

[76] *Id.*

that case was too "expansive," "setting forth a smorgasbord of law-enforcement interests assertedly justifying its holding."[77] Because, in his view, the interests in preventing flight and in opening locked containers were "nothing more than the ordinary interest in investigating crime," he concluded that "[t]he *Summers* exception is appropriately predicated only on law enforcement's interest in carrying out the search unimpeded by violence or other disruptions."[78]

In dissent, Justice Breyer argued that all of the *Summers* law-enforcement interests applied with full force to situations like the one in *Bailey*.[79] He focused on two main points. First, he argued that the majority failed to provide an "easily administered bright line" but would instead "invite[] case-by-case litigation."[80] Second, he contended that allowing police to wait to detain departing occupants was the better rule, because departing occupants may be armed or may see the police and notify persons inside the home of the impending search.[81] Although acknowledging the majority's argument that police are not required to detain a departing person, Justice Breyer opined that police may feel compelled to detain anyone emerging from a home prior to the execution of a warrant because they will not know if that person has spotted them.[82]

Analysis

The Need to Ensure That Exceptions Don't Swallow the Rules

Rights have costs. Enshrining a command into constitutional text takes certain options off the table—even where adherence to that rule seems inconsistent with some other attractive value. The Confrontation Clause forbids the use of testimonial hearsay at a criminal trial if the defendant has no opportunity to confront the declarant—even if the testimony has all the indicia of reliability.[83] The Double Jeopardy Clause bars appeal of an acquittal—even one that is

---

[77] *Id.* at 1044.

[78] *Id.* at 1044–45.

[79] *Id.* at 1046–47 (Breyer, J., dissenting).

[80] *Id.* at 1047.

[81] *Id.* at 1047–48.

[82] *Id.* at 1048.

[83] Crawford v. Washington, 541 U.S. 36 (2004).

obviously erroneous.[84] The Sixth Amendment insists that juries, not judges, determine whether the government has proven the elements of an offense beyond a reasonable doubt—even if there is little doubt what a properly instructed jury would decide.[85] Such commands are the product of a constitutional settlement in which it was resolved that the overall benefits of adhering to these guarantees are worth the costs they produce.

The Fourth Amendment is no different. By barring "unreasonable" searches and seizures, the amendment does not merely require reasonableness in the abstract but enshrines, at least to some extent, a particular vision of reasonable police practices into law. An important part of that vision, even though not explicit in the constitutional text, is the requirement that arrests must be based on probable cause.[86] That rule has strong historical support and has been repeatedly reaffirmed by the Court. And it's a rule that makes good sense; if the ban on unreasonable seizures means anything, it should, under normal circumstances, prevent police from depriving a person of his liberty without at least some reason to think he has committed a crime. That requirement, by its nature, makes law enforcement more difficult. But our society decided, when it enshrined the amendment

---

[84] Fong Foo v. United States, 369 U.S. 141 (1962).

[85] Sullivan v. Louisiana, 508 U.S. 275, 280–81 (1993). But see Neder v. United States, 527 U.S. 1, 8–15 (1999) (holding that trial court's failure to instruct jury on element of materiality is susceptible to harmless-error analysis on appeal from conviction).

[86] There is significant disagreement over whether the Fourth Amendment's reasonableness requirement simply constitutionalizes the search-and-seizure rules existing in 1791 or instead invites judges to engage in common-law reasoning, with the power to fashion rules in light of changed circumstances. Justice Scalia has forcefully advocated the first position. See, e.g., County of Riverside v. McLaughlin, 500 U.S. 44, 60–66 (1991) (Scalia, J., dissenting). For opposing views, see, e.g., David A. Sklansky, The Fourth Amendment and Common Law, 100 Colum. L. Rev. 1739 (2000); Carol S. Steiker, Second Thoughts About First Principles, 107 Harv. L. Rev. 820 (1997). That debate has significant implications about many areas of Fourth Amendment doctrine, such as the warrant requirement. See, e.g., Akhil Reed Amar, Fourth Amendment First Principles, 107 Harv. L. Rev. 757, 762–81 (1994) (arguing that the warrant requirement lacks a historical basis). However one comes down on that dispute, it is of no moment here. The rule that arrests require probable cause has strong historical roots, see *supra* notes 4 & 5 and accompanying text, but also has strong support in modern practice and precedent, see, e.g., Sklansky, *supra*, at 1764 (noting that the Supreme Court reaffirmed the probable-cause requirement "when the ahistoric approach to the Fourth Amendment was at its apogee").

into law, that those costs were worth the benefits of personal liberty and security.

Precisely because the Fourth Amendment is worded so vaguely, however, it poses special difficulties in judicial application. The language of reasonableness can make the Fourth Amendment seem like an open-ended invitation to figure out what seems reasonable on the unique facts of each case. And even where there is agreement that the amendment envisions some baseline rules, it's also widely understood that those rules must bend under some circumstances.

There's a risk, then, that judges will come to view rules like the probable-cause requirement as little more than weak suggestions, capable of being trumped whenever, in a judge's view, they seem like more trouble than they are worth. If so, it becomes all too easy for judges to throw up their hands, unwilling to second-guess the judgments of police officers. That's especially true given that most Fourth Amendment litigation occurs in the context of suppression rulings. In such situations, police actually found evidence of crime; to a reviewing court, police choices will often appear sensible in retrospect.[87]

Yet to the extent that the Fourth Amendment actually imposes meaningful constraints on police officers, requirements like the probable-cause rule must have bite. That is, they must prevent police from doing things that they would otherwise do—things that, in a world without a Fourth Amendment, might even seem to a judge like *reasonable* things to do. That means judges must not ignore the amendment's commands simply because they make it harder for police to catch criminals. Judges who do so inappropriately substitute their own preferences for the choices made in the Constitution.[88]

Avoiding that possibility requires clear rules governing how courts should fashion Fourth Amendment doctrine itself—specifically, principles governing when courts can and should recognize exceptions to commands like the probable-cause requirement. By way of analogy, consider the First Amendment. America today has almost certainly the most speech-protective laws on the planet.

[87] See William J. Stuntz, Warrants and Fourth Amendment Remedies, 77 Va. L. Rev. 881, 911–13 (1991).

[88] Cf. John F. Manning, Separation of Powers as Ordinary Interpretation, 124 Harv. L. Rev. 1939, 1946 (2011) ("An interpreter . . . must not invoke background purpose as a way to convert rules into standards or standards into rules.").

That fact is usually attributed to the First Amendment. But the First Amendment itself has not done the work. A key element in shaping America's vibrant free-speech culture is the fact that the Supreme Court has developed, and continues to refine, legal doctrines that preclude courts from deciding what speech merits protection based on "an ad hoc balancing of relative social costs and benefits."[89] The doctrine not only limits when and why government can restrict speech, but also largely prohibits the possibility that courts could recognize exceptions to those protections.[90]

A similar approach for the Fourth Amendment would seek to ensure that judicial decisionmaking doesn't just boil down to ad hoc judgments about what seem like reasonable police practices, all things considered. What's necessary are principled and objective norms about when, exactly, exceptions to baseline rules like the probable-cause requirement are permissible. Those norms must create some flexibility, but they cannot allow the exceptions to swallow the rules themselves and replace them with fact-specific interest balancing in each case.

Such principles governing proper Fourth Amendment analysis are important not merely because they constrain lower courts vis-à-vis the Supreme Court (although they do);[91] as important, over time, is their effect in limiting the types of arguments the Supreme Court will consider in a given context. In that sense, I submit that such rules are critical to taking the Fourth Amendment seriously as *law*— that is, as a source of rules that has objective, discernible content distinct from a particular judge's assessments of costs and benefits in a specific case.

When it comes to the probable-cause requirement for seizures of the person, taking that rule seriously means that judges need to have guidance about what kinds of arguments are in bounds and what kinds of governmental interests should count as legitimate reasons for an exception. If the probable-cause rule—which, by definition,

[89] United States v. Stevens, 130 S. Ct. 1577, 1585 (2010); see also Brown v. Entertainment Merchants Ass'n, 131 S. Ct. 2729, 2734 (2011).

[90] See, e.g., Brown, 131 S. Ct. at 2734 (rejecting the possibility of "new categories of unprotected speech" beyond those previously recognized).

[91] See, e.g., Toby J. Heytens, Doctrine Formulation and Distrust, 83 Notre Dame L. Rev. 2045, 2057–59 (2008) (explaining how appellate courts use clear rules to constrain lower courts).

makes the job of police harder—doesn't apply whenever it makes policing more difficult, it is no rule at all.

Under Justice Scalia's view, an exception "is only permissible where . . . 'some governmental interest independent of the ordinary interest in investigating crime and apprehending suspects'" is at stake.[92] This assertion seems not quite right as a descriptive matter (which may explain why its only cited support is Justice Stewart's dissent in *Summers*). The *Terry* doctrine, the most significant exception to the probable-cause requirement, gives police authority briefly to detain and question individuals based only on articulable suspicion, a lower standard than probable cause. And the doctrine's justification for those detentions is the ordinary interest in detecting and preventing crime.[93] (Perhaps *Terry* is best thought of as less of an exception to and more of an application of the probable-cause rule—when police have a little bit less than probable cause, they can effect a brief detention that is much less intrusive than a real arrest. One can accept *Terry* while still largely accepting Justice Scalia's approach.[94])

Putting *Terry* to one side, however, Justice Scalia's approach has much to recommend it. The Fourth Amendment's probable-cause requirement reflects a tradeoff between liberty and privacy on the one hand and the government's interest in fighting crime on the other. To allow the rule to give way simply because it gets in the way of law enforcement would miss the whole point of the rule—it would fail to respect the rule *as a rule*.

---

[92] Bailey, 133 S. Ct. at 1044 (quoting Summers, 452 U.S. at 707 (Stewart, J., dissenting)).

[93] To be sure, *Terry* noted that "more than the governmental interest in investigating crime" was present when it analyzed the *search* (the frisk for weapons) at issue in that case, recognizing "the more immediate interest of the police officer in taking steps to assure himself that the person with whom he is dealing is not armed." Terry v. Ohio, 392 U.S. 1, 23 (1968). That interest, however, comes into play only once police have detained the person to be questioned. In most instances, it provides no justification for the initial *seizure*, which will typically be motivated solely by the desire to investigate potential criminal activity.

[94] Justice Scalia's rationale for permitting *Terry* stops is that, on his reading of the common law, "it had long been considered reasonable to detain suspicious persons for the purpose of demanding that they give an account of themselves." Minnesota v. Dickerson, 508 U.S. 366, 380 (1993) (Scalia, J., concurring in the judgment). He has, however, expressed skepticism that frisks authorized by *Terry* have a historical analogue. See *id.* at 381 ("I frankly doubt . . . whether the fiercely proud men who adopted our Fourth Amendment would have allowed themselves to be subjected, on mere *suspicion* of being armed and dangerous, to such indignity.").

By contrast, permitting exceptions only where the government can point to a legitimate reason separate from its ordinary law-enforcement interests—a reason that explains why an exception is justified here, but not everywhere—helps prevent the doctrine from sliding down that slippery slope. Acknowledging that some strong government interest *other than* the ordinary interest in law enforcement might justify a limited exception does not question the balance struck by the Fourth Amendment between investigative needs and personal liberty and privacy—it does not effectively "revise the judgment [of] the American people . . . that the benefits of [the Fourth Amendment's] restrictions on the Government outweigh the costs."[95]

Of course, Justice Scalia's approach does not take all discretion out of judges' hands. Even where legitimate law-enforcement interests potentially justifying an exception exist, courts must balance those interests against the intrusions on privacy and liberty that an exception would create. Fourth Amendment analysis cannot be entirely mechanized. Nonetheless, requiring the government to articulate a special interest justifying an exception provides a significant constraint on judges' ability to disregard the probable-cause requirement whenever it seems inconvenient. And to the extent that the probable-cause requirement is a rule worthy of respect, some constraint is better than none at all.

The Right Result

In light of the foregoing analysis, *Bailey* reached the right bottom line. As Justice Scalia correctly concluded in his concurrence, the *only* legitimate interest at stake—the only one that was distinct from ordinary law enforcement—was the government's interest in effectuating the search without interference.[96] And that interest essentially disappeared as soon as Bailey left the vicinity of his apartment. Accordingly, the normal probable-cause requirement applied with full force.

The majority was not so explicit, but its opinion seemed to recognize that the sweeping array of interests recognized in *Summers* was too broad. Given that the majority acknowledged that both the

---

95 Cf. Brown, 131 S. Ct. at 2734 (internal quotation marks omitted; first alteration in original).

96 Bailey, 133 S. Ct. at 1044–45 (Scalia, J., concurring).

flight rationale and the government interest in opening locked doors and containers would have "no limiting principle" if extended outside the immediate vicinity of the home,[97] and instead emphasized "the law enforcement interests in conducting a safe and efficient search,"[98] it appeared, more or less, to track Justice Scalia's analysis.

By contrast, the reasoning of the many lower courts that relied on *Summers* to uphold detentions of departing occupants demonstrates why principled constraints like Justice Scalia's are needed. Without them, judges may be irresistibly tempted to water down probable-cause requirements whenever they pose an obstacle to police. Take the Second Circuit's assertion that police would be in an "impossible position" if they lacked authority to detain occupants who had left the premises.[99] Certainly, police executing search warrants after *Bailey* may sometimes face a difficult choice between detaining an occupant before he leaves the premises or letting the occupant leave and waiting to begin the search. But the choice between those two alternatives is not a "Hobson's choice" simply because the government finds both imperfect.[100] Police will inevitably face such choices because the Fourth Amendment takes certain options off the table.

The Fourth Circuit's recent decision in *United States v. Montieth*[101] provides another good example of similarly problematic reasoning. In that case, police had a warrant to search a home where the defendant, a suspected drug dealer, resided. "In an effort to minimize both the trauma to family as well as the safety risks of a search," police officers planned to detain the defendant away from the home and then "secure his cooperation to execute the warrant."[102] The plan worked; Montieth, once detained, agreed to cooperate with the search "to avoid an abrupt or forcible entry into the house while his wife and children were inside."[103] Police asked Montieth's wife

[97] *Id.* at 1040.

[98] *Id.* at 1042.

[99] United States v. Bailey, 652 F.3d 197, 205 (2d Cir. 2011).

[100] *Id.* at 206. Indeed, this is not even a proper use of the idiom. A "Hobson's choice" is not a choice between two imperfect alternatives, but is instead "the option of taking the one thing offered or nothing." See "choice, n.," Oxford English Dictionary Online, http://www.oed.com/view/Entry/32111 (accessed Aug. 1, 2013).

[101] 662 F.3d 660 (4th Cir. 2011).

[102] *Id.* at 663.

[103] *Id.*

to leave the home with her children; once the family had departed, police brought Montieth into the home and he showed them where his drugs were located.[104] The Fourth Circuit found this technique permissible: "To require officers to bypass less dangerous and disruptive methods of executing a search warrant and push them to harsher and more forcible modes of entry would be at odds with the Fourth Amendment's ultimate command of reasonableness."[105]

The Fourth Circuit seemed strangely untroubled by the way police so obviously wielded their authority under *Summers* as a cudgel to coerce the defendant into revealing the location of his drugs. Why was either Montieth's detention or his consent necessary to avoid an "abrupt or forcible entry,"[106] given that police could simply have asked the family members to leave after Montieth departed? The most plausible interpretation, at least to this reader, seems to be that police detained Montieth away from the residence precisely so they could threaten him with an unnecessarily violent entry into the home, with its ensuing trauma to his wife and children (perhaps the police would even have placed them in handcuffs too), in order to get him to agree to cooperate with their investigation. *Montieth*, then, is an especially stark example of how courts sometimes decline to follow the probable-cause requirement when police show that adhering to it would make their jobs more difficult.

Justice Breyer's dissent, for the most part, added little to the arguments previously made by the Second Circuit and other courts that adopted the "as soon as reasonably practicable" rule. He endorsed all of the interests recognized in *Summers*, including the flight interest, without seriously engaging Justice Scalia's arguments or explaining why, in his view, those interests were legitimate.[107] The best justification he could muster for his rule was that it was possible an emerging occupant might notice officers preparing to execute the warrant and then notify those inside the house, who in turn could flee with or destroy the evidence or prepare to attack officers as they enter the home.[108] This particular argument, at least, relies on law-

---

[104] *Id.*

[105] *Id.* at 667.

[106] *Id.*

[107] Bailey, 133 S. Ct. at 1046–47 (Breyer, J., dissenting).

[108] *Id.* at 1047–48.

enforcement interests that are distinct from "ordinary" ones. But it is nonetheless unpersuasive.

First of all, the argument relies on a sequence of speculative possibilities: "[T]hose emerging occupants might have seen the officers outside the house. And they might have alerted others inside the house. . . . Suppose that an individual inside the house (perhaps under the influence of drugs) had grabbed the gun and begun to fire through the window."[109] Simply because a judge can concoct a hypothetical scenario in which adhering to a Fourth Amendment rule could conceivably fail to prevent harm cannot be enough, in and of itself, to justify an exception to that rule. The situation must be at least somewhat likely to occur in order to justify a blanket exception from a general Fourth Amendment rule, and Justice Breyer's elaborate hypothetical was anything but.

Putting that objection to one side, however, there's an even more basic problem: It's not at all clear how allowing police to detain a recent occupant *a mile away from the premises* would prevent the harm Justice Breyer postulated. If, indeed, Bailey had noticed police outside his apartment—he didn't—and if there had been a confederate of Bailey's inside the apartment—there wasn't—and if Bailey had intended to alert that person as to an imminent search so that he could destroy evidence or arm himself—why on earth would Bailey have waited until he was nearly a mile away from his apartment to phone or text a warning? Wouldn't he (or his passenger) have done so almost immediately, in which case detaining Bailey after he had driven for several minutes would have done nothing to prevent the sequence of events Justice Breyer worried about? That this was Justice Breyer's strongest argument is perhaps all the evidence needed to show that his position was wrong on the merits.

A Missed Opportunity

Although the Court reached the correct result in *Bailey*, both the majority opinion and Justice Scalia's concurrence are, in one way, frustrating: The reasoning in each, if followed to its conclusion, would require narrowing the *Summers* rule itself. Yet neither the majority nor the concurrence was willing even to suggest that possibility.

[109] *Id.*

Take the majority opinion first. In purporting to apply the *Summers* interests, the Court subtly modified them. It emphasized that police have an interest in maintaining their own safety during the search, but recognized that occupants who are not inside the home during the search pose much less risk.[110] It cited the interest in "the orderly completion of the search" but emphasized that "[i]f occupants are permitted to wander around the premises, there is the potential for interference with the execution of the search warrant" while largely dismissing *Summers*'s acknowledged interest in opening locked doors and containers.[111] And it reduced the flight interest to one that "serves to preserve the integrity of the search by controlling those persons who are on the scene. If police officers are concerned about flight, and have to keep close supervision of occupants who are not restrained, they might rush the search, causing unnecessary damage to property or compromising its careful execution."[112]

Yet if *Bailey* is correct about which government interests are properly relevant, it's difficult to understand why the *Summers* rule is as broad as it is. Why, if the legitimate law-enforcement justifications boil down to the interest in maintaining control over the site of the search, shouldn't police have to give an occupant the choice between leaving freely (in which case the occupant, like Bailey, would not be in a position to wander through the home, harm officers, destroy evidence, or otherwise interfere with the search) or remaining in the home but being detained (which would preclude any interference)? Indeed, Summers himself was detained outside his home, while he was in the process of leaving; given that fact, it's far from clear that the legitimate interests *Bailey* relied on actually shake out differently on the facts of the two cases.

The Court took the position that there was something magical about the line demarcating the "immediate vicinity" of the premises. But it seems like the more sensible line, for purposes of the detention power, would be between those who choose to remain present at the site of the search and those who do not. Of course, there's a possibility that a person who chooses to leave the site of a search might later return and harm police. But as *Bailey* explained, police

---

[110] Bailey, 133 S. Ct. at 1039.

[111] *Id.* at 1040.

[112] *Id.*

could "mitigate that risk . . . by taking routine precautions, for instance by erecting barricades or posting someone on the perimeter or at the door."[113]

Drawing the constitutional line between occupants who choose to remain and those who do not has two key virtues. First, it's easier to administer than the majority's line. There is no need to evaluate "the lawful limits of the premises, whether the occupant was within the line of sight of his dwelling," or "the ease of reentry from the occupant's location."[114] Second, and more importantly, it avoids intrusions on liberty that—as the Court's opinion in *Bailey* tells us—are justified by *no* government interest that should legitimately trump the Fourth Amendment's presumptive requirements.

Justice Scalia can usually be relied upon for candor, especially when writing separately; he is more willing than most justices are to criticize precedent.[115] Yet he too declined to question the *Summers* rule despite implicitly recognizing its flaws. He criticized the Court's opinion in *Summers* for setting forth a "smorgasbord" of interests, only one of which ("carrying out the search unimpeded by violence or other disruptions") he deemed legitimate.[116] But he accepted the substance of the original *Summers* rule and the majority's "immediate vicinity" limitation without qualification. And he did so even though, as explained above, the interest in executing the search free of disruptions would seem to justify only a narrower power to detain those who *choose* to remain on premises. More's the pity; an opinion by Justice Scalia questioning the *Summers* rule could have laid the groundwork for its rollback in a later case.[117]

There are times, of course, when it is not worth revisiting past decisions. Perhaps we should be grateful that the Court declined to extend a dubious precedent into new territory and leave it at that. *Summers*, however, seems especially deserving of reconsideration. The intrusions on liberty that it authorizes are significant. Although *Summers* asserted that detentions pursuant to search warrants are

[113] 133 S. Ct. at 1039.

[114] *Id.* at 1042.

[115] See, e.g., Thornton v. United States, 541 U.S. 615, 630–32 (2004) (Scalia, J., concurring in the judgment) (criticizing *Belton*).

[116] Bailey, 133 S. Ct. at 1044 (Scalia, J., concurring).

[117] Cf. Arizona v. Gant, 556 U.S. 332, 344–43 (2009) (limiting *Belton* and endorsing Justice Scalia's separate opinion in *Thornton v. United States*, 541 U.S. 615 (2004)).

less intrusive than arrests, it's clear today that that isn't so. Why should the government have a categorical power to keep an occupant of a home in handcuffs for hours during a search—like in *Muehler v. Mena*—simply because she had the bad luck to be within the "immediate vicinity" of her home when police showed up to perform the search? Why couldn't police ensure the integrity of the search scene and their own safety by giving her the opportunity to leave before starting the search?

Second, the moment seems especially ripe for the Court to do more than it has to rein in, or at least question, aggressive police search tactics. As journalist Radley Balko has ably demonstrated, violent, military-style SWAT team raids are becoming the norm when police execute search warrants—even for minor crimes.[118] Such tactics lead to trauma, injuries, and sometimes death for residents of the homes being searched—many of whom turn out to be innocent of any crime. Although *Bailey* did not deal with such a fact pattern, now might have been as good a time as any to suggest to police that their need to "exercise unquestioned command"[119] during a search must be balanced against the constitutional rights of those present at homes being searched.

Despite the foregoing criticism of *Bailey*'s specifics, however, I don't mean to lose sight of all that is good about *Bailey*—for there is much to like. *Bailey* got the correct result, and in doing so both the majority and the concurrence approached the case the right way, focusing attention on what made the search-warrant context special, rather than relying on reasoning that could undercut the probable-cause requirement across the board. And although the Court didn't say anything explicitly to undermine the breadth of the *Summers* rule, it's possible someday that *Bailey*'s reasoning—which, as noted, significantly undermines *Summers* itself—will eventually lead to the Court's narrowing the *Summers* rule. Perhaps, as Justice Scalia recently predicted in a dissent in a different Fourth Amendment case, "At the end of the day, *logic will out*."[120] We can only hope.

---

[118] See generally Radley Balko, Rise of the Warrior Cop: The Militarization of America's Police Forces (2013).

[119] Summers, 452 U.S. at 703.

[120] Maryland v. King, 133 S. Ct. 1958, 1989 (2013) (Scalia, J., dissenting) (emphasis in original).

Conclusion: The Bigger Picture

Much more important than the result in *Bailey* itself is what the case demonstrates about the current state of Fourth Amendment doctrine. Consider the difference between *Summers* and *Bailey*. *Summers* relied on an incoherent mishmash of government interests to justify the detention in that case. And it suggested no limiting principle to ensure that exceptions can't swallow the probable-cause requirement entirely. In *Bailey*, by contrast, six justices recognized, implicitly or explicitly, the need for principled limits for exceptions to Fourth Amendment rules.

And *Bailey* is no isolated example. Just four years ago, *Gant* significantly narrowed the *Belton* rule. And consider some of the decisions from just the last two terms. In *United States v. Jones*, the Court unanimously concluded that police installation of a GPS device on a vehicle constituted a search.[121] So is the use of a drug-sniffing dog on the porch of a house, according to *Florida v. Jardines*.[122] *Missouri v. McNeely* rejected a per se rule that nonconsensual blood tests in drunken-driving cases always constitute exigent circumstances making a warrant unnecessary.[123]

At least part of the credit for these results belongs to a renewed interest on the Court in looking to the Fourth Amendment for clear principles that can be applied to individual cases—what I call taking the amendment seriously as law. *Gant* insisted that exceptions to the probable-cause requirement for searches cannot become untethered from their legitimate justifications. Rather than conducting fuzzy balancing tests, *Jones* and *Jardines* both rested on property-law rationales. A "property-rights baseline" doesn't let the scope of the Fourth Amendment's protection depend on judges' assessments of societal interests in privacy but instead "keeps easy cases easy."[124] A plurality in *McNeely* hewed to previously recognized Fourth Amendment principles, rejecting a "modified *per se* rule" in favor of the traditional exigent circumstances doctrine.[125]

---

[121] 132 S. Ct. 945, 949 (2012).
[122] 133 S. Ct. 1409, 1417–18 (2013).
[123] 133 S. Ct. 1552, 1563 (2013).
[124] Jardines, 133 S. Ct. at 1417.
[125] 133 S. Ct. at 1563 (plurality op.).

And while *Maryland v. King* declared that DNA testing of all those arrested for serious offenses is reasonable,[126] perhaps what's surprising about that case is that the vote was so close. Many people have gut reactions that the government's crime-solving interest strongly outweighs the privacy intrusion to arrestees of having their cheeks swabbed. Yet Justice Scalia's dissent was one vote away from declaring such searches impermissible. What's more, the majority felt compelled to argue the case on the dissent's terms. Thirty years ago, the Court might simply have balanced the interests and declared the swabs reasonable in light of the government's strong interest in solving crimes, notwithstanding the lack of articulable suspicion. Today, however, the Court had to at least try to come up with justifications (such as "identifying arrestees"[127]) distinct from the ordinary interest in solving crime (although its attempt to do so was not particularly persuasive).[128]

The Fourth Amendment developments highlighted here should be seen as part of a broader effort on the Court in recent years, led by Justice Scalia, to be more rigorous about identifying and consistently enforcing the specific rights protected by constitutional provisions governing the criminal process. The Court has recognized that what the Confrontation Clause protects is not "reliability" writ large, but instead the specific right to confront those who bear testimony against you.[129] The right to a criminal jury means that all findings necessary to increase the maximum sentence authorized by law must be made by a jury, regardless of whether those findings are labeled "elements" or "sentencing factors."[130] Violations of the Sixth Amendment right to one's chosen counsel cannot be declared harmless whenever the defendant receives a fair trial, for "[t]he right to counsel of choice . . . commands not that a trial be fair, but that *a particular guarantee of fairness be provided*—to wit, that the accused be

---

[126] 133 S. Ct. 1958, 1980 (2013).

[127] *Id.* at 1976.

[128] Similarly, *Florence v. Board of Chosen Freeholders of County of Burlington* upheld the right of prison officials to conduct strip searches of arrestees who enter into a jail's general population based on the government's prison-specific security interests. 132 S. Ct. 1510, 1520 (2012).

[129] Crawford v. Washington, 541 U.S. 36, 61–62 (2004) (overruling Ohio v. Roberts, 448 U.S. 56 (1980)).

[130] Apprendi v. New Jersey, 530 U.S. 466, 494 (2000).

defended by the counsel he believes to be best."[131] As *Bailey* demonstrates, that movement has made great inroads into Fourth Amendment doctrine. Although one can certainly argue about some of the specifics,[132] as a general matter that development is welcome—at least for those who believe that the Fourth Amendment should impose real constraints on police action.

This isn't to say that defenders of a robust Fourth Amendment have no reason to worry. Recent cases may conceal underlying disagreement over remedial questions; although Justice Scalia has forged a coalition with Justices Ginsburg, Sotomayor, and Kagan, he almost certainly disagrees with them on the scope—perhaps even the legitimacy—of the exclusionary rule.[133] Moreover, Justice Scalia will not be on the Court forever, and the next generation of conservative justices seems to have less interest in a principled approach to Fourth Amendment analysis. That's especially true of Justice Alito, who has yet to demonstrate that he believes that the Fourth Amendment imposes meaningful constraints on police. Nor is the liberal bloc solid; Justice Breyer's pragmatic methodology has seemed recently to be leading him to favor the government on Fourth Amendment issues.[134] The pendulum could certainly swing back.

That uncertain future aside, however, *Bailey* shows how much the Court's approach has changed since the days of *Belton*, *Summers*, and similar cases. Freeform, all-things-considered reasonableness assessments are out of fashion. The Court is taking that "doggone Fourth Amendment"[135] seriously as a source of binding rules.

---

[131] United States v. Gonzalez-Lopez, 548 U.S. 140, 146 (2006) (emphasis added).

[132] See *supra* note 86 (discussing disagreement over whether Fourth Amendment doctrine incorporates common-law rules).

[133] See, e.g., Hudson v. Michigan, 547 U.S. 586 (2006) (Scalia, J.) (holding, over four dissenting votes, including that of Justice Ginsburg, that violations of knock-and-announce requirement do not require suppression).

[134] This past term, Justice Breyer sided with the prosecution in every divided Fourth Amendment case: *Bailey*, *King*, *McNeely*, and *Jardines*; earlier, he had also dissented in *Gant*.

[135] Transcript of Oral Argument, *supra* note 53, at 57.

Two Steps Forward for the "Poor Relation" of Constitutional Law: *Koontz, Arkansas Game & Fish,* and the Future of the Takings Clause

*Ilya Somin**

Introduction

Despite occasional judicial protestations to the contrary, property rights protected by the Fifth Amendment's Takings Clause have long been "relegated to the status of a poor relation" in Supreme Court jurisprudence.[1] Since the 1930s, federal courts have rarely given them the level of protection routinely accorded most other constitutional rights.[2] Over the last 25 to 30 years, however, Takings Clause issues have been more seriously contested in the Court than previously, and property rights have had a modest revival. During the 2012–2013 Supreme Court term, property rights advocates won three notable victories: *Arkansas Game & Fish Commission v. United States,*[3] *Koontz v. St. Johns River Water Management District,*[4] and *Horne v. Department of Agriculture.*[5] These decisions stop well short of completely ending the

*Professor of Law, George Mason University School of Law. For helpful suggestions and comments, I would like to thank James Ely, Rick Hills, Tim Mulvaney, and Ilya Shapiro. I would also like to thank Nate Pettine for excellent research assistance.

[1] Dolan v. City of Tigard, 512 U.S. 374, 392 (1994).

[2] See Ilya Somin, Taking Property Rights Seriously? The Supreme Court and the "Poor Relation" of Constitutional Law, George Mason Law & Econ. Research Paper No. 08-53 (2008), available at http://ssrn.com/abstract=1247854 (discussing this trend and the rationales offered to justify it); see also James W. Ely Jr., The Guardian of Every Other Right: A Constitutional History of Property Rights 125–42 (9th ed. 2008) (discussing the origins of this trend in the New Deal era).

[3] 133 S. Ct. 511 (2012).

[4] 133 S. Ct. 2586 (2013).

[5] 133 S. Ct. 2053 (2013).

"poor relation" status of the Takings Clause, but they are noteworthy steps in the right direction.

This article considers the significance of *Arkansas Game & Fish* and *Koontz*, arguing that both cases are potentially important victories for property rights, and that the Court decided both correctly. But because both rulings also left some key issues unresolved, their full impact may not be evident for some time to come. Unlike the other two cases, *Horne* focuses primarily on procedural issues and is therefore covered in Joshua Hawley's contribution to this volume.[6]

In Part I, I discuss *Arkansas Game & Fish*, the less controversial of the two cases. The Court's unanimous decision makes clear that when the government repeatedly and deliberately floods property owners' land, it is possible that the resulting damage qualifies as a taking for which "just compensation" must be paid under the Fifth Amendment. The Court's unanimity is a rebuke to the extreme position taken by the federal government in the case. But it also leaves a number of crucial issues for later resolution by lower courts, and perhaps future Supreme Court decisions.

Part II considers *Koontz*, which ruled that there can potentially be a taking in a situation where a landowner was refused a permit to develop his land by a government agency, unless he agreed to, among other things, pay for off-site repair and maintenance work on other land in the area that he did not own.[7] *Koontz* thereby limits the government's ability to use permit processes and other land-use restrictions as leverage to force property owners to perform various services. The case could turn out to be the most important property rights victory in the Supreme Court in some time. In part for this reason, the Court was much more divided than in *Arkansas Game & Fish*, with the justices splitting 5–4 along ideological lines. Like the term's other major Takings Clause case, *Koontz* leaves some crucial issues for later determination, including the question of what kinds

---

[6] See Joshua Hawley, The Beginning of the End? *Horne v. Department of Agriculture* and the Future of *Williamson County*, 2012-2013 Cato Sup. Ct. Rev. 245 (2013). For my own thoughts on *Horne*, see Ilya Somin, A Modest, But Potentially Significant Supreme Court Victory for Property Rights, Volokh Conspiracy, Jun. 10, 2013, http://www.volokh.com/2013/06/10/a-modest-but-potentially-significant-supreme-victory-for-property-rights.

[7] *Koontz*, 133 S. Ct. at 2591–93.

of remedies property owners are entitled to in cases where their Takings Clause rights are violated by permit denials.

Finally, the conclusion briefly discusses the implications of these decisions for the future of constitutional property rights. Although both cases represent incremental progress, there is still a long way to go before property rights cease to get second-class treatment from the Court. Moreover, the deep ideological division over *Koontz* reinforces the reality that judicial enforcement of Takings Clause property rights lacks the kind of cross-ideological support needed to firmly establish it in the long run. At the same time, these cases show that protection for property rights is making incremental gains.

I. *Arkansas Game & Fish Commission v. United States*

Arkansas Game & Fish addressed a case that arose from the U.S. Army Corps of Engineers' repeated, deliberate flooding of forest land owned by an Arkansas state agency responsible for management of public wildlife habitats. Between 1993 and 2000, the Army Corps repeatedly engaged in deliberate flooding of the Dave Donaldson Black River Wildlife Management Area, owned by the Arkansas Game & Fish Commission; as a result, some 18 million board feet of timber were damaged or destroyed, and the area's function as a habitat for migratory birds and other animals was significantly impaired.[8]

At the trial stage, the Court of Federal Claims ruled that this deliberate flooding qualified as a taking.[9] But the U.S. Court of Appeals for the Federal Circuit reversed this ruling, concluding that because the floods created by the Corps of Engineers "were only temporary, they cannot constitute a taking."[10]

A. *The Court's Holding and Its Limits*

In a narrowly drawn opinion written by Justice Ruth Bader Ginsburg, the Supreme Court reversed the Federal Circuit decision but limited its holding to the proposition that "recurrent floodings, even if of finite duration, are not categorically exempt from Takings Clause liability."[11] As the Court's opinion emphasizes, "We

[8] Ark. Game & Fish Comm'n, 133 S. Ct. at 515–18.

[9] Ark. Game & Fish Comm'n v. United States, 87 Fed. Cl. 594 (2009).

[10] Ark. Game & Fish Comm'n v. United States, 637 F.3d 1366, 1378 (Fed. Cir. 2011).

[11] Ark. Game & Fish Comm'n, 133 S. Ct. at 515.

rule today, simply and only, that government-induced flooding temporary in duration gains no automatic exemption from Takings Clause inspection."[12]

The ruling leaves open a large number of other issues relevant to the determination of what kinds of government-induced flooding qualify as takings. Justice Ginsburg does note several factors that are relevant to such determinations, including the duration of the flooding, "the character of the land at issue and the owner's 'reasonable investment-backed expectations' regarding the land's use," and "the degree to which the invasion is intended or is the foreseeable result of authorized government action."[13] But the Court does not tell us how long the flooding must continue before it is long enough to qualify as a taking, what degree of intent or foreseeability is required, in what ways "the character of the land" matters, how much in the way of "investment-backed expectations" the owner must have, or how these four factors should be weighed against each other in cases where they cut in opposite directions.

Brian Hodges of the Pacific Legal Foundation, a leading pro-property rights public interest firm, argues that the Court's brief citation of these four factors may confuse litigants and lower court judges because it "lists, without any differentiation, various tests that have been developed over the years to determine different types of takings in very different circumstances."[14] Hodges further suggests that *Arkansas Game & Fish* may perpetuate preexisting confusion in the lower courts over the distinction between temporary and permanent physical occupation takings cases.[15]

The Court also did not even clearly address the federal government's extremely dubious argument that damage inflicted by flooding on downstream owners is categorically excluded from qualifying

---

[12] *Id*. at 522.

[13] *Id*. at 522–23 (quoting Palazzolo v. Rhode Island, 533 U.S. 606, 618 (2001)).

[14] Brian T. Hodges, Will *Arkansas Game & Fish Commission v. United States* Provide a Permanent Fix for Temporary Takings?, Boston College Environmental Affairs L. Rev. (forthcoming), available at http://papers.ssrn.com/sol3/papers.cfm?abstract_id=2262908, at 18. Hodges was also lead counsel on the joint PLF-Cato Institute-Atlantic Legal Foundation amicus brief in the case. Brief for Pacific Legal Foundation et al. as Amici Curiae in Support of Petitioner, Ark. Game & Fish Comm'n v. United States, 133 S. Ct. 511 (2012) (No. 11-597), available at http://www.cato.org/publications/legal-briefs/arkansas-game-fish-commission-v-united-states-1.

[15] *Id*. at 19–23.

as a taking, even though the justices expressed great skepticism about this claim at the oral argument.[16] It similarly remanded for further consideration the federal government's argument that much of the flood damage inflicted on Arkansas' property was not really caused by the Corps' actions.[17] These and other issues will have to be dealt with by the lower court on remand, and by other federal and state courts in future cases.

Quite possibly, the justices bought unity at the expense of clarity. This ruling could be an example of Chief Justice John Roberts's much-discussed efforts to seek unanimity by limiting the scope of holdings. As Roberts explained in 2006, he believes that "[t]he more cautious approach, the approach that can get the most justices to sign onto it, is the preferred approach," in part because it "contributes . . . to stability in the law."[18] But we probably will not have real "stability" in this area of law until the Court develops clearer standards for determining what kinds of flooding qualify as takings. In the meantime, it seems clear that *Arkansas Game & Fish* will result in further litigation in the lower courts, as property owners and government agencies advance competing interpretations of the Court's vague criteria.

B. What the Court Got Right—Without Going Far Enough

As far as it goes, the Court's decision is clearly correct. There is no good reason to hold that temporary flooding can never count as a taking. This is especially true if the flooding was deliberate and inflicted permanent damage on the property owner's land. Other temporary physical invasions of property, such as overflights by aircraft,[19] qualify as takings, and there is nothing special about flooding that should lead the Court to create a categorical exception for it.

---

[16] See Ark. Game & Fish Comm'n, 133 S. Ct at 521–22 (declining to reach this issue). For my analysis of the discussion of this claim in the oral argument, see Ilya Somin, Today's Oral Argument in Arkansas Game and Fish Commission v. United States, Volokh Conspiracy, Oct. 3, 2012, http://www.volokh.com/2012/10/03/todays-oral-argument-in-arkansas-game-and-fish-commission-v-united-states.

[17] *Id.* at 522–23.

[18] Quoted in Mark Sherman, Roberts Touts Unanimity on Court, Wash. Post, Nov. 17, 2006, available at http://www.washingtonpost.com/wp-dyn/content/article/2006/11/17/AR2006111700999.html.

[19] United States v. Causby, 328 U.S. 256 (1946).

To the contrary, allowing the government to temporarily flood private property without paying any compensation whatsoever would severely undermine the purpose of the just-compensation element of the Takings Clause, which, as a 1960 decision put it, is to "bar Government from forcing some people alone to bear public burdens which, in all fairness and justice, should be borne by the public as a whole."[20] If temporary flooding was completely exempted from Takings Clause scrutiny, the government would have free rein to flood and destroy property at will any time it furthered a policy objective or advanced the interests of politically influential interest groups, like the agricultural interests that benefited from the Corps' actions in this case.[21]

But the Court should have gone further and recognized that what ultimately matters is not the duration of the flooding, but that of the damage inflicted. If the government deliberately damages and destroys private property by physically occupying it with water or anything else, it has no less "taken" it if the destruction occurs quickly than if it takes a longer time. Either way, the effect is permanent and private property has been taken and destroyed by the government in order to advance some policy objective. As the Supreme Court explained in the 1871 case of *Pumpelly v. Green Bay Co.*, interpreting Wisconsin's state constitutional takings clause (the wording of which is nearly identical to the federal one):

> It would be a very curious and unsatisfactory result if in construing a provision of constitutional law always understood to have been adopted for protection and security to the rights of the individual as against the government, and which has received the commendation of jurists, statesmen, and commentators as placing the just principles of the common law on that subject beyond the power of ordinary legislation to change or control them, it shall be held that if the government refrains from the absolute conversion of real property to the uses of the public it can destroy its value entirely, can inflict irreparable and permanent injury to any extent, can, in effect, subject it to total destruction without making any compensation, because, in the narrowest

[20] Armstrong v. United States, 364 U.S. 40, 49 (1960).

[21] See Ark. Game & Fish Comm'n, 87 Fed. Cl. at 599–605 (describing the role of different interest groups in influencing the Corps' plans).

sense of that word, it is not taken for the public use. Such a construction would pervert the constitutional provision into a restriction upon the rights of the citizen, as those rights stood at the common law, instead of the government, and make it an authority for invasion of private right under the pretext of the public good, which had no warrant in the laws or practices of our ancestors.[22]

For this reason, the Supreme Court ruled that the government was liable under Wisconsin's takings clause when it deliberately flooded a property owner's land by building a dam that directed water toward it.[23] The key factor, as Justice Samuel Miller recognized, was the infliction of "irreparable and permanent injury," which can occur irrespective of the duration of the flooding.[24] The federal Takings Clause, of course, is "almost identical in language" to Wisconsin's,[25] and has much the same purposes.

Arkansas Game & Fish could thus have made a stronger statement than simply concluding that "government-induced flooding temporary in duration gains no automatic exemption from Takings Clause inspection."[26] It might instead have held that such deliberate flooding is always a taking if it inflicts significant permanent damage on the property in question.

Despite the very limited nature of the Court's holding, some commentators worry that the Court went too far, rather than not far enough. For example, Jon Kusler of the Association of State Wetland Managers claims that the decision will result in large amounts of "time-consuming, expensive, and technical" litigation, because "[l]andowners subject to even limited amounts of temporary flooding caused or exacerbated by governments may now claim (whether successful [sic] or not) a temporary taking."[27] Professor Timothy Mulvaney worries that, in rejecting arguments that the "sky is falling" if

---

[22] Pumpelly v. Green Bay Co., 80 U.S. 166, 177–78 (1871).

[23] *Id.* at 176–82.

[24] *Id.* at 177.

[25] *Id.* Compare U.S. Const. amend. V ("nor shall private property be taken for public use, without just compensation") with Wisc. Const. art. I, § 13 ("The property of no person shall be taken for public use without just compensation therefore.").

[26] Ark. Game & Fish Comm'n, 133 S. Ct. at 522.

[27] John Kusler, Implications to Floodplain and Wetland Managers of Arkansas Game & Fish Commission v. United States, Wetland News (Dec. 2012), at 2–3.

courts allow takings claims in temporary flooding cases, "the Court significantly understated the impact of its takings jurisprudence on the efforts of government officials charged with protecting the public health, safety, and the environment through the regulation of land uses."[28]

As discussed above, *Arkansas Game & Fish* will indeed likely lead to additional litigation, in part because of the vagueness of the Court's standards for determining what counts as a taking in temporary flooding cases. But there is no reason to believe that such cases will be inherently more difficult than takings cases in other contexts, or cases involving the adjudication of many other constitutional rights. For example, Fourth Amendment cases, free-speech cases, freedom-of-religion cases, and numerous others all often involve complex circumstances that vary from case to case and locality to locality.[29] If such difficulties should not lead us to abandon judicial review in these areas, then they should not deter courts from protecting Takings Clause property rights.[30]

Moreover, the amount of litigation is likely to decline over time as courts establish clearer rules in the course of addressing new cases. Even initially, it is likely that only landowners whose property has suffered fairly extensive damage will file suit. Even if there is a reasonable probability of winning, few will want to litigate cases where the damages that might be obtained are outweighed by the substantial costs of litigation itself.

Finally, allowing liability in such cases does not prevent beneficial regulation, and may actually improve the quality of regulatory policy. After all, requiring compensation for takings caused by temporary flooding does not actually bar such flooding, but merely requires the government to compensate landowners whose property has been damaged as a result. If the government is sensitive to costs,

---

[28] Timothy Mulvaney, Takings Case Set for Oral Argument at the SCOTUS on January 15th, Envtl. L. Prof Blog, Jan. 13, 2013, http://lawprofessors.typepad.com/environmental_law/2013/01/takings-case-set-for-oral-argument-at-the-scotus-on-january-15th-.html. But see Ark. Game & Fish Comm'n, 133 S. Ct. at 521 (rejecting this kind of "slippery slope argument").

[29] See Ilya Somin, Federalism and Property Rights, 2011 U. Chi. Legal Forum 53, 80–84 (discussing these complexities and comparing them to those in takings cases).

[30] *Id.* at 80–87 (discussing why there should not be a double standard cutting against property rights in this field).

this will strengthen its incentives to resort to flooding only when the benefits outweigh the costs. If it does not have to pay compensation, the government has incentives to ignore the damage caused by its regulations, except perhaps in cases where the victims are politically powerful. As Professor Jonathan Adler has explained, requiring the government to pay takings compensation can actually improve environmental policy by incentivizing officials to focus regulatory efforts on initiatives that are likely to create the greatest benefits at the least total cost to society, including property owners.[31]

Such benefits will not materialize in situations where government agencies are indifferent to the fiscal costs of their actions, of course. But where that is the case, it is also unlikely that requiring compensation will deter officials from engaging in beneficial flooding.

Ultimately, the slippery-slope objections against *Arkansas Game & Fish* fail, because they could just as easily be made against enforcement of the Takings Clause in other contexts. As Justice Ginsburg writes in her opinion:

> Time and again in Takings Clause cases, the Court has heard the prophecy that recognizing a just compensation claim would unduly impede the government's ability to act in the public interest. . . . We have rejected this argument when deployed to urge blanket exemptions from the Fifth Amendment's instruction. While we recognize the importance of the public interests the Government advances in this case, we do not see them as categorically different from the interests at stake in myriad other Takings Clause cases. The sky did not fall after *Causby* [allowed takings liability for plane overflights] and today's modest decision augurs no deluge of takings liability.[32]

There is a strong case that the Court should have gone further than it did in protecting property rights in *Arkansas Game & Fish*. But it is hard to argue that it went too far, without simultaneously rejecting judicial enforcement of a wide range of other constitutional rights.

---

[31] Jonathan Adler, Money or Nothing: The Adverse Environmental Consequences of Uncompensated Regulatory Takings, 49 B.C. L. Rev. 301 (2008); see also James W. Ely Jr., Property Rights and Environmental Regulation: The Case for Compensation, 28 Harv. J. L. & Pub. Pol'y 51 (2004) (making a similar argument).

[32] Ark. Game & Fish Comm'n, 133 S. Ct. at 521.

A final argument that the Court went too far is based on claims that it should not have gone against the rule outlined in the 1924 case of *Sanguinetti v. United States*,[33] the main precedent relied on by the United States. *Sanguinetti* states that an "overflow" must "constitute an actual, permanent invasion of the land" in order to be considered a taking.[34] However, that case primarily turned on the fact that there was "no permanent impairment of value" to the owner's land, and that any injury he suffered was "indirect and consequential."[35] As Justice Ginsburg notes, "[N]o distinction between permanent and temporary flooding was material to the result in *Sanguinetti*."[36] It is not clear that the 1924 Court would have reached the same decision if the landowner's property had suffered permanent damage as a result of temporary government-created flooding.

In addition, as Ginsburg emphasizes, the *Sanguinetti* Court did not assume that temporary flooding cases should be treated any differently from other cases where the government damages private property by means of a deliberate but temporary physical invasion of land. In sum, the *Arkansas Game & Fish* Court was justified in going against this passage in *Sanguinetti*, even if one assumes that it had a strong obligation to defer to precedent. The passage in question was not essential to the outcome of the 1924 case.

Furthermore, the relevant statement was not supported by any detailed textual, historical, or logical reasoning. The only authorities the Court cited to support this statement in *Sanguinetti* were two earlier cases that actually cut the other way, even if not conclusively.[37] One of them held that "where the government by the construction of a dam or other public works so floods lands belonging to an individual as to substantially destroy their value there is a taking within the scope of the Fifth Amendment."[38] This suggests that the crucial factor is the destruction of value rather than the duration of the flooding that caused it. The second case concluded that "[t]here is no

[33] 264 U.S. 146 (1924).

[34] *Id*. at 149.

[35] *Id*. at 149–50.

[36] Ark. Game & Fish Comm., 133 S.Ct. at 520.

[37] See Sanguinetti, 264 U.S. at 149 (citing United States v. Lynah, 188 U. S. 445 (1903) and United States v. Cress, 243 U. S. 316 (1917)).

[38] Lynah, 188 U.S. at 470.

difference of kind, but only of degree, between a permanent condition of continual overflow by backwater and a permanent liability to intermittent but inevitably recurring overflows."[39] While this statement does not cover intermittent flooding that is *not* "inevitably recurring," the same logic surely applies: The difference between "inevitably recurring overflows" and recurring overflows whose future continuation is not inevitable is also one of degree rather than kind.

C. Using the Takings Clause to Protect Public Property as Well as Private

One interesting anomaly in *Arkansas Game & Fish* that has not gotten much attention is the fact that the flooded land was owned by the state of Arkansas, rather than a private owner. The text of the Fifth Amendment protects only "private property" against takings without "just compensation." However, the Supreme Court has long treated federal takings of state property the same way as takings of private property,[40] and the United States did not challenge these longstanding precedents in this case. The relevant precedents are not very persuasive in explaining the reasons why a Takings Clause that only refers to "private property" should be used to protect public property as well. For example, a 1946 Supreme Court decision suggests that public property is protected because the Takings Clause is merely "a tacit recognition of a preexisting power to take private property for public use, rather than a grant of new power."[41] But even if the power to take private property for public use is "preexisting,"[42]

[39] Cress, 243 U.S. at 328.

[40] See, e.g., United States v. Carmack, 329 U.S. 230, 241–42 (1946) ("The Fifth Amendment . . . imposes on the Federal Government the obligation to pay just compensation when it takes another's property for public use in accordance with the federal sovereign power to appropriate it. Accordingly, when the Federal Government thus takes for a federal public use the independently held and controlled property of a state or of a local subdivision, the Federal Government recognizes its obligation to pay just compensation for it."); City of St. Louis v. Western Union Tel. Co., 148 U.S. 92, 101 (1893) (holding that the Takings Clause bars uncompensated federal takings of "property whose ownership and control is in the state [because] it is not within the competency of the national government to dispossess the state of such control and use, or appropriate the same to its own benefit, or the benefit of any of its corporations or grantees, without suitable compensation to the state").

[41] Carmack, 329 U.S. at 241.

[42] For a recent critique of the conventional wisdom that the federal government has broad, inherent authority to condemn property within states, see William Baude, Rethinking the Federal Eminent Domain Power, 122 Yale L. J. 1738 (2013).

the constraint on that power imposed by the requirement of just compensation comes from the Fifth Amendment—and that amendment seems to apply it only to takings of private property.

Longstanding as it is, the Supreme Court's position that the Takings Clause protects government as well as private property is an obvious deviation from the text of the Fifth Amendment. It should perhaps be revisited in an appropriate future case. Be that as it may, the Court was probably justified in not considering this issue in *Arkansas Game & Fish* given that neither party sought to overturn longstanding precedent on the subject.

II. *Koontz v. St. Johns River Water Management District*

The *Koontz* case arose from a situation where Coy Koontz Sr., a Florida property owner, was refused a permit to develop his land by a government agency unless he agreed to, among other things, perform off-site repair and maintenance work on other properties he did not own, which were miles away from his land.[43] When Koontz sought to get a permit to develop his 14.9 acre property, the St. Johns River Water Management District asked him to either cede it a conservation easement over more than 90 percent of the land or "hire contractors to make improvements to District-owned land several miles away."[44] Koontz argued that these demands violated his rights under the Takings Clause. During the course of the prolonged litigation on the subject, Coy Koontz Sr. passed away, and the claims of his estate continued to be asserted by his son, Coy Koontz Jr.[45]

In *Nollan v. California Coastal Commission* (1987)[46] and *Dolan v. City of Tigard* (1994),[47] the Supreme Court ruled that, under the Takings Clause, there must be a connection between the purpose behind a government-imposed physical invasion of property and the objectives of any permit scheme where development permits are conditioned on allowing the invasion. In *Nollan*, the Court held that a

---

[43] Koontz, 133 S. Ct. at 2591–93.

[44] Koontz himself had previously offered to forego development on 11 acres of the land. But the district's offer of barring it on 13.9 acres would still have banned him from developing over 70 percent of the area he sought to build on. *Id*. at 2592–93.

[45] *Id*. at 2591.

[46] 483 U.S. 825 (1987).

[47] 512 U.S. 374 (1994).

requirement that beachfront property owners allow the public to pass through their property lacked an "essential nexus" to their building-permit application.[48] In *Dolan*, the Court extended the logic of *Nollan* by ruling that there must be "rough proportionality" between the degree of the imposition and the government's objectives.[49] Under the *Nollan-Dolan* framework, if either an "essential nexus" or "rough proportionality" is lacking, then a taking has occurred, and the Takings Clause requires that the property owner get just compensation.

These rules are essential to enforcement of the Takings Clause. Without them, the government could essentially wipe out owners' rights to control their property simply by refusing them the right to develop their land in any way unless they do whatever the state demands. Absent the essential-nexus requirement or something like it, the government could use permit schemes as leverage to force owners to give up their property rights for virtually any purpose. Absent rough proportionality, the government could do the same thing in any instance where the landowner's property has even a slight connection to the legitimate purposes of a permit scheme.

Koontz addresses two major issues that previous Supreme Court cases had not covered: (1) Whether the requirements of *Nollan* and *Dolan* apply when the government denies a permit, as opposed to approving it with attached conditions; and (2) whether those requirements apply to cases where the burden imposed by the government is a financial obligation—in this case, paying for improvements on other government-owned land—as opposed to requiring the property owner to allow a physical invasion of his own property. Koontz had prevailed on both issues in a Florida trial court and intermediate appellate court, but lost in the state supreme court.[50]

In an opinion written by Justice Samuel Alito, the Supreme Court answered "yes" to both questions, though it did not determine whether the conditions demanded of Koontz actually violated the requirements of *Nollan* and *Dolan*.[51] The Court was unanimous in rejecting the idea that the *Nollan-Dolan* framework does not apply

[48] Nollan, 483 U.S. at 837–38.

[49] Dolan, 512 U.S. at 391.

[50] Koontz v. St Johns Water Mgmt. Dist., 5 So.3d 8 (Fla. Dist. Ct. App. 2009), rev'd 77 So.3d 1220 (Fla. 2011).

[51] This latter issue will have to be determined by the Florida courts on remand. Koontz, 133 S. Ct. at 2603.

to permit denials, but split 5-4 on the issue of whether it applies to financial exactions. In addition, the Court ruled that permit denials that violate the *Nollan-Dolan* framework qualify as per se takings, as opposed to regulatory-takings cases where the *Penn Central* three-factor balancing test must be applied.[52] This was a crucial conclusion, since the *Penn Central* test is usually applied in ways that are highly favorable to the government, making it difficult for property owners to vindicate their rights.[53]

A. Permit Denials vs. Permit Approvals

Rejection of the federal government's argument that permit denials should be exempt from the Takings Clause scrutiny given to approvals was the one important question in *Koontz* on which all nine justices agreed.[54] Justice Alito's opinion for the Court puts forward several strong arguments for subjecting permit denials to *Nollan-Dolan* Takings Clause scrutiny. As he points out, this distinction has been rejected when applied to constitutional rights other than the Takings Clause.[55] These include freedom of speech and the right to travel, among others.[56] If the St. Johns River Water Management District refused to issue Koontz a permit unless he refused to stop criticizing its land use regulations, few would deny that his First Amendment rights were violated. The same logic applies to situa-

[52] *Id.* at 2600 (citing Penn. Central Transp. Co. v. City of New York, 438 U.S. 104, 124 (1978)).

[53] A 2003 study found that property owners prevail in fewer than 10 percent of cases where the *Penn Central* test is applied (including 13.4 percent of cases that reached the merits stage). See F. Patrick Hubbard et al., Do Owners Have a Fair Chance of Prevailing Under the Ad Hoc Regulatory Takings Test of Penn Central Transportation Company?, 14 Duke Env. L. & Pol'y F. 121, 141–42 (2003). The authors claim that the 13.4 percent success rate is not especially low when one considers that all but one of the cases where property owners lost were ones where low litigation costs or high potential rewards justified pursuing a case with a low probability of success. *Id.* However, the fact that nearly all of the *Penn Central* cases in the authors' sample involved instances where plaintiffs had incentives to go forward with even a low probability of success merely underscores the reality that the test is tilted against owners.

[54] See Koontz, 133 S. Ct. at 2594–97 (majority's rejection of the approval-denial distinction); *id.* at 2603 (Kagan, J., dissenting) (stating that "I think the Court gets the first question it addresses right").

[55] Koontz, 133 S. Ct. at 2594–95.

[56] See *id.* (citing Perry v. Sindermann, 408 U.S. 593 (1972) (freedom of speech) and Memorial Hospital v. Maricopa County, 415 U.S. 250 (1974) (right to travel)).

tions where the government denies permits to property owners who refuse to surrender their constitutional right to compensation for the taking of their property by the state. As Alito puts it:

> We have said in a variety of contexts that "the government may not deny a benefit to a person because he exercises a constitutional right . . . ." Those cases reflect an overarching principle, known as the unconstitutional conditions doctrine, that vindicates the Constitution's enumerated rights by preventing the government from coercing people into giving them up.[57]

Justice Alito also correctly points out that "[a] contrary rule would be especially untenable in this case because it would enable the government to evade the limitations of *Nollan* and *Dolan* simply by phrasing its demands for property as conditions precedent to permit approval."[58] If the federal government had prevailed on this issue, "a government order stating that a permit is 'approved if' the owner turns over property would be subject to *Nollan* and *Dolan*, but an identical order that uses the words 'denied until' would not."[59] It should be emphasized that virtually any other constitutional right could be undermined in the same way. For example, a government seeking to use permit systems to restrict freedom of speech or religion could simply draft orders stating that land-use permits (or any other type of permit) are "denied until" the applicant stops criticizing the government or practicing a particular religion.

Despite the Court's unanimity on this issue, its rejection of the approval-denial distinction has drawn a certain amount of criticism. University of Vermont law professor John Echeverria, a leading critic of judicial enforcement of restrictions on land-use regulation and eminent domain, worries that this part of the decision "will very likely encourage local government officials to avoid any discussion with developers related to permit conditions that, in the end, might have let both sides find common ground on building projects that are good for the community and environmentally sound. Rather than risk a lawsuit through an attempt at compromise, many

---

[57] *Id.* at 2594 (quoting Regan v. Taxation with Representation of Wash., 461 U.S. 540, 545 (1983)).

[58] *Id.* at 2596.

[59] *Id.*

municipalities will simply reject development applications outright—or, worse, accept development plans they shouldn't."[60]

This criticism can, of course, be applied to judicial enforcement of *any* restrictions on government's ability to use permit denials as leverage to extract concessions from landowners, or private individuals seeking other kinds of permits. If the government is not allowed to demand restrictions on freedom of speech, religion, Fourth Amendment rights, or any other constitutional rights when it negotiates with private parties, there is a chance that it will instead refuse to negotiate and simply deny permits—or, alternatively, issue them unwisely.

In practice, however, governments can deal with the danger of lawsuits by restricting the demands they impose on landowners to those that are unlikely to violate the Takings Clause—just as they currently try to avoid making demands that would force landowners to give up other constitutional rights. Even demands that would otherwise implicate the Takings Clause would be constitutionally permissible under *Koontz*, so long as they were coupled with an offer of adequate compensation. In this respect, the enforcement of Takings Clause just-compensation rights actually imposes *fewer* constraints on permit processes than enforcement of most other constitutional rights. The government cannot remedy violations of free-speech rights or freedom of religion by offering financial rewards to people who are willing to give up those rights in exchange for permits. In the case of the Takings Clause's just compensation element, however, such a strategy is perfectly permissible, because the payment

---

[60] John D. Echeverria, A Legal Blow to Sustainable Development, N.Y. Times, June 27, 2013, available at http://www.nytimes.com/2013/06/27/opinion/a-legal-blow-to-sustainable-development.html. Echeverria attributes this concern to Justice Elena Kagan's dissent, but, as discussed below, the dissent actually endorses this part of the majority's decision. Kagan does, however, raise a similar concern about the majority's resolution of the second issue. Koontz, 133 S. Ct. at 2610 (Kagan, J., dissenting). Cf. Timothy Mulvaney, Koontz: 5-4 Supreme Court Sides with Landowner in Takings Case, Env. L. Prof Blog, June 25, 2013, http://lawprofessors.typepad.com/environmental_law/2013/06/koontz-5-4-supreme-court-sides-with-landowner-in-takings-case.html (*Koontz* "is nearly certain to place a significant chilling effect on regulator-landowner coordination. Governmental officials may be forced into uncommunicative rejections or unconditioned approvals of development applications when a more amenable compromise may have been available"); see also Mark Fenster, Failed Exactions, 36 Vt. L. Rev. 623, 643–44 (2012) (arguing that imposing *Nollan-Dolan* scrutiny on government demands that are rejected would unduly impede negotiations).

of compensation for restrictions on property rights is precisely the right at issue.

B. *Extending the* Nollan-Dolan *Framework to Cover Financial Exactions*

Although the Court's rejection of the approval-denial distinction was not completely uncontroversial, far more criticism has been leveled at its holding that the *Nollan-Dolan* framework applies to financial exactions imposed on property owners, not just direct physical invasions of their land.

1. *A Flood of Litigation?*

In a forceful dissenting opinion written on behalf of the four liberal justices, Justice Elena Kagan warns that "the majority's approach . . . threatens significant practical harm" because it would lead to Takings Clause litigation over the "many kinds of permitting fees" that state and local governments "impose every day," including those that mitigate pollution, pay for public services such as sewage, and "limit the number of landowners who engage in a certain activity."[61] New York University law professor Roderick Hills similarly fears that *Koontz* will lead to a "quagmire" by "enlist[ing] federal courts to duplicate the work of state courts in policing conditions on literally hundreds of thousands of land-use permits."[62] For his part, John Echeverria warns that the ruling is a "revolutionary and destructive step" that undermines the "traditional court approach of according deference to elected officials and technical experts on issues of regulatory policy" and "will result in a huge number of costly legal challenges to local regulations."[63]

A key problem with this sort of criticism of *Koontz* is that it can just as readily apply to federal judicial protection of a wide range of other constitutional rights that might be infringed by state and local government action. To adapt Professor Hills's terminology, federal courts "duplicate the work of state courts" in enforcing Fourth Amendment

---

[61] Koontz, 133 S. Ct. at 2606–07 (Kagan, J., dissenting).

[62] Roderick Hills, Koontz's Unintelligible Takings Rule: Can Remedial Equivocation Save the Court from a Doctrinal Quagmire?, Prawfsblawg, June 25, 2013, http:// prawfsblawg.blogs.com/prawfsblawg/2013/06/koontzs-unintelligible-takings-rule-can-remedial-equivocation-make-up-for-an-incoherent-substantive-.html.

[63] Echeverria, *supra* note 60.

restrictions on searches and seizures despite the fact that local law enforcement agencies conduct "literally hundreds of thousands" of raids and searches every year. By the early 2000s, there were an estimated 40,000 SWAT team raids alone every year, to say nothing of the much larger number of ordinary searches.[64] Similarly, as Justice Kagan might put it, federal courts enforce First Amendment rights against state and local officials, despite the fact that "many kinds of permitting" schemes—including those regulating the use of streets, parks, movie theaters, and lecture halls—impinge on free-speech rights to varying degrees.[65]

Obviously, judicial enforcement of Fourth Amendment rights, speech rights, and numerous other constitutional protections necessarily involves nondeferential judicial scrutiny of what Echeverria describes as "elected officials and technical experts' [decisions] on issues of regulatory policy."[66] In many cases, these decisions are just as dependent on technical expertise and knowledge of varying local conditions as land-use decisions are.[67] If such concerns are not a sufficient reason to abandon judicial oversight of other constitutional rights, they also should not stand in the way of judicial enforcement of the Takings Clause.

Obviously, judicial protection of any constitutional right necessarily involves greater litigation than would exist if the courts simply let government officials do as they please. This situation is particularly true when the courts first begin to intervene in an area, and the application of doctrine to particular cases is often still unclear. Thus, it would not be surprising if *Koontz*, like other decisions expanding protection for constitutional rights of various kinds, led to an initial increase in litigation. Such an increase is, however, as much a feature as a bug. It can help clarify applicable legal standards and deter officials from future rights violations.

Moreover, it is far from clear that *Koontz* really will result in as great a flood of litigation as feared by Kagan, Hills, and Echeverria. As Justice Alito points out in his majority opinion, no such deluge

[64] Radley Balko, Overkill: The Rise of Paramilitary Police Raids in America 11 (2006).

[65] See, e.g., Timothy Zick, Speech out of Doors: Preserving the First Amendment Liberties in Public Places (2009) (discussing federal judicial review of numerous types of permit policies restricting outdoor speech).

[66] Echeverria, *supra* note 60.

[67] For details, see Somin, Federalism and Property Rights, *supra* note 29, at 80–84.

has occurred in the many states whose supreme courts adopted rules similar to *Koontz* in interpreting their state constitutions.[68] Indeed, at least seven state supreme courts have made similar decisions since 1991, including those of highly populated states such as California, Illinois, Ohio, and Texas.[69] UCLA law professor Jonathan Zasloff points out that California's experience, in particular, undercuts the notion that *Koontz* is likely to lead to a flood of litigation that blocks beneficial regulation.[70]

Professor Hills worries that reliance on state-level experience is misleading, because federal courts, unlike state courts, lack the "decentralized flexibility" and expertise needed to make appropriate adjustments to local conditions.[71] But that has generally not been the case with federal court enforcement of other constitutional rights that involve complex local policy decisions. Moreover, there is little reason to believe that the average state judge is significantly more knowledgeable about local land-use policy and property law than the average federal judge. Federal district judges usually come from the states where they hear cases, and many have prior experience as state judges, state officials, or practitioners.[72] Few federal judges are property-law experts. But the same is true of most state judges. On average, there is little reason to believe that state judges are likely to do a systematically better job of handling takings cases than federal

---

[68] Koontz, 133 S. Ct. at 2602–03.

[69] See Ehrlich v. Culver City, 911 P.2d 429 (Cal. 1996); Home Builders Ass'n v. City of Beavercreek, 729 N.E.2d 349 (Ohio 2000); Kirk v. Denver Publishing Co., 818 P.2d 262 (Colo. 1991); N. Illinois Homebuilders Ass'n, Inc. v. Cnty. of du Page, 649 N.E.2d 384 (Ill. 1995); Smith v. Price Dev. Co., 125 P.3d 945 (Utah 2005); Town of Flower Mound v. Stafford Estates Ltd P'ship, 135 S.W.3d 620 (Tex. 2004); Trimen Dev. Co. v. King Cnty., 877 P.2d 187 (Wash. 1994). For a detailed discussion of some of these cases and their relationship to *Koontz*, see Brief of Owners Counsel of America as Amicus Curiae in Support of Petitioner, Koontz v. St. Johns River Water Management District, 133 S. Ct. 2586 (2013), at 9–11.

[70] See Jonathan Zasloff, Koontz and Exactions: Don't Worry, Be Happy, Legal Planet: Env. L. & Pol'y Blog, June 27, 2013, at http://legalplanet.wordpress.com/2013/06/27/koontz-and-exactions-dont-worry-be-happy.

[71] See Hills, *supra* note 62.

[72] For a discussion of various reasons why federal judges are not likely to be significantly worse than state judges at addressing property rights issues, see Somin, Federalism and Property Rights, *supra* note 29 at 84–86; see also Ilya Somin, *Stop the Beach Renourishment* and the Problem of Judicial Takings, 6 Duke J. Const. L. & Pub. Pol'y 91, 101-03 (2011) (symposium on judicial takings)

judges in the same region. On the other hand, in some instances state judges may be systematically *worse,* if they have been put into their positions by the same interest groups that also promote harmful government policies at the state level. Especially in states where judges are elected, state judges sometimes have close ties to the local political establishment, which in turn may be susceptible to interest-group lobbying.[73]

2. Will Koontz *Impede Beneficial Regulation?*

Closely related to the "flood of litigation" critique of *Koontz* are claims that it will impede beneficial regulation by convincing officials to desist from beneficial regulation that might now lead to takings lawsuits.[74] If some demands that regulatory agencies could previously impose without paying any costs might now be compensable takings, it is certainly possible that the frequency of such demands will be reduced. There is no way to definitively prove that such risk aversion will never lead to the abandonment of potentially beneficial regulatory policies.

But, as discussed above in addressing similar criticisms of *Arkansas Game & Fish,* this constraint is likely to lead to better, rather than worse, regulatory policies. Forcing governments to internalize the costs that their regulations impose on landowners, will strengthen incentives to adopt only those regulations whose benefits are likely to exceed their costs. Whereas these officials previously did not need to consider costs imposed on landowners in their calculus—unless the landowners could force them to do so through political lobbying—compensation requirements will impose tighter discipline and incentivize officials to concentrate regulatory expenditures in areas where they are likely to do the most good.

Interestingly, a 2001 analysis of a survey of land-use planners in California suggests that they perceive the impact of *Nollan-Dolan* restrictions on land-use policy in roughly this way.[75] Some 74 percent of California city planners and 81 percent of county planners agreed

---

[73] See Somin, *Stop the Beach Renourishment* and the Problem of Judicial Takings, supra note 72 at 99–100 (discussing this problem in more detail).

[74] See Echeverria, *supra* note 60; Mulvaney, *supra* note 60.

[75] See Ann E. Carlson & Daniel Pollak, Takings on the Ground: How the Supreme Court's Takings Jurisprudence Affects Local Land Use Decisions, 35 U.C. Davis L. Rev. 103 (2001).

with the statement that "[t]he nexus and rough proportionality standards established by the *Nollan* and *Dolan* decisions, when followed carefully, simply amount to good land use planning practice."[76] The planning officials endorsed the decisions despite the fact that a majority of them reported that concern about takings issues had led them to reevaluate their fee and exaction standards over the previous decade.[77] The authors of the study suggest that this positive response to the decisions may be because planners support their "tendency to favor a comprehensive, long-range approach to planning that avoids ad hoc decision-making."[78] This beneficial effect occurred despite the fact that many lower court decisions have interpreted *Nollan* and *Dolan* relatively narrowly, exempting some types of exactions from the essential-nexus and rough-proportionality requirements.[79] Stronger enforcement of these rulings might yield greater efficiency benefits, by increasing government planners' incentives to take account of the costs their policies impose.

Like *Arkansas Game & Fish*, *Koontz* does not actually forbid regulatory measures, but merely requires the government, in some cases, to pay compensation to landowners whose property rights have been impaired. As will be discussed below, regulatory agencies may not have to pay compensation in cases where they ultimately choose not to impose a particular condition, perhaps even if they also ultimately deny the permit in question. But in cases where the relevant demand fails the requirements of *Nollan* and *Dolan*, they will have to offer compensation if they hope to make the condition stick. A *Koontz*-like rule thus sometimes increases the efficiency of regulation in ways that even planning officials welcome.

In addition, *Koontz* largely gives the government free rein in cases where monetary exactions are used to prevent landowners from engaging in activities that harm the property of others, including that

76 *Id*. at 142.

77 *Id*. at 143.

78 *Id*.

79 See, e.g, J. David Breemer, The Evolution of the Essential Nexus: How State and Federal Courts Have Applied *Nollan* and *Dolan* and Where They Should Go from Here, 59 Wash. & Lee L. Rev. 373, 374–75 (2002) (describing this trend); David L. Callies, Regulatory Takings and the Supreme Court: How Perspectives on Property Rights Have Changed from *Penn Central* to *Dolan* and What State and Federal Courts Are Doing About It, 28 Stetson L. Rev. 523, 567–75 (1999) (same).

of the state. Justice Alito's majority opinion emphasizes that "[i]nsisting that landowners internalize the negative externalities of their conduct is a hallmark of responsible land-use policy, and we have long sustained such regulations against constitutional attack."[80]

3. Doctrinal Criticisms of the Koontz Majority

As we have seen, much of the criticism aimed at *Koontz* in Justice Kagan's dissent and by academic commentators focuses on policy considerations. But Kagan's most powerful attacks on the majority are primarily doctrinal in nature. She suggests that "the *Nollan-Dolan* test applies only when the property the government demands during the permitting process is the kind it otherwise would have to pay for—or, put differently, when the appropriation of that property, outside the permitting process, would constitute a taking."[81] Kagan notes that a demand that a citizen spend money for public purposes, outside the permitting process, would not in itself constitute a taking, and therefore the Water Management District's demand that Koontz spend money on refurbishing public lands cannot be a taking.[82]

This is an important point. But it runs afoul of the reality that the monetary payment was demanded as the price for allowing Koontz to avoid having to cede a conservation easement covering more than 90 percent of his property, and for allowing him to develop at least some substantial part of the property. Forcing a property owner to allow an easement surely would be a taking even outside the permitting process; *Nollan* and *Dolan* themselves both involved government demands for easements.[83] As the *Dolan* Court noted, an easement differs from a mere regulatory restriction on the use of property because it constitutes "a requirement that [the owner] deed portions of the property to the city."[84]

---

[80] Koontz, 133 S. Ct. at 2595.

[81] Koontz, 133 S. Ct. at 2605 (Kagan, J., dissenting).

[82] *Id.* at 2605–06.

[83] Nollan, 483 U.S. at 828; Dolan, 512 U.S. at 385–86.

[84] Dolan, 512 U.S. at 385. But see Smith v. Town of Mendon, 822 N.E.2d 1214, 1217–21 (N.Y. 2004) (holding that the *Nollan-Dolan* framework does not apply to a permanent "conservation restriction" imposed as a condition of a development permit because it is not an "exaction" that involves the "dedication of 'property'" to public use). In my view, *Smith* is a serious misinterpretation of *Nollan* and *Dolan* because the permanent assignment of conservation rights to the government pretty clearly does involve

To be sure, there is a potential distinction between easements allowing public access, as in *Nollan* and *Dolan*, and the conservation easement demanded of Koontz. However, in both scenarios the government's demands would have largely eliminated the landowner's ability to determine the uses of his own property, and forced him to devote it to serving the government's purposes. Indeed, by barring virtually any development on the land it covers, a conservation easement actually exerts greater control over the landowner's property than merely giving the public the right to pass through a beachfront area, as in *Nollan*.[85] The same applies to a categorical permanent ban on development, at least if it destroys virtually all of the economic value of the land.[86]

In addition, as Justice Alito emphasizes, exempting demands for monetary payments from *Nollan-Dolan* scrutiny would make it "very easy for land-use permitting officials to evade the limitations of *Nollan* and *Dolan*. Because the government need only provide a permit applicant with one alternative that satisfies the nexus and rough-proportionality standards, a permitting authority wishing to exact an easement could simply give the owner a choice of either surrendering an easement or making a payment equal to the easement's value."[87]

I should add that the same kind of argument can easily be used to undermine other constitutional rights. If demands for monetary payments can be used to circumvent the Takings Clause, they can also be used to get around the First Amendment, the Fourth Amendment, and most other individual rights. For example, the government could circumvent protection for freedom of speech by demanding that speakers either refrain from criticizing political leaders or pay a

---

the seizure of an important property right—often a more significant element of the owner's "bundle of sticks" than that at stake in *Nollan* and *Dolan* themselves. Cf. *id.* at 1219 (unpersuasively claiming that the right at stake in a permanent conservation restriction "is trifling compared to the rights to exclude or alienate"). As Judge Read explained in his dissenting opinion in *Smith*, "A conservation easement is a nonpossessory 'interest in real property' . . . which imposes use restrictions on the landowner for purposes generally of 'conserving, preserving and protecting' the State's 'environmental assets and natural and man-made resources' for the benefit of the public." *Id.* at 1225 (Read, J., dissenting) (citations omitted).

[85] *Nollan*, 483 U.S. at 828.

[86] *Lucas v. South Carolina Coastal Council*, 505 U.S. 1003, 1015 (1992).

[87] *Koontz*, 133 S. Ct. at 2599.

fine for doing so. It could use the threat of fines to force homeowners to allow searches that would otherwise violate the Fourth Amendment. And so on. As with many of the other criticisms of *Koontz*, the claim that the use of financial exactions as leverage against landowners cannot violate the Takings Clause is one that few would accept if applied to other constitutional rights.

Alito also seeks to distinguish the water district's demands from taxes, user fees, and other typical financial exactions imposed by the government, by emphasizing that this "monetary obligation burdened petitioner's ownership of a specific parcel of land."[88] Here, Justice Kagan makes a good point where she notes that property taxes and some types of fees for public services also burden ownership of a specific parcel of land.[89] Thus, the majority's attempt to exclude such taxes and user fees from *Nollan-Dolan* scrutiny seems arbitrary. Justice Alito's claim that "teasing out the difference between taxes and takings is more difficult in theory than in practice" is far from fully reassuring.[90] Both property owners and local governments could benefit from clearer judicial guidance than this.

One possible answer is to take up Professor Richard Epstein's suggestion to bite the bullet, admit that taxes can be takings, and apply the *Nollan-Dolan* framework to them.[91] This approach would not lead to the wholesale invalidation of all property taxes and user fees. Many such exactions could easily pass the essential-nexus and rough-proportionality tests, since there is surely both (1) an essential nexus between property ownership and financing for basic

---

[88] *Id.* This is also Alito's reason for distinguishing the Court's earlier decision in Eastern Enter. v. Apfel, 524 U.S. 498 (1998), where five justices on a badly splintered Court concluded that the Takings Clause does not apply to situations where the government imposes monetary exactions that "d[o] not operate upon or alter an identified property interest." *Id.* at 540 (Kennedy, J., concurring); see also *id.* at 554–56 (Breyer, J., dissenting) (agreeing with Kennedy on this point on behalf of the four dissenting justices).

[89] *Id.* at 2607–08 (Kagan, J. dissenting).

[90] *Id.* at 2601.

[91] See Richard Epstein, Koontz v. St. Johns River Water Management District: Of Issues Resolved—and Shoved Under the Table, PointofLaw.Com, Jun. 26, 2013, http://www.pointoflaw.com/archives/2013/06/koontz-v-st-johns-river-water-management-district-of-issues-resolved--and-shoved-under-the-table.php. See also Richard A. Epstein, Takings: Private Property and the Power of Eminent Domain 283–305 (1985) (arguing that taxes qualify as takings).

functions of local government that benefit the owners and (2) a rough proportionality between the amounts charged and the services provided. This dynamic is even more true for user fees calibrated to the amount of services the property owner consumes.

But courts need not take such a radical step to address the problem raised by Justice Kagan. Although it may not be possible to draw an absolutely precise line between takings and taxes, some guidance is provided by the purpose of the Takings Clause's just-compensation requirement, which is to "bar Government from forcing some people alone to bear public burdens which, in all fairness and justice, should be borne by the public as a whole."[92] This creates an important distinction between broad-based property taxes or user fees that apply to all property owners, or to all users of a particular public service, and narrowly targeted exactions that single out individual landowners or small groups.[93] Although the precise line between the two may be elusive, most real-world cases are likely to fall clearly on one side or the other of this continuum.

Ultimately, Justice Alito was right to point out that the problem of distinguishing taxes from takings is not unique to this case, but "is inherent in this Court's long-settled view that property the government could constitutionally demand through its taxing power can also be taken by eminent domain."[94] Although there is a genuine difficulty here, the only way to completely avoid it is either to abandon judicial enforcement of the Takings Clause in all cases where the government uses monetary exactions to coerce property owners, or to embrace Richard Epstein's position that taxes qualify as takings.

Finally, Justice Kagan argues that the water district did not really demand a monetary payment from Koontz.[95] If her understanding of the facts is correct, it is possible that the district did not run afoul of the *Nollan-Dolan* framework. But the majority was likely correct

[92] Armstrong v. United States, 364 U.S. 40, 49 (1960).

[93] Cf., Epstein, PointofLaw.com, *supra* note 91 (criticizing Kagan's dissent and pointing out that "[a] general real estate tax is imposed on all parcels of land based on value in order to fund common improvements from which the community at large benefits. This particular exaction is imposed on a single parcel of land at the time of its possible development and thus singles out one owner for excessive burdens from which it gets no special return benefits.").

[94] Koontz, 133 S. Ct. at 2601.

[95] *Id.* at 2609–11 (Kagan, J., dissenting).

in ruling that this sort of factual dispute should be settled by lower courts.[96]

C. The Problem of Remedy

A key point left unaddressed in Koontz is the question of what sort of remedy is available to landowners who successfully challenge conditions linked to permit denials. The usual remedy for a Takings Clause violation is the payment of fair-market-value compensation.[97] In Koontz and similar permit-denial cases, however, "there is an excessive demand but no taking" and the possible constitutional problem is "an unconstitutional conditions violation."[98] The issue is not that the government has directly violated the Takings Clause, but that it has undermined it indirectly by trying to force property owners to surrender their Takings Clause rights as a condition of getting a permit. For this reason, the Court did not address the issue of what kind of remedy Koontz may be entitled to. If the lower court concludes that the requirements demanded of Koontz violated the standards of Nollan and Dolan, Florida courts will have to determine the appropriate remedy.

Professor Hills, a leading critic of Koontz, believes that, if the federal courts leave the remedy issue up to state courts, and the latter "continue to define the Nollan-Dolan remedy as invalidation of the illegal condition and denial of the zoning permission, then Koontz will be a practical dead letter."[99] Hills believes this possibility is "a good thing," since he would prefer that federal courts abandon the exercise of judicial review over Takings Clause violations created by permit systems.[100]

This analysis is either unduly pessimistic (from my point of view) or unduly optimistic (from Hills's). It is not clear that restoration of the pre-permitting status quo is the remedy lower courts and the Supreme Court will ultimately settle on. For example, Richard Epstein

[96] Id. at 2598.

[97] See, e.g., Kirby Forest Indus. Inc. v. United States, 467 U.S. 1, 10 (1984) (noting that this is the remedy "in most cases").

[98] Koontz, 133 S. Ct. at 2597.

[99] Hills, supra note 62; see also Fenster, supra note 60, at 642–43 (making a similar argument).

[100] Id.

suggests that courts could instead award property owners "damages for economic losses attributable to what is temporary taking of land given that no development could take place."[101]

Even if invalidation of the permit condition does turn out to be the sole remedy, that approach is far from completely toothless. It disincentivizes states and localities from adopting land-use restrictions whose main purpose is precisely to be used as leverage in forcing landowners to accept extortionate conditions in exchange for lifting them. It should also incentivize localities to offer compensation in cases where they wish to impose permit conditions that would otherwise violate the rules of *Nollan* and *Dolan*. Just as *Nollan* and *Dolan* previously incentivized California land-use planners to revamp their approval policies, so *Koontz* may incentivize them to either moderate their demands or offer compensation in cases where the *Nollan-Dolan* standard would otherwise be violated.

Conclusion

Both *Arkansas Game & Fish* and *Koontz* are significant victories for property rights advocates. The former ruling prevents the government from "temporarily" flooding property owners' land virtually at will, without paying compensation. The latter restricts the power of government agencies to use permit processes to impose "[e]xtortionate demands" on landowners.[102]

To some extent, these cases are part of a recent trend of property rights victories in the Supreme Court. *Arkansas Game & Fish* was the second of three unanimous Supreme Court defeats for the federal government in property rights cases within a 15-month period, following *Sackett v. EPA*,[103] and preceding *Horne v. Department of Agriculture*.[104]

At the same time, both rulings have significant limitations. We are still far short of achieving the goal of enforcing property rights on the same terms as those accorded most other constitutional rights. The Obama administration's three unanimous defeats were in part a result of the extreme nature of the positions adopted by the federal

---

[101] Richard Epstein, PointofLaw.com, *supra* note 91.

[102] Koontz, 133 S. Ct. at 2595.

[103] 132 S. Ct. 1367 (2012).

[104] 133 S. Ct. 2053 (2013).

government in these cases.[105] This intransigence is likely what led liberal justices normally inclined to be skeptical of property rights claims to vote against the government in these three instances. In addition, *Horne* and *Sackett* were both decided on statutory rather than constitutional grounds, and both merely involved property owners' rights of access to judicial review of their takings claims, rather than a substantive decision on the merits.

As previously discussed, *Arkansas Game & Fish* and *Koontz* do not address crucial issues the resolution of which is likely to be a major factor in determining their ultimate real-world impact. *Arkansas Game & Fish* is vague on the standards that determine which types of temporary government-induced flooding qualify as takings, and which do not. *Koontz* did not address the issue of remedy and side-stepped the question of "how concrete and specific a demand must be to give rise to liability under *Nollan* and *Dolan*."[106] If, as Justice Kagan suggests, the "demand must be unequivocal,"[107] government officials could potentially evade *Koontz* by cloaking their demands in euphemisms.

Another troubling aspect of *Koontz* is that it was a close decision, with all four liberal justices not only dissenting but being willing to exempt nearly all demands for monetary exactions from Takings Clause scrutiny under *Nollan* and *Dolan*. In reaching this conclusion, they—and prominent academic commentators—advanced a range of arguments that few would credit outside the property rights context. The widespread acceptance of such claims is a sign of the continuing second-class status of property rights in much of our constitutional discourse.

The ideological division evident in the debate over *Koontz* is a further sign that most liberal jurists are unwilling to support anything more than extremely limited judicial enforcement of constitutional property rights—a standard of protection far below that extended to

---

[105]For a brief discussion of this aspect of these cases, see Ilya Somin, Supreme Court Shutouts Reveal Reckless Decisions, USA Today, July 23, 2013, at 8A; see also Ilya Shapiro, Why Obama Keeps Losing at the Supreme Court, Bloomberg View, Jun. 6, 2013, http://www.bloomberg.com/news/2013-06-06/why-obama-keeps-losing-at-the-supreme-court.html (describing administration's unanimous losses in several areas, including property rights).

[106]Koontz, 133 S. Ct. at 2598.

[107]*Id.* at 2610 (Kagan, J., dissenting).

most other enumerated constitutional rights.[108] As long as this ideological division persists, the status of constitutional property rights will remain tenuous: In the long run, no constitutional right is likely to get robust judicial protection unless there is at least some substantial bipartisan and cross-ideological consensus in favor of it.

At the same time, it is also clear that property rights advocates have won some important victories over the last 25 years. The 2012–2013 Supreme Court term is a continuation of that trend. Even painful defeats such as *Kelo v. City of New London*[109] have often been much closer and more controversial than similar decisions would have been a generation ago.[110] Property rights are still the "poor relations" of constitutional law. But the case for bringing them back into the family fold is now being taken more seriously.

---

[108] For a more detailed discussion of this aspect of modern liberal jurisprudence, see Somin, Taking Property Rights Seriously?, *supra* note 2.

[109] 545 U.S. 469 (2005).

[110] On the massive controversy generated by *Kelo*, a close 5–4 decision, see, e.g., Ilya Somin, The Limits of Backlash: Assessing the Political Response to *Kelo*, 93 Minn. L. Rev. 2100 (2009) (documenting the political and legislative response to the decision); and Somin, The Judicial Reaction to *Kelo*, 4 Albany Gov't L. Rev. 1, 7–10 (2011) (symposium on eminent domain) (documenting skeptical reaction by several state supreme courts).

The Beginning of the End?
Horne v. Department of Agriculture and the Future of *Williamson County*
Joshua D. Hawley*

Introduction

Horne v. Department of Agriculture exposes a fundamental confusion right at the nerve of the Supreme Court's contemporary takings jurisprudence. For nearly 30 years—since, to be precise, its 1985 decision in *Williamson County Regional Planning Commission v. Hamilton Bank*—the Court has insisted that a property owner who wants to raise a takings claim in federal court must first exhaust any post-deprivation remedies made available by state or federal law.[1] The idea is that, in the words of *Williamson County*, "[t]he Fifth Amendment does not proscribe the taking of property; it proscribes taking without just compensation."[2] So if the government, whichever government it is, provides "an adequate process for obtaining compensation," the claimant has no takings case until he uses that process and is denied relief.[3] And the federal court has no jurisdiction because the claim "is not yet ripe."[4] Therein the confusion.

More than one commentator has noticed that this is a strange definition of ripeness.[5] Traditionally understood, the Article III ripeness

---

* Associate Professor, University of Missouri School of Law.

[1] Williamson Cnty. Reg'l Planning Comm'n v. Hamilton Bank, 473 U.S. 172, 194–95 (1985).

[2] *Id.* at 194.

[3] *Id.*

[4] *Id.*

[5] See, e.g., J. David Breemer, Overcoming *Williamson County*'s Troubling State Procedures Rule: How the England Reservation, Issue Preclusion Exceptions, and the Inadequacy Exception Open the Federal Courthouse Door to Ripe Takings Claims, 18 J. Land Use & Envtl. L. 209 (2003); Peter A. Buchsbaum, Should Land Use Be Different?

doctrine bars claims for injuries that have not yet occurred or are purely speculative.[6] But a property invasion that has already happened, or is bound to happen by the operation of state or federal law, hardly fits that description. There is nothing speculative about it.

In fact, the availability of post-deprivation process has nothing to do with *ripeness*; it has to do with *remedies*. Before *Williamson County*, courts had held for two centuries that if the government took private property but provided no mechanism for compensating the owner, the owner could obtain equitable relief if the taking was not yet complete, or damages if it were. If the government, on the other hand, provided compensation at the time of the invasion or adequate process for obtaining it afterward, equitable relief was not available. The existence of an adequate compensation process determined what sort of remedy the claimant could get. It had nothing to do with whether the property owner's claim was ripe. Indeed, in no case before *Williamson County* did any federal or state court ever suggest that it lacked jurisdiction to hear a takings claim, or that the claim was somehow premature, merely because the claimant had not yet attempted to obtain compensation from the government.

But then that is because earlier American jurists understood the takings principle not primarily as a government promise to pay for certain acts, but as a structural limit on government power—a governmental disability.[7] If the state severely burdened private property without paying a fair price, the takings rule declared the action *ultra vires*, beyond the power of law and void, just as if it had conflicted with the Contracts Clause or the First Amendment.[8] That declaration rendered government actors subject to injunction and perhaps liable

---

Reflections on *Williamson County Regional Planning Board v. Hamilton Bank*, in Taking Sides on Takings Issues: The Public & Private Perspective 471, 473–74 (Thomas E. Roberts, ed. 2002) ("This underlying premise [that the government has not acted illegally until you ask for compensation and then it is denied] is, of course, untrue.").

[6] 13B Charles A. Wright et al., Federal Practice & Procedure § 3532 (3d ed. 2008); see Younger v. Harris, 401 U.S. 37, 41–42 (1971) (holding contingent threat of prosecution under state law inadequate to create ripe controversy).

[7] That distinction between government "disabilities" and "duties" belongs to H.L.A. Hart. See H.L.A. Hart, The Concept of Law 64–69 (1961). Robert Brauneis first noticed the applicability of this taxonomy to takings jurisprudence. See Robert Brauneis, The First Constitutional Tort: The Remedial Revolution in Nineteenth-Century State Just Compensation Law, 52 Vand. L. Rev. 57, 60 (1999).

[8] Brauneis, *supra* note 7, at 60–61.

for damages when needed to make the claimant whole.[9] But owners were never required to seek compensation from the government before bringing suit. The burden was rather on the government to demonstrate that it had not exceeded its lawful authority and intended to compensate the owner.

Williamson County decisively broke with this understanding of the Takings Clause and converted the "adequate compensation" inquiry—formerly about whether the government had acted lawfully or not—into a jurisdictional test. The effect was to introduce distortions and doctrinal anomalies up and down the length of takings law. Property owners with claims against state governments suddenly found themselves shut out of federal court, thanks to the pairing of *Williamson County*'s exhaustion requirement with federal preclusion doctrines.[10] Federal courts meanwhile struggled to determine whether the exhaustion requirement applied to suits challenging the direct transfer of funds from a property owner to the government,[11] or whether it precluded claimants from raising the Takings Clause as a defense,[12] or what compensation precisely Congress intended to make available under the Tucker Act.[13] Even the Supreme Court found the jurisdictional line too difficult to hold and soon retreated

---

[9] *Id.* at 67–68.

[10] See San Remo Hotel, L.P. v. City & County of San Francisco, 545 U.S. 323, 351 (2005) (Rehnquist, C.J., concurring). For scholarly commentary, see Stephen E. Abraham, *Williamson County* Fifteen Years Later: When Is a Takings Claim (Ever) Ripe?, 36 Real Prop. Prob. & Tr. J. 101, 104 (2001); Michael M. Berger, Supreme Bait & Switch: The Ripeness Ruse in Regulatory Takings, 3 Wash. U. J.L. & Pol'y 99, 102 (2000); Max Kidalov & Richard Seamon, The Missing Pieces of the Debate over Federal Property Rights Legislation, 27 Hastings Const. L.Q. 1, 5 (1999); Thomas E. Roberts, Ripeness and Forum Selection in Fifth Amendment Takings Litigation, 11 J. Land Use & Envtl. L. 37, 37 (1995).

[11] See Asociación de Subscripción Conjunta del Seguro de Responsabilidad Obligatorio v. Flores Galarza, 484 F.3d 1, 19–20 (1st Cir. 2007); Wash. Legal Found. v. Tex. Equal Access to Justice Found., 270 F.3d 180, 192–93 (5th Cir. 2001); Washlefske v. Winston, 234 F.3d 179 (4th Cir. 2000); Student Loan Mktg. Ass'n v. Riley, 104 F.3d 397, 401–02 (D.C. Cir. 1997); Bay View, Inc. v. AHTNA, Inc., 105 F.3d 1281 (9th Cir. 1997); In re Chateaugay Corp., 53 F.3d 478, 493 (2d Cir. 1995).

[12] Horne v. Dept of Agric., 673 F.3d 1071, 1078–80 (9th Cir. 2011).

[13] Eastern Enterprises v. Apfel, 524 U.S. 498 (1998); see also Hinck v. United States, 550 U.S. 501, 506 (2007); Lion Raisins, Inc. v. United States, 416 F.3d 1356, 1370 (Fed. Cir. 2005).

to the claim that the exhaustion requirement was a matter of "prudential ripeness," though the Court never quite explained why.[14]

Which brings us to *Horne v. Department of Agriculture.* Here was a case that brought the *Williamson County* confusion to the fore. The Hornes raised the Takings Clause as a defense in a federally initiated enforcement action seeking a transfer of funds from them to the government. The U.S. Court of Appeals for the Ninth Circuit dismissed the case for want of jurisdiction: the Hornes' claim was not ripe, the court concluded, because they had not availed themselves of the post-deprivation hearing on offer under the Tucker Act in the Court of Federal Claims.[15] When the Supreme Court granted certiorari, it looked as if it intended finally to address the disordered state of its takings jurisprudence—or make a start anyway. Instead, the Court (unanimously) avoided the central doctrinal issues and ruled on a narrow statutory ground.

This was, to say the least, an opportunity missed. Still, the case is worth attending to for the spotlight it casts on *Williamson County's* critical confusion. And the opinion of the Court had at least one intriguing element: In a footnote, the Court suggested for the first time that the central jurisdictional holding of *Williamson County* may be mistaken.[16] If the Court pursues that thought, *Horne* could be the first step on a way forward.

I. The *Horne* Litigation

Marvin and Laura Horne farm raisins in California's central valley, where they have owned a small operation since 1969. Under a New Deal-era statute called the Agricultural Marketing Agreement Act of 1937 (AMAA) and a subsequent order enforcing it, the Department of Agriculture (USDA) requires "handlers" of raisins to turn over a certain portion of their annual crop to the federal government, which then distributes the raisins for use in school lunches, export stimulation efforts, and other government programs. The aim of the statute and the "marketing order" is to stabilize prices by limiting the volume of raisins available on the open market. Sometimes growers are compensated for the share of their crop they turn over,

[14] Suitum v. Tahoe Regional Planning Agency, 520 U.S. 725, 733–34 (1997).
[15] 673 F.3d at 1080.
[16] Horne v. Dep't of Agric., 133 S. Ct. 2053, 2062 n.6 (2013).

sometimes not. For the two growing seasons at issue in this case, 2002-03 and 2003-04, the USDA required producers to remit first 47 and then 30 percent of their crops, respectively. For the 2002-03 season, the government paid farmers less than the cost of production. For the 2003-04 season, it paid nothing at all.[17]

The Hornes dutifully remitted whatever percentage of their raisins the government required for 30 years. But eventually they grew disillusioned with a system they believed amounted to "involuntary servitude"[18] and decided to reorganize their business in an attempt to avoid government exactions. Since the statute and the USDA's marketing order applied only to raisin "handlers," which the order defined to include "[a]ny processor or packer," the Hornes stopped using third-party packers and distributors.[19] Instead, they purchased equipment to process the raisins themselves, and then sold the finished product directly to food-processing companies and bakeries without relying on an intermediary. Their revamped operation was functional by 2002, and because they believed they no longer qualified as "handlers" under the statute, the Hornes declined to turn over any percentage of their crop from 2002 to 2004.[20]

The USDA did not share the Hornes' interpretation of the statute. It directed the Hornes to remit the designated percentage of their crop and when they did not, filed an administrative enforcement action against them in 2004. The USDA argued that the Hornes continued to count as "handlers" within the marketing order. The Hornes, for their part, disputed the USDA's statutory interpretation. They also raised, as an affirmative defense, the Fifth Amendment Takings Clause.[21]

Administrative-review officials rejected both the Hornes' statutory claim and their Fifth Amendment defense and ordered them to pay the dollar value of the raisins they would otherwise have

---

[17] See 133 S. Ct. at 2058–60; Brief for Petitioners at 2–4, Horne v. Dep't of Agric., 133 S. Ct. 2053 (2013) (No. 12-123).

[18] 133 S. Ct. at 2058 n.3.

[19] Brief for Petitioners, *supra* note 17, at 5.

[20] 133 S. Ct. at 2058–60; Brief for Petitioners, *supra* note 17, at 2–4.

[21] 133 S. Ct. at 2059.

withheld, in addition to a civil penalty. The total came to nearly $700,000, more than the value of the Hornes' entire raisin crop.[22]

The Hornes then appealed to the federal district court, which ruled against them on the merits, including on the Takings Clause question. On appeal again, the Ninth Circuit also adjudicated the takings question and concluded that the Hornes could not make out a violation. The court initially affirmed the district court in full.[23] But after the Hornes moved for rehearing, the government argued for the first time that the court lacked jurisdiction.[24] The Ninth Circuit agreed. It withdrew its first panel opinion and substituted one dismissing the appeal for lack of jurisdiction. Although the court acknowledged that the AMAA provides an administrative-review procedure for raisin "handlers" that effectively withdraws Tucker Act jurisdiction—and thus the need to exhaust one's takings claim in the Court of Federal Claims—it found that for purposes of their Takings Clause defense, the Hornes counted as raisin "producers" under the statute.[25] The AMAA does not provide an administrative remedy for producers. Consequently, the court held that the rule of *Williamson County* mandated that the Hornes pay their fine and then seek reimbursement in the Court of Federal Claims.[26] Until that time, their takings defense was not ripe.[27]

In a unanimous decision written by Justice Clarence Thomas, the Supreme Court reversed. "The Ninth Circuit's jurisdictional ruling flowed from its determination that petitioners brought their takings claim as producers rather than handlers," Thomas wrote in the opinion's key passage.[28] "This determination is not correct."[29] All parties agreed that the AMAA imposed duties on the Hornes only in their capacity as handlers. The Hornes' takings defense, then, functioned as an alternative to their statutory argument: the Hornes claimed that if they lost the statutory question and were deemed handlers, the Fifth

---

[22] *Id.*

[23] Brief for Petitioners, *supra* note 17, at 3.

[24] *Id.*

[25] 673 F.3d at 1080.

[26] *Id.* at 1079–80.

[27] *Id.*

[28] 133 S. Ct. at 2060.

[29] *Id.*

Amendment should bar the government from imposing the fines.[30] Both the district court and the Ninth Circuit had ruled that the Hornes were indeed handlers, Justice Thomas pointed out.[31] And as the Ninth Circuit admitted, the AMAA's "comprehensive remedial scheme" available to handlers withdraws Tucker Act jurisdiction.[32] That ruling meant the Hornes had "no alternative remedy, and their takings claim was not 'premature' when presented to the Ninth Circuit."[33]

This statutory holding relieved the Court of any need to grapple with the substance of the *Williamson County* ripeness rule, postponing that question to another day. Justice Thomas did, however, sound a brief but potentially significant note of skepticism. "[W]e have recognized," he wrote after rehearsing *Williamson County*'s exhaustion requirement, "that [this rule] is not, strictly speaking, jurisdictional."[34] He continued the thought in a footnote: "A 'Case' or 'Controversy' exists once the government has taken private property without paying for it. Accordingly, *whether an alternative remedy exists does not affect the jurisdiction of the federal court.*"[35]

These observations did not matter to the disposition of the case. But they did and do represent the Court's first acknowledgment, however oblique, that what *Williamson County* called ripeness may in fact be a question of remedies. That is no small thing. Because as the extensive briefing in *Horne* ably explained, the history of takings doctrine makes abundantly clear that *Williamson County*'s jurisdictional holding is a novelty—and an unfortunate one at that. A return to this history may show the way forward.

II. Rights, Remedies, and the Power of Eminent Domain

To unravel *Williamson County*, we must begin in the past. The takings jurisprudence of state and federal courts from the early Republic through the middle of the 20th century casts considerable doubt on *Williamson County*'s principal claims. In holding that no takings action was ripe until the government had affirmatively refused to

[30] *Id.* at 2060–61.

[31] *Id.* at 2061.

[32] *Id.* at 2062.

[33] *Id.* at 2063.

[34] *Id.* at 2062.

[35] *Id.* at 2062 n.6 (emphasis in original).

pay, *Williamson County* directly implied that injunctive relief was never available as a takings remedy, not even when the takings claim was raised as a defense. Yet courts from the Founding period forward routinely granted equitable relief to property owners. And they never required claimants to first ask the government for payment before bringing suit.

Behind *Williamson County's* holding was the idea that the Takings Clause functions, most fundamentally, as a promise by the government to pay for certain activities.[36] Not until the government fails to make the promised payment has the clause been violated.[37] The earlier cases work from a different understanding. They pictured the takings rule, whether located in state law, common law, or the federal Constitution, as a structural limit on government power. That conception, as it turns out, makes far better sense of the takings jurisprudence *Williamson County* struggled to apply and it might, if recovered now, help bring some order to our misshapen takings law.

A. The Early Understanding: The Takings Clause as Structural Limit

From the first, both equitable relief and damages were available to takings claimants in American courts. As Robert Brauneis has explained, owner-initiated takings claims before the Civil War typically proceeded in three stages.[38] First, the aggrieved property owner would bring a suit at common law for trespass or trespass on the case, alleging a burden on his property beyond that the government was authorized to impose to protect the general welfare or curb nuisances. The defendant, usually a government official or corporation, would then plead as a defense public law authorizing the action.[39] That left the court to decide, in the final stage, whether the

---

[36] 473 U.S. at 194–95 ("If the government has provided an adequate process for obtaining compensation, and if resort to that process yields just compensation, then the property owner has no claim against the Government for a taking.") (quotations omitted).

[37] *Id.* at 195.

[38] Brauneis, *supra* note 7, at 67–68. This taxonomy describes the process claimants pursued in state courts, where nearly all takings claims were brought until the late 19th century. State courts decided hundreds of just-compensation cases in the 19th century, while the U.S. Supreme Court decided only a handful. See *id.* at 61.

[39] Immunity doctrines prevented suit against the states directly, and against most counties, townships, and municipalities. *Id.* at 72–74.

authorizing law provided adequate compensation to the owner. If it did not, the court invalidated the law as unconstitutional or otherwise void.[40] That judgment in turn freed the successful owner to pursue the remedies for trespass available at common law, including injunctive relief to prevent permanent harm to the property or, if the invasion had already occurred, retrospective damages.[41]

In none of these cases did the court demand that property owners first submit to the taking and bring suit thereafter to retrieve payment. And for good reason. Courts read the Takings Clause, and its state and common-law equivalents, as a strict limitation on the types of burdens the government was permitted to impose in the first instance. Put another way, they read the Takings Clause as a disability on government action. On this view, the government was authorized to burden property in order to protect the health or safety or general welfare of the public. This authority was of a piece with the government's power to abate public nuisances.[42] But if the government went further and imposed on property severe burdens, akin to a trespass at common law, it had to pay the property owner for the property invasion at the time the invasion occurred. The government's action was only *lawful* if it was accompanied by compensation: the power of eminent domain was the power of takings-with-compensation. Failure to observe the bounds of that power rendered the government action null and void.[43]

In *Thacher v. Dartmouth Bridge Company*, for example, decided in 1836, the Massachusetts Supreme Judicial Court held that a state act that "confer[red] a power on [a] corporation to take private property for public use, without providing for . . . the payment of an adequate indemnity" would contravene the Massachusetts constitution's bar on takings, and "the wrongful act would stand unjustified by legislative grant."[44] As a consequence, the aggrieved party was empow-

---

40 *Id*. at 67–68.

41 Thacher v. Dartmouth Bridge Co., 35 Mass. (18 Pick.) 501, 502 (1836).

42 See Morton J. Horwitz, The Transformation of American Law, 1870–1960, at 27–28 (1992).

43 Brauneis, *supra* note 7, at 60.

44 35 Mass. (18 Pick.) at 502. See also Sinnickson v. Johnson, 17 N.J.L. 129 (1839) (defendants liable in nuisance and trespass on the case for flooding because statute authorized construction of a dam but provided no compensation); Bloodgood v. Mohawk & Hudson R.R. Co., 18 Wend. 9, 78 (N.Y. 1837) (trespass action prohibiting

ered to pursue the traditional remedies of common law.[45] The New Jersey Supreme Court reached a parallel conclusion in *Bonaparte v. Camden & A.R. Company* in 1830, when it enjoined railroad officials acting under the auspices of a state charter authorizing them to take land for railroad construction.[46] "If the law is unconstitutional, it can give no authority," the court concluded, and "the person who acts by colour of law merely is a trespasser."[47]

It made no sense on this view to require property owners to submit to the taking and then bring a later suit for recompense. The government held no general power to burden property in this way. It possessed rather a limited power to take property for public use with compensation. For that reason, the central question in all the early cases was whether the government had exceeded its power of eminent domain. Courts decided that question by asking another one: had the government provided adequate payment at the time of the taking? The onus was not on the property owner to secure compensation after the fact, but on the government to prove it had not acted unlawfully to begin with. The California Supreme Court summarized this view in 1875, explaining that "a taking of private property for public use in the sense in which that phrase is used in the Constitution . . . can only be effected upon the conditions prescribed in the Constitution—that is, upon just compensation being simultaneously made."[48]

B. A New Synthesis

In the years before the Civil War, the Takings Clause (and its state equivalents) was enforced primarily through the common law of torts. That changed in the 1870s, as more and more states and the federal government adopted statutes conferring the power of condemnation on private entities, railroads most conspicuously. Sometimes,

---

railway that claimed authorization from corporate charter to take property with damages to be paid later from entering land "until [plaintiff's] damages were appraised and paid"); Perry v. Wilson, 7 Mass. 393, 395 (1811) (holding defendant liable in trespass because law purportedly authorizing taking of logs failed to provide just compensation and was thus void).

[45] 35 Mass. (18 Pick.) at 502.

[46] 3 F. Cas. 821 (C.C.D.N.J. 1830).

[47] *Id.* at 827.

[48] San Mateo Waterworks v. Sharpstein, 50 Cal. 284, 285 (1875).

these statutes explicitly created a private right of action for burdened property owners; other times the courts implied one. And quite frequently, the new statutes created a mechanism for owners to obtain compensation for their property after the taking had occurred. The upshot was to displace the common law as the ground of the action and, potentially, as the source of the remedy.

This transition naturally raised the question whether the new statutes fit with the dictates of the Takings Clause, as well as what sort of relief property owners could now secure in a takings claim. The canonical answer to both questions came from the Supreme Court in 1890, in a case called *Cherokee Nation v. Kansas Railway Company.*[49] Congress had delegated to a private railroad the right of eminent domain over lands held in part by the Cherokee Indian tribe. The statute afforded the tribe certain procedures for obtaining compensation following the taking. The tribe sued and asked for a permanent injunction. The Supreme Court held first that the statute did not offend the Takings Clause and second that the tribe was not entitled to injunctive relief.[50] Both holdings rested on the same reason: the statute provided an adequate remedy at the time of the taking.

Under the statute, the Court found, "the owner is entitled to reasonable, certain, and adequate *provision* for obtaining compensation before his occupancy is disturbed."[51] That was enough to satisfy the Takings Clause. Previous cases had emphasized that to be a valid exercise of eminent domain, the government action had to be accompanied by payment. This was the structural limit the takings principle imposed on the state. The Court in *Cherokee Nation* continued to think of the Takings Clause as a governmental disability, but now held that the clause could be satisfied by providing a *mechanism* to the property owner to obtain payment. The Constitution "does not provide or require that compensation shall be actually paid in advance of the occupancy of the land to be taken," the Court reasoned.[52] The Constitution required that the government take only with compensation. The provision of a sure mechanism for payment would satisfy that restraint.

[49] 135 U.S. 641 (1890)

[50] *Id.* at 659.

[51] *Id.* (emphasis added).

[52] *Id.*

Assuming, that is, the mechanism was adequate. "Whether a particular provision be sufficient to secure the compensation to which, under the constitution, [the property owner] is entitled," the Court went on, "is sometimes a question of difficulty."[53] Not just any compensation procedure would do. For one thing, it had to be in place at the time of the taking. The owner was entitled to "a reasonable, certain, and adequate provision for obtaining compensation *before his occupancy is disturbed*."[54] Moreover, the procedure had to afford owners full and fair payment. Just over a decade later, in *Western Union Telegraph Company v. Pennsylvania Railroad*,[55] the Court invalidated a congressional act conferring condemnation power on a telegraph company because the act did not provide an appropriate amount of compensation. In the years following *Cherokee Nation*, the Court similarly invalidated statutes that included compensation procedures too uncertain or too meager.[56]

That left the question of remedies, the sort of relief a property owner could secure from the court if the statute appropriately provided for compensation. *Cherokee Nation* answered this second question by reference to the first. If the payment mechanism was truly and constitutionally "adequate," then claimants were limited to the remedy the statute provided.[57] They could not obtain injunctive relief because they had a remedy at law. If the procedure were inadequate, however, either because it was not in place at the time of the taking or did not provide for fair compensation, courts could grant equitable relief.[58] In other words, an injunction was never available

---

[53] *Id.*

[54] *Id.* (emphasis added).

[55] 195 U.S. 540 (1904).

[56] See United States v. Sioux Nation of Indians, 448 U.S. 371 (1980) (awarding retrospective damages for taking because Congress previously provided constitutionally inadequate means to obtain compensation in conjunction with treaty); Macfarland v. Poulos, 32 App. D.C. 558, 562–63 (D.C. Cir. 1909) (holding provision for compensation inadequate under *Cherokee Nation*); see also Conn. River R.R. v. Franklin Cnty. Comm'rs, 127 Mass. 50 (1879), cited in Sweet v. Rechel, 159 U.S. 380, 401 (1895) (holding inadequate compensation for taking when it was to be paid "out of the earnings of" private railroad).

[57] 135 U.S. at 659.

[58] See, e.g., Smyth v. Ames, 169 U.S. 466, 549–50 (1898) (enjoining enforcement of rate regulation as unconstitutional taking), overruled on other grounds, Fed. Power Comm'n v. Hope Natural Gas Co., 315 U.S. 575, 605 (1942); Tindal v. Wesley, 167 U.S.

if the government acted lawfully, pursuant to its eminent domain power, but was available if the government exceeded that authority. In this way, the rule of *Cherokee Nation* paralleled the Supreme Court's decision in *Ex Parte Young* that injunctive relief is available to enjoin state officials who violate the Constitution when there is no adequate remedy at law.[59]

Cherokee Nation changed the contours of takings suits, but the basic premise of the earlier cases remained intact. The Takings Clause continued to function as a structural restraint on government power. Justice Oliver Wendell Holmes voiced the post-*Cherokee Nation* consensus in 1922 in his opinion for *Morrisdale Coal Company v. United States*.[60] Government regulation was a valid exercise of the takings power when it "provides compensation for obedience to [its] orders."[61] To be sure, the government was not obliged to compensate affected property owners for every regulation it issued, for "no lawmaking power promises by implication to make good losses that may be incurred by obedience to its commands."[62] Rather, the government was obliged to refrain from taking property unless it intended to pay a fair price. If the government exceeded its lawful authority, injunctive relief was available. "If the law requires a party to give up property . . . without adequate compensation the remedy is, if necessary, to refuse to obey it."[63]

C. The Causby Connection

As the century wore on, however, courts increasingly characterized the Takings Clause as a government duty to purchase particularly severe property intrusions, rather than a disability from pursuing those intrusions in the first place. With that shift, the earlier notion of the clause as a structural restraint fell into obscurity. The Supreme Court's increasingly expansive interpretation of the Tucker

---

204, 222–23 (1897) (holding that state officers were subject to ejectment where state had not acquired property by paying just compensation); D.M. Osborne & Co. v. Missouri Pac. Ry. Co., 147 U.S. 248, 258–59 (1893) (injunctive relief available "in view of the inadequacy of legal remedy").

[59] 209 U.S. 123, 163 (1908).

[60] 259 U.S. 188 (1922).

[61] *Id*. at 190.

[62] *Id*.

[63] *Id*.

Act helped drive this trend, typified and accelerated by a mid-century case called *United States v. Causby*.[64] The Court was on the road to *Williamson County*.

First adopted in 1887,[65] the Tucker Act gives the Court of Federal Claims exclusive jurisdiction over any "claim against the United States for money damages exceeding $10,000" when that claim is "founded either upon the Constitution, or any Act of Congress or any regulation of an executive department . . . in cases not sounding in tort."[66] This capacious language was susceptible to more than one interpretation. It might be read to provide a general damages remedy to any claimant for any takings claim brought against the federal government. For the first 70 years of the act's life, however, courts interpreted it in line with the prevailing distinction between lawful government exercises of the eminent domain power and *ultra vires* takings of property, holding that the act provided a mechanism for obtaining fair payment in the former set of cases only. Courts read the act to work like this: If the government acknowledged that its action constituted a taking and that compensation was due, the Court of Claims (later renamed the Court of Federal Claims) had jurisdiction and injunctive relief was not available. If the government contested the obligation to provide payment, on the other hand, the district court retained jurisdiction and the claimant could win equitable relief.[67]

The textual anchor for this reading was the language limiting Tucker Act jurisdiction to cases "not sounding in tort."[68] The Supreme Court treated cases in which the government challenged the duty to compensate as a species of tort action, while those in which the government acknowledged that its activity constituted a

---

[64] 328 U.S. 256 (1946).

[65] A predecessor statute had established the Court of Claims in 1855. 10 Stat. 612 (1855).

[66] 28 U.S.C. § 1491(a)(1).

[67] Plaintiffs might also challenge government action as failing to meet the "public use" requirement of the Takings Clause. Jurisdiction—and equitable relief—were available for that claim in the federal district court, regardless of whether the government had provided a mechanism for compensation. See City of Cincinnati v. Vester, 281 U.S. 439 (1930) (public use challenge against state government adjudicated in district court); Brown v. United States, 263 U.S. 78 (1923) (public use challenge against federal government adjudicated in district court).

[68] 28 U.S.C. § 1491(a)(1).

taking—and that compensation was due—were treated as a type of implied contract.[69] The Tucker Act provided jurisdiction only over the latter. The idea was that Congress meant to provide a damages remedy only for those instances in which the government intended to use the power of eminent domain. As the Supreme Court put it in 1925, "There can be no recovery under the Tucker Act if the intention to take is lacking."[70]

Then in 1946, the Court unceremoniously changed its mind in *United States v. Causby.* A homeowner alleged that Army and Navy planes flying low over his property disturbed the peace—and his chicken farming—so thoroughly as to constitute a taking.[71] The federal government denied that it had or intended to take the owner's property.[72] Under the prevailing rule, that meant that Tucker Act jurisdiction was unavailable. Nevertheless, the Court held that jurisdiction was proper in the Court of Claims because the case was "founded upon the Constitution."[73] "We need not decide," the Court concluded, "whether repeated trespasses might give rise to an implied contract."[74] Without further discussion, the Court announced that any time "there is a taking, the claim is . . . within the jurisdiction of the Court of Claims to hear and determine."[75]

The likely impetus for this holding was to ensure that the homeowner in the case could have his day in court; besides the Tucker Act,

---

[69] See, e.g., Tempel v. United States, 248 U.S. 121, 129–30 (1918) ("[U]nder the Tucker Act, the consent of the United States to be sued is (so far as here material) limited to claims founded 'upon any contract, express or implied'; and a remedy for claims sounding in tort is expressly denied. . . . [I]n the case at bar, both the pleadings and the facts found preclude the implication of a promise to pay."); Herrera v. United States, 222 U.S. 558, 563 (1912) ("the record does not show a 'convention between the parties' or circumstances from which a contract could be implied, and that therefore the case is one sounding in tort, and claimants have no right of recovery"); Bigby v. United States, 188 U.S. 400, 406–08 (1903) (stating that the Tucker Act requires a "meeting of the minds of the parties," that is, "an agreement to pay for that which was used for the government").

[70] Mitchell v. United States, 267 U.S. 341, 345 (1925).

[71] 328 U.S. at 258–59.

[72] The government claimed that it already owned the relevant property, the airspace above the petitioner's acreage. See *id.* at 260.

[73] *Id.* at 267 (quoting 28 U.S.C. § 250(1)).

[74] *Id.* at 267.

[75] *Id.*

no other law provided the claimant a forum. But the implications were far broader. If the Tucker Act provided a forum—and a damages remedy—for *any* sort of takings claim brought by a property holder, regardless of whether the government invoked its power of eminent domain, then the Tucker Act might serve as a "reasonable, certain, and adequate" remedy at law for any government burden on property.

That meant, for one thing, that equitable relief might no longer be available in takings claims against the federal government, ever: there would always be a remedy at law. But further, reading the Tucker Act in this way effectively dissolved the longstanding distinction between lawful government exercises of the eminent domain power and government action beyond the power of law. Read in the manner of the *Causby* Court, the Tucker Act would mean that the government always offered to pay for its actions—all of them. If this were true, it would be difficult to go on thinking of the Takings Clause as a structural limit on government power. Takings claims instead were a matter of getting the government to make good on its universal promise to pay.

The full meaning of the *Causby* turn took some while to be felt. In the years immediately following the case, the Supreme Court continued to limit Tucker Act jurisdiction, now based less on principle than on practicality. When a claimant challenged a government action that was already complete, the Court directed the case to the Court of Claims. No equitable relief was available. If the challenged government act was not yet complete, and the government disclaimed any intent to compensate, jurisdiction remained in the district court, and the claimant could seek injunctive relief.[76]

Still, whether the Court recognized it or not, the logic of *Causby* thoroughly undermined the foundations of the *Cherokee Nation* takings jurisprudence, and the pre-Civil War tradition before it. *Williamson County* made these implications plain.

D. Rereading Williamson County

Considering *Causby* and the doctrinal change it helped instigate, it is not so hard to see how *Williamson County* arrived at the result it did—or why that result seemed, to the Court, entirely plausible.

---

[76] See Duke Power Co. v. Carolina Envtl. Study Grp., Inc., 438 U.S. 59, 71 n.15 (1978); Reg'l Rail Reorganization Act Cases, 419 U.S. 102, 149 n.36 (1974); Youngstown Sheet & Tube Co. v. Sawyer, 343 U.S. 579, 584–85 (1952).

Williamson County concerned a suit brought by a land developer in federal district court after a regional planning commission rejected his preliminary plat proposal.[77] At the time of suit, the developer had not requested variances from the commission, nor had he appealed the commission's denial of the preliminary plat to the zoning board of appeals. Not surprisingly on those facts, the Court held that the developer's takings claim was premature, but for two independent reasons. The first was that the decision the developer challenged was not final; the commission had denied only the preliminary plat. Because the developer never sought variances, the commission's denial was "not a final, reviewable decision."[78]

The Court might have stopped there; that was surely enough to decide the case. Instead, it pressed on to give a "second reason the taking claim is not yet ripe," having to do with the claimant's failure to use available state compensation procedures.[79] The Court began its analysis on this point by referring to the *Cherokee Nation* rule that compensation need not "be paid in advance of, or contemporaneously with, the taking; all that is required is that a reasonable, certain and adequate provision for obtaining compensation exist at the time of the taking."[80] This reason was unremarkable enough; *Cherokee Nation* had been commonplace for 100 years. But the next sentence appended a new conclusion: If the government provided adequate process, the Court went on, "then the property owner has no claim against the Government for a taking."[81] This was logic influenced by *Causby*. Earlier cases had held that the availability of a compensation mechanism determined whether the government acted lawfully and what sort of relief was available to claimants. Now the Court was saying something different, that the availability of a damages remedy at law determined whether there was a claim at all. Unless the government refused to pay, the property holder could not even invoke the Takings Clause—she had "no claim against the Government for a taking."[82]

---

[77] 473 U.S. at 190.

[78] *Id.* at 194.

[79] *Id.*

[80] 473 U.S. at 194 (quotations omitted).

[81] *Id.* (quotations omitted).

[82] *Id.*

On this view, the Takings Clause did not disable the government from pursuing certain classes of activity, with remedies available to aggrieved owners should the government transgress its bounds. Rather, it gave individuals a cause of action to recover payment from the government after the fact if the government's action was sufficiently burdensome. The *Causby* Court had hinted that the Tucker Act might be a standing promise to pay; *Williamson County* now read the Takings Clause in the same fashion. The clause represented a commitment by government to compensate individuals who complained about a severe property burden. "As we have explained," the Court said, "because the Fifth Amendment proscribes takings *without just compensation,* no constitutional violation occurs until just compensation has been denied."[83]

With that logic in place, the rest followed easily enough. The Takings Clause was a promise, a duty to make good, and the government did not violate it until it failed to pay. "The nature of the constitutional right therefore requires that a property owner utilize procedures for obtaining compensation before bringing" suit, the Court concluded.[84] There simply was no takings problem unless the government denied payment. And this reasoning led the Court to its fateful conclusion that "takings claims against the Federal Government are *premature* until the property owner has availed itself of the process provided by the Tucker Act."[85] Until an owner specifically asked the government to make good, the owner had no claim—because until the government actually failed to pay, it had done nothing wrong. The same reasoning applied to state claims. "[I]f a State provides an adequate procedure for seeking just compensation, the property owner cannot claim a violation of the Just Compensation Clause until it has used the procedure and been denied just compensation."[86]

No case had held this before, not *Causby* nor the others the Court cited.[87] *Ruckelshaus v. Monsanto* perhaps came closest, though even it held only that the statute involved in that case, the Federal Insec-

---

[83] *Id.* 194 n.13 (emphasis in original).

[84] *Id.*

[85] 473 U.S. at 195 (emphasis added).

[86] *Id.*

[87] *Id.*

ticide, Fungicide, and Rodenticide Act, implemented an arbitration exhaustion requirement as a precondition to a Tucker Act suit for takings.[88] It did not hold what *Williamson County* did, that the very availability of a Tucker Act suit prevents a Takings Clause violation from occurring.[89]

It was a transformative holding, reworking two centuries of doctrine. It was also wrong. Just two years after *Williamson County*, the Court admitted that liability under the Takings Clause arises at the time the government interferes with property rights, not at some later date when the government refuses to pay for it.[90] Or as Justice Ruth Bader Ginsburg succinctly put it, dissenting some years later in *Wilkie v. Robbins*, the Takings Clause "confers on [the property owner] the right to insist upon compensation *as a condition* of the taking of his property."[91]

The Court's confusion about these points in *Williamson County* led it, and eventually all of takings law, down a doctrinal cul-de-sac. It is time for a new turn.

III. Beyond *Williamson County*

If the *Horne* decision gives any reason to hope, it is that it suggests the Court understands this turn is necessary. The mere availability of a damages remedy, the Court noted in footnote 6, cannot "affect the *jurisdiction* of the federal court."[92] That is a start. A different decision of the Court points to the next step.

That case is called *Eastern Enterprises v. Apfel*, decided in 1998.[93] *Apfel* concerned federal regulations on property owners imposed via the Coal Act, a 1992 law that compelled coal companies to pay money into a healthcare fund run for the benefit of coal-industry employees.[94] Eastern Enterprises, a company formerly involved in the mining industry and consequently liable under the act, brought suit

[88] 467 U.S. 986, 1018 (1984).

[89] 473 U.S. at 194.

[90] First English Evangelical Lutheran Church v. Los Angeles Cnty., 482 U.S. 304, 319 (1987).

[91] 551 U.S. 537, 583 (2007) (Ginsburg, J., dissenting) (emphasis added).

[92] 133 S. Ct. at 2062 n.6 (emphasis in original).

[93] 524 U.S. 498 (1998).

[94] *Id*. at 514–15.

in federal district court challenging the payment mandate as a taking without compensation.[95] The Supreme Court was thus obliged to decide whether the Tucker Act required Eastern Enterprises first to file a reverse-condemnation suit in the Court of Federal Claims. In an opinion by Justice Sandra Day O'Connor, a plurality of the Court concluded that it did not.[96] The plurality's reasoning is illuminating.

The Tucker Act appeared to provide a damages remedy for Eastern Enterprises to pursue. After *Williamson County* it was, after all, a standing offer to pay. But O'Connor and the plurality concluded that reading the Tucker Act that way, in this context, yielded nonsensical results. "Congress could not have contemplated that the Treasury would compensate coal operators for their liability under the Act," O'Connor pointed out, "for every dollar paid pursuant to a statute would be presumed to generate a dollar of Tucker Act compensation."[97] That would render the statutory scheme utterly pointless. If government compensation was available to reimburse the property owners for all the monies they paid in, the private healthcare fund would become a public fund financed by the government—just the opposite of what the statute was designed to create.[98] Given this fact, Congress surely had no intention of paying coal companies for their contributions.

And if that were true, if the government had already determined that it was not going to pay, Justice O'Connor reasoned, "a claim for compensation" in the Court of Federal Claims "would entail an utterly pointless set of activities."[99] The presumption of Tucker Act availability had to be reversed.

With this, the plurality reasoned its way to an important insight. The reading of the Tucker Act first suggested by *Causby* and assumed by *Williamson County* made little sense in practice: It simply could not be that the federal government affirmatively intended to pay any time for any infringement found to be a taking. Scores of statutory schemes would be rendered absurdly contradictory. Surely

---

[95] *Id.*

[96] *Id.* at 521.

[97] *Id.* (quotations omitted).

[98] *Id.*

[99] *Id.*

the Tucker Act applied only to a more limited set of claims—but which ones?

The plurality thought it clear that "the presumption of Tucker Act availability must be reversed where the challenged statute, rather than burdening real or physical property, requires a direct transfer of funds."[100] Congress could not have meant to reimburse property owners in those cases. It made more sense to think that, in those cases, Congress would sooner abandon the project at issue rather than see its character fundamentally transformed by the requirement of government reimbursement.

The plurality did not say more; nothing more was required to decide the case. But it was on to more than perhaps it knew. In focusing again on the government's intent to provide a remedy, the plurality had inadvertently recovered one of the leading features of the *Cherokee Nation* synthesis and the older, structural understanding of the takings power that informed it. According to *Cherokee Nation,* the existence of statutory compensation demonstrated that the government intended to use its power of eminent domain. If the compensation provided was adequate, the power had been used appropriately.[101] The *Apfel* case demonstrates that this focus on the government's intent to invoke eminent domain (or not) can solve the riddle of Tucker Act jurisdiction and also clarify the remedies available to federal takings claimants. It can, that is, lead the law out of the *Williamson County* cul-de-sac.

In a word, the Tucker Act creates jurisdiction in the Court of Federal Claims when the government intends to deploy the power of eminent domain. Absent such intention, jurisdiction in the Court of Federal Claims is unavailable. In practice, this understanding would mean using the ordinary tools of statutory interpretation to discern when Congress has evinced, in a given statute, affirmative intent to compensate aggrieved property owners. *This* is when Congress can be said to have invoked its eminent domain authority. Congress's intent also determines the remedy. If the statute demonstrates an intent to compensate property holders, then the Tucker Act provides a remedy at law and claimants must seek damages in the Court of Federal Claims. If the statute demonstrates no such intent, there is

---

[100] *Id.*

[101] 135 U.S. at 659.

no remedy at law. The claimant may then bring suit in the federal district court and obtain damages or equitable relief as appropriate.

This reasoning might have decided the *Horne* case, had the Court so chosen. The AMAA imposes financial penalties on property owners for their refusal to comply with the government's marketing program.[102] The statute gives no indication that Congress intended to make those penalties reimbursable. Consequently, Congress did not intend to use its power of eminent domain. The Tucker Act therefore does not provide a remedy, and the Hornes were perfectly entitled both to raise a takings claim in federal district court and to seek injunctive relief.

Before *Causby* and *Williamson County*, the principal question of takings law was whether the government had lawfully deployed its power of eminent domain, which was another way of asking whether the government had complied with the structural limits placed on it by the Takings Clause. Not only does this approach fit with the takings doctrine's history, but it is error-reducing today. It makes sense of Tucker Act jurisdiction and the remedies that follow from it. And more broadly, it explains why the mere availability of a remedy at law never renders a takings claim *premature*. The reason is that the Takings Clause is not fundamentally a promise to pay for certain types of property burdens. It is a limit on the government's power to impose those burdens in the first place.

If the *Horne* case represents the first step toward recovering that understanding, it will be a case worth remembering.

---

[102] Horne, 133 S. Ct. at 2057–58.

Patents at the Supreme Court: It Could've Been Worse

*Gregory Dolin**

I. Introduction

Since the formation of the U.S. Court of Appeals for the Federal Circuit in 1984, the Supreme Court has taken a mostly "hands-off" approach to patent cases. Indeed, in the first 20 years of the Federal Circuit's existence, the Supreme Court heard only 10 cases dealing with substantive patent law (and two of these cases dealt with rather esoteric issues of plant patents). Since 2004, however, the Court has shown increased interest in engaging with patent law and has granted at least 16 substantive patent cases on issues as varied as patent-eligible subject matter and the interaction of patent and FDA law. In taking these cases, the Supreme Court has been widely viewed as attempting to "rein in" the overly patent-friendly Federal Circuit. Whether or not this was the Supreme Court's goal or intent, it is undeniable that, on balance, its rulings have been far less solicitous of patentees than those emanating from the Federal Circuit.

In the last few years in particular, the Court has expanded the zone of exclusion from patent eligibility,[1] limited the availability of injunctive relief for patentees whose patents have been adjudged to be valid and infringed,[2] and broadened the scope of the patent exhaustion doctrine.[3] To be sure, not all of the Supreme Court's decisions were "anti-patent." For example, the Court chose to adhere to the rule that

*Associate Professor of Law, Co-Director, Center for Medicine & Law, University of Baltimore School of Law; Adjunct Associate Professor of Emergency Medicine, Johns Hopkins University School of Medicine. Many thanks to Irina Manta, Tara Helfman, and Adam Mossoff for their help in drafting this article.

[1] Mayo Collaborative Servs. v. Prometheus Labs., Inc., 132 S. Ct. 1289 (2012); Bilski v. Kappos, 130 S. Ct. 3218 (2010).

[2] eBay Inc. v. MercExchange, LLC, 547 U.S. 388 (2006).

[3] Quanta Computer, Inc. v. LG Electronics, Inc., 553 U.S. 617 (2008).

anyone seeking to challenge an issued patent's validity may do so only by the standard of "clear and convincing evidence," rather than by the lower "preponderance of the evidence" standard, as many law professors have been urging it to do.[4] Nonetheless, the overall trajectory of the Court's patent jurisprudence has been toward a narrower set of patent rights. Thus, there was significant trepidation in the patent bar and the academy when the Supreme Court decided to hear three patent cases this term: *Bowman v. Monsanto*,[5] *Association for Molecular Pathology v. Myriad Genetics*,[6] and *FTC v. Actavis*.[7] Each of the cases had the potential to rewrite decades of patent law and significantly upend major industries that have come to rely on patents. Ultimately, however, the Court adopted an incremental approach to each of the problems it addressed. And though the overall outcome in this term's patent cases leaves quite a lot to be desired, the worst fears of the patent-dependent industries did not come to pass.

II. *Bowman v. Monsanto*

Bowman turned out to be perhaps the least controversial of the intellectual property cases before the Court—though the case certainly elicited much attention because Monsanto Company was the other party to a dispute that involved genetically modified organisms (GMOs). Yet it is precisely because the issue seemed so clear-cut that the decision to hear *Bowman* raised significant worries about the direction that the Supreme Court might take.

At issue in the case was a type of soybean produced by Monsanto. By modifying the soybean's genetic makeup, the company was able to create and patent a bean that is resistant to certain pesticides—specifically to Monsanto's own Roundup. In other words, a farmer planting these particular soybeans (known as Roundup Ready) can spray his field with Roundup pesticide confident that the chemical will kill unwanted weeds but will leave the soybean cash crop unaffected. It should come as no surprise that Monsanto charges a premium for the

---

[4] Microsoft Corp. v. i4i Ltd. Partnership, 131 S. Ct. 2238 (2011).

[5] Bowman v. Monsanto Co., 133 S. Ct. 1761 (2013).

[6] Ass'n for Molecular Pathology v. Myriad Genetics, Inc., 133 S. Ct. 2107 (2013).

[7] FTC v. Actavis, Inc., 133 S. Ct. 2223 (2013). This article will not discuss *Actavis* beyond noting that in that case, as in the other two, the Court, though taking an anti-patent step, made sure that that step was rather modest.

advantage that the pesticide-resistant seed provides. A seed bought from Monsanto is thus significantly more expensive than a seed bought from a grain elevator.

When the farmer buys a Roundup Ready seed, he ends up growing more identical seeds, owing to the genetic features of the initial seed. That is, a farmer who planted one seed will, at the end of the season, end up with several dozen identical seeds borne by the plant that sprouted from the original. Absent unexpected (and unlikely) genetic mutations, these new seeds have the same features as the original seed—they too are Roundup-proof. Theoretically, then, a farmer wishing to grow Roundup Ready soybeans only needs to buy seeds from Monsanto once with every subsequent generation being regrown from that original purchase.

Monsanto recognized this problem and sought to address it through contractual arrangements. When selling its patented soybeans either to farmers directly or to authorized dealers, the company secures a contractual promise from buyers that they will use the purchased seeds to grow only a single generation of soybean plants and won't use the resultant seeds to plant a second generation of plants. Vernon Bowman, a commercial farmer, purchased Roundup Ready seeds from Monsanto's authorized dealer and signed the appropriate contract. He honored the terms of the contract with respect to the seeds that he purchased from Monsanto and its dealers. The seeds that Bowman grew from this original purchase were all harvested and sold to a grain elevator, with none kept for additional replanting. Bowman, however, found what he thought was an ingenious way of circumventing Monsanto's contractual restrictions. After selling his own harvest of soybeans, he purchased more soybeans, but this time not from Monsanto or any of its dealers but from a grain elevator. Though the grain elevator had a mixture of beans, it was fairly easy for Bowman to separate the progeny of the original Monsanto seeds from that of unmodified seeds. All Bowman had to do was to plant the seeds bought from the grain elevator and then spray them with Roundup. The second-generation Roundup Ready seeds would survive, whereas the second-generation unmodified seeds would not. Bowman would then be able to harvest the surviving seeds and sell the bulk of them while keeping a sufficient amount for planting the following year, when he would be able to repeat the process.

This subterfuge allowed Bowman to avoid paying Monsanto's high premium for its patented soybean and instead to pay the regular commodity price for soybeans. The grain elevator, meanwhile, couldn't charge the premium for the patented soybean as opposed to the unmodified natural one because it's not in the business of selling soybeans for future agricultural use. Indeed, federal law explicitly prohibits grain elevators from packaging or marketing their wares as agricultural products.[8] Thus, from the perspective of a grain elevator, a modified soybean is identical to an unmodified soybean, and is worth exactly the same. For that reason, all soybeans are stored together and the same commodity price is charged for all of them—regardless of whether they're descendants of the originally patented seed. Accordingly, the grain elevator (unlike Monsanto or any of its authorized dealers) could not and would not insist on a contractual promise that purchased seeds not be used for multiple generations of agricultural use.

Eventually, Monsanto discovered Bowman's operation and filed suit alleging that his activities infringed Monsanto's patents, which claimed (in one form or another) a modified gene that encoded for the herbicide resistance.[9] Monsanto argued that by growing new seeds that contain the patented gene, Bowman was infringing Monsanto's exclusive rights to "make[], use[], offer[] to sell, or sell[]" the patented invention.[10] Given that he was in fact producing seeds containing the patented gene, Bowman was forced to concede that he indeed "makes, uses, offers to sell, or sells" the patented product. The statute, however, makes an infringer only out of an individual who "makes, uses, offers to sell, or sells" the patented invention *without authority*.[11] Bowman argued that his production of new seeds was authorized by the doctrine of patent exhaustion—which holds that once the patentee has made an authorized sale of a patented invention, the purchaser can use the sold product or resell it to others as he sees fit and on whatever terms he sees fit. Bowman argued that the doctrine prevents Monsanto from objecting to downstream uses

---

[8] See 7 U.S.C. § 1571; Ind. Code § 15-15-1-32 (2012); Bowman, *supra* note 5, at 1765.

[9] U.S. Patent Nos. 5,352,605 (filed Oct. 28, 1993) and RE39,247 E (filed Aug. 22, 2006); Monsanto Co. v. Bowman, 657 F.3d 1341, 1344 (Fed. Cir. 2011) (describing the patented technology).

[10] 35 U.S.C. § 271(a).

[11] *Id.*

of its patented seed because Monsanto exhausted its patent rights via the original sale of the modified soybean. He also argued that whatever contractual restrictions Monsanto tried to place on the use of the seed post-sale were void because they were inconsistent with the nature of the transaction between Monsanto and the dealers or farmers, thus constituting an "end run" around the patent exhaustion doctrine.

Bowman lost the infringement suit and the subsequent appeal to the Federal Circuit.[12] The Supreme Court granted Bowman's petition for the writ of certiorari to address whether the Federal Circuit erred when it created "an exception to the doctrine of patent exhaustion for self-replicating technologies."[13] Given the unanimity of the Federal Circuit panel—which included a judge generally regarded as a skeptic of broad patent law claims—the cert grant was somewhat of a surprise. As the old adage goes, the Supreme Court doesn't grant cases to affirm, and that has been especially true as of late with cases emanating from the Federal Circuit.

The question was whether the Supreme Court would take a broader view of patent exhaustion than did the lower courts, thus potentially undermining the very business model of companies making GMOs. Had the Court adopted Bowman's argument, it would necessarily follow that companies like Monsanto would be able to enjoy their exclusive rights to make and sell their technology for only a year or two (rather than the statutory 20 years of the patent term) because after the first year of sales, downstream purchasers would be able to reproduce the patented GMOs and sell them in competition with the patentee. Each subsequent year would potentially bring in more and more competitors until the price for the patented GMO soybean would be equivalent to the cost of raising *any* soybean. In other words, the patent holder would be unable to charge a premium and so would reap a much lower profit than it can now, perhaps to the point of not even being able to recoup the initial investment in creating the seed. The Supreme Court then was in a perfect position to do considerable damage to an industry that is dependent on patent protection for its business model.

---

[12] Monsanto Co. v. Bowman, 686 F. Supp. 2d 834 (S.D. Ind. 2009), aff'd, 657 F.3d 1341.

[13] Bowman v. Monsanto Co., 133 S. Ct. 420 (2012).

What made the grant all the more suspicious was the attack on a 1992 Federal Circuit case, *Mallinckrodt, Inc. v. Medipart, Inc.*[14] Bowman's cert petition expressly asked the Court to overrule *Mallinckrodt*. The United States, appearing as amicus curiae, though ostensibly supporting affirmance of the decision below, endorsed Bowman's argument on this point. The *Mallinckrodt* case is interesting because it stands for the proposition that the patentee can avoid triggering the patent exhaustion rights if it contractually restricts the post-sale use of the patented device. In *Mallinckrodt*, the Federal Circuit held that when the patentee sold certain medical devices imprinted with "single-use only" notice, disregarding such notice and reusing the devices constituted patent infringement. The *Mallinckrodt* decision has come under much criticism over the last 20 years, so the Supreme Court's decision to review Bowman's lawsuit was viewed as a signal that perhaps the Court not only would broaden the scope of patent exhaustion doctrine, but also would limit the licensing arrangements that have grown common between purveyors and users of various patented goods.

Ultimately, however, the Court dashed those fears—or hopes, depending on which side of the issue you happen to be on—by issuing a short and almost playful unanimous opinion that explicitly declined to address the particular problems posed by self-replicating technologies.[15] The ruling was altogether silent on the permissible scope of licensing arrangements that are meant to counterbalance the patent exhaustion doctrine. Instead, the Court merely reaffirmed the uncontroversial proposition that the patent exhaustion doctrine "restricts a patentee's rights only as to the 'particular article' sold, it leaves untouched the patentee's ability to prevent a buyer from making new copies of the patented item."[16] This proposition was so uncontroversial that Bowman readily conceded it in his brief and at oral argument. This concession proved fatal to Bowman's case.[17] Simply put, the Court concluded that by growing successive generations of Roundup Ready soybean seeds, Bowman was making new, additional patented soybeans—an activity beyond the scope of the

---

[14] Mallinckrodt, Inc. v. Medipart, Inc., 976 F.2d 700 (Fed. Cir. 1992).

[15] Bowman, *supra* note 5, at 1769.

[16] *Id.* at 1766.

[17] *Id.*

patent exhaustion doctrine. And though the Court agreed that seeds are generally meant to be planted and thus Monsanto would likely be unable to restrict the planting (or other use) of the very seeds purchased from itself or an authorized dealer had it attempted to do so, the *re*planting of new seeds and growing additional generations of the patented product were outside the safe harbor provisions of the exhaustion doctrine.

The Court unquestionably got the answer right. As Justice Elena Kagan recognized in her unanimous opinion, under a contrary holding:

> Monsanto's patent would provide scant benefit. After inventing the Roundup Ready trait, Monsanto would, to be sure, "receiv[e] [its] reward" for the first seeds it sells. But in short order, other seed companies could reproduce the product and market it to growers, thus depriving Monsanto of its monopoly. And farmers themselves need only buy the seed once, whether from Monsanto, a competitor, or (as here) a grain elevator. The grower could multiply his initial purchase, and then multiply that new creation, *ad infinitum*— each time profiting from the patented seed without compensating its inventor.[18]

The trouble, though, is that the question the Court answered was not of particular importance to anyone. Both Bowman and Monsanto agreed "that the exhaustion doctrine does not extend to the right to 'make' a new product."[19] The answer to that question in no way depends on various contractual arrangements that Monsanto and its dealers entered into with farmers like Bowman. Bowman would have been adjudged an infringer even absent the restrictive covenants in the sale, because what he violated was not a contractual clause—after all, he bought his seeds from a grain elevator and not from Monsanto—but Monsanto's exclusive right to make new, additional copies of the patented product.

Two far more interesting questions remained unanswered after *Bowman*. First, can a patentee sidestep the exhaustion doctrine via restrictive contractual covenants attendant to the sale of a patented device? Second, in the case of self-replicating technologies, can a party whose wares, through no fault of his own, were contaminated by a

---

[18] *Id*. at 1767 (citations omitted).
[19] *Id*. at 1766 (citations omitted).

patented product be an "infringer" within the meaning of 35 U.S.C. § 271? In other words, had Monsanto's soybeans been blown over onto Bowman's field and cross-pollinated his plants—causing some of Bowman's seeds to contain the patented gene—would Bowman still be liable for infringement? The Court chose not to answer either of these questions in its opinion, perhaps because this case was a poor vehicle to address those issues. After all, Bowman was not an innocent party whose fields were simply contaminated by Monsanto's product. Nor did he plant his seeds in violation of a contractual obligation with the patent holder. Thus, there was no need to delve into these matters.

But that does not mean that these issues simply disappear. Instead, they have been deferred. When they come up—and they will—the Court will need to consider seriously how to reconcile the strict liability nature of infringement with the unavoidable infringement resulting from actions of the *patentee* (and forces of nature) alone. It's quite possible that the doctrine of patent exhaustion at issue in *Bowman* isn't the best tool to resolve this problem, and therefore this question was best left unaddressed in the present case. However, companies like Monsanto may need to develop legal arguments in anticipation of future cases. Similarly, the patent world is now on notice that the federal government views *Mallinckrodt* as incorrectly decided and should expect that argument to be made in due course to the Supreme Court. Patent-reliant companies should be prepared to adjust their business models accordingly. For now, though, industries that rely heavily on patented technology can breathe a little more easily knowing that the Court didn't expand the doctrine of patent exhaustion to the point at which it would undermine the de facto term of the patent and therefore the economic incentives to innovate.

III. *Association for Molecular Pathology v. Myriad Genetics*

Whereas *Bowman* ultimately broke no new ground by relying exclusively on well-established and agreed-upon precedent and deferring the hard questions for later, *Myriad* did none of those things, instead plunging head-on into scientific issues that the Court, judging from oral arguments, clearly did not understand. The result was an incoherent opinion instead of a clear exposition of patent law. That said, the ultimate outcome in *Myriad* is not as bad or as radical as claimed by the petitioners and by a large segment of legal academia.

Myriad Genetics is a company located in Salt Lake City. In the late 1980s, scientists worldwide, realizing that certain forms of breast and ovarian cancer have a genetic component, began searching for genes that increase the likelihood of developing these maladies. Among the hundreds of scientists searching for the answer, Myriad was first to find the location of the gene and first to decode its chemical structure or, in the words of molecular genetics, its "sequence." Myriad managed to separate the cancer-causing gene from the thousands of other genes located on the same chromosome and to develop a test capable of confirming the presence or absence of mutations in that gene. Between 1997 and 2000, Myriad obtained a number of patents on the method of testing for breast cancer and on the isolated gene itself. Because the company had these patents, it possessed exclusive rights to conduct genetic testing for the particular genes known as BRCA1 and BRCA2 (pronounced "brack-uh one" and "brack-uh two"). Myriad did license a number of laboratories to conduct the same tests, but it was under no legal obligation to do so and extracted a price for its license. Unsurprisingly, Myriad charged a higher price than it would have been able to if it had multiple competitors providing the same testing service.

Unhappy with this state of affairs, a collection of doctors, patients, and medical organizations sued Myriad and sought to declare these patents invalid. Throughout the litigation, the challengers essentially argued that genetic materials are not human "inventions," but rather "products of nature" and thus beyond the scope of patent protection. This argument was accepted wholesale by the district court, but rejected, in a split decision, by the Federal Circuit, which held that isolated DNA isn't a product of nature and is therefore eligible for patent protection.[20] In 2012, the Supreme Court vacated that decision and remanded the case to the Federal Circuit in light of a case it had just decided, *Mayo Collaborative Servs. v. Prometheus Labs.*, which limited the scope of patent-eligible subject matter.[21] On remand, the Federal Circuit reissued its original decision with only minor changes.[22] The Supreme Court again granted cert.

[20] Ass'n for Molecular Pathology v. U.S. Patent & Trademark Office, 702 F. Supp. 2d 181 (S.D.N.Y. 2010), aff'd in part & rev'd in part, 653 F.3d 1329 (Fed. Cir. 2011).

[21] Ass'n for Molecular Pathology v. Myriad Genetics, Inc., 132 S. Ct. 1794 (2012).

[22] Ass'n for Molecular Pathology v. U.S. Patent & Trademark Office, 689 F.3d 1303 (Fed. Cir. 2012).

To understand the nature of the legal dispute in *Myriad*, it is necessary to understand the basic science underlying the case. Bear with me through this section, because grasping it is key to understanding what's going on here and evaluating the Supreme Court's ruling.[23]

A DNA molecule consists of two strands of a repetitive sugar-phosphate chain called deoxyribose. Each strand is a long molecule (called a polymer) composed of four types of subunits molecular bases known as adenine, cytosine, guanine, and thymine—("A," "C," "G," and "T," respectively, if you recall your high school biology)—leading to a structure resembling four kinds of beads strung on a necklace. Each adenine base on one strand is paired with a thymine base on the other, and each cytosine base is paired with a guanine base, generating strands that are complementary, not identical. The DNA molecule can be visualized as a zipper with each strand serving as tape and the A, C, T, G base pairs forming the teeth. Unlike a regular zipper, a molecule of DNA is neither straight nor flat. Instead, in its "native" state—the state it assumes naturally inside a living organism—the DNA molecule is twisted into a spiral ladder shape, giving rise to the famous "double helix" model. The chemical and physical properties of native DNA emerge from this combination of factors: the entire sequence of base pairs (rather than a particular isolated fragment); the chemical modification of its nucleotides; the association with proteins such as "histones"; and the overall packaging into superstructures such as chromosomes. Each of these factors plays a role in defining and controlling native DNA's molecular weight, chemical charge, three-dimensional structure, responsiveness to particular chemicals and enzymes, availability of electrons for other chemical reactions, and every other property.

The function of DNA is to provide a set of genetic instructions for the production of other critical molecules: proteins. Amino acids are the building blocks of proteins, and DNA codes for amino acids. This coding operates by grouping nucleotides together in groups of three. Mathematically, each triad drawn from the set of four nucleotides defines a potentially distinct code, yielding 64 distinct possible values, or "codons."[24] For reasons not wholly understood, genes

[23] For a more detailed exposition see Gregory Dolin, Exclusivity Without Patents: The New Frontier of FDA Regulation for Genetic Materials, 98 Iowa L. R. 1399, 1407–17 (2013).

[24] Because there are only 20 amino acids, several codons may code for the same amino acid.

have noncoding regions (known as "introns") that are interspersed among coding regions (known as "exons"). Indeed, the majority of genetic material consists of noncoding regions. Mutations in a codon sequence—which may occur, for example, by adding or deleting a nucleotide or by changing one nucleotide into another—often result in coding for an incorrect amino acid, leading to a defective or completely nonfunctional protein. Thus, when diagnosing genetic disorders, it is important to compare the subject sequence with both the normal sequence and all known mutations. Furthermore, though DNA is composed of two strands, only one strand codes for proteins, while the other simply binds the coding strand. Which strand is coding and which is merely binding can change from one gene to another, however, and even occasionally within a single gene.

DNA doesn't directly code for proteins. Instead, an intermediary molecule known as RNA is used. Thus, the process of "decrypting" the DNA's code begins when the DNA region containing the relevant active gene is "transcribed" into a corresponding RNA molecule. RNA is composed of nucleotides attached to a single strand of a sugar molecule called ribose (as opposed to the dual strands of deoxyribose in DNA). In a similar vein, single-stranded RNA transcribes only the coding strand, never the binding strand. RNA and DNA differ in several other significant ways as well. Unlike the native DNA strand that contains multiple genes, only some of which are active, an RNA molecule contains only a single active gene. Also unlike DNA, RNA lacks the bound histones that fold DNA into the complex chromosomal structures. RNA strands also possess several chemical modifications that native DNA lacks.

Finally, before protein production can begin, a further preprocessing step, known as "RNA splicing," removes noncoding introns from the RNA and splices the remaining exons together in an uninterrupted string known as "messenger RNA," or mRNA. That sets the stage for the "translation" step, where cellular mechanisms read the mRNA, one codon at a time, to produce the final protein structure.

Myriad's patents claimed two types of DNA structures. First, they claimed an isolated gene coding for BRCA1 and BRCA2.[25] In other words, the claim covered a gene excised from the chromosome, separated from various associated proteins and neighboring genes, and

---

[25] See, e.g., claim 1 of U.S. Patent No. 5,747,282 (filed on May 5, 1998).

otherwise purified.[26] It's important to understand that contrary to various press accounts, Myriad did not attempt to patent genes that are carried by individuals as part of their genetic makeup. Instead, Myriad created and patented a small molecule that, standing alone, isn't carried by any individual. The second set of claims was directed to a yet further-refined molecule: Myriad constructed a DNA molecule that was complementary to the sequence of mRNA. In other words, like mRNA (and unlike the native-state DNA) this molecule no longer had any noncoding introns. Instead, it had only the coding exon regions. In all other respects, it had features of DNA rather than RNA. This molecule, because it is *complementary* to the RNA molecule, is known as cDNA.[27]

The petitioners in *Myriad* argued that neither isolated DNA nor cDNA are patent-eligible because both are products of nature. Under longstanding patent principles, only inventions created by human ingenuity are eligible for a patent, while naturally occurring products—for example, gold, trees, and so forth—are not patent-eligible.[28] The petitioners' argument rested on the premise that, isolated or not, these pieces of DNA ultimately perform the same function as naturally occurring DNA: they code for proteins. In other words, native DNA, isolated DNA, and cDNA all carry the same information. In the petitioners' view, DNA's information-carrying capacity rendered *all* DNA molecules carrying that information patent-ineligible subject matter.

Myriad, on the other hand, pointed out that these precise molecules (whether isolated DNA or cDNA) never existed in nature until isolated from larger structures. The company argued, and the Federal Circuit agreed, that the molecules described in the patents have vastly different chemical properties—such as molecular weight, ionic charge, and ability to react with other reagents—than naturally

---

[26] Technically, the claim went to a wholly synthetic DNA molecule that merely had the same nucleotide sequence that an excised piece of a chromosome would have had. This fact alone should have sufficed to settle the patent-eligibility question. The Court chose to read the claim more broadly, however, so that it would cover not just synthetic constructs but also genetic material excised from the chromosome. I engage the Court's reasoning on its own terms.

[27] See, e.g., claim 2 of U.S. Patent No. 5,747,282 (filed on May 5, 1998).

[28] See, e.g., Diamond v. Chakrabarty, 447 U.S. 303, 309 (1980).

occurring molecules. In short, the dispute centered on whether DNA should be judged on its chemical or biological functions.

The solicitor general, arguing the case as amicus curiae, took a "split the baby" approach. With respect to native DNA, he argued that isolated DNA is too similar to what occurs in nature to qualify for patent protection. With respect to cDNA, however, he argued that human intervention was of sufficient magnitude to make the resultant product patent-eligible.

The Court's opinion ultimately adopted the solicitor general's position and held isolated DNA to be patent-ineligible but cDNA to be patent-eligible. Surprisingly, this split decision prompted news media worldwide to announce that the Court "invalidated gene patents."[29] That isn't what the Court did, although the media's confusion is understandable given the incoherent nature of the opinion. In concluding that isolated DNA is *not* patent-eligible subject matter, the Court, per Justice Clarence Thomas, concluded that

> Myriad's claims [are not] saved by the fact that isolating DNA
> from the human genome severs chemical bonds and thereby
> creates a nonnaturally occurring molecule. Myriad's claims
> are simply not expressed in terms of chemical composition,
> nor do they rely in any way on the chemical changes that
> result from the isolation of a particular section of DNA.
> Instead, the claims understandably focus on the genetic
> information . . . . [I]ts claim is concerned primarily with the
> information contained in the genetic *sequence*, not with the
> specific chemical composition of a particular molecule.[30]

The Court apparently agreed with the petitioners' argument that DNA is primarily an information-carrying molecule, not subject to the same rules as other chemical molecules. But a mere page later, in a single, cursory paragraph, Justice Thomas wrote that the "creation of a cDNA sequence from mRNA results in an exons-only molecule that is not naturally occurring," making "cDNA . . . distinct from the DNA from which it was derived. As a result, cDNA is not a 'product

[29] See, e.g., David G. Savage, Supreme Court Rejects Gene Patents, L.A. Times, Jun. 14, 2013, at 1.

[30] Myriad, *supra* note 6, at 2118 (emphasis in original).

of nature' and is patent eligible."[31] There is no mention of cDNA's information-carrying capacity.

The legal analysis leading to the conclusion of patent ineligibility for isolated DNA is thus irreconcilable with the legal analysis leading to the conclusion of patent eligibility for cDNA. Whereas the former looks to the information encoded in the DNA molecule, the latter looks at its chemical structure. No explanation is given as to why such different approaches are appropriate.

The concluding section of the opinion makes the matter even more opaque. There, Justice Thomas states that the methods used by Myriad to find and isolate BRCA1 and BRCA2 genes "were well understood, widely used, and fairly uniform insofar as any scientist engaged in the search for a gene would likely have utilized a similar approach."[32] But it's unclear why this is legally significant. Methods for creating cDNA are also "well understood, widely used, and fairly uniform." But it has long been the law that the method of arriving at an invention isn't relevant to the inquiry of whether the invention is novel or patent-eligible. The inclusion of this phrase only adds confusion to the requirements for patent eligibility going forward. Will the courts below now be required not only to identify the amount of difference between a lab-created product and naturally occurring substances, but also to determine whether "enough effort" went into creating these differences? If so, how much effort will be "enough"? It remains to be seen how the Federal Circuit and district courts apply this decision to new facts, but the creation of these problems was entirely unnecessary.

The reason for this confusion is the Court's accepting the erroneous argument that DNA is somehow unique with respect to its information-carrying function and capacity. In fact, there's nothing particularly unique about DNA. It's true that DNA carries information that the cellular mechanisms then use to make RNA and proteins. But the same can be said about a number of other molecules. For example, a number of molecules work by binding to cellular proteins on the outside of the cell, which results in a chain reaction inside the cell leading to very particular outcomes. Such molecules could be easily described as "information-carrying" because they carry instructions for the cell to act a certain way at a certain time. Other proteins bind

[31] *Id.* at 2119.
[32] *Id.* at 2120.

to DNA itself in order to activate or deactivate certain genes. This process too could be described as "information-carrying" because only as a result of such binding do cellular mechanisms know when to express a particular gene and when to leave it quiescent.

Much medical research is centered on intervening in these processes to modify the expression of certain deleterious genes or to enhance the expression of beneficial genes. Laboratory-designed molecules must have the same "informational" capacity as naturally occurring molecules to work. Consider laboratory-made insulin. Most of it is either identical or nearly identical to naturally occurring insulin,[33] and for good reason. If the laboratory-designed molecule were different, it wouldn't be insulin at all, and could not treat diabetes. This similarity to the naturally occurring product is to be celebrated and rewarded rather than held as the basis for patent ineligibility. If the identity of informational function were to serve as a bar to patent eligibility, such research will grind to a halt.

The Supreme Court should instead have focused on the fact that isolated DNA and cDNA are merely research, diagnostic, and treatment tools in much the same way as various dyes that are used to stain biopsies or centrifuges that are used to separate blood products. There is little doubt that dyes, centrifuges, pipettes, and the like are all patent-eligible subject matter. The fact that new tools are biological rather than mechanical should not change the analysis. Yet this fact was lost on the Supreme Court, the petitioners, the solicitor general, and even, in some respects, on Myriad itself. This misconception led to the illogical and disjointed opinion.

The Court's opinion, though problematic and at war with itself, was not a total loss. The Court did reject the more extreme version of the argument pressed by the petitioners and a number of amici, which urged the Court to declare all DNA to be patent-ineligible on the theory that the functionality of the invented product should decide its eligibility for a patent. Had the Court adopted that argument, it would have created significant problems for the biotechnology industry by essentially declaring that medical innovations that rely on biologic solutions (rather than traditional chemical pills) are beyond the reach of the Patent Act. The perverse result of such a decision

[33] See FDA, NovoLog Insulin Aspart Label (2013), available at http://www.accessdata.fda.gov/drugsatfda_docs/label/2005/020986s033lbl.pdf.

would have been to incentivize less desirable forms of medical treatments while disincentivizing the more desirable kind. Luckily, the Court did not go that far, leaving plenty of room for innovation and patent protection in biotechnology and biopharmaceuticals.

But the Court's opinion does sow confusion where none was necessary, especially in light of the previous term's extraordinarily broad anti-patent opinion in *Mayo*. But given the choice between confusion remediable in lower courts by careful application of *Myriad* to new facts and complete prohibition on patenting the fruits of genetic research, the former is clearly better.

IV. Conclusion

This past term, the Supreme Court faced a number of complicated patent questions. Given the Court's recent performance on patent law, the industry had much to be concerned about. The Court seemed poised to: (1) expand the patent exhaustion doctrine significantly, giving a new and broad shield to infringers; (2) limit the scope of patent eligibility, potentially taking an entire industry outside the ambit of patent protection; and (3) restrict the ability of patentees to enforce their patents not only through litigation, but also through settlement.[34] At the end of the term, however, each industry could breathe a little easier. Though the Court did manage to make the law a little less patentee-friendly, and did create confusion where none was necessary, the outcome was far from the worst-case scenario. That's not to say that patentees can fully relax because it remains to be seen how lower courts and eventually the Supreme Court answer the questions left open and resolve the confusion stemming from this term's decisions. But at least patentees will live to fight another day—an outcome that was not a given when these cases were set for argument. In short, for patentees, the Supreme Court's October Term 2012 can best be characterized by an old Jewish saying: "It could've been worse."

---

[34] See Actavis, *supra* note 7. In that case, the Supreme Court did not adopt a bright line, per se rule that under antitrust laws, patentees cannot enter certain types of settlement agreements with patent challengers. Instead, the Court settled on a "rule of reason" analysis that, though more restrictive than the current practice, continues to allow the patentees to protect their patents through settlement agreements. Nonetheless, the Court's decision sowed much confusion about how to actually apply this new rule. In that sense, *Actavis*'s incremental approach is similar to the one taken in *Bowman* and *Myriad*.

Patent Protection for Genetic Innovation: *Monsanto* and *Myriad*

*David S. Olson**

Genetic science is increasingly important to the economy and people's individual lives. Among other things, genetic scientists have contributed to the ongoing Green Revolution that began in the 1950s and continues making agriculture ever more efficient. The study of genetics can also inform people about their risks for disease and develop therapies to treat many of the health scourges of our time. Of course, the genetic research that brings forth such advances (or sometimes endangers our health, according to some critics of genetically modified organisms (GMO)) is complex and costly to conduct. Thus, since at least the 1980s, companies have turned to patents to protect their innovations in genetics.

This term, the Supreme Court ruled on two cases involving patents in the field of genetics. In the first case, the Court upheld a decision preventing a farmer from reproducing Monsanto's Roundup Ready soybeans for subsequent plantings. In the second case, the Court ruled that natural DNA, as it exists in living organisms, is not patentable, but that complementary DNA ("cDNA"), which is produced in laboratories, is patentable even though cDNA is very similar to DNA.

In practical effect, this term the Court maintained protection for genetic crop modifications that are passed on in successive generations of the plants ("self-replicating" genetically modified plants). In disallowing patents on DNA but allowing them on cDNA, the Court decreased the patent rights given to researchers who discover genetic mutations that correlate with disease, but did not fully eliminate them. As to the effects on substantive patent law, the Court explained that the legal doctrine of patent exhaustion does not operate to permit the "making" of new copies of a patented genetic seed,

* Associate Professor, Boston College Law School. I thank Sarandos Markopolous for able research assistance.

even if the method of making the new copy is merely planting the patented seed and letting it grow more seeds that contain the patented genetic trait. The Court also continued to grapple with one of the most amorphous and intellectually unsatisfying areas in patent law—the question of what types of innovation and discovery should qualify for patentability. The Court has not clearly stated a uniform statutory interpretation and policy rationale for what should be patentable, and thus continues to make piecemeal decisions in individual cases without providing clear guidelines or predictability in this area of law. Notwithstanding that, this term the Court probably arrived at a decision that is good policy when it comes to patents on genetic material that occurs in nature.

Bowman v. Monsanto

In *Bowman v. Monsanto,* the Supreme Court upheld a Federal Circuit decision holding a farmer liable for patent infringement for buying and replanting patented seeds.[1] The farmer, Vernon Hugh Bowman, bought seed from a grain elevator deliberately so as to get the advantage of Monsanto's genetically modified soybeans without having to pay Monsanto a patent license fee for each use of a new batch of seeds.

Monsanto created and patented[2] a genetic modification to soybean plants that makes them resistant to glyphosate, which is the active ingredient in Monsanto's herbicide Roundup (as well as many other herbicides). Monsanto markets the seed as "Roundup Ready" seed. Monsanto sells the seed to farmers with a license agreement that allows the farmers to plant the seed and then harvest and consume or sell the crop of soybeans as a commodity, generally to grain elevators who resell to soybean processors. The license agreement is important because the soybeans grown from the seeds purchased from authorized Monsanto retailers are themselves seeds. These soybeans can be consumed, or they can be planted and will reproduce a new crop of Roundup Ready soybean plants. Thus, but for the license agreement, a farmer could buy a single planting's worth of Roundup Ready seed and then replant a portion of the resulting

---

[1] Bowman v. Monsanto Co., 133 S. Ct. 1761, 1763 (2013).

[2] Monsanto claims its Roundup Ready soybean is covered by U.S. Patent Nos. 5,352,605 and RE39,247E.

crop to produce generation after generation of Roundup Ready soy-beans without ever having to buy more from an authorized Mon-santo retailer.

Monsanto has seen widespread adoption of its Roundup Ready seed because it saves farmers considerable time and effort in eradi-cating weeds from their fields. By using Roundup Ready seed, farm-ers can plant the seed and then spray the herbicide glyphosate on their fields, which kills weeds and leaves the soybean plants intact. This method has been very popular with farmers, who find it a con-siderable improvement over prior methods of dealing with weeds.

Bowman bought Roundup Ready seed pursuant to a license from an authorized Monsanto dealer for his spring plantings but did not buy it for his fall planting. Instead, he bought soybeans from his local grain elevator at a price significantly lower than Monsanto dealers charge and planted those seeds in the fall. He then treated the result-ing plants with glyphosate, which killed the weeds and any non-glyphosate-resistant soybean plants. Because the vast majority of farmers use Monsanto's patented seed, most of his soybean plants survived. Of these surviving soybean plants, all of them contained the patented genetic trait of resistance to glyphosate. Bowman then used some of the soybeans from his fall crop to continue planting soybeans, and he continued in this way for successive generations. By the time Monsanto sued, Bowman had grown eight generations of soybeans containing the glyphosate-resistant trait that Monsanto had patented.

Bowman did not deny that the soybeans he was using to plant suc-cessive generations of plants contained the genetic trait covered by Monsanto's patents on glyphosate-resistant soybean plants. Rather, Bowman defended himself by invoking the doctrine of patent ex-haustion. This doctrine limits patent rights to an initial authorized sale of a patented item.[3] The authorized buyer then has "the right to use [or] sell" the item in whatever way the buyer chooses. The policy rationale underlying the patent exhaustion doctrine is that the pat-ent owner only gets to receive the reward from its patent monopoly at the initial sale of an item covered by the patent. The buyer may

---

[3] Quanta Computer, Inc. v. LG Electronics, Inc., 553 U.S. 617, 625 (2008) (noting that "the initial authorized sale of a patented item terminates all patent rights to that item").

then use and further convey the item free of the risk of a patent infringement suit to himself or subsequent purchasers.[4]

Patent law gives the patent owner the right to exclude others from making, using, selling, or importing a patented invention.[5] The law is clear that patent exhaustion bars only the assertion of patent rights against successive sales of a patented item after a first authorized sale.[6] The exhaustion doctrine does not allow an authorized buyer to make additional copies of the patented item, or even to reconstruct the item when it has become sufficiently degraded.[7] The policy behind this is simple: to allow a buyer to make copies or reconstruct the patented item "would impinge on the patentee's right to exclude others from making" the patented item.[8]

Monsanto accused Bowman of making, using, and selling Monsanto's patented seeds without authorization by his actions of buying soybeans that he knew to contain the patented trait, planting them, applying glyphosate to them, and then planting and reusing subsequent generations of the soybeans. Bowman argued that he had not made copies of the patented soybeans. Rather, he argued that the soybeans were "self-replicating" and that they made copies of themselves when they were placed in the ground. He argued in addition that because soybeans are seeds that naturally reproduce when planted, Monsanto's initial sale of patented soybean seeds exhausted Monsanto's patent rights because the only way to use the patented soybean seed was to produce more soybeans.[9]

In a unanimous decision, the Court made short work of Bowman's asserted patent exhaustion defense. The Court held that Bowman's planting of new generations of soybean plants definitively qualified as making new instances of the patented plants. In doing so,

---

[4] See United States v. Univis Lens Co., 316 U.S. 241, 251 (1942) ("[T]he purpose of the patent law is fulfilled with respect to any particular article when the patentee has received his reward . . . by the sale of the article.").

[5] 35 U.S.C. § 271(a) ("Except as otherwise provided in this title, whoever without authority makes, uses, offers to sell, or sells any patented invention, within the United States or imports into the United States any patented invention during the term of the patent therefor, infringes the patent.").

[6] 35 U.S.C. § 154.

[7] Aro Mfg. Co. v. Convertible Top Replacement Co., 365 U.S. 336, 346 (1961).

[8] Wilbur-Ellis Co. v. Kuther, 377 U.S. 422, 424 (1964) (internal quotation omitted).

[9] Bowman, 133 S. Ct. at 1765.

the Court noted that a contrary holding would leave Monsanto with "scant protection" because Monsanto would only be able to sell its patented seed once, and then the buyer could create and sell successive generations of plants with the patented trait.[10] The Court averred that it was deciding only the case at issue and reserved judgment on other patent exhaustion issues that might arise from self-replicating products, such as self-replication that occurs outside a purchaser's control, or that is a necessary but incidental step in using the item for another purpose.[11]

The Court also did not have occasion to address a harder question that has remained open since its 2008 decision in *Quanta v. LG Electronics*[12]: the boundaries of patent exhaustion and whether parties can contract around exhaustion. In *Quanta*, the Court held that patent owner LG's sale of computer chips to chip manufacturer Intel exhausted all patent rights embodied in the chips. Thus, the patentee could not seek license fees from Quanta, which bought chips from Intel and then used them to build computers. The contract at issue in *Quanta* licensed only the manufacturer Intel's use of the patented chips with other Intel components; it did not authorize the combination of the licensed chips with non-Intel components (such as the data buses and memory that Quanta connected to the chips to build computers). But importantly, the license agreement did not prohibit Intel from selling the patented chips to buyers that Intel knew would combine the chips with other, non-Intel parts, thus exceeding the scope of Intel's license.

The Court held that LG's license to Intel authorizing Intel to make and sell chips embodying the patents exhausted LG's patent rights, and the Court prohibited LG from suing Quanta or other computer manufacturers who bought chips from Intel. Because the license agreement did not prohibit Intel from selling chips to computer manufacturers that LG wanted to separately license, the case left open two questions: First, could a contract claim lie against a manufacturer if the manufacturer's license agreement with the patent

---

[10] *Id.* at 1763.

[11] *Id.* at 1769 (citing 17 U.S.C. § 117(a)(1) ("[I]t is not [a copyright] infringement for the owner of a copy of a computer program to make . . . another copy . . . of that computer program provide[d] that such a new copy . . . is created as an essential step in the utilization of the computer program.")).

[12] Quanta, 553 U.S. at 625.

owner prohibited the manufacturer from selling to buyers who it knew would use the products in prohibited manners (for example, to combine with their components to make computers)? Second, could a patent claim lie against both the manufacturer and anyone who bought from the manufacturer if the license agreement with the manufacturer prohibited sales to those who the manufacturer knew would make unauthorized uses of the patented component? In a nutshell, is patent exhaustion a default that can be contracted around, or is it a hard rule that negates attempts to contract to a different result?

The *Bowman* case does not address these questions because the soybeans at issue were new instances of the patented invention. The logic of *Quanta*, however, suggests that even careful drafting of contracts will not accomplish making successive buyers of patented items infringers, especially if they were not in privity with the initial contract. The Court in *Quanta* disallowed LG from doing just that. LG wanted to license Intel to use its patents for certain authorized uses, but it attempted to draft its contract so that successive users of the patented components would not have the right to use the components without negotiating separate licenses with LG. The Court rejected such restraints on alienation in patent rights, and it seems very unlikely that it would be enough to avoid exhaustion to merely change the contract so that subsequent buyers of components have notice of the purported limited license.

On the other hand, if a contract authorizes a buyer only to use the patents but does not allow the sale of products incorporating the patents to others, could this be enforced in contract and patent law? It would certainly be a breach of contract for a manufacturer to sell components in contravention of the contract. Would patent exhaustion negate the contract claim? Further, if the patent owner only licensed the manufacturer to make and use items embodying the patent, would it be patent infringement for the manufacturer to sell to a third party and for that third party to combine the patented components and resell?

In some areas, courts have upheld license terms restricting the use of patented or copyrighted materials to an initial user. Such license agreements have been widely upheld for computer software. Likewise, courts have generally upheld license agreements that restrict uses of a patented item to a single use. Such restrictions are popular for patented medical devices such as stents, for instance. The difference between these cases and *Quanta*, however, is that software and medical devices are sold to end users, and thus the license restrictions merely prevent resale to other end users. In *Quanta*, the patents were licensed to chipmaker Intel, and LG knew that Intel would make chips using the patented technology and sell them to other manufacturers for use in computers. Thus, the contract term in *Quanta* acted to disrupt the vertical chain of manufacturing. Are such restrictions in vertical manufacturing chains preempted by patent exhaustion? Again, because *Bowman* deals with a new instance of a patented product, it does not answer any of these lingering questions from *Quanta*. We will have to wait to see how the Court addresses these issues as future contracting arrangements are tried and challenged.

Association for Molecular Pathology v. Myriad Genetics, Inc.

In *Association for Molecular Pathology v. Myriad Genetics*, the Supreme Court dealt with a more fundamental question: is DNA patentable? The Court unanimously held that DNA as it occurs in nature is not patentable, even if a particular section of DNA is extracted from an organism and isolated. Yet the Court also held that cDNA, a non-naturally occurring synthetic creation, is patentable. Because cDNA is commonly used in laboratories when working with DNA, the right to exclude others from making cDNA may still give cDNA patent owners substantial control over working with genetic sequences. As more laboratories work with native DNA, however, the practical commercial advantage of cDNA patents may decrease. The Court expressly reserved judgment on whether human-created DNA that does not have a counterpart in nature can be patented.

The patents at issue in *Myriad* claim, in various forms, two human genes, BRCA1 and BRCA2, and some of their common mutations.[13] The claims cover both DNA and cDNA sequences. Myriad's claimed "invention" was not a new genetic sequence, but rather discovering both the location and sequence of the BRCA1 and BRCA2 genes (pronounced "brack-uh one" and "brack-uh two"), as well as mutations of those genes that can significantly increase a person's risk of breast and ovarian cancer. Myriad's patents claimed the genes and portions

---

[13] Ass'n for Molecular Pathology v. Myriad Genetics, Inc., 133 S. Ct. 2107, 1308 n.2 (2008). The patents and claims at issue were claims 1, 2, 5, 6, and 7 of U.S. Patent 5,747,282, claim 1 of U.S. Patent 5,693,473, and claims 1, 6, and 7 of U.S. Patent 5,837,492.

thereof, either in a form extracted and isolated from the human body or in the form of cDNA, which is created in the laboratory from messenger RNA ("mRNA").[14]

Because the Court's opinion as to patentability turns on the differences between DNA and cDNA, a brief description of the science is in order. The human genome contains approximately 22,000 genes in 23 pairs of chromosomes.[15] Each gene is encoded as DNA. DNA is made up of four nucleotides: adenine (A), thymine (T), cytosine (C), and guanine (G).[16] DNA occurs in a double helix in which each nucleotide on one side of the helix binds with only one other nucleotide from the other side of the helix. A binds with T and C binds with G.[17] The ordering of the nucleotides in the DNA determines an organism's genetic makeup.[18] Sequences of DNA nucleotides contain the genetic code to create strings of amino acids from which the body builds proteins.[19] Not all DNA sequences code for amino acids, however. The sequences that have the information to produce amino acids are called "exons." The sequences that do not code for amino acids are called "introns."[20]

DNA produces proteins by the processes of transcription and translation. Transcription occurs when the organism is ready to produce proteins from a sequence of DNA. During this process, the DNA double helix separates into two individual strands. The strands of DNA then interact with enzymes to create complementary ribonucleic acid ("RNA") strands.[21] RNA contains the same four nucleotides as DNA, except that RNA substitutes the nucleotide base uracil (U) for thymine (T).[22] The result of transcription is called pre-RNA. This is an inverse image of the DNA strand with which it bonded. Pre-RNA corresponds to the entire strand of DNA from which it was

---

[14] Id. at 1975.

[15] Jane B. Reece & Neil A. Campbell, Campbell Biology 102 (6th ed. 2011).

[16] Id. at 9.

[17] Id. at 88.

[18] Id. at 26.

[19] Id. at 335.

[20] Id. at 335.

[21] Id. at 328.

[22] Id. at 88.

created, and thus contains both exons and introns.[23] In the next step, the pre-RNA separates from the DNA, and the intron portions of the RNA strands are discarded, leaving only an RNA strand in which the exon portions are spliced together. The result is mRNA.[24] Amino acids are produced in the next part of the process, called translation. During translation, ribosomes read the mRNA strand three nucleotides at a time. These groups of three nucleotides are called "codons." Each codon tells the corresponding ribosomes to create 1 of 20 possible amino acids or to stop production of amino acids. The resulting amino acids are then used to create proteins that are used to fulfill the specific function for which the DNA codes.[25]

Researchers can extract DNA from the human body and study it in the lab.[26] Researchers can also create cDNA in the laboratory by reverse transcription from mRNA.[27] Reverse transcription occurs when scientists use the enzyme known as reverse transcriptase ("RT"), which contains nucleotides, to make an inverse copy of mRNA.[28] Because each nucleotide base pairs only with one other base, RNA is, in effect, a mirror image of DNA, and cDNA is a mirror image of mRNA. Thus, cDNA is identical to DNA except in one significant aspect: because all introns are removed from mRNA, the cDNA that results from reverse transcription with mRNA contains only the exon-encoding sequences of the original DNA.[29] All intron portions are omitted. The resulting cDNA can be used to create mRNA and the resulting amino acids and proteins, but it is not chemically identical to the DNA that occurs in nature because it contains only exons.[30]

Research scientists find cDNA very useful.[31] Scientists use cDNA to create cDNA libraries of mRNA, which allows them to have libraries of the genetic sequences that code for the proteins of the cor-

---

[23] *Id.* at 329.

[24] *Id.* at 328.

[25] *Id.* at 329.

[26] *Id.* at 10.

[27] *Id.* at 401.

[28] *Id.*

[29] *Id.*

[30] *Id.* at 403.

[31] *Id.* at 401.

responding mRNA.[32] Reverse transcription to produce cDNA is also a common and cost-effective way to produce a significantly greater volume of the genetic material with which scientists are working.[33] This process is called "amplification," and it is crucial to gene cloning and to creating gene probes to test for the presence of specific genetic material.[34] It is important to note that cDNA does not occur in nature, but for one exception—certain viruses create cDNA and then insert it into host cells as a way to program the cells to create proteins to replicate the virus.[35] This cDNA does not occur naturally in the host organism, but rather is created by the virus's invasion of the organism and interaction with mRNA.[36]

Mutations in segments of DNA occur when the order of nucleotides is altered.[37] Mutations of even a single nucleotide can produce entirely different amino acids, or can end amino acid production.[38] Mutations can also occur on larger scales in which hundreds or millions of nucleotides are missing, rearranged, or repeated.[39] Large-scale mutations can result in the elimination of certain genes, or in their misplacement or duplication.[40] Some mutations have no effect. Others have debilitating consequences. Strictly speaking, there is not a single, "normal" sequence for a gene. Rather, some variation occurs across individuals. On the whole, the sequence is similar enough that the gene is the same. Common variants of DNA sequences for a gene are called "wild types" of that gene.[41] "Mutations" are changes in the sequence that are more significant or that cause significant effects.[42]

Myriad's discovery of the location and sequence of the BRCA1 and BRCA2 genes allowed it to study and classify the various wild types

---

[32] *Id.*

[33] *Id.* at 409.

[34] *Id.*

[35] *Id.* at 401.

[36] *Id.*

[37] *Id.* at 344.

[38] *Id.*

[39] *Id.* at 298.

[40] *Id.* at 345.

[41] *Id.* at 288.

[42] *Id.*

of the genes. It also made it possible for Myriad to categorize common mutations of the genes and to study the increased risk of cancer from various mutations. Myriad used its patents to exclude others from using the BRCA1 and BRCA2 genes to test for and provide information to patients as to their risk factors for breast and ovarian cancer.[43] Myriad followed an enforcement practice to preserve its place as the sole test provider for BRCA1 and BRCA2 genes.[44] Myriad charged $4,000 per test,[45] and it did not allow others to test for BRCA1 and BRCA2 mutations, even if only to provide "second opinions" as to the risk from mutation.[46]

The plaintiffs in the case included women who wanted their BRCA1 and BRCA2 genes tested to determine their cancer risk and Dr. Harry Osterer, a genetic researcher who sent patients' DNA samples to a competing lab until Myriad sent letters informing the lab that testing patients' BRCA1 and BRCA2 genes infringed its patents.[47] Dr. Osterer asserted that he would resume sending patients' DNA samples to competing labs for testing if Myriad's patents were ruled invalid. The Federal Circuit found that only Dr. Osterer had standing to bring the instant suit,[48] and the Supreme Court did not consider whether any other plaintiffs had standing.[49] Instead, the Supreme Court proceeded directly to the question of the patentability of DNA and cDNA.

The Court held that naturally occurring DNA is not patentable because it falls within the longstanding exception to patentability for natural phenomena. The Court held that cDNA is patentable, however, because it is not "naturally occurring."[50]

[43] *Id.*

[44] *Id.* at 1340.

[45] David B. Agus, The Outrageous Cost of a Gene Test, N.Y. Times, May 20, 2013, at A25.

[46] Reece & Campbell, *supra* note 15, at 1339.

[47] *Id.* at 1340.

[48] *Id.* at 7.

[49] *Id.*

[50] The Court noted that cDNA may be created in certain cases by viruses, but it held that fact to be lacking in material significance. The cDNA of genes found in the human genome generally cannot be found naturally in the body, and the Court held that the possible introduction of some cDNA by invasive viruses too rare, random, and unpredictable to disqualify cDNA from categorization as a man-made "synthetic DNA." Myriad, 133 S. Ct. at 1350.

Myriad is the latest in a train of Supreme Court cases dealing with patentable subject matter. Notwithstanding very broad language in the patent statute as to what types of innovations and discoveries are patentable, the Supreme Court has—at least until recently—always understood itself to be vested with the power to determine what sorts of innovation are and are not patentable. In the early years of the Republic, the Supreme Court took on what amounted to a common-law approach to patentable subject matter.[51] From the outset, the Court announced three exceptions to patentable subject matter: "laws of nature, natural phenomena, and abstract ideas."[52] These exceptions to what can be patented are not found in either the constitutional grant to Congress of the right to grant patents, or in the Patent Act itself. Rather, the Court has called these "important implicit exceptions" to what can be patented.[53] Over the years, courts have invented additional tests to exclude certain types of innovation from patentability. The Supreme Court and the Federal Circuit (or its predecessor, the Court of Claims and Patent Appeals) came up with the physical transformation test (meaning that a process had to result in a physical transformation of matter to qualify for patenting), the mathematical algorithm exception to patentability, and the mental steps doctrine (holding unpatentable processes that could also be performed as a series of mental steps). For a time, methods of doing business were also presumed to be unpatentable, but in the 1998 *State Street Bank* case, the Federal Circuit ruled that business methods are patentable, and that statements to the contrary over the years were merely dicta.[54]

The Court has justified its exceptions to patentable subject matter on policy grounds. First, the Court has said that laws of nature, natural phenomena, and abstract ideas "are the basic tools of scientific

[51] David S. Olson, Taking the Utilitarian Basis of Patent Law Seriously: The Case for Restricting Patentable Subject Matter, 82 Temp. L. Rev. 181 (2009).

[52] See Diamond v. Diehr, 450 U.S. 175, 185 (1981); Diamond v. Chakrabarty, 447 U.S. 303, 309 (1980); Le Roy v. Tatham, 55 U.S. 156, 175 (1852); O'Reilly v. Morse, 56 U.S. 62, 112–20 (1853).

[53] Mayo Collaborative Servs. v. Prometheus Laboratories, Inc., 132 S. Ct. 1289, 1293 (2012).

[54] State St. Bank & Trust Co. v. Signature Fin. Group, Inc., 149 F.3d 1368 (Fed. Cir. 1998).

and technological work."[55] Second, and more practically, the Court has claimed that to allow patents in these areas would "tie up" these basic building blocks of science and research, and therefore "inhibit future innovation premised upon them."[56] Indeed, if one examines the case law carefully, one sees that for the majority of U.S. history, the Supreme Court decided what sorts of innovation should be patentable and what should not. These determinations were based on a rough, implicit calculus as to whether patentability for a certain type of innovation would likely benefit society with enough increased invention to outweigh the costs of granting patents—in terms of both higher prices to consumers and possible holdups to research from the difficulties in licensing all of the necessary patents.[57]

Historically, the Court's approach to patentable subject matter was very much like its approach to making antitrust law—the Court seemed to view the broad patentable subject matter section of the Patent Act as an invitation for judicial lawmaking. While this view was never explicitly endorsed by an act of Congress, it was never rejected by Congress either. In fact, Congress has never substantially changed the patentable subject-matter section of the Patent Act. Instead, Congress has seemed content to let the courts hash out what types of innovation should and should not be patentable.

The historic approach to judges shaping the law of patentable subject matter faded in recent decades until, in *Bilski v. Kappos*,[58] the Court explicitly rejected any substantial role in developing the law

---

[55] Mayo, 132 S. Ct. at 1293.

[56] *Id.* at 1301. The Supreme Court's concern that patents in these areas would deter science and innovation rests upon two implicit assumptions. First, the Court assumes that an adequate level of research and innovation in these areas is possible without the incentive effects of patent grants. Second, the Court assumes that the transaction costs of clearing rights to successive and overlapping patents would be great enough to deter a significant amount of socially beneficial research that would occur but for these patent rights. Basically, the Court assumes that patents are not needed for adequate innovation in these areas and/or that, to the extent that patents might spur more innovation in these areas, the subsequent costs of licensing the patent rights to allow further research would be great enough to deter more scientific advancement than they encourage. Although these assumptions seem reasonable and even intuitive, there is little and conflicting empirical support for them.

[57] See Olson, Taking the Utilitarian Basis of Patent Law Seriously, *supra* note 51. But note that either a low-transaction-cost licensing environment or widespread unpunished infringement can overcome problems of patent thickets.

[58] Bilski v. Kappos, 130 S. Ct. 3218, 3221 (2010).

of patentable subject matter.[59] Instead, the Court in *Bilski* announced that it was going to interpret the Patent Act according to the ordinary meaning of the text of the act.[60] Moreover, the Court has "more than once cautioned that courts 'should not read into the patent laws limitations and conditions which the legislature has not expressed.'"[61] The Court made its textual approach to Section 101 even more clear in *Bilski* when it said, "In patent law, as in all statutory construction, '[u]nless otherwise defined "words will be interpreted as taking their ordinary, contemporary, common meaning.""[62]

There are two problems with the Court's hard turn to textualism in the Patent Act. First, while there is great merit to textualism—in that it allows Courts to enforce the law rather than say what the law is—a sudden swerve to textualism in patentable subject-matter determinations is problematic if Congress has basically concluded that it has delegated patentable subject-matter determinations to the Court. Second, and more fundamentally, the plain text of the Patent Act reads to make everything patentable.

Section 101 of the Patent Act lays out the requirements for patentable subject matter.[63] The statute says: "Whoever invents or discovers any new and useful process, machine, manufacture, or composition of matter, or any new and useful improvement thereof, may obtain a patent therefor, subject to the conditions and requirements of this title."[64] This statutory text is very broad. The plain text of those words makes everything patentable. Every physical item in the world is a composition of matter.[65] And just about everything that is

---

[59] *Id.*

[60] *Id.* at 3225.

[61] *Id.* at 3221 (quoting Diamond v. Diehr, 450 U.S. at 182).

[62] Bilski, 130 S. Ct. at 3226 (2010) (quoting Perrin v. United States, 444 U.S. 37, 42 (1979)).

[63] 35 U.S.C. § 101.

[64] *Id.*

[65] The *American Heritage Dictionary* defines "matter" as: "1.a. Something that occupies space and can be perceived by one or more senses; a physical body, a physical substance, or the universe as a whole." It defines "composition" as: "The combining of distinct parts or elements to form a whole." When you put these definitions together, you get that anything that has physical matter, or can be described as a process, is patentable.

not a composition of matter can be called a process. Thus, when you put these terms together, everything is patentable.[66]

Moreover, a textual definition of Section 101 should make even naturally occurring matter patentable, because Section 101 says that inventions and discoveries are patentable so long as they are newly "discovered."[67] Indeed, the Court in *Bilski* recognized that the plain text of Section 101 did not support and require the three exceptions to patentability. The Court instead said that they were "consistent" with the statute: "[w]hile these exceptions are not required by the statutory text, they are consistent with the notion that a patentable process must be 'new and useful.'"[68] But consistency is not enough; under a textual approach to patentable subject matter, the text of the statute must prohibit patentability for something to be unpatentable. The Court in *Bilski* recognized that Section 101 does not do that. Instead, the Court relied on the fact that the judicial exceptions to patentable subject matter go back 150 years.[69] The Court thus said that it was granting the exceptions "statutory *stare decisis.*"[70]

The problem with a plain-text approach to patentable subject matter, or any other approach that does not balance the costs of patents for certain types of innovation against their benefits, is that such approaches result in bad patent policy and indeterminacy. At the end of the day, we should only grant patents for areas of innovation in which the availability of patents gives us enough additional innovation to outweigh the inherent costs of patents in terms of higher prices on patented goods and potential patent thickets that clog research and development.

The Court should resurrect its historic approach to patentable subject matter. Instead of trying to decide patentability for cDNA

---

[66] Michael Risch, Everything Is Patentable, 75 Tenn. L. Rev. 591 (2008).

[67] Some argue that naturally occurring substances are foreclosed by the text of Section 101, because the text grants patents only to "new and useful" processes, compositions of matter, etc. Thus, according to this argument, previously existing matter cannot be patentable. *Id.* This argument ignores, however, that Section 101 also says "invents or discovers." The plainest reading of the text is that someone may invent something new, or discover something previously unknown by others, and that either of these is patentable.

[68] Bilski, 130 S. Ct. at 3225 (2010).

[69] *Id.*

[70] *Id.*

based on whether cDNA is man-made even though it is sometimes naturally created by viruses, the Court should ask the simple and central question: Will society on net benefit from patents on DNA and cDNA? The answer to this question should determine patentability of genetic material, not nuanced discussions of what constitutes "natural phenomena."

The *Myriad* case touches upon two important areas of genetic research and innovation. First, it is very beneficial to society for scientists to determine the location and sequence of genes, and mutations thereto, that have significant health effects. Second, genetic therapies aimed at repairing mutated genes have great potential to improve health and save lives. The fundamental question to be asked about these two areas of genetic research is whether allowing them to be patented will benefit society more in terms of increased innovation than it costs society in terms of increased consumer prices and decreased research due to excessive patents in a field. In other words, do we need patents on genes, or are they a drag on research and innovation?

Under current law, gene therapies that involve synthesized, nonnaturally occurring genetic sequences are patentable subject matter as man-made products. Likewise, discovering a process to administer genetic therapy using existing genetic material is also patentable in that it qualifies as a new use of a known product. Under *Myriad*, however, discovering a new gene, including its location, sequence, function, and dangerous mutations, is not patentable.

The question as a matter of policy is whether this distinction makes sense. Without the reward of patentability, will enough scientists engage in enough research to discover relevant genes, their health effects, and effects of mutations thereto? Will keeping naturally occurring genes free of patents make it easier for researchers to make discoveries unencumbered by potential patent infringement?[71] These are ultimately empirical questions to which we can never know the answers to a certainty. Nevertheless, it would be worthwhile for the Court to make its best attempt at determining the answers to the empirical questions and decide patentability from those

---

[71] But note that it is uncommon for patent holders to sue researchers, especially if the research would make the patent more valuable. Myriad itself only sued rival testing providers, not scientists studying BRCA1 and BRCA2 mutations.

answers. If an adequate amount of research into the correlations be-tween specific genes and disease will not be done but for the patent grant, then society is better off with patents on even naturally occur-ring genetic material. If such patents hurt more then they help, then non-patentability is in order.

The Court seemed to recognize this balancing act in *Myriad*,[72] but did not embrace it as the best test for patentable subject mat-ter. Rather, the Court mentioned the balance and then inquired as to whether DNA and cDNA are naturally occurring. The Court could simply adopt this test and uphold patents on naturally occurring ge-netic material if it thinks doing so will be beneficial. After all, noth-ing in the plain text of the Patent Act disallows patentability for nat-ural phenomena. That exception to patentability is merely judicially created and can be eliminated in the same way.

Although the Court in *Myriad* did not adopt the most straightfor-ward and efficient way of determining patentable subject matter, its parsing of patentability for DNA and cDNA may have served the function of granting enough patent rights to incentivize research, but not so many patents as to cause very high consumer costs and research blockages. By preserving naturally occurring DNA in the public domain, the Court made sure this material is free of patents and available to all. By allowing cDNA to be patented, the Court en-sured that some incentives flow to genetic researchers for their dis-coveries of important gene-disease correlations. At least until a DNA-based test is perfected, Myriad seems to have a patent on the most effective way of conducting BRCA1 and BRCA2 tests.[73] Indeed, since the Supreme Court's decision, Myriad has already filed suit against two competing lab companies that are seeking to offer BRCA1 and BRCA2 testing. The company has asserted some of the claims that

---

[72] Myriad, 133 S. Ct. at 2116 ("As we have recognized before, patent protection strikes a delicate balance between creating incentives that lead to creation, invention, and discovery and impeding the flow of information that might permit, indeed spur, invention.") (internal quotation omitted).

[73] See John Timmer, Supreme Court Blocks Patenting of Genomic DNA, Ars Tech-nica, Jun. 13, 2013, http://arstechnica.com/tech-policy/2013/06/supreme-court-blocks-patenting-of-genomic-dna; Megan Krench, New Supreme Court Decision Rules That cDNA Is Patentable—What It Means for Research and Genetic Testing, Scientific American Blogs, Jul. 9, 2013, http://blogs.scientificamerican.com/guest-blog/2013/07/09/new-supreme-court-decision-rules-that-cdna-is-patentablewhat-it-means-for-research-and-genetic-testing.

the Supreme Court upheld and has also asserted method-of-testing claims from some of the 24 other patents it owns related to BRCA1 and BRCA2 genes. In its filings, Myriad claims that the competing testing companies cannot test for BRCA1 and BRCA2 genes without creating the cDNA to which Myriad has exclusive right.[74]

Conclusion

The Supreme Court this term maintained protections for genetic patents in terms of both genetically modified seeds and synthetic versions of genes. As a practical matter, these decisions uphold patent rights and incentives of genetic scientists to both create new GMOs and to continue to research gene-disease correlations. As to the development of patent law, in *Bowman* the Court left us without significant answers to persistent questions about the boundaries of the patent exhaustion doctrine. The Court unanimously rejected the argument that patent exhaustion should govern new plants containing patented genetic material, but did not venture further than that on the questions of contract versus exhaustion doctrine. As to patentable subject matter, in *Myriad* the Court declined the opportunity to set forth a comprehensive cost-benefit approach to what sorts of things should be patentable. Instead, the Court's decision extended the uncertainty in patentable subject matter that has been in existence for some time, and that *Bilski*'s textualist approach exacerbated. Nevertheless, the Court's decision allowing patents on man-made cDNA but not on naturally occurring DNA probably threads nicely the needle of encouraging investment in studying genetic disease while leaving open to others the use of DNA. In all, the Court's decisions this term should maintain conditions for the encouragement of important genetic science.

---

[74] See, e.g., Motion for Prelim. Injunctive Relief, University of Utah Research Foundation v. Ambry Genetics Corp., No. 2:13-cv-00640-RJS (D. Utah filed Jul. 9, 2013).

Common Problems for the Common Answers Test: Class Certification in *Amgen* and *Comcast*

*Mark Moller**

Introduction

Just a few years ago, class-action law was, by all accounts, a terrible mess. The origins of that mess were various. Its deepest roots lay in Federal Rule of Civil Procedure 23's vague requirements for class certification, which offer little insight into how its framers thought the rule ought to be applied. But an even deeper source lay in the astounding fact that, for decades, the Supreme Court had provided lower courts with minimal clarification about how those requirements should be interpreted. Worse, the guidance the Court had offered seemed inconsistent. The result was a three-decade-long babble of different approaches to class certification across the circuits, as lower courts struggled, without meaningful direction, to put Rule 23 into effect.

Hope arrived in 2011, when the Supreme Court, after more than a decade of silence, entered the fray in *Wal-Mart Stores, Inc. v. Dukes*[1] and attempted to, finally, sort out the mess. The solution *Wal-Mart* offered was a new guiding principle that could discipline the class-certification inquiry across its various domains.

That principle declared that the goal of certification is to determine "the capacity of a classwide proceeding to generate common answers apt to drive the resolution of the litigation."[2] Of course, on its face, this statement raises as many questions as it answers. Its promise as a source of discipline for class-action law lay not in its words, but in its origin. The test was drawn from a series of elegant,

---

* Associate Professor of Law, DePaul University College of Law.
[1] 131 S. Ct. 2541 (2011).
[2] *Id.* at 2550.

rigorous articles by the late Professor Richard Nagareda.[3] By drawing on Nagareda's work, the Court, in the process, self-consciously harnessed his larger explanatory framework as a source of future guidance for lower courts.

The special value of Nagareda's work lay not only in its detail and rigor, but in Nagareda's focus on one of the deepest legitimacy problems plaguing the class-action procedure: its widely acknowledged, and much criticized, capacity to alter or abridge plaintiffs' and defendants' substantive rights. Professor Nagareda's framework was self-consciously, as he put it, "pro law"—that is, designed to put substantive law back in charge of judicial uses of the class procedure.[4]

This term provides an opportunity to assess how that project is working out. In two of the term's most important class-action cases, *Amgen v. Connecticut Retirement Plans and Trust Funds*[5] and *Comcast v. Behrend*,[6] the Court revisited the common answers test, extending it to new problems in the fields of securities and antitrust law.

For those keeping score of which side, plaintiffs or defendants, won this term, *Amgen* goes to the plaintiffs and *Comcast* to defendants. But for those watching to find out if the common answers test would mark a new "pro law" direction that can rescue substantive law from procedural distortion, both decisions proved to be modest disappointments. In different respects, both decisions reflect a continuation rather than a break with the procedure-driving-substance problem that Professor Nagareda's work tried to combat.

Part I starts by reviewing the state of law on the eve of *Wal-Mart* and then summarizes Nagareda's "common answers" framework, which *Wal-Mart* adopted. This part takes some time to tease out different principles that guide that framework, which is necessary to make sense of *Amgen* and *Comcast*. Part II proceeds to walk through

---

[3] In particular, it drew on Nagareda's article *Class Certification in the Age of Aggregate Proof*, 84 N.Y.U. L. Rev. 97 (2009) [hereinafter Aggregate Proof]. Nagareda also summarized some of the main points of that article in what was basically a "Reader's Digest" version, which was published shortly after his death in *Vanderbilt Law Review*'s online supplement, as the Court deliberated about *Wal-Mart*. See Richard A. Nagareda, Common Answers for Class Certification, 63 Vand. L. Rev. En Banc 149 (2010).

[4] Nagareda, Aggregate Proof, *supra* note 3, at 135.

[5] 133 S. Ct. 1184 (2013).

[6] 133 S. Ct. 1426 (2013).

Amgen and *Comcast* in turn, providing a brief reader's guide to the ways the decisions apply that framework and fumble in the process.

I. The Common Answers Test: A Guide for the Perplexed

A. Origins

At the turn of the millennium, the circuits were riven by a jumble of conflicting approaches to class certification. The source of the problem lay partly in Rule 23's famously vague standards and partly in the Supreme Court's spare, cross-cutting directions about how to apply those requirements.

One significant source of confusion turned on when the underlying "merits"—that is, questions bearing on defendants' ultimate liability—should be considered in the course of deciding to certify a class. Initially, federal courts synthesized the class-action rule to more familiar joinder devices, particularly Rule 20, whose permissive joinder provisions had long been assessed initially based on the pleadings. Following that model, "first-generation" class-action law, approached certification questions in the same pleading-focused way.[7]

In these early years, the Supreme Court did not control so much as observe the developments in the lower courts, tinkering on the margins. The Court's first major contribution in the first two decades of class-action law's development came in its 1974 opinion in *Eisen v. Carlisle & Jacquelin*, where it announced that district courts cannot condition certification on an assessment of the plaintiff's likely success on the merits.[8] The meaning of *Eisen* was muddied by another Supreme Court decision several years later, 1982's *General Telephone Co. v. Falcon*.[9] There, the Court directed that certification demands "actual, not presumed" compliance with Rule 23's requirements,

---

[7] Nagareda, Aggregate Proof, *supra* note 3, at 111–12.

[8] 417 U.S. 156, 177 (1974) ("We find nothing in either the language or history of Rule 23 that gives a court any authority to conduct a preliminary inquiry into the merits of a suit in order to determine whether it may be maintained as a class action."). Because *Eisen*'s specific holding concerned who bears the cost of notice to class members that a class has been certified, and not the certification of the class itself, the statement, applied to class certification, was, as the Court recently put it, the "purest dictum." See Wal-Mart, 131 S. Ct. at 2552 n.6.

[9] 457 U.S. 147 (1982).

and added that Rule 23 sometimes demands "prob[ing] behind the pleadings."[10]

Together, *Eisen* and *Falcon* produced confusion and a substantial constellation of different approaches among the circuits, particularly with respect to the relation between certification and the merits, which persisted for over two decades.[11] Surveying the mess just a decade ago, Robert Bone and David Evans lamented that class certification cases reflected "a patchwork of discretionary decisions difficult to justify on principled grounds."[12]

In 2011, the Supreme Court re-entered the fray in *Wal-Mart Stores v. Dukes* and attempted to sort out the mess. For help, it turned to the work of Professor Nagareda, who in a series of articles, had set out to synthesize the existing law in the lower courts while articulating some underlying principles that fit its basic contours and could give it some larger theoretical coherence.

The lower courts, he argued, had been evolving toward an understanding of Rule 23's requirements that he paraphrased as an inquiry into the "capacity" of a "unified proceeding" to generate "common answers" that can "resolve" class members' dispute with the defendant.[13] This "common answers" test for certification was not, in his telling, meant as an explanation for one of Rule 23's discrete certification requirements. Instead, building on the observation that

---

[10] *Id.* at 160.

[11] The confusion was exacerbated by the fact that it wasn't clear what *Falcon* was trying to get at in these passages. To take just one example, *Falcon*'s suggestion that district courts may sometimes need to "probe behind the pleading" was followed immediately by a recommendation that courts ought to demand more *specificity* in class pleadings before coming to rest on certification, which suggested less a rejection of a pleading-focused approach to certification than a qualification that courts should not accept overly vague pleadings bearing on the propriety of certification. *Id.* at 160–61 (emphasizing "the need for 'more precise pleadings'" because "'without reasonable specificity the court cannot define the class, cannot determine whether the representation is adequate'") (quoting Johnson v. Georgia Highway Express, 417 F.2d 1122, 1125–27 (5th Cit. 1969) (Godbold, J., dissenting)).

[12] Robert G. Bone & David S. Evans, Class Certification and the Substantive Merits, 51 Duke L.J. 1251, 1254 (2002).

[13] Nagareda, Aggregate Proof, *supra* note 3, at 131–32 (the focus of certification is on "the prospects for joint resolution of class members' claims through a unified proceeding"); *id.* ("What matters to class certification . . . is not the raising of common 'questions'—even in droves—but, rather the capacity of a classwide proceeding to generate common *answers* apt to drive the resolution of the litigation.").

those requirements (commonality, typicality, adequacy, predominance, and so forth) all point to a larger set of underlying organizing principles unstated in the rule itself,[14] Nagareda's work, brilliantly, presented itself as a synthesis of one of those underlying organizing principles.[15]

In *Wal-Mart*, the Supreme Court lifted his common answers test into Rule 23 into class-action doctrine verbatim. "What matters to class certification . . . is not the raising of common 'questions'—even in droves," said the Court, quoting Nagareda. It is "the capacity of a classwide proceeding to generate common *answers* apt to drive the resolution of the litigation."[16]

B. Applications

1. The Common Answers Test as a Practical Inquiry

Understanding the common answers test requires appreciating its roots in one of the original purposes of Rule 23: ensuring, before the resources and time of the parties are consumed by class litigation on the merits, that a class proceeding can actually produce a judgment that will resolve the underlying dispute.[17] This prejudgment screening is a comparatively recent innovation in class-action procedure. Eighteenth- and nineteenth-century equitable practice did not provide one.[18] Rather, the primary avenue for challenging the pro-

---

[14] See, e.g., General Telephone Co. v. Falcon, 457 U.S. 147, 157–58 & n.13 (1982) (noting the rule's requirements "tend to merge" into an underlying inquiry into whether "maintenance of a class action is economical" and "the class claims are so interrelated that the interests of class members will be fairly and adequately protected in their absence").

[15] See, e.g., Nagareda, Aggregate Proof, *supra* note 3, at 131 (framing the common answers test as one that gets at the "overarching picture" of class cohesion, toward which Rule 23's various requirements point). For this reason, Justice Ginsburg construed Nagareda too narrowly when she suggested, in her *Wal-Mart* dissent, that his common answers test was a limited explication of Rule 23(b)(3)'s predominance requirement. See Wal-Mart, 131 S. Ct. at 2566 (Ginsburg, J., dissenting).

[16] 131 S. Ct. at 2551 (emphasis in original).

[17] The test has its origin in a key insight by Allan Erbsen about the connection between Rule 23 and the "resolvability" of the claims. Allan Erbsen, From "Predominance" to "Resolvability": A New Approach to Regulating Class Actions, 58 Vand. L. Rev. 995 (2005).

[18] For the seminal treatment of the class-action rule's equitable precursors, see Stephen C. Yeazell, From Medieval Group Litigation to the Modern Class Action (1987).

ceeding's propriety came after the fact, in subsequent collateral suits targeting the defendant in which individual class members sought to avoid the preclusive effect of the class judgment.[19]

In these collateral attacks on the class judgment, the class member might try to avoid that judgment by showing that she had not been adequately represented because the class representative's interests conflicted with hers.[20] Or, if the class were unsuccessful, she might assert an alternative theory of relief for the same wrong, one not advanced in the class proceeding because it could not have been litigated on a class basis.[21] Too many of such after-the-fact challenges to a class judgment, and the result is that the original class proceeding would have ended up settling nothing—a monumental waste of time for all concerned.

Rule 23, by contrast, moves the scrutiny of the class proceeding forward, before the class judgment, by requiring a front-end determination that the class device can produce a fair, accurate judgment entitled to binding effect at the back end. By doing so, Rule 23 economizes on judicial process, by screening out proposed actions in which the class device is incapable of facilitating a fair and accurate resolution of the underlying dispute.[22]

The common answers test is, in turn, derived from this economizing purpose. Rather than ask whether the claims are amenable to common proof in the abstract, the test asks whether claims are capable of being "productively litigated at once."[23] The key word here is "productively"—the test boils down to whether, as a practical matter, class members are situated such that the question of defendants' liability to the class can be "resolved in a unified proceeding."[24]

---

[19] A classic example of this pattern is *Hansberry v. Lee*, a collateral attack on an Illinois state law class judgment entered, after the fashion of traditional equitable practice, without any "prejudgment" certification process. See Hansberry v. Lee, 311 U.S. 32 (1940).

[20] *Id.* at 44–45.

[21] See, e.g., Restatement (Second) of the Law of Judgments § 26(c); Cooper v. Federal Reserve Bank of Richmond, 467 U.S. 867 (1984) (holding that class members' individualized claims are not merged and barred by a prior class judgment arising out of the same transaction or occurrence).

[22] See Erbsen, From "Predominance" to "Resolvability," *supra* note 17, at 1023–50.

[23] 131 S. Ct. at 2551.

[24] Nagareda, Aggregate Proof, *supra* note 3, at 131.

The test's practical focus is illustrated by the basic reasoning of the Court in *Wal-Mart*. There, the named plaintiffs alleged Wal-Mart was liable to the class based on allegations of gender discrimination, but class members might have proven that liability in more than one way. One would be through proof of a top-down corporate-wide policy or practice, either adopted by Wal-Mart with an impermissible discriminatory motive or, in operation, yielding an impermissible discriminatory impact. The other would turn on proof of store-level, rather than company-wide, gender discrimination for which Wal-Mart could be held vicariously liable.[25]

Obviously, then, if plaintiffs were unable to offer sufficient proof of a company-wide discriminatory policy, class members' rights to relief would collapse into a welter of dissimilar investigations into store-level practices that could not be resolved in a single proceeding. Accordingly, the Court rightly made class certification contingent on whether plaintiffs could demonstrate the existence of a company-wide corporate discriminatory practice at the outset.[26] And, finding plaintiffs were unable to produce proof of such a policy, it reversed the certification of the class.

2. Two Mistakes in Application: "Underreaching" and "Overreaching"

In the course of explaining the common answers test, Nagareda also highlighted two common ways that lower courts fall into error when applying it.[27] The first, which he called "underreaching," involves judicial efforts to ascertain the "fit" between class procedure and the substantive law applied through it. The resolvability of claims as a class depends on the amenability of the claims to common proof. And often the amenability of claims to common proof turns on a contested question of substantive law about how the claims can be proven. Yet sometimes, he noted, courts certified a class without resolving that question. The sources of this abdication are too various to summarize here. The gist is that judges may have

[25] 131 S. Ct. at 2552. See also Cooper v. Federal Reserve Bank of Richmond, 457 U.S. at 881 (noting that class claims premised on a company-wide pattern or practice and individual claims targeting particular supervisors present alternative theories for remedying the same underlying injury).

[26] 131 S. Ct. at 2552.

[27] Nagareda, Aggregate Proof, *supra* note 3, at 135 (noting "judicial errors" taking two forms: "underreaching" and "overreaching").

been led by a heavily fact-focused certification process to lose sight of broader legal questions bearing on whether claims are actually amenable to common proof.[28]

Wal-Mart again offers an example. There, Nagareda noted, the plaintiffs presented "common proof," in the form of statistical analysis and anecdotal evidence, purporting to show company-wide gender discrimination. The U.S. Court of Appeals for the Ninth Circuit, focusing on the "commonality" of the proof developed by plaintiffs to the class claims, certified the class. Yet, Nagareda noted, that proof reflected a highly contested view of the type of discrimination proscribed in Title VII. It was, in effect, a "stalking horse" for a larger legal theory of proscribed sex discrimination. By certifying the class without first examining whether that theory was right, the Court advanced that contested account of the law "in real-world operational terms, if not explicitly in doctrine."[29]

At least two concerns follow when courts certify claims but ignore the substantive questions that bear on the availability of common proof. First, the case-ending nature of a certification order means that when courts refuse to resolve important questions of substantive law concerning whether common proof of plaintiffs' claims is possible, plaintiffs in effect get to dictate both the law and the result of their case (that is, a settlement at a premium reflecting the *in terrorem* effect of certification).[30] This is obviously inconsistent with the basic impartiality constraint to which all fair processes of dispute resolution must conform.

Second, when courts, in the course of certifying a class, refuse to resolve substantive questions bearing on class members' rights to relief, they violate norms favoring transparent and accountable law declaration. This second point also follows from the link between certification and settlement. Other defendants in different but factually analogous cases will, in the interest of avoiding being pressed into a similar settlement, treat such certification orders much like a judicial decision declaring the contested substantive question in

---

[28] *Id.* at 125–30 (discussing this problem).

[29] *Id.* at 161–62.

[30] *Id.* at 128 (noting that when courts certify claims based on the existence of common proof supporting the class claims, without deciding whether that proof is consistent with the governing law, class certification "proceeds only upon the say-so of one side").

plaintiffs' favor, even though the certification order does not, as a matter of doctrine, announce itself as such.[31] Thus, the result is akin to lawmaking in operation, if not in doctrine, because its effect on potential defendants' incentives and behavior is law-*like*.[32] Yet this "operational" law reform avoids the critical constraints of public judicial deliberation, accountability, and transparency to which above-board acts of law declaration are subject.

Accordingly, Nagareda argued that courts must take care to resolve questions of law that bear on how the claims can be proven at the outset of the certification inquiry.[33] He suggested, in turn, the best practice is to address those legal questions first, and "only then" turn to apply the common answers test.[34] The legal determination informs which factual dissimilarities among class members are material to the liability question. And thus it guides the subsequent inquiry into whether resolution of class members' claims in a single proceeding is possible.

The second form of judicial error that Nagareda highlighted involved not "underreaching," by failing to decide questions of law that bear on the amenability of the claims to common answers, but "overreaching," by pushing the merits inquiry beyond the scope of the Rule 23 common answers test.[35] Thus, he said, courts miscarry by deciding mixed law-fact questions related to the merits when their resolution is not necessary to determine the resolvability of the dispute in a class-wide proceeding.[36] This type of overreaching is par-

---

[31] *Id.* at 137–38 (noting that when courts certify claims based on evidence organized around contested but generalizable principles, the result assumes a "law-like character" in operation).

[32] *Id.* at 161 (criticizing the tendency of class-action law toward "law transformation" through "class certification and the well-nigh inevitable denouement of class settlement . . . [which] achieve in practical terms what the legislative process has not yet delivered and, indeed, may be disinclined to provide").

[33] *Id.* at 125, 133.

[34] *Id.* at 164 ("the notion of declaring the governing law and, only then, ascertaining compliance with Rule 23 requirements . . . would lend coherence to the law of class certification").

[35] *Id.* at 135.

[36] *Id.* at 132–33 ("[c]ourts today properly engage aggregate proof as a question of class certification . . . when disputes concerning that proof pertain to whether there exist disabling dissimilarities" that would "prevent common resolution" of the claims); *id.* at 130, 135 (warning of "judicial overreach" in the form of "the displacement

ticularly problematic because plaintiffs must prove that they meet the requirements of Rule 23 by a preponderance of the evidence, a higher standard than they must meet to survive summary judgment. As a result, forcing plaintiffs to prove issues relating to the merits when doing so is not required by Rule 23 undoes the careful judge-jury balance struck by the federal rules.[37]

Securities fraud claims offer a ready example. A plaintiff asserting such a claim must prove not only that a securities issuer made material representations that inflated her stock's price, but she must also prove that she sold the security at a loss that was proximately caused by the misrepresentation.[38] The defendant is thus not liable to the plaintiff if the defendant shows that the collapse in the price of plaintiff's stock was caused by some intervening event that triggered a market-wide sell-off and ensuing general collapse in stock prices affecting both plaintiff and purchasers of unrelated securities indiscriminately.[39]

Securities-fraud defendants have sought to argue that this question of "loss causation" bears on certification, largely in the hope of taking advantage of a potentially case-ending judicial assessment under the more demanding preponderance standard applicable to certification. Still, because disentangling the relative contributions of the disclosure and larger market trends to the injurious price reduction is often an issue inherently common to the class, the issue of

---

of summary judgment" when consideration of the merits does not "bear upon the application of a Rule 23 requirement"); *id.* at 114 ("the concept that does the work" in the common answers test "consists of what one might dub a 'tethering' doctrine," under which a court "oversteps its proper bounds" if it conducts a merits inquiry "untethered" to Rule 23's resolvability requirements).

[37] *Id.* at 140–41 ("The distinction between a class certification question and a summary judgment question is far from trivial. A requirement of a genuine issue of material fact remains much easier for plaintiffs to satisfy" than Rule 23's preponderance standard); *id.* at 149 ("law declaration" in conjunction with certification is warranted only to the extent it can reveal dissimilarities in the class; going beyond this intrudes on the "proper domain of summary judgment, such as to implicate the role of the court vis-à-vis the factfinder at trial"). Nagareda also emphasized the party neutrality accomplished by tethering the merits inquiry to a resolvability analysis—"[p]roper delineation of the law-declaring component of class certification" along these lines "does not uniformly favor either plaintiffs or defendants." *Id.* at 136.

[38] Erica P. John Fund, Inc. v. Halliburton, 131 S. Ct. 2179, 2186 (2011).

[39] Dura Pharmaceuticals, Inc. v. Broudo, 544 U.S. 336, 342–43 (2005).

loss causation is frequently amenable to common answers.[40] When that is so, the competing merits of the causation issue should have no bearing on whether the class exhibits "fatal dissimilarities" that could impede, as a practical matter, the capacity of a single class proceeding to resolve the underlying dispute. Rather, the loss-causation issue is a matter fit for the summary judgment phase.[41] This was exactly the conclusion to which the Court came in *Erica P. John Fund v. Halliburton*, decided the same term as *Wal-Mart*.[42]

II. Checking in on the Common Answers Test: A Look at *Amgen* and *Comcast*

Between the two biggest class-action cases this term, *Amgen v. Connecticut Retirement Plans and Trust Funds* and *Comcast v. Behrend*, every justice signed onto majority opinions that applied some version of the common answers test, confirming that the test is here to stay. Yet for those hoping that the Court's adoption of the test would curtail the class procedure's warping effect on substantive law, both are modest disappointments. Between the two cases, both the liberal and conservative wings separately indulged in precisely what Professor Nagareda's framework was designed to prevent: law reform without accountability.

A. Lawmaking via Procedure in Amgen

1. Some Securities Law Background

Amgen involved a lawsuit, filed by an institutional investor, targeting a biotechnology company's public statements about its "flagship drugs."[43] As is characteristic of securities-fraud suits, the plaintiffs alleged that these statements were false and misleading, inflating the value of Amgen's stock and leading to financial losses for the company's shareholders when the misrepresentations were later corrected.[44] A central problem in the case concerned proof of the "reliance" element of claims alleging securities fraud under Section 10(b)

---

[40] Nagareda, Aggregate Proof, *supra* note 3, at 139–40.

[41] *Id*. at 140.

[42] 131 S. Ct. 2179 (2011).

[43] Amgen, 133 S. Ct. at 1193.

[44] *Id*. (describing the allegations of the complaint).

of the Securities Exchange Act of 1934 and so it helps to review the contours of that element before looking at the case.[45]

Proof of securities fraud under Section 10(b), as with all claims of fraud, requires not only identifying misrepresentation but showing that the misrepresentation *caused* the plaintiff's injury. Causation, in traditional fraud claims, is proven by showing the plaintiff knew of the misrepresentation and reasonably relied on it to her detriment. Yet, mostly to facilitate class enforcement of securities-fraud actions, the Supreme Court, in *Basic v. Levinson*,[46] dispensed with the ordinary common law burden of proving individualized reliance in Section 10(b) fraud actions.

Basic reasoned that securities purchasers do not rely directly on representations about a company when purchasing its stock. Instead, they rely on the "integrity of the market price" for the security.[47] They are, that is, willing to pay for the stock not because of any specific representation about the company that issued it, but because they assume that, thanks to the efficient operation of the market and the watchful eye of regulators, the security's price reflects a fair valuation of the company embodying accurate public information disseminated about it. Given this, the Court relaxed plaintiff's traditional burden of proving they directly relied on the misrepresentation sued upon and held that, instead, "an investor's reliance on any public material misrepresentations . . . may be presumed for purposes of a [securities fraud] action [under Section 10(b)]."[48]

---

[45] Section 10(b) of the Securities Exchange Act proscribes the "use or employment, in connection with the purchase or sale of any security . . . [of] any manipulative or deceptive device or contrivance in contravention of such rules and regulations as the Commission may prescribe." 15 U.S.C. § 78j(b). Pursuant to Section 10(b), the SEC promulgated Rule 10b-5, which makes it illegal "to make any untrue statement of a material fact or to omit to state a material fact necessary in order to make the statements made in the light of the circumstances under which they were made, not misleading . . . in connection with the purchase or sale of any security." 17 C.F.R. § 240.10b-5(b). Relying on both Section 10(b) and Rule 10b-5, federal courts inferred a private right of action for securities fraud with the Supreme Court's eventual approval. See Blue Chip Stamps v. Manor Drug Stores, 421 U.S. 723, 729–31 (1985) (reviewing history of the implied right of action for securities fraud under Section 10(b)).

[46] 485 U.S. 224 (1988).

[47] *Id.* at 247.

[48] *Id.*

Since *Basic*, it has been understood that class plaintiffs may take advantage of this presumption only if they establish three things: (1) that the securities they and class members purchased were in fact traded in an open and efficient market capable of translating public information into the security's price; (2) that misrepresentations were disseminated publicly;[49] and, (3) that the representations were "material," meaning a reasonable investor would have relied on the representation when deciding whether to purchase it.[50]

Of the three elements on which the presumption depends, materiality, though, is special. Unlike questions about the efficiency of the market in which the security was traded or about the publicity of the representation, materiality is essential to establishing the defendant's liability to each class member, even if plaintiffs are *not* legally entitled to the *Basic* reliance presumption.

To understand *Amgen*, this last point bears emphasis. If plaintiff is unable to prove either that the market in which the security is traded is efficient or that the representation was disseminated to the market, that dooms the availability of the *Basic* presumption. Without the presumption of reliance, a plaintiff must establish reliance individually, the old-fashioned way: by showing that she in fact knew of the representation and relied on it when deciding to purchase the security at a given price. But even in that case, the Section 10(b) fraud action, like the common-law fraud actions on which it is modeled, requires proof that the defendant's representations were materially false or misleading.[51] Thus, even in the absence of the *Basic* presumption, the issue of materiality remains in the case. And so, even in the

[49] Another requirement often associated with the presumption—that the class members must have purchased the securities "between the time the misrepresentations were made and the time the truth was revealed"—is, as the Court noted, technically relevant to the class definition and the Rule 23(a) requirements of typicality and adequacy of representation, rather than the presumption itself. Amgen, 133 S. Ct. at 1198.

[50] *Id.* at 1195.

[51] Specifically, Rule 10b-5 makes it illegal "to make any untrue statement of a material fact or to omit to state a material fact necessary in order to make the statements made in the light of the circumstances under which they were made, not misleading . . . in connection with the purchase or sale of any security." 17 C.F.R. § 240.10b-5(b). Based on the text of Rule 10b-5, the Court has treated materiality as a separate element that must be satisfied regardless of whether plaintiff can take advantage of *Basic*'s presumption. See Matrixx Initiatives v. Siracusano, 131 S. Ct. 1309, 1317 (2011).

absence of the presumption, if plaintiffs are unable to prove that the misrepresentation would be material to a reasonable investor, they lose.

2. Justice Ginsburg's Common Answers Analysis

The certification question in *Amgen* focused on proof relating to the *Basic* presumption. Amgen conceded that the market in which the class securities were sold was efficient, but it contested the materiality of the representations at issue.[52] As a result, materiality was the sole issue on which the availability of the *Basic* presumption hinged.

Amgen argued that materiality is an issue that must be resolved as part of the inquiry into whether the claims could be certified. Its reasoning was straightforward: If materiality is decided against the class, the reliance element would depend on individualized inquiries into whether each class member actually saw the representation and relied on it, impeding common answers to the liability question.

In an opinion by Justice Ruth Bader Ginsburg, the *Amgen* majority, however, held that the question of materiality can be kicked down the road and resolved *after* the class is certified, either at the summary judgment stage or at trial.[53] Although surprising at first glance, the majority's holding turns out to be a straightforward application of the common answers test.

The key is to remember that, under the common answers test, an inquiry into the underlying merits of the claims must be "tethered" to determining whether, as a practical matter, dissimilarities among class members will impede the ability of the class device to resolve the underlying dispute in a single proceeding.[54] Under the test, some elements of the *Basic* presumption, like market efficiency, clearly must be resolved in plaintiffs' favor in order to render the case resolvable on a class basis. If the question of the market's efficiency were resolved against the class, defendants' liability to the class would necessarily collapse into individual inquiries about each class

---

[52] 133 S. Ct. at 1190 (noting "Amgen has conceded the efficiency of the market for the securities at issue and has not contested the public character of the allegedly fraudulent statements").

[53] *Id.* at 1196.

[54] Nagareda, Aggregate Proof, *supra* note 3, at 114 (discussing the requirement that a peek at the merits must be "tethered" to a common answers analysis).

member's subjective reliance. Therefore, resolving that substantive question up front is necessary to decide whether the claims form an efficient trial unit that is capable of being resolved in a single proceeding.[55]

By the same logic, however, resolving the materiality question is *not* necessary to determining whether the claims are resolvable in a single proceeding. The point flows from the special nature of the materiality issue. Determined in favor of the class, materiality will cement the availability of the *Basic* presumption, eliminating individualized issues of reliance across the class. Yet, because materiality is so irreducibly essential to establishing fraud liability, a determination that representations are not material will simply doom the claims on the merits altogether, again as a unit.[56] They will be "dead on arrival," presumption of reliance or no.[57] Since its resolution will thus have no effect on the resolvability of the class claims in a single proceeding, the merits of the materiality issue are irrelevant to certification.

Justice Clarence Thomas, in a portion of the dissent joined only by Justice Anthony Kennedy, sharply criticized this reasoning. Rule 23's certification standards, he argued, mandate that plaintiffs show "that the elements of the claim are susceptible to classwide proof."[58] "Without that proof," he wrote, "there is no justification for certifying a class because there is no 'capacity of a classwide proceeding to generate common *answers* apt to drive the resolution of the litigation.'"[59]

Because, Justice Thomas continued, the element of reliance is susceptible to "common proof" only if plaintiffs are entitled to rely on the *Basic* presumption, and because the presumption depends on a prior determination that the misrepresentations are material,

---

[55] Wal-Mart Stores v. Dukes, 131 S. Ct. 2541, 2552 n.6 (2011).

[56] *Id.* ("Absent proof of materiality, the claim of the Rule 10b-5 class will fail in its entirety; there will be no remaining individual questions to adjudicate."); *id.* (noting that "failure to present evidence of materiality to defeat a summary-judgment motion or to prevail at trial" would not "cause individual reliance questions to overwhelm questions common to the class" but "would end the case for one and all; no claim would remain in which individual reliance issues could potentially predominate").

[57] Amgen, 133 S. Ct. at 1211 (Thomas, J., dissenting).

[58] *Id.* at 1210 (citing Wal-Mart, 131 S. Ct. at 2552 n.6).

[59] *Id.* (quoting Wal-Mart, 131 S. Ct. at 2551) (emphasis in original).

the district court ipso facto must determine the materiality issue in plaintiffs' favor in order to certify the class. As he put it, a "plaintiff who cannot prove materiality does not simply have a claim that is 'dead on arrival'" once the case proceeds to summary judgment or trial. He "has a class that should never have arrived at the merits at all because it failed Rule 23(b)(3) certification from the outset."[60]

If Nagareda's work and *Wal-Mart's* holding are any guide, though, the majority would seem to have the better of the argument. The fact that materiality has a metaphysical bearing on whether the reliance element can be conceptualized as governed by "common proof" is simply beside the point. The common answers test does not require that courts decide that every element of the claim is amenable in theory to common proof. It requires that the claims must be "productively . . . *litigated*" in a class proceeding because they are susceptible to common resolution *in practice*.[61] Because resolving the materiality issue one way or another has no bearing on that practical question, it is just not relevant to certification.

3. A Problem the Court Ignored

Although the dissent's argument misfires, lurking behind it was one point of valid criticism. That criticism lies in the fact that hidden away behind *Amgen* was a significant contested legal question bearing on how the *Basic* presumption is proven. Because the decision to certify the claims is practically case-ending, the majority's approach in turn avoids transparently addressing that legal question. This is the kind of unaccountable lawmaking via procedure that Professor Nagareda warned against.

This lurking question of law relates to how evidence of "price distortion"—the effect of the misrepresentation on the market price of the security—ought to bear on the merits of a securities fraud claim. Evidence of price distortion can be said to shed light on two different questions. One is the question of loss causation discussed in the last part of this essay. If misrepresentation doesn't cause movement in the price of the security, then class members' losses are not attributable to the misrepresentation. In *Erica P. John Fund v. Halliburton Co.*, the Court settled, consistent with the common

---

[60] *Id.* at 1211.

[61] Wal-Mart, 131 S. Ct. at 2551 (emphasis added).

answers test, that loss causation raises a question of generalizable proof appropriately considered at the summary judgment—not the class-certification—stage.[62]

Even so, defendants have argued that price distortion is separately relevant to the *Basic* presumption. The argument turns on the idea that the *Basic* presumption is premised on the market's incorporation of the misrepresentation into the price of the security. Through its incorporation into the price, investors are treated as relying on the misrepresentation indirectly. This is where evidence of price distortion becomes relevant. If the presumption reflects the idea that plaintiffs rely indirectly on the misrepresentation because it is embedded in the stock's price, then the premise supporting the presumption is defeated if evidence shows that the representation does not affect the price at all. If it is not embedded in the price, then purchasers do not rely on it, even "indirectly."

Defendants have framed their argument about the relevance of price distortion as a question that goes to the "materiality" of the misrepresentation to the market. From defendants' standpoint, the tactical wisdom of the push to bring price distortion evidence through the materiality element is impeccable: The problem for defendants, as Professor Donald Langevoort explains, is that evidence of price distortion or a lack thereof is rarely clear-cut.[63] As a result, it is difficult to defeat plaintiffs on the issue under the lenient summary judgment standard, which requires plaintiffs to show only that a reasonable jury might decide for them on the price distortion issue. The result is that the conflicting evidence goes to the jury, which defendants fear tend to skew heavily in plaintiffs' favor.

Defendants would prefer to get a judge to pass on the merits of the issue, unshackled from the plaintiff-friendly summary judgment standard. This is the basic impetus behind efforts to bring proof of price distortion into the *Basic* presumption. By doing so, defendants have hoped to make price distortion relevant to class certification. At the class-certification stage, the judge can get out from under the

---

[62] 131 S. Ct. at 2186.

[63] Donald C. Langevoort, *Amgen* and the Fraud-on-the-Market Class Action: Frozen in Time?, at 8–9, available at http:ssrn.com/abstract=2281910 (explaining that "once the inquiry extends to a potentially lengthy period of time between the original lie and the corrective disclosure" it is "hard—if not impossible—to disentangle all the effects with an econometric rigor").

restraints of the summary judgment standard and determine the price distortion question based on the preponderance standard applicable to certification. A determination of the issue in defendants' favor at the certification stage will, in turn, end the case as a practical matter.[64]

Smart tactics aside, the merits of the conception of materiality are open to question. Based on a careful reading of *Basic*, Langevoort has argued at length—in terms too involved to review here—that the *Basic* presumption might make much more conceptual sense if price distortion were not viewed as a "predicate to" the presumption of reliance. Instead, on his carefully argued view, *Basic* reflects the simple idea that plaintiffs are entitled to rely on the integrity of the stock price. Proof that the price was "distort[ed]," on this view, "merely establishes the injury from the misplaced reliance," rather than doing the double work of establishing the reliance element itself.[65]

The majority dodged the merits question about how price distortion bears on the presumption by kicking that question to later stages of litigation that, in practice, will be superseded by settlement. One suspects that the justices who joined the majority opinion did so because they saw Amgen's procedural position for what it was: a transparent attempt to manipulate the interface between securities fraud's substance and class-action procedure in order to gut much of the presumption's power "in operation, if not in doctrine."[66]

---

[64] *Id.* at 2–3 (discussing these concerns).

[65] *Id.* at 16 (summarizing the argument). See also Donald C. Langevoort, *Basic* at Twenty? Rethinking Fraud on the Market, 2009 Wisc. L. Rev. 151, 198. Langevoort's argument is that *Basic* should not be read as adopting the theory that purchasers rely on the misrepresentation "indirectly" because it is embedded in the stock price. He argues that *Basic*'s holding would make more sense if it is instead read as holding the reliance "is on the presumed absence of distortion (price integrity)," so that "distortion merely establishes the injury from the misplaced reliance." Langevoort, Frozen in Time?, *supra* note 63, at 16.

Of course, many think *Basic* was simply wrongly decided and that it is time to reconsider the *Basic* presumption entirely. *Basic* indeed has been a durable part of the conservative anti-canon. To his credit, Justice Samuel Alito, who joined the majority, specially concurred to note that the decision turned on an assumption about the rightness of *Basic* that the Court ought to reconsider in a more appropriate case. 133 S. Ct. at 1204 (Alito, J., concurring) ("I join the opinion of the Court with the understanding that the petitioners did not ask us to revisit *Basic*'s fraud-on-the-market presumption.").

[66] See also Langevoort, Frozen in Time, *supra* note 63, at 16 (noting that separation-of-powers concerns relating to Congress's control over securities litigation reform "seem[] crucial to assembling the majority").

But if that was the concern driving some justices in the majority, that concern tends to underscore the *strength* of Justice Thomas's call for some assessment of the price distortion issue—albeit one limited to the legal theory that explains how it is relevant, and not its factual merits—in advance of certification. By deferring that issue until *after* the invariably case-ending certification decision, the majority has done something equal to Amgen's gambit, but with opposite effect: it has "in operation, if not in doctrine" *pruned* price distortion from the elements of proof relating to the *Basic* presumption.[67] That this pruning might be desirable is the position that Langevoort thoughtfully presented.[68] But it is one that the majority effectively made through a procedural ruling, rather than through the kind of forthright interpretation of the substantive law illustrated by Langevoort's parsing of *Basic*.

Reasonable minds can differ about whether Langevoort's theory of *Basic* is right, or whether it is time to reconsider the *Basic* presumption altogether. But the impulse to fend off what many justices surely viewed as a transparent attempt to manipulate the procedure-substance interface cuts both ways. If you don't like what Amgen was trying to do, then it ought to be hard to feel sanguine about what the majority did in *Amgen*: manipulating the procedure-substance interface to avoid taking the time to justify a desired substantive outcome with reference to the usual substantive sources.[69]

The procedural tail should not wag the substantive dog, even if you happen to think the tail is, in fact, wagging the dog in the right direction. This was one of Nagareda's principal themes.[70] This larger

[67] Cf. *id.* (discussing hints in the majority's opinion that it thinks "[p]rice distortion is not a predicate to . . . reliance").

[68] See Langevoort, *Basic* at Twenty?, *supra* note 65, at 198.

[69] See also Langevoort, Frozen in Time?, *supra* note 63, at 24–25 (agreeing that "the majority . . . responds to the defense-side request to allow them an early shot at materiality . . . by invoking old school procedure," rather than substantive sources that might have supported the same conclusion).

[70] Nagareda, Aggregate Proof, *supra* note 3, at 164 (emphasizing that the certification process should not serve as a vehicle for "development of the law" "*sub silentio*"). Admittedly, *Amgen* presents a case where the legal issue was not necessary to assess the propriety of certification, and so is different from the cases that were Nagareda's focus. *Id.* at 171 (noting his focus was on "[l]aw declaration . . . necessary to assess the propriety of class certification"). The concern in *Amgen* is more general: by relying on procedural rules to resolve the case, when the result also could have been justified by reference to the substantive law, the Court impoverishes the public's understanding of important legal principles in play. That is not merely a theoretical concern in this

transparency and accountability concern with *Amgen*, in turn, underscores the wisdom of Nagareda's advice: Courts ought to resolve threshold questions of law bearing on how the class claims can be proven first, and "only then" turn to apply the common answers test.[71] Doing so helps check the temptation, to which the Court succumbed here, to shove substantive questions with larger importance beyond the case at hand under the procedural rug.

B. Lawmaking via Procedure in Comcast

If *Amgen* saw a coalition of liberal justices (plus Chief Justice John Roberts and Justice Samuel Alito) engaged in what amounted to lawmaking via procedure, in *Comcast* it was the conservative justices' turn—suggesting a tendency around which the entire Court is, if on nothing else, united.

1. The Majority's Analysis

Comcast v. Behrend involved a proposed class action against the cable television provider Comcast. The complaint, brought on behalf of more than two million present and former Comcast cable television subscribers in the Philadelphia area, attacked the cable company's use of a so-called "clustering" strategy in the Philadelphia cable market.[72] "Clustering" is antitrust lingo for a company's efforts to concentrate its operations in a particular market, and Comcast pursued such a strategy in the Philadelphia area through a series of acquisitions approved by antitrust regulators.[73] Plaintiffs, however, alleged that the strategy violated federal antitrust law by monopolizing the Philadelphia cable market.[74]

---

case. As Langevoort notes, the majority, by avoiding addressing how price distortion matters to proof of securities fraud, missed an opportunity to address a larger, related question with far-reaching implications: whether the 1995 Private Securities Litigation Reform Act "froze" the "balance between plaintiffs and defendants" in the mid-1990s into place, leaving further adjustments to Congress. See Langevoort, Frozen in Time?, *supra* note 63, at 24–35 (noting the Court's view of this "frozen in time" concept of securities fraud "will determine much about the future of private securities class actions").

[71] Nagareda, Aggregate Proof, *supra* note 3, at 164.

[72] 133 S. Ct. at 1429–30.

[73] *Id.* (describing Comcast's clustering strategy).

[74] Plaintiffs, specifically, alleged Comcast entered into illegal swap agreements in violation of § 1 of the Sherman Act and had monopolized or attempted to monopolize services in the Philadelphia area in violation of § 2. See, e.g., *id.* at 1430.

Proving an antitrust claim requires not simply showing the defendant engaged in anti-competitive conduct, but proving that this conduct injured class members by inflating the prices of goods they bought, resulting in measurable damages.[75] And plaintiffs' complaint, of course, alleged this was so: Comcast's clustering strategy, the complaint contended, allowed the cable company to obtain a dominant market position, eliminating competition and allowing the company to charge the entire class of Philadelphia-area consumers inflated prices for inferior cable subscriptions and service.[76]

In a 5–4 decision, the Court, in an opinion by Justice Antonin Scalia and joined by the other four conservatives, sided with Comcast. For the majority, the question concerning how Comcast's monopoly affected the prices paid by class members doomed the plaintiffs' class-action theory. The trouble stemmed from the plaintiffs' efforts to prove how Comcast's clustering strategy affected the entire class. Plaintiffs had proposed four scenarios that explained how Comcast's clustering strategy affected prices in the Philadelphia area. To quote Justice Scalia:

> First, Comcast's clustering made it profitable for Comcast to withhold local sports programming from its competitors, resulting in decreased market penetration by direct broadcast satellite providers. Second, Comcast's activities reduced the level of competition from "overbuilders," companies that build competing cable networks in areas where an incumbent cable company already operates. Third, Comcast reduced the level of "benchmark" competition on which cable customers rely to compare prices. Fourth, clustering increased Comcast's bargaining power relative to content providers. Each of these forms of impact, respondents alleged, increased cable subscription rates throughout the Philadelphia [Designated Market Area].[77]

The district court held that based on the evidence only one of these scenarios—the so-called "overbuilding theory"—could possibly

[75] See, e.g., In re Hydrogen Peroxide Antitrust Litigation, 552 F.3d 305, 311 (3d Cir. 2008).

[76] 133 S. Ct. at 1430 ("Petitioners' clustering scheme, respondents contended, harmed subscribers in the Philadelphia cluster by eliminating competition and holding prices for cable services above competitive levels").

[77] Id. at 1430–31.

support an award of damages on a class-wide basis.[78] Even if the scenarios described in the other theories may have had some price effects in some parts of the Philadelphia market (which the trial court doubted), they also did not plausibly affect the entire market and so could not support an award of class-wide damages.[79]

To connect the one surviving theory to measurable damages incurred by the class, the plaintiffs retained a statistician, Dr. James McClave. McClave attempted to quantify the damages to the class using a multiple regression that "compar[ed] actual cable prices in the Philadelphia [area] with hypothetical prices that would have prevailed but for petitioners' allegedly anticompetitive activities."[80] Although his model's calculations yielded an estimate of over $875 million in damages "for the entire class,"[81] the model did not attempt to isolate damages attributable solely to Comcast's deterrence of overbuilding. In effect, his $875 million damages figure reflected damages attributable to the cumulative impact of Comcast's anticompetitive conduct "as a whole" across the class, including *but not limited to* deterrence of overbuilding.[82]

It was this point on which the majority seized. "If respondents prevail on their claims," said the Court, "they would be entitled only to damages resulting from reduced overbuilder competition, since that is the only theory of antitrust impact accepted for class-action treatment by the District Court."[83] It follows that "the model . . . must

---

[78] *Id.* at 1431 ("The District Court accepted the overbuilder theory of antitrust impact as capable of classwide proof and rejected the rest.").

[79] This seems, anyway, to be the majority's understanding of the district court's reasoning. See *id.* at 1434–35 (speculating that "[f]or all we know, cable subscribers in Gloucester County may have been overcharged because of petitioners' alleged elimination of satellite competition (a theory of liability that is not capable of classwide proof); while subscribers in Camden County may have paid elevated prices because of petitioners' increased bargaining power vis-à-vis content providers (another theory that is not capable of classwide proof); while yet others . . . may have paid rates produced by the combined effects of multiple forms of alleged antitrust harm"). It bears noting, however, that the district court largely dismissed the other three theories as implausible sources of *any* price effects. See Behrend v. Comcast, 264 F.R.D. 150, 162–81 (E.D. Pa. 2010).

[80] 133 S. Ct. at 1431.

[81] *Id.*

[82] *Id.* at 1434.

[83] *Id.* at 1433.

measure only those damages attributable to that theory."[84] Because the model did not attempt to do so, the Court concluded, "it cannot possibly establish that damages are susceptible of measurement across the entire class for purposes of Rule 23(b)(3)."[85]

The defense bar is already vigorously trying to cement the perception that *Comcast* broadly holds that damages must be susceptible of "common" calculation, and the claim finds support in the language of the opinion.[86] If that is right, *Comcast* is quite a significant case that pushes the common answers test deep into the damages phase of class litigation. Courts must now closely scrutinize admissibility of expert evidence bearing on calculation of damages during the certification stage to determine its reliability as a method of common damages measurement, and the decision would seem to doom certification in a host of different cases where modeling cannot reliably capture significant variation in damages within the class. [87] Understood this way, the case would significantly restrict damages class actions in ways that, arguably, may go beyond even what Nagareda envisioned.[88]

---

[84] *Id.*

[85] *Id.*

[86] This broader interpretation draws some support from the Court's framing of its inquiry as, variously, "[w]hether individual damage calculations" defeat predominance (*id.*); and whether plaintiffs satisfy "commonality of damages" (*id.* at 1435 n.6); and from its suggestion (seemingly added to the opinion at the last minute, complete with typos) that "even if the model had identified subscribers who paid more solely because of the deterrence of overbuilding, it still would not have established the requisite commonality of damages unless it plausibly shows that the extent of overbuilding .... would have been the *same* in all counties, or that the extent is irrelevant to effect upon ability [sic] to charge supra-competitive prices." See, e.g., *id.* (emphasis added). The last point, in particular, connects to the concern articulated by the dissent in the Third Circuit that "no model can calculate class-wide damages because any damages—such as they may be—are not distributed on anything like a similar basis throughout the [Philadelphia area]," but rather exhibit "wide variations" owing to significant differences in conditions across segments of the market. See Behrend v. Comcast, 655 F.3d 152, 224 & n.35 (3d. Cir. 2011) (Jordan, J., dissenting).

[87] See, e.g., 133 S. Ct. at 1435 n.6 (suggesting that where damages may be based on a single source but vary widely in impacts across the class, "commonality of damages" is defeated).

[88] One common solution to problems of individualized damages, which Nagareda did not question, is bifurcating trial into separate liability and damages phases and then certifying the common liability issues on a class-wide basis, while leaving damages calculation issues to more individualized proceedings. See, e.g., Behrend, 655 F.3d at

It is doubtful, though, that the lower courts will all read the decision so broadly. First, the plaintiff never challenged the idea that damages must be "susceptible of classwide measurement."[89] Many of the broadest pronouncements in the decision therefore reflect what amount to statements of stipulated law.[90] Second, the result can be rationalized without reference to this broader principle, since, at several junctures, the Court seemed particularly concerned that the expert evidence simply failed to prove that the theory of liability in the case actually applied to the class as a unit. Accordingly, *Comcast* can be viewed, like *Wal-Mart*, as one more case in which plaintiffs simply have not shown they can prove the existence of a single classwide wrong that holds the class together.[91]

Both features provide reasons to suspect that lower courts, particularly those in circuits hewing to the traditional view that

---

209 & 224 n.35 (Jordan, J., dissenting) (proposing a variation on this solution, and suggesting the damages phase could be practically managed through the certification of damages subclasses encompassing different segments of the market). *Comcast's* broadest language (e.g., stating that failure of "commonality of damages" defeats certification of a "single class," 133 S. Ct. at 1435), coupled with its pointed refusal to recommend bifurcation, may cast doubt on this practice, although it perhaps may alternatively reflect the Court's implicit agreement with Comcast that the number of subclasses needed to deal with variations in damages at the remedial stage would raise separate problems under Rule 23(b)(3)'s manageability requirement. See Oral Arg. Tr. at 9–10, Comcast v. Behrend, 133 S. Ct. 1426 (2013) (No. 11-864) ("MR. ESTRADA: There are cases, indeed, in which . . . the variances of the classes can be dealt with, with subclasses . . . . [T]here is considerable basis for skepticism in thinking that could ever be accomplished [here] because we are talking about 649 franchise areas with different competitive conditions.").

[89] See, e.g., 133 S. Ct. at 1437 (Ginsburg, J., dissenting) (noting "[t]he oddity of this case, in which the need to prove damages on a classwide basis through a common methodology was never challenged by respondents").

[90] See Gary Lawson, Stipulating the Law, 109 Mich. L. Rev. 1191 (2011).

[91] Compare Wal-Mart Stores, Inc. v. Dukes, 131 S. Ct. 2541, 2551 (2011) (articulating the need for class members' to identify the "same injury," meaning a legal wrong capable of being remedied "at once") with Comcast, 131 S. Ct. at 1435 (noting that "[f]or all we know," some class members in different counties had incurred damages resulting exclusively from separate "wrong[s]" associated with the Comcast monopoly that had not been certified for class treatment—and holding that given the failure to demonstrate damages resulting from a single classwide wrong, "Rule 23(b)(3) cannot authorize treating subscribers within the Philadelphia cluster as members of a single class").

individualized damages calculations do not defeat predominance, may not feel bound to follow *Comcast*'s broadest pronouncements.[92]

2. *Conservatives Do It Too:* Comcast's *Lawmaking Problem*

While the exact import of *Comcast*'s procedural holding remains to be seen, the case does seem to mark a significant *substantive* shift in the way the Court understands some key points of antitrust law. This point, which hasn't received much attention, also suggests an overlooked point of comparison between *Amgen* and *Comcast*.

In a post about *Comcast* on the *Point of Law* blog, Richard Epstein articulates the conventional view of plaintiffs' substantive rights: To demonstrate a right to damages, class members need only prove that monopolization caused some price impact affecting each member of the class, but do not need to prove the specific mechanisms for the impact. [93] The remedy in antitrust cases can then take the form of an average of the damage caused consumers as a group.[94]

On that view of the substantive law, Epstein notes, plaintiffs met their burden of proof in *Comcast*. The fact of a classwide price increase attributable to Comcast's monopoly could be proven through the type of multiple regression submitted by Dr. McClave.[95] And once a classwide impact was proven, the amount of damages at the

---

[92] For one early example of what is likely to be a broader phenomenon, see Glazer v. Whirlpool Corp., 2013 U.S. App. LEXIS 14519 (6th Cir. July 18, 2013) (upholding certification limited to common liability issues and distinguishing *Comcast*).

[93] Richard A. Epstein, The Precarious Status of Class Action Antitrust Litigation after *Comcast v. Behrend*, Point of Law, Apr. 8, 2013, http://pointoflaw.com/columns/2013/04/the-precarious-status-of-class-action-antitrust-litigation-after-comcast-v-behrend.php.

[94] *Id.*

[95] *Id.* ("[T]he information on the four possible sources of the increase should not be looked at in the alternative; if examined at all, the theories should be treated at most as cumulative descriptive evidence that is weaker in kind than the quantitative evidence in the regression itself. It is therefore a *plus* that the regression is not tied to the overbuilding theory . . . . [T]he numbers tell the key story, as each of the four theories mentioned could offer a partial explanation as to . . . how the antitrust injury came to pass."). See also Sergio Campos, *Comcast* Puzzles, Mass Tort Litigation Blog, http://lawprofessors.typepad.com/mass_tort_litigation/2013/04/comcast-puzzles.html (April 8, 2013) (noting that the McClave model reflected "a standard method of determining an overcharge in an antitrust case" and wondering whether "it makes sense to isolate one antitrust violation [i.e., the overbuilding theory] to determine the 'but for' price").

individual level could be established using the class-friendly imprecision of econometrics and averaging.[96]

The majority in *Comcast* implicitly adopted a different understanding of antitrust law's contours. The tip-off is the Court's assumption that plaintiffs must prove a specific impact theory detailing a particular chain of events set in motion by the monopoly (here, deterrence of overbuilding) that led to *their* price increase.[97] That makes sense only if antitrust law adopts an individualized form of damages liability. If so, class members can't just offer blunt proof of a group impact to prove their entitlement to damages. That impact is the sum of a number of discrete *impact scenarios*, each of which may cause damages that are not evenly distributed across the class.[98] To isolate the individualized damages to which she, specifically, is entitled, a class member must accordingly isolate the specific impacts that affected *her*.[99] Put simply, an individualized conception of the remedy leads to an individualized conception of liability.

By treating class members' rights in this individualized way, the certification problem in *Comcast* follows as a matter of course, and the decision links up with Nagareda's concern that the class procedure ought to follow the contours of the substantive law. If each class member may recover only those damages attributable to specific harmful events affecting her, then showing class members' claims are resolvable on a class basis requires demonstrating that class members' claims flow from a single harmful impact that affected the class as a unit. McClave's study, which fails to isolate class damages attributable to any specific harmful chain of events, doesn't make this showing.[100] Finding plaintiffs are entitled to damages based on his study, would, indeed, *alter* class members' substantive rights

[96] Epstein, Precarious Status, *supra* note 93.

[97] *Id.* (damages could be calculated "by taking the total amount of antitrust injury that [defendants'] actions caused across the market and dividing it among the plaintiffs in a form that is certain *not* to reflect the exact injuries that each member of the class sustained") (emphasis in original).

[98] See, e.g., 131 S. Ct. at 1435 (noting the effects of the four different theories of "antitrust harms" may be confined to different parts of the class; "[t]he permutations involving four theories of liability and 2 million subscribers located in 16 counties are nearly endless").

[99] *Id.* at 1434 (raising concern that the model will identify damages that are "not the result of reduced overbuilding").

[100] *Id.*

by allowing some class members to recover damages that have no proven relation to any events that actually affected them.[101]

The cleavage between these two views of antitrust might be roughly described as one between public and private rights. The conventional modern view treats antitrust law as creating a quasi-public *group* remedy that can be proven easily on a class basis.[102] The majority, by contrast, views the antitrust civil damages remedy in the narrow terms of the traditional private rights: as a remedy anchored by the real-world scope of each class member's individual injuries. Because, on this view, the focus of antitrust is the real-world experience of each individual, there is little doubt that private antitrust actions will qualify for class treatment less frequently (even if the details of the exact difficulties after *Comcast* remain to be worked out). The dissent characterized this latter conception as a "remarkable" shift in antitrust law's perspective.[103]

This article takes no view about which conception of the substantive law is right (and, indeed, I confess some initial sympathy for the individualized view). The problem that I want to highlight here is a variant on the procedural problem in *Amgen*. *Amgen* reflected an old-fashioned use of procedure to engage in lawmaking "in operation, if not in doctrine." At first glance, *Comcast* might not seem to be comparable—as just suggested, Justice Scalia's opinion seems to reflect a shift in the way the Court understands antitrust law. And, indeed, his opinion even explicitly acknowledges the ruling flows from a determination of "law" about how antitrust claims are proven.[104]

Yet the essence of the problem in cases like *Amgen* is that procedure enables substantive transformation without the usual accountable process of substantive *justification*. On a closer, second look, something similar in kind, if subtly different in operation, seems to

---

[101] See, e.g., Brief of Petitioners, Comcast v. Behrend, 133 S. Ct. 1426 (2013) (No. 11-864) ("allowing gross damages by treating unsubstantiated claims of class members collectively" would "significantly alte[r] substantive rights").

[102] See Epstein, Precarious Status, *supra* note 93.

[103] 133 S. Ct. at 1440 (Ginsburg, J., dissenting) (noting the Court's premise, that plaintiffs are entitled only to damages attributable to reduced overbuilder competition, as a "remarkable" interpretation of antitrust law that "it could not mean to apply in other cases").

[104] See *id*. at 1433 n.5 (noting that "while the data contained within an econometric model may well be 'questions of act' in the relevant sense, what those data prove" is a question of law).

be happening in the antitrust arena. As the procedural search for dissimilarities dictated by a search for common answers has taken hold, so lower courts have increasingly shifted in the direction of articulating a more individualized burden of proof in antitrust, but without any frank assessment of the usual substantive sources (text, legislative history, purpose and the like) that justify that shift.[105]

The majority seemed to follow this trend. It pivots from fear that class members' inflated prices have their source in several different scenarios to the conclusion that the named plaintiff must dispel this fear by showing damages can be traced to a single scenario affecting the class as a whole. Yet that conclusion depends on the premise that the feared dissimilarities would actually impede class-wide resolution of class members' claims. That premise, in turn, properly depends on a substantive theory of antitrust that no court in the course of this litigation has squarely tried to justify.[106]

The pattern, indeed, is the mirror image of one identified by Nagareda in the pre-*Wal-Mart* case law. Before *Wal-Mart*, he noted, some lower courts were led by plaintiffs' proffer of aggregate proof to assume the legal materiality of that proof—a phenomenon that he termed "conforming the law to the proof."[107] This practice obviously predetermines the conclusion that certification is appropriate. The antitrust cases seem to exhibit the same pattern but from a different starting point and cutting in the opposite direction: presuming, based on defendants' proffer of proof showing various dissimilarities within the class, that this individualized proof is material to plaintiffs' recovery, leading to the predestined conclusion that the claims cannot be grouped together. Here, again, the law is being conformed to proof—but this time, to proof of dissimilarities rather than of sim-

---

[105] *See* Nagareda, Aggregate Proof, *supra* note 3, at 103.

[106] One good starting point for a broader justification would be the Court's subsequent observation, this term, in *American Express Co. v. Italian Colors Restaurant*, that "[t]he Sherman and Clayton Acts . . . . were enacted decades before the advent of [Rule 23]" and so did not originally presuppose a group litigation unit. 133 S. Ct. 2304, 2309 (2013). The point in this article is not that the substantive theory on which certification analysis is implicitly premised is wrong or incapable of meaningful support from the usual legal sources, but that the courts in the case seemed, improperly, to rely on the dissimilarities framework of procedural doctrine to do much of the above-board work justifying a conclusion that depended, in significant part, on a missing substantive analysis.

[107] Nagareda, Aggregate Proof, *supra* note 3, at 104.

ilarities. Both miss the necessary step—a "definitive assessment" of the "precise delineation of the right at stake,"[108] which determines how the claims can be proven and so identifies "at the outset" of the certification inquiry which dissimilarities are legally relevant.[109]

One can only speculate on the reason why the case law exhibits this pattern. Perhaps part of the story is an anchoring effect, in which a procedural analysis framed around a search for a certain type of proof (proof of similarities pre-*Wal-Mart*, or of dissimilarities post-*Wal-Mart*) biases courts toward attributing substantive importance willy-nilly to proof of that type identified in the record.[110] Whatever the cause, *Comcast* is suggestive of an ironic turn. A reformulation of the class-action test, designed to promote accountability and transparency, may be replicating the same old bad tendency: conforming the law to procedure, rather than the other way around.

Conclusion

Because of the intense interest in class-action law, and the huge practical import of class-action cases for some of the country's largest corporations, popular coverage of class-action law tends to treat class-action cases as a horse race between plaintiffs' lawyers and corporate defendants. That focus, though, misses some less practical, but important, questions lurking behind the scenes.

Behind the immense "who's up, who's down" tactical commentary that surrounds *Amgen* and *Comcast*, this term's two key class-action cases both squarely presented examples of a larger problem—the implication of the class device in disguised acts of judicial lawmaking. It's tempting to dismiss this problem as one relating to middling process values not worth getting exercised over. Conforming to those values would have simply required putting the lawmaking taking place in both cases up-front. That would not necessarily have changed the outcomes in either case.

---

108 *Id.* at 151.

109 *Id.* at 129, 164.

110 "Anchoring" is the term for a common form of cognitive bias in which the starting point for a chain of reasoning colors subsequent analysis. For discussion, see Amos Tversky & Daniel Kahneman, Judgment under Uncertainty: Heuristics and Biases, 185 Science 1124, 1128 (1974).

Why, then, make a fuss? Some fuss is warranted because transparency and accountability are important. These process values restrain and discipline federal courts and empower more appropriate lawmakers. The stakes in the long run are significant, especially in the class-action field.[111]

Hence the room for some concerns this term. Both *Amgen* and *Comcast* illustrate that together the conservative and liberal wings of the Court are, when the opportunity arises, susceptible to the kind of lawmaking-without-accountability that class procedure enables. Of course, perhaps both cases are just bumps in a long road toward a larger realignment of class-action procedure in a "pro law" direction. One can hope. For now, this term illustrates that such a realignment remains very much a work in progress.

---

[111] Indeed, it is no exaggeration to say that class procedure has been an engine for reshaping the role of courts and litigation in the business of regulation. One commentator argues it has created the "litigation state," a judicial rival to the executive "administrative state." See Sean Farhang, The Litigation State: Public Regulation and Private Litigation in the U.S. (2010). The point helps link the rule-of-law concerns explored in this article to those that have long been a part of the administrative-law conversation. See Antonin Scalia, *Vermont Yankee*: The APA, the D.C. Circuit, and the Supreme Court, 1978 Sup. Ct. Rev. 345, 406 (noting, with a focus on the administrative field, that "procedural elaboration . . . [is] a means of adjusting [agencies'] power," and advocating a "truly stable framework of administrative procedure" subject to Congress's control). In this regard, it is worth noting Justice Scalia's comment, from a term ago, disparaging the "judge-empowering" image of administrative procedure as part of "a partnership between legislators and judges," who "working [together would] produce better law than legislators alone could possibly produce." See United States v. Home Concrete & Supply, 132 S. Ct. 1836, 1848 (2012) (Scalia, J., concurring). The same image, this term suggests, still casts a long shadow over the separate field of class-action analysis.

City of Arlington v. FCC: Justice Scalia's Triumph

*Andrew M. Grossman**

The Court's opinion in *City of Arlington v. FCC*[1] may mark the most "avulsive"[2] change in administrative law in at least the last 13 years. But it is not the revolution that anyone, save its author, was expecting. While the Court may, from time to time, engage in misdirection to pull rabbits out of hats, this case was more like pulling a trout out of a pencil-case.

Yes, the Court did answer the question presented, holding that agencies are due deference under the two-step framework of *Chevron v. Natural Resources Defense Council* for reasonable statutory constructions resolving ambiguity concerning the scope of their jurisdiction.[3] Had the Court come out the other way, that certainly would have been avulsive too, giving courts the opportunity in nearly every regulatory challenge to resolve statutory ambiguities de novo, taking no or little account of the administering agency's views. But that, at least, would have been predictable, because it was among the answers to the question before the Court.

Instead, *City of Arlington* could be the landmark that Justice Antonin Scalia has always maintained that *Chevron* was. His majority opinion announces a broad rule of judicial deference to agency statutory construction, when within the bounds of permissible interpretation. In this new formulation, gone is the "flabby" multi-factor inquiry that preceded application of *Chevron* deference. In its place is a simple, easily administrable rule of deference to agencies that reasonably and authoritatively

---

* The author practices appellate litigation in the Washington, D.C., office of BakerHostetler LLP and is a visiting fellow in the Edwin Meese III Center for Legal and Judicial Studies at the Heritage Foundation.

[1] 133 S. Ct. 1863 (2013).

[2] See *infra* § I.B.

[3] City of Arlington, 133 S. Ct. at 1874–75 (citing Chevron, U.S.A., Inc. v. Natural Resources Defense Council, 467 U.S. 837 (1984).

interpret ambiguities in the statutes that they administer—the rule that Scalia has promoted for years, as often as not in dissent.

Scalia's majority opinion sets the stage for a heated debate with Chief Justice John Roberts, writing in dissent, on the role of the courts in policing the administrative state. Where Scalia is concerned about marking the boundary between the judicial branch and the political branches, the chief justice frets over Congress's unbounded delegations of authority to administrative agencies, which themselves are barely checked by the president or the courts. Just when it seems the chief justice is ready to breathe life into the non-delegation doctrine and put the lot of them on notice, he turns in a different direction, concluding that agencies are due no deference on their authority to interpret different provisions of the statutes they administer—a question substantially narrower than the one the Court agreed to hear.

What to make of it all? It may be that Scalia and Roberts share the same concern, each struggling for a way to assert control over an administrative state that does not fit the Constitution's separation of powers but is, at this late date, a fact of life. Scalia, ever the formalist, would keep the courts away from decisions that smack of policymaking, while using the heavy artillery of thoughtful statutory interpretation to limit the bounds of permissible agency action. Roberts, meanwhile, would have the courts take on more statutory questions themselves, strictly construing agencies' freedom of action and, ultimately, their authority. Each is a second-best solution, and neither is without its problems. Somewhat counterintuitively, Scalia's approach may be the more durable and, ultimately, the more effective at protecting individual liberty.

This article proceeds in four sections. The first presents a thumbnail sketch of the Court's approach to applying deference to agencies' statutory constructions. The second describes the *City of Arlington* litigation and the different parties' positions, which are essential to understanding the Court's resolution of the case. The third analyzes the justices' opinions. And the fourth concludes with several observations on the decision's impact

I. A Brief History of Deference

A. *The* Chevron *Revolution*

The only thing that has ever been clear about the "doctrine" enunciated in *Chevron* is that it is contained in the following paragraph, surely the most cited in administrative law:

> When a court reviews an agency's construction of the statute which it administers, it is confronted with two questions. First, always, is the question whether Congress has directly spoken to the precise question at issue. If the intent of Congress is clear, that is the end of the matter; for the court, as well as the agency, must give effect to the unambiguously expressed intent of Congress. If, however, the court determines Congress has not directly addressed the precise question at issue, the court does not simply impose its own construction on the statute, as would be necessary in the absence of an administrative interpretation. Rather, if the statute is silent or ambiguous with respect to the specific issue, the question for the court is whether the agency's answer is based on a permissible construction of the statute.[4]

These things are "well-settled," the Court explained.[5] But left unsettled and unanswered were at least a few minor points: Which types of "construction[s]" are entitled to such deference? How is a court to decide when the "intent of Congress is clear"? What is a "permissible construction of the statute"? And above all, what is *Chevron's* domain? That is, "[t]o what sorts of statutes and what sorts of agency interpretations should the mandatory deference doctrine of *Chevron* apply?"[6] Thirty years into this project, *Chevron's* contours and substance remain uncertain.

That would be a strike against *Chevron* if the Court that decided it had intended it to work any great change in the law. It did not. The Court's focus at argument and conference was the precise question before it: whether the Environmental Protection Agency could allow states to treat all pollution-emitting devices within a plant-wide "bubble" as a single "stationary source" under the Clean Air Act's Prevention of Significant Deterioration preconstruction review program, thereby allowing sources more flexibility to "trade" emission increases and decreases among different emitting units within the "bubble."[7] At conference, Justice John Paul Stevens, *Chevron's* author,

---

[4] 467 U.S. at 842–43 (footnotes omitted).

[5] *Id.* at 845.

[6] Thomas W. Merrill & Kristin E. Hickman, *Chevron's* Domain, 89 Geo. L.J. 833, 835 (2001).

[7] William N. Eskridge, Jr., & Lauren E. Baer, The Continuum of Deference: Supreme Court Treatment of Agency Statutory Interpretations from *Chevron* to *Hamdan*, 96 Geo. L.J. 1083, 1086 (2008) (quoting Memorandum from Justice Sandra Day O'Connor to

had no firm opinion on that question and was sympathetic to the agency's exercise of discretion in an area fraught with competing legal and policy considerations: "When I am so confused, I go with the agency."[8] And so he did.

And in so doing, *Chevron* seemingly supplanted the disparate approaches that the Court had, until then, applied to agencies' interpretations of their governing statutes. Judge Henry Friendly described the complicated state of the law in a 1976 opinion:

> We think it is time to recognize . . . that there are two lines of Supreme Court decisions on this subject which are analytically in conflict, with the result that a court of appeals must choose the one it deems more appropriate for the case at hand. Leading cases supporting the view that great deference must be given to the decisions of an administrative agency applying a statute to the facts and that such decisions can be reversed only if without rational basis . . . . However, there is an impressive body of law sanctioning free substitution of judicial for administrative judgment when the question involves the meaning of a statutory term.[9]

Indeed, in the freewheeling spirit of the era, the Supreme Court routinely conducted open-ended "totality of the circumstances" inquiries before deciding to go with its own view of a statute's "most natural or logical" meaning,[10] and the lower courts considered themselves empowered to order executive agencies to create new regulatory programs out of whole cloth.[11] No more, post-*Chevron*. Its "equa-

---

the Conference (June 14, 1984) (in Papers of Harry A. Blackmun, Library of Congress, Madison Building, Box 397, Folder 7); see generally Thomas W. Merrill, The Story of *Chevron*: The Making of an Accidental Precedent, in Administrative Law Stories 398 (Peter L. Strauss ed., 2006).

[8] Eskridge & Baer, *supra* note 7, at 1086.

[9] Pittston Stevedoring Corp. v. Dellaventura, 544 F.2d 35, 49 (2d Cir. 1976), aff'd, Northeast Marine Terminal Co., Inc. v. Caputo, 432 U.S. 249 (1977); see also Natural Resources Defense Council, Inc. v. EPA, 725 F.2d 761, 767 (D.C. Cir. 1984) ("[T]he case law under the Administrative Procedure Act has not crystallized around a single doctrinal formulation which captures the extent to which courts should defer to agency interpretations of law.").

[10] See, e.g., Securities and Exchange Commission v. Sloan, 436 U.S. 103 (1978).

[11] See, e.g., Sierra Club v. Ruckelshaus, 344 F. Supp. 253 (D.D.C. 1972), aff'd, 4 ERC 1815 (D.C. Cir. 1972), aff'd by an equally divided court sub nom., Fri v. Sierra Club, 412 U.S. 541 (1973) (ordering EPA to create the Prevention of Significant Deterioration

tion of gaps and ambiguities with express delegations turned the doctrine of mandatory deference . . . into a ubiquitous formula," effecting "a fundamental transformation in the relationship between courts and agencies under administrative law."[12]

But if *Chevron* marked a revolution, the Court didn't immediately recognize it, applying the two-step framework only inconsistently, at best, in subsequent terms.[13] But the timing was right: *Chevron's* rise reflected a sea change in the politics and policies of judging. The doctrine quickly gained currency on the U.S. Court of Appeals for the D.C. Circuit, particularly among Reagan appointees like thenjudges Antonin Scalia and Kenneth Starr, who recognized it as a "landmark"[14] and a "watershed," respectively, for deregulation.[15] Under *Chevron*, no longer would courts impose artificial "obstacles" "when an agency that has been a classic regulator decides to go in the other direction" or when it "simply sits on its hands and does not choose to do additional things that could be done."[16] Yet even Starr admitted that its "revolutionary effect is not apparent from a quick examination of the opinion itself. The opinion on its face signals no break with the past; it does not explicitly overrule or disapprove of a single case."[17] It would be several more years before the lower courts' view of *Chevron* bubbled up to the high court, pushed along by the elevation of Justice Scalia in 1986. This delay was also a reflection, perhaps, of the Reagan and George H. W. Bush administrations' efforts to tread lightly for fear that the Supreme Court would undermine the gains it had made in the courts of appeals.[18]

Program based on a statutory purpose provision and some cherry-picked excerpts of legislative history). For background, see generally Jack L. Landau, *Alabama Power Co. v. Costle*: An End to a Decade of Controversy over the Prevention of Significant Deterioration of Air Quality?, 10 Envtl. L. 585, 589–92 (1980).

[12] Merrill & Hickman, *supra* note 6, at 834.

[13] Thomas W. Merrill, Judicial Deference to Executive Precedent, 101 Yale L.J. 969, 980–81 (1992) (presenting statistics).

[14] Antonin Scalia, The Role of the Judiciary in Deregulation, 55 Antitrust L.J. 191, 193 (1986).

[15] Kenneth W. Starr, Judicial Review in the Post-*Chevron* Era, 3 Yale J. On Reg. 283 (1986).

[16] Scalia, *supra* note 14, at 191.

[17] Starr, *supra* note 15, at 284.

[18] Eskridge & Baer, *supra* note 7, at 1087; see Peter H. Schuck and E. Donald Elliott, To the *Chevron* Station: An Empirical Study of Federal Administrative Law, 1990 Duke L.J.

B. The Counterrevolution

That fear was not misplaced, because there was resistance. In *Immigration and Naturalization Service v. Cardoza-Fonseca*, Justice Stevens wrote for the Court that agencies are due no special deference when they face "a pure question of statutory construction for the courts to decide," rather than a "question of interpretation [in which] the agency is required to apply [a legal standard] to a particular set of facts."[19] Although this statement was arguably dicta, given that the Court had already held the agency's interpretation to be flatly inconsistent with the statutory text, it provoked a fiery response from Justice Scalia, who recognized Justice Stevens's attempt to realign his *Chevron* opinion with the less-deferential approaches that had preceded it.[20]

Although this aspect of *Cardoza-Fonseca* was a dead end—in the Supreme Court, at least; it caused no little confusion in the lower courts—it was a prelude to the Court's decision in *United States v. Mead Corporation*.[21] Where *Chevron* expressed a presumption that statutory "gaps" indicate an implicit delegation of interpretative authority to the administering agency, *Mead* held that a "gap" alone was not enough and that delegation must be supported by an "indication of a . . . congressional intent," basically flipping the presumption of congressional intent the other way:

> Congress . . . may not have expressly delegated authority or responsibility to implement a particular provision or fill a particular gap. Yet it can still be apparent from the agency's generally conferred authority and other statutory circumstances that Congress would expect the agency to be able to speak with the force of law when it addresses ambiguity in the statute or fills a space in the enacted law.[22]

Those circumstances "may be shown in a variety of ways, as by an agency's power to engage in adjudication or notice-and-comment

---

984, 1031 (1990) (discussing the federal government's "win rate" in the lower courts post-*Chevron*); see Eskridge & Baer, *supra* note 7, at 1121–22 (discussing the Supreme Court).

[19] 480 U.S. 421, 448 (1987).

[20] *Id.* at 453–55 (Scalia, J., concurring).

[21] 533 U.S. 218 (2001).

[22] *Id.* at 227, 229.

rulemaking, or by some other indication of a comparable congressional intent."[23] Under this formula, even "express congressional authorizations to engage in the process of rulemaking or adjudication that produces regulations or rulings" would be only a "very good indicator of delegation meriting *Chevron* treatment."[24] As to the agency construction at issue—a ruling letter by the Customs Headquarters Office concluding that Mead's imported day planners were subject to the statutory tariff classification for "diaries"—the Court denied it *Chevron* deference based on a laundry list of factors, including the lack of notice-and-comment practice, the letter's inapplicability to third parties, the many Customs offices issuing such letters, and so on.[25]

But the agency was not necessarily out of luck. The Court exhumed the doctrine of *Skidmore v. Swift & Company*,[26] which some believed *Chevron* had interred. Under this approach, the weight accorded an administrative judgment in a particular case "will depend upon the thoroughness evident in its consideration, the validity of its reasoning, its consistency with earlier and later pronouncements, and all those factors which give it power to persuade, if lacking power to control."[27] The Court described this fallback as necessary "to tailor deference to variety" in the spectrum of possible agency actions.[28]

Justice Scalia, in lone dissent, explained that the *Mead* majority worked "an avulsive change" in administrative law, replacing *Chevron*'s presumption of agency delegation with "a presumption that agency discretion does not exist unless the statute, expressly or impliedly, says so."[29] Compounding that dislocation was the Court's "wonderfully imprecise" test for whether or not agency interpretations would be entitled to deference, made worse by a "virtually

---

[23] *Id.* at 227.

[24] *Id.* at 229. In this, the Court backed away from its statement of just a year earlier, in *Christensen v. Harris County*, 529 U.S. 576, 586–87 (2000), that *Chevron* held "that a court must give effect to an agency's regulation containing a reasonable interpretation of an ambiguous statute"—and even that was a retreat from *Chevron*'s reference to "an agency's construction of the statute which it administers," without limitation as to the form the construction takes. See 467 U.S. at 842.

[25] 533 U.S. at 232–34.

[26] 323 U.S. 134 (1944).

[27] Mead, 533 U.S. at 228 (quoting Skidmore, 323 U.S. at 140).

[28] *Id.* at 236.

[29] *Id.* at 239–40 (Scalia, J., dissenting).

open-ended exception" meant to incorporate all of the Court's prior case law.

Scalia had particularly harsh words for the majority's embrace of *Skidmore* deference:

> [I]n an era when federal statutory law administered by federal agencies is pervasive, and when the ambiguities (intended or unintended) that those statutes contain are innumerable, totality-of-the-circumstances *Skidmore* deference is a recipe for uncertainty, unpredictability, and endless litigation. To condemn a vast body of agency action to that regime (all except rulemaking, formal (and informal?) adjudication, and whatever else might now and then be included within today's intentionally vague formulation of affirmative congressional intent to "delegate") is irresponsible.[30]

Chevron, Scalia argued, although "rooted in a legal presumption of congressional intent," actually concerns the "division of powers between the Second and Third Branches"—that is the executive and the judicial.[31] Rather than fixing the balance of power between Congress and the agencies it has authorized, *Mead* adopted a "background rule . . . that ambiguity in legislative instructions to agencies is to be resolved not by the agencies but by the judges."[32] But, as *Chevron* explained, administration of "a congressionally created . . . program necessarily requires the formulation of policy and the making of rules to fill any gap left, implicitly or explicitly, by Congress."[33] Now judges, rather than agency administrators, would exercise that policy discretion in an increasing number of cases. This would cause "ossification of large portions of our statutory law" in cases where agency interpretations that would have been permissible under *Chevron* are denied that deference and the court fixes statutory meaning de novo.

Scalia's warnings proved prescient. *Mead* did cause confusion in the lower courts, which adopted a variety of inconsistent approaches to when an agency's interpretative positions are entitled

[30] *Id.* at 250.
[31] *Id.* at 241.
[32] *Id.* at 243.
[33] *Id.* at 256 (quoting Chevron, 467 U.S. at 843).

to deference.[34] In some cases, reasonable agency resolutions of statutory ambiguities prevail; in others, courts "read *Mead* as a sort of abstract instruction . . . to decide, on an all-things-considered basis, and without affording any deference to agency views at all, whether Congress expressly delegated to the agency the power to take the very action it did take."[35] That dissonance—between substantial deference in one class of cases and open-ended inquiries up to and including outright judicial policymaking in another, with no clear line between the two—has largely prevailed in the post-*Mead* world, despite the Court's several attempts to clarify and backfill the "*Mead* doctrine."[36] As Adrian Vermeule observed early on, "*Mead*'s compromise position, suspended uneasily between *Chevron*'s relatively clear global presumption and a genuine totality-of-the-circumstances test, is intrinsically unstable."[37]

[34] See Lisa Schultz Bressman, How *Mead* Has Muddled Judicial Review of Agency Action, 58 Vand. L. Rev. 1443, 1445 (2005) ("Years have passed since *Mead* was decided, and we still lack a clear answer to the question when an agency is entitled to *Chevron* deference for procedures other than notice-and-comment rulemaking or formal adjudication.").

[35] Adrian Vermeule, Introduction: *Mead* in the Trenches, 71 Geo. Wash. L. Rev. 347, 352 (2003).

[36] See, e.g., Nat'l Cable & Telecomm. Ass'n v. Brand X Internet Servs., 545 U.S. 967, 982 (2005) (holding that a prior judicial interpretation of a statute is necessarily binding on an agency "only if the prior court decision holds that its construction follows from the unambiguous terms of the statute and thus leaves no room for agency discretion"); Long Island Care at Home, Ltd. v. Coke, 551 U.S. 158, 173–74 (2007) (explaining that Congress would have expected deference "[w]here an agency rule sets forth important individual rights and duties, where the agency focuses fully and directly upon the issue, where the agency uses full notice-and-comment procedures to promulgate a rule, where the resulting rule falls within the statutory grant of authority, and where the rule itself is reasonable"); Barnhart v. Walton, 535 U.S. 212, 221–22 (2002) (deferring to an agency interpretation, despite that it had not been promulgated through rulemaking, due to "interstitial nature of the legal question, the related expertise of the Agency, the importance of the question to administration of the statute, the complexity of that administration, and the careful consideration the Agency has given the question over a long period of time"). On the other hand, some decisions have only added to the confusion. See, e.g., Gonzales v. Oregon, 546 U.S. 243, 258–68 (2006) (denying *Chevron* deference for reasons that are basically impossible to summarize in a squib).

[37] Vermeule, *supra* note 35, at 353.

C. Chevron *and Agency Jurisdiction*

As Justice Scalia's *Mead* dissent intimates, one consequence of *Chevron*'s accidental landmark status is that its theoretical basis is unclear. The decision itself pays lip service to notions of democratic accountability and agency competence.[38] Later decisions like *Mead* have stated that *Chevron* rests (principally? entirely?) on legislative intent.[39] (Its plain incompatibility with the Administrative Procedures Act notwithstanding.[40]) Others, like Scalia, imply that *Chevron* stems from Article III and is a limitation of the judicial power and on the role of judges in deciding matters that are not properly justiciable or are committed to the political branches. The lack of any firm theoretical grounding for the *Chevron* framework makes answering questions about its proper application difficult.

In particular, there has been uncertainty from nearly the beginning about whether *Chevron* applies to agencies' constructions regarding their own jurisdiction. When the issue was first broached in *Mississippi Power & Light Co. v. Mississippi* in 1988, the Court ducked it, holding that a prior case resolved that the jurisdiction of the Federal Energy Regulatory Commission extended to power allocations among utilities that affect wholesale rates, such that states are preempted from barring regulated utilities from passing through to retail consumers wholesale rates resulting from FERC-mandated power allocations.[41] The majority opinion does not mention *Chevron* or the concept of deference.

But in concurrence, Justice Scalia addressed the issue head-on. The question, as he framed it, was "whether FERC has jurisdiction to determine the prudence of a particular utility's participation in [a pooling arrangement with other utilities]."[42] This, in turn, required application of the *Chevron* framework to FERC's interpretation of its "statutory authority or jurisdiction" under the Federal Power Act—this was, Scalia

---

[38] Chevron, 467 U.S. at 866 ("[F]ederal judges—who have no constituency—have a duty to respect legitimate policy choices made by those who do.").

[39] Mead, 533 U.S. at 230 n.11 & accompanying text.

[40] See 5 U.S.C. § 706 ("[T]he reviewing court shall decide all relevant questions of law . . . ."); Mark Seidenfeld, *Chevron*'s Foundation, 86 Notre Dame L. Rev. 273, 278–79 (2011).

[41] 487 U.S. 354, 370–74 (1988). Notably, Justice Stevens, who also authored *Chevron*, wrote for the majority.

[42] *Id.* at 378 (Scalia, J., concurring).

wrote, "settled law."[43] In this, Justice Scalia laid down a marker, characterizing *Mississippi Power* and a swath of the Court's prior cases for a proposition that had never quite been addressed.[44] *Commodity Futures Trading Commission v. Schor*, for example, had held that the CFTC was due deference for its choice to exercise jurisdiction over counterclaims arising out of the same transaction as disputes over which the agency had been expressly conferred jurisdiction.[45] And *City of New York v. FCC* upheld the Federal Communications Commission's view that it could preempt state and local authorities from imposing stricter technical standards governing the quality of cable television signals than those imposed by the FCC.[46] But like the majority opinion in *Mississippi Power*, neither case devoted a word to addressing the appropriate degree of deference, if any, due an agency's interpretation of its statutory jurisdiction. The most that could be said is that the Court simply assumed that deference would apply to such determinations.

Scalia identified two justifications for granting deference. The first was pragmatic:

> [T]here is no discernible line between an agency's exceeding its authority and an agency's exceeding authorized application of its authority. To exceed authorized application is to exceed authority. Virtually any administrative action can be characterized as either the one or the other, depending upon how generally one wishes to describe the "authority."[47]

The second was doctrinal: "Congress would naturally expect that the agency would be responsible, within broad limits, for resolving ambiguities in its statutory authority or jurisdiction."[48] In other words, deference to jurisdictional determinations rests on the same basis as any other application of the *Chevron* framework: the legal presumption that Congress would expect agencies, not the courts, to exercise policymaking discretion in choosing among permissible interpretations of statutory authority.

---

[43] *Id.* at 381.

[44] *Id.* at 381–83.

[45] 478 U.S. 833, 845–46 (1986).

[46] 486 U.S. 57, 64 (1988).

[47] 487 U.S. at 381 (Scalia, J., concurring).

[48] *Id.* at 381–82.

Justice William Brennan took issue with those points in a forceful dissent. To begin with, jurisdictional issues "do not reflect conflicts between policies that have been committed to the agency's care, but rather reflect policies in favor of limiting the agency's jurisdiction that, by definition, have not been entrusted to the agency."[49] For that reason, "agencies can claim no special expertise in interpreting a statute confining its jurisdiction."[50] Accordingly, there was no basis to presume that Congress intended agencies to fill gaps in a jurisdictional statute, "since by its nature such a statute manifests an unwillingness to give the agency the freedom to define the scope of its own power."[51]

There the issue stood for the next 15 years, as the Supreme Court continued its habit of unmentioned "drive-by" deference to agency jurisdiction determinations.[52] The lower courts, meanwhile, were divided, sometimes even among panels within the same circuit.[53]

II. A Tempest over Transmission Towers

A. Municipalities Challenge FCC's Authority to Regulate the Timing for Antenna Zoning Decision

City of Arlington arose under the Communications Act of 1934, which in a 1996 amendment sought to address the problem of undue interference by state and local government in the placement and construction of wireless communications facilities like the antennae used for cellular phone and wireless data services.[54]

---

[49] *Id.* at 387 (Brennan, J., dissenting).

[50] *Id.*

[51] *Id.* In support of this last point, Brennan cites *Schor*'s discussion of the CFTC's governing statute, ignoring that *Schor* was undertaking a *Chevron* step one inquiry. 478 U.S. at 844–45.

[52] E.g., United States v. Eurodif S.A., 555 U.S. 305, 316 (2009); FDA v. Brown & Williamson Tobacco Corp., 529 U.S. 120, 132 (2000); MCI Telecomm. Corp. v. American Telephone & Telegraph Co., 512 U.S. 218, 224, 229, 231 (1994); Reiter v. Cooper, 507 U.S. 258, 269 (1993).

[53] See Nathan A. Sales & Jonathan H. Adler, The Rest Is Silence: *Chevron* Deference, Agency Jurisdiction, and Statutory Silences, 2009 U. Ill. L. Rev. 1497, 1518 (2009) (citing cases among the circuits and noting that the "D.C. and Eighth Circuit appear to have resolved the issue both ways.").

[54] Telecomm. Act of 1996, Pub. L. No. 104-104, 110 Stat. 56, codified at 47 U.S.C. § 332.

The provision at issue, Section 332(c)(7), contains three relevant subparagraphs. The first, a savings clause, generally preserves local zoning authority, except for the few exceptions that follow.[55] The second, which contains one of the exceptions, requires that a state or locality must act on any request for authorization to site wireless facilities "within a reasonable period of time after the request is duly filed."[56] And the third provides that persons adversely affected by such an unreasonable delay may file suit in federal court within 30 days. Through this scheme, Congress sought to reconcile two competing interests: the "desire to preserve the traditional role of state and local governments in regulating land use and zoning and Congress's interest in encouraging the rapid development of new telecommunications technologies by removing the ability of state and local governments to impede the construction and modification of wireless communications facilities through delay or irrational decisionmaking."[57]

As is often the case, Congress's handiwork was not entirely successful at achieving its intended ends. In 2008, CTIA—The Wireless Association[58] filed a petition with the FCC complaining that the local zoning process for siting wireless facilities remained "extremely time-consuming," frustrating operators' ability to deploy wireless systems.[59] It proposed that the agency clarify the meaning of Section 332(c)(7)(b)(ii)'s requirement that zoning authorities act on siting requests "within a reasonable amount of time" by setting a presumptively reasonable time limit of 45 days for the addition of an antenna to an existing facility (known as "collocation") and 75 days for a new facility.[60]

In November 2009, the commission issued a declaratory ruling granting, in part, the CTIA petition.[61] Its legal discussion proceeded in two steps. First, it addressed the FCC's authority to interpret Section 332(c)(7), which had been challenged in comments submitted

---

[55] 42 U.S.C. § 332(c)(7)(A).

[56] 42 U.S.C. § 332(c)(7)(B)(ii).

[57] City of Arlington, Texas v. FCC, 668 F.3d 229, 234 (5th Cir. 2012).

[58] See City of Arlington, 133 S. Ct. 1863 at 1867 n.1 ("This is not a typographical error.").

[59] 24 FCC Rcd. 13994, 13996 (2009).

[60] *Id.* at 13997.

[61] *Id.* at 13996.

by state and local governments as inconsistent with congressional intent to deny the FCC such authority.[62] Predictably, the agency disagreed. Section 1 of the Communications Act, it explained, directs the commission to "execute and enforce the provisions of this Act" in order to regulate and promote communication "by wire and radio" on a nationwide basis, and its authority was supported by various provisions like Section 203(b) conferring rulemaking and adjudicatory power as may be necessary to carry out the act.[63] In its second step, the agency declared its interpretation of Section 332(c)(7)(b)(ii): a reasonable time presumptively would be 90 days for applications regarding collocated antennae and 150 days for all other applications, with the exceptions that (1) the wireless provider and locality could agree to extend the time frame and (2) the locality could, in court, seek to rebut the presumption of unreasonableness.[64]

The City of Arlington, Texas, filed a petition for review of the FCC's declaratory ruling in the U.S. Court of Appeals for the Fifth Circuit challenging, among other things, the FCC's statutory authority to adopt the presumptive time limits.[65] The court held, applying circuit precedent, that the *Chevron* framework applied to the agency's determination of its own statutory jurisdiction and that, under *Chevron*, the statute was ambiguous with respect to the FCC's authority to establish presumptively reasonable time limits and the agency's claim to possess such authority was a permissible interpretation of the statute.[66] It proceeded, also applying the *Chevron* framework, to uphold the time limits themselves as reasonable resolutions of a statutory ambiguity.[67]

The City of Arlington asked the Supreme Court to consider both the appropriate degree of deference and the FCC's authority in this instance, but the Court accepted only the first question: "Whether . . . a court should apply *Chevron* to review an agency's determination of its own jurisdiction."[68]

---

[62] *Id.* at 14000.

[63] *Id.* at 14001.

[64] *Id.* at 14003–05.

[65] City of Arlington, 668 F.3d at 236.

[66] *Id.* at 254.

[67] *Id.* at 255–60.

[68] City of Arlington v. FCC, 133 S. Ct. 524 (2012).

B. The Confusion Begins

Presumably for strategic reasons, the City of Arlington chose, in its merit briefing, to address a potentially narrower issue: the deference due to the FCC's determination that it possessed "interpretive authority" over Section 332(c)(7).[69] Because agencies possess only that power which Congress has conferred upon them, it argued, "the scope of an agency's legal authority is for a court to determine."[70] Leaning heavily on *Mead*, Arlington argued that courts must conduct a threshold "*Chevron* Step 0" inquiry, without affording any deference to the agency, to "determin[e] whether Congress intended to assign the agency authoritative interpretative power over the statute."[71] This inquiry, proceeding on a provision-by-provision basis, would assess "factors such as whether Congress empowered the agency to make rules with the force of law, whether the agency's expressed views are authoritative, and whether the agency's position is well-reasoned, to name a few."[72] In support of this proposition, Arlington cited a number of cases carrying out *Mead*'s threshold inquiry into congressional intent.[73] *Forget about the broad question that we asked you to consider*, the brief seems to say, *this is just a straightforward application of* Mead. Indeed, apparently playing for Justice Scalia's vote, Arlington actually *distinguishes* its "interpretative authority" argument from cases concerning agency "jurisdiction."[74]

Having punted on the question that it asked the Court to consider, Arlington proceeded to brief the question that the Court had specifically declined to hear: the FCC's authority to interpret Section 322(c)(7), in particular. The illustration is instructive. That provision begins with "jurisdiction-limiting language" (that is, the savings clause), concerns

[69] Brief for Petitioner at 12, City of Arlington, Texas v. FCC, 133 S. Ct. 1863 (2013) (No. 11-1545) [hereinafter "Arlington Br."]. Confusingly, the brief alternatively refers to this concept as "interpretive jurisdiction." For clarity's sake, this article sticks with "interpretive authority" to refer to Arlington's argument, and "agency jurisdiction" to refer to the broader question.

[70] *Id.* at 15.

[71] *Id.* at 16–17.

[72] *Id.* at 19.

[73] *Id.* at 19–20 (citing, *inter alia*, Long Island Care at Home, Ltd., 551 U.S. at 165; Gonzales, 546 U.S. at 258–68; National Cable, 545 U.S. at 980–81; Barnhart, 535 U.S. at 221–22; Mead, 533 U.S. at 233–34; Christensen, 529 U.S. at 587).

[74] *Id.* at 24–26.

a matter of traditional state police power, lacks any clear statement that Congress intended the FCC to intrude on that state authority, and places judicial review of unreasonable delays in approving antenna siting not in the FCC, but in the courts.[75] So while Congress did generally confer rulemaking authority on the agency, its interpretative authority does not extend to this particular provision. That was the issue, Arlington argued, that the Fifth Circuit should have addressed de novo at the outset.[76] Truth be told, that was the issue that the FCC had addressed at the outset of its declaratory ruling.[77]

The International Municipal Lawyers Association, which had intervened in support of Arlington before the Fifth Circuit, was not quite so retiring, filing a forceful brief on the "agency jurisdiction" issue that the Court had actually agreed to hear. That question, the IMLA argued, implicates both the horizontal and vertical separation of powers. As to the horizontal, "*Chevron* deference is premised on the necessary precondition that Congress has granted the agency authority to administer the statute being construed."[78] Therefore, "[i]t would make nonsense of *Chevron*'s logic to grant an agency deference on the very question of whether it is entitled to deference."[79] On that basis, the IMLA proposed a hard line governing when to accord agencies deference:

> Jurisdictional questions concern the *who, what, where,* and *when* of regulatory power: which subject matters may an agency regulate and under what conditions. Substantive interpretations entitled to *Chevron* deference concern the *how* of regulatory power: in what fashion may an agency implement an administrative scheme.[80]

Implicitly acknowledging the scant case law in support of this approach, the IMLA argued that this distinction was compelled by "separation of powers principles."[81] Agencies would always act to

[75] *Id.* at 35–40.

[76] *Id.* at 34.

[77] 24 FCC Rcd. at 14000 (discussing the agency's "interpretive authority").

[78] Brief for Respondent IMLA at 17, City of Arlington, Texas v. FCC, 133 S. Ct. 1863 (2013) (No. 11-1545) [hereinafter "IMLA Br."].

[79] *Id.* at 17.

[80] *Id.* at 18–19 (emphasis in original).

[81] *Id.* at 27.

aggrandize their power, "broadly constru[ing] ambiguous statutes in favor of agency jurisdiction."[82] As a check, and to place such authority in a more accountable branch, Congress, the rule should be to deny "agencies deference in interpreting the metes and bounds of their own authority."[83]

And as to the vertical separation of powers, the IMLA argues that there is "no room for *Chevron* deference where, as here, an agency claims jurisdiction over local governmental procedures."[84] Instead, such jurisdiction must be presumed lacking in the face of statutory silence. Any other rule "would unnecessarily place *Chevron* and the clear statement rule on a collision course."[85]

The government, in response, urged the Court to reject arguments to create an exception for "jurisdictional" statutory provisions that "would be inadministrable in practice."[86] It addressed the agency-jurisdiction and interpretative-authority arguments, in turn. As to the former, after reciting the Court's cases applying the *Chevron* framework to jurisdictional questions,[87] the government embraced the rationale of Justice Scalia's *Mississippi Power* concurrence, arguing that the same presumption of legislative intent underlying *Chevron* applies equally to jurisdictional interpretations and that maintaining a "statutory authority" exception would be "unworkable."[88] The IMLA's proposed distinction, in addition to being "flatly inconsistent with this Court's precedents," is unnecessary to protect against

---

[82] *Id.* at 28.

[83] *Id.* at 30.

[84] *Id.* at 36.

[85] *Id.* at 38. See Gregory v. Ashcroft, 501 U.S. 452, 461 (1991) ("In traditionally sensitive areas, such as legislation affecting the federal balance, the requirement of clear statement assures that the legislature has in fact faced, and intended to bring into issue, the critical matters involved in the judicial decision." (quotation marks omitted)); Jones v. United States, 529 U.S. 848, 858 (2000) ("[U]nless Congress conveys its purpose clearly, it will not be deemed to have significantly changed the federal-state balance . . . ." (quotation marks omitted)).

[86] Brief for the Federal Respondents at 11, City of Arlington, Texas v. FCC, 133 S. Ct. 1863 (2013) (No. 11-1545).

[87] *Id.* at 18–19.

[88] *Id.* at 21–22.

agency usurpations, which the Court had policed in prior cases through ordinary statutory interpretation under *Chevron* step one.[89]

Arlington's narrower interpretative-authority argument, the government argued, was simply inconsistent with the reality of statutory delegations, which are typically phrased in broad terms reaching the entirety of an agency's governing statute.[90] Where Congress wishes to rebut the presumption that it meant what it said, it can and has done so "by enacting a specific exception to a general grant of regulatory authority."[91] A "provision-by-provision search for delegation," as urged by Arlington, was therefore "obviated" by broad grants of rulemaking authority, as even *Mead* had recognized.[92] Accordingly, because Section 332(c)(7) had not expressly negated the FCC's general interpretative authority, the agency's resolution of any ambiguity in that section is entitled to deference.[93] Finally, that this provision concerns the relationship between state and federal power was of no moment, given that the FCC had done nothing more than "interpret[] a statutory phrase that explicitly constrains the discretion of state and local zoning authorities."[94] In other words, the balance of power had already been set by the statute, and the FCC's interpretation therefore created no additional federal requirement.

Oral argument began with the admission of Arlington's counsel, Tom Goldstein, that the case was "complicated" because "the word 'jurisdiction' means a lot of different things to a lot of different people"[95]—and the argument did indeed reflect the confusion between the different questions briefed by Arlington and the IMLA. Goldstein, Justice Elena Kagan noted, was "running as fast as [he could] away from the arguments that IMLA has presented," attempting to present his position as a modest application of *Mead*.[96] But as

[89] *Id.* at 27–28 (discussing Food and Drug Admin. v. Brown & Williamson Tobacco Corp., 529 U.S. 120 (2000), Dole v. United Steelworkers, 494 U.S. 26 (1990), and Massachusetts v. EPA, 549 U.S. 497 (2007)).

[90] *Id.* at 30–31.

[91] *Id.* at 31–32.

[92] *Id.* at 32–33.

[93] *Id.* at 36.

[94] *Id.* at 37.

[95] Oral Arg. Tr. at 4, City of Arlington, Texas v. FCC, 133 S. Ct. 1863 (2013) (No. 11-1545).

[96] *Id.* at 60.

to his point that the Court must decide first whether "the FCC [has] the power to implement this statute," the Court was largely unreceptive.[97] Justice Kagan's dismissive response was representative: "[A]t one level, you are right. It's just a level that doesn't help you very much," because the Court had always looked first to an agency's organic statute to determine whether it provided the agency with general administrative authority before proceeding to apply the *Chevron* framework.[98]

The solicitor general, in turn, warned the Court of a "Pandora's Box situation" if it accepted either Arlington's or the IMLA's argument, because of the hopelessness of drawing "a clear, neat dividing line" between issues of jurisdiction or interpretative authority and issues of substance.[99] Of course, he conceded, "there is *de novo* review of the question of whether Congress has delegated authority to the agency, generally, to act with the force of law and whether the interpretation claiming deference is an exercise of that delegated authority."[100] But after that, "*Chevron* kicks in."[101]

"*Chevron* is at an end. It's unraveled," quipped Justice Anthony Kennedy as Goldstein launched into his rebuttal.[102]

III. *Chevron* Unchained . . . and That Jurisdiction Thing, Too

A. *The End of the Line for* Mead *and* Skidmore?

Twenty-nine years after the Court announced its accidental landmark in *Chevron*, that case's eponymous doctrine finally has a principled basis agreed to by a majority of the Court: "Statutory ambiguities will be resolved, within the bounds of reasonable interpretation, not by the courts but by the administering agency."[103] This is "a stable background rule against which Congress can legislate"; it is not a presumption or fiction about what Congress actually intended when

---

[97] *Id.* at 14.
[98] *Id.* at 14–15.
[99] *Id.* at 33.
[100] *Id.* at 35.
[101] *Id.*
[102] *Id.* at 59.
[103] City of Arlington, 133 S. Ct. at 1868.

it did.[104] And this rule applies whenever "a court reviews an agency's construction of the statute which it administers."[105]

If those concepts sound familiar, that is because they echo Justice Scalia's *Mead* dissent. As the senior justice in the majority, Scalia assigned to himself the opinion of the Court, which was joined by Justices Clarence Thomas, Ruth Bader Ginsburg, Sonia Sotomayor, and Kagan.[106]

Yes, that's right, the Court has apparently reversed *Mead*. *Mead*, Justice Scalia's opinion breezily explains, requires only that, "for *Chevron* deference to apply, the agency must have received congressional authority to determine the particular matter at issue in the particular manner adopted."[107] Of course, if that were all that had been at issue in *Mead*, the case would have come out the other way, Congress clearly having authorized the Customs Service to "'fix the final classification and rate of duty applicable to . . . merchandise.'"[108] To be sure, the majority opinion distinguishes *Mead* on the basis that it denied "deference to action, by an agency with rulemaking authority, that was not rulemaking."[109] But that is not a rule, it is a distinction.[110]

And what happens when an agency interpretation is not entitled to *Chevron* deference? According to the majority, the statute then apparently falls within the "scope for *de novo* judicial review."[111] *Skidmore* deference? The majority has never heard of it. Nor is the possibility broached in Chief Justice Roberts's opinion in dissent, joined by Justices Kennedy and Samuel Alito. The dissent states that, in

[104] *Id.*

[105] *Id.*

[106] *Id.* at 1865.

[107] *Id.* at 1874.

[108] Mead, 533 U.S. at 222 (quoting 19 U.S.C. § 1500(b)).

[109] 133 S. Ct. at 1874.

[110] Even for those who may be skeptical of this conclusion, there can be no question that *City of Arlington* at the least undermines any suggestion that a "rulemaking proceeding is neither a necessary nor a sufficient condition for according *Chevron* deference," Brand X, 545 U.S. at 1004 (Breyer, J., concurring). Cf. City of Arlington, 133 S. Ct. at 1874 ("What the dissent needs, and fails to produce, is a single case in which a general conferral of rulemaking or adjudicative authority has been held insufficient to support *Chevron* deference for an exercise of that authority within the agency's substantive field. There is no such case.").

[111] 133 S. Ct. at 1873–74.

Mead, "[t]he Court did not defer to the agency's views" at all.[112] That might come as a surprise to anyone who has read *Mead*, which actually "h[e]ld that under *Skidmore*, the [agency] ruling is eligible to claim respect according to its persuasiveness."[113] If there were any doubt, the dissent states plainly that an "agency's interpretive authority, entitling the agency to judicial deference, acquires its legitimacy from a delegation of lawmaking power from Congress to the Executive"—in other words, the *Chevron/Mead* formula.[114] Adding it up, that is eight of nine justices apparently denying that *Skidmore* deference maintains any vitality.

The lonely voice in this debate is Justice Stephen Breyer, writing in concurrence, who remains faithful to *Mead* in every respect. To Justice Breyer, statutory ambiguity standing alone is "not enough" to warrant deference.[115] Instead, to determine whether to apply the *Chevron* framework, a court should consider, among any number of other things, "'the interstitial nature of the legal question, the related expertise of the Agency, the importance of the question to administration of the statute, the complexity of that administration, and the careful consideration the Agency has given the question over a long period of time.'"[116] And when all else fails, "sometimes an agency interpretation, in light of the agency's special expertise, will still have the 'power to persuade, if lacking power to control'"[117]—in other words, *Skidmore* deference. Considering the totality of the circumstances—and ducking the interpretative/jurisdictional deference question presented—Breyer would defer in this case because there is no "good reason" not to.[118] With apparent exasperation, Breyer states that he "consequently join[s] the majority's judgment and such portions of its opinion as are consistent with what I have written here."[119]

---

[112] *Id.* at 1882 (Roberts, C.J., dissenting).

[113] Mead, 533 U.S. at 221.

[114] City of Arlington, 133 S. Ct. at 1886 (Roberts, C.J., dissenting).

[115] *Id.* at 1875 (Breyer, J., concurring).

[116] *Id.* (Breyer, J., concurring) (quoting Barnhart, 535 U.S. at 222).

[117] *Id.* at 1876 (Breyer, J., concurring) (quoting Skidmore, 323 U.S. at 140).

[118] *Id.* at 1877 (Breyer, J., concurring).

[119] *Id.* (Breyer, J., concurring).

B. The Jurisdiction Thing

Justice Scalia's majority opinion, no surprise, rejects the agency jurisdiction argument raised by the IMLA, much along the lines of Scalia's *Mississippi Power* concurrence.

To begin with, "the distinction between 'jurisdictional' and 'non-jurisdictional' interpretations is a mirage" as it concerns agency action. In every case, the question is simple: "whether the agency has stayed within the bounds of its statutory authority."[120] With a court, "a jurisdictionally proper but substantively incorrect . . . decision is not ultra vires," because the court had the power to issue the decision. But with agencies, "[b]oth their power to act and how they are to act is authoritatively prescribed by Congress, so that when they act improperly, no less than why they act beyond their jurisdiction, what they do is ultra vires."[121]

And that, the majority contends, causes the practical difficulty of distinguishing between jurisdictional and non-jurisdictional provisions. "The ['jurisdictional'] label is an empty distraction because every new application of a broad statutory term can be reframed as a questionable extension of the agency's jurisdiction."[122] For example: "Who is an 'outside salesman'? What is a 'pole attachment'? Where do the 'waters of the United States' end?"[123] "Make no mistake," Scalia warns, "the ultimate target here is *Chevron* itself," because "[s]avvy challengers of agency action would play the 'jurisdictional' card in every case."[124]

Of the risk that affording agencies deference as to their statutory jurisdiction will permit them to aggrandize their powers, the majority counsels greater attention to the art of statutory interpretation:

> The fox-in-the-hen-house syndrome is to be avoided not by establishing an arbitrary and undefinable category of agency decisionmaking that is accorded no deference, but by taking seriously, and applying rigorously, in all cases, statutory limits on agencies' authority. Where Congress has established a clear line, the agency cannot go beyond it; and where

[120] *Id.* at 1868 (emphasis omitted).
[121] *Id.* at 1869.
[122] *Id.* at 1870.
[123] *Id.*
[124] *Id.* at 1873.

> Congress has established an ambiguous line, the agency can go no further than the ambiguity will fairly allow.[125]

Finally, the majority dismisses the vertical separation-of-powers concerns here as "faux-federalism," for much the reason provided by the government. Given that the agency is doing nothing more than clarifying an ambiguity in a statute already subject to federal court review, "[t]hese lines will be drawn either by unelected federal bureaucrats, or by unelected (and even less politically accountable) federal judges. It is hard to spark a passionate 'States' rights' debate over that detail."[126]

Chief Justice Roberts, of course, dissents on these points, albeit in characteristically modest fashion. (Which is not to say that the entirety of his dissent is modest—more on that anon.) Rather than address the agency jurisdiction question taken on by the majority, Roberts would resolve the case on the narrower ground, interpretative authority, proposed by Arlington. He begins with a simple enough proposition: "[a] court should not defer to an agency until the court decides, on its own, that the agency is entitled to deference."[127] The obligatory citation to *Marbury* follows.[128] And, from there, it is a short leap to *Mead*:

> In *Mead*, we again made clear that the "category of interpretative choices" to which *Chevron* deference applies is defined by congressional intent. *Chevron* deference, we said, rests on a recognition that Congress has delegated to an agency the interpretive authority to implement "a particular provision" or answer "a particular question." An agency's interpretation of "a particular statutory provision" thus qualifies for *Chevron* deference only "when it appears that Congress delegated authority to the agency generally to make rules carrying the force of law, and that the agency interpretation claiming deference was promulgated in the exercise of that authority."[129]

---

[125] *Id.* at 1874.

[126] *Id.* at 1873 (quotation marks omitted).

[127] *Id.* at 1877 (Roberts, C.J., dissenting).

[128] *Id.* at 1880 (Roberts, C.J., dissenting) (quoting Marbury v. Madison, 5 U.S. (1 Cranch) 137, 177 (1803) ("It is emphatically the province of the judicial department to say what the law is.")).

[129] *Id.* at 1882 (Roberts, C.J., dissenting) (citations omitted) (quoting Mead, 533 U.S. at 229, 226–27).

This is so, Chief Justice Roberts continues, because *"Chevron* deference is based on, and finds legitimacy as, a congressional delegation of interpretive authority"—the presumption rejected by the majority.[130] On that basis, it is the court's duty to ascertain, de novo, whether a congressional delegation of interpretative authority extends to the specific statutory ambiguity at issue. That inquiry, Roberts argues, would be no more difficult in any case than in the present one, where even the agency identified the issue properly.

Finally, the dissent responds to the majority's charge that *Chevron* is in its crosshairs:

> The Court touches on a legitimate concern: *Chevron* importantly guards against the Judiciary arrogating to itself policymaking properly left, under the separation of powers, to the Executive. But there is another concern at play, no less firmly rooted in our constitutional structure. That is the obligation of the Judiciary not only to confine itself to its proper role, but to ensure that the other branches do so as well.[131]

So who has the better of this argument, Scalia or Roberts? That question should be answered on two dimensions: adherence to the Court's precedents and doctrinal soundness.

On the former, Scalia stands on firm ground. From *Chevron* on, the Court has always looked to an agency's general administrative authority, rather than conducting any sort of provision-by-provision inquiry into congressional intent. Although the language in *Adams Fruit Co., Inc. v. Barrett*[132] and *Gonzales v. Oregon*[133] is arguably to the contrary, it is less apparent that those cases do any more than recognize express limitations on interpretative authority.[134] In other words, the "Step 0" analysis is still conducted at a relatively high level, fo-

---

[130] Compare *id.* at 1883 (Roberts, C.J., dissenting) with *id.* at 1868 (majority opinion).

[131] *Id.* at 1883 (Roberts, C.J., dissenting).

[132] 494 U.S. 638, 649–50 (1990) ("[I]t is fundamental that an agency may not bootstrap itself into an area in which it has no jurisdiction." (quotation marks omitted)).

[133] 546 U.S. at 258–60 ("To begin with, the rule must be promulgated pursuant to authority Congress has delegated to the official.").

[134] Adams Fruit Co., 494 U.S. at 650 (noting that the delegation at issue "does not empower the Secretary to regulate the scope of the judicial power vested by the statute"); Gonzales, 546 U.S. at 259 ("The CSA gives the Attorney General limited powers, to be exercised in specific ways.").

cusing on the delegation provision itself. Neither case conducts the kind of detailed, contextual search for interpretative authority that Arlington urged the Court to do with respect to Section 332(c)(7).[135] Instead, such limitations on agency authority have generally been recognized under *Chevron* step one.[136] In this respect, the chief justice's approach is a definite break with precedent, giving litigants two bites at the apple in every regulatory challenge: (1) contest the agency's interpretative authority de novo based on statutory context and then (2) contest the agency's interpretation under *Chevron* step one, on more or less the same basis. Justice Scalia does have a point that the dissent's "ultimate target here is *Chevron* itself."[137]

As for doctrinal soundness, there is literally no comparison—the majority and dissent chose to address different arguments, and each has its merits and faults. Scalia's claim that any distinction between jurisdictional and non-jurisdictional provisions would be "illusory" is overblown. As Michael Greve memorably put it, jurisdiction "concerns a regulatory agency's question, 'Can we screw 'em?,'" while "[s]ubstance goes to, 'Screw 'em *how?*'"[138] This line—effectively the one urged by the IMLA—is certainly administrable. But is it the right one? If Congress authorizes an agency to exercise "jurisdiction over emissions of pollutants that threaten human health and welfare" is it really likely that it intended the courts to decide, on a de novo basis, what is and is not a "pollutant," without substantial deference to the agency's views? And what if the statute expressly confers rulemaking authority on the agency to interpret that term? Its rules would still be jurisdictional. One could argue, more modestly, that *Chevron*'s presumption regarding *implicit* grants of interpretative authority should not apply to jurisdictional provisions, but it is not apparent that that was even at issue in this case or in most cases—after all, Congress did authorize the FCC to "prescribe such rules and

---

[135] See *supra* § II.B.

[136] E.g., FDA v. Brown & Williamson Tobacco Corp., 529 U.S. 120, 126 (2000); MCI Telecommunications Corp. v. American Telephone & Telegraph Co., 512 U.S. 218, 229–31 (1994).

[137] City of Arlington, 133 S. Ct. at 1873.

[138] Michael S. Greve, From *Chevron* to *Arlington*: The Court and the Administrative State at Sea, Liberty Law Blog, Jan 19, 2013, http://www.libertylawsite.org/2013/01/19/from-chevron-to-arlington-the-court-and-the-administrative-state-at-sea.

regulations as may be necessary in the public interest to carry out [the Communication Act's] provisions."[139] It is the rare case where an agency proffers a putatively authoritative interpretation of a statute that is not its to administer.

Meanwhile, the dissent's "interpretative authority" line avoids the absurdity of a hard jurisdictional rule at the expense of administrability. It is all well and good to say that, before applying the *Chevron* framework, a court "must on its own decide whether Congress . . . has in fact delegated to the agency lawmaking power over the ambiguity at issue,"[140] but how does that work in practice if, as here, *an express grant of rulemaking authority* over the act in question apparently is not enough? At best, this under-determinative approach would foment the same kind of confusion as *Mead* in the lower courts, robbing *Chevron* of one of its chief virtues: predictability. At worst, it would give courts a plausible rationale to address any statutory ambiguity de novo, taking important decisions from agencies (in the hypothetical above, for example, whether water vapor is a regulable "pollutant") because they are important. Manipulation of the standard of review is not an uncommon charge,[141] and giving courts another lever to do so in administrative cases would only cause it to be leveled more often, likely with some basis.

But if the keystone of deference is what Congress actually intended, then Chief Justice Roberts has the upper hand, because that is precisely what he would plumb—even where doing so is at odds with the whole *Chevron* approach. If, however, deference is meant to confine the courts to questions that are entirely legal in nature, and thereby leave matters of implementation and policy to the political branches, then Justice Scalia's near-blanket presumption of deference to an administering agency fits the bill. Once again, the dispute is over the fundamental purpose of *Chevron* and, more broadly, judicial review of agency action.

---

[139] 47 U.S.C. § 201(b).

[140] City of Arlington, 133 S. Ct. at 1880 (Roberts, C.J., dissenting).

[141] See, e.g., Amanda Peters, The Meaning, Measure, and Misuse of Standards of Review, 13 Lewis & Clark L. Rev. 233, 236 (2009) (empirical study illustrating "how appellate judges sometimes disregard or manipulate the various standards of review").

C. Roberts's Radical Turn

Chief Justice Roberts's dissent does address that broader question, in a manner that is anything but modest. To say that his "disagreement with the Court is fundamental," as he does,[142] may be the understatement of this term and perhaps of his tenure to date.

The target of Roberts's concern is nothing less than the administrative state. It "'wields vast power and touches almost every aspect of daily life.'"[143] Indeed, the Framers of the Constitution "could hardly have envisioned today's 'vast and varied federal bureaucracy' and the authority administrative agencies now hold over our economic, social, and political activities."[144] It is unchecked by presidential control, because "'no President (or his executive office staff) could, and presumably none would wish to, supervise so broad a swath of regulatory activity.'"[145] And too often "Congressional delegations to agencies are often ambiguous—expressing 'a mood rather than a message.'"[146] Only rarely are the agencies checked in how they resolve those ambiguities thanks to *Chevron* deference, "a powerful weapon in an agency's regulatory arsenal."[147] "It would be a bit much to describe the result as 'the very definition of tyranny,'" Roberts allows, "but the danger posed by the growing power of the administrative state cannot be dismissed."[148]

---

[142] City of Arlington, 133 S. Ct. at 1877 (Roberts, C.J., dissenting).

[143] *Id.* at 1878 (Roberts, C.J., dissenting) (quoting Free Enter. Fund v. Public Co. Accounting Oversight Bd., 130 S. Ct. 3138, 3156 (2010)).

[144] *Id.* (Roberts, C.J., dissenting) (quoting Free Enterprise Fund, 130 S. Ct. at 3156).

[145] *Id.* (Roberts, C.J., dissenting) (quoting Elena Kagan, Presidential Administration, 144 Harv. L. Rev. 2245, 2250 (2001), and citing Stephen Breyer, Making Our Democracy Work 110 (2010)).

[146] *Id.* at 1879 (Roberts, C.J., dissenting) (quoting Henry J. Friendly, Administrative Agencies: The Need for a Better Definition of Standards, 75 Harv. L. Rev. 1263, 1311 (1962)).

[147] *Id.* (Roberts, C.J., dissenting).

[148] *Id.* (Roberts, C.J., dissenting) (quoting The Federalist No. 47, at 324 (James Madison) (J. Cooke ed., 1961)). On this point, the chief justice's dissent specifically notes that the "PPACA 'creates, requires others to create, or authorizes dozens of new entities to implement the legislation.'" *Id.* at 1878 (Roberts, C.J., dissenting) (quoting Congressional Research Service, New Entities Created Pursuant to the Patient Protection and Affordable Care Act 1 (2010)). But see NFIB v. Sebelius, 132 S. Ct. 2566, 2593–2600 (2012) (Roberts, C.J.) (finding it "fairly possible" that the PPACA's core individual mandate is an exercise of the taxing power and therefore not *ultra vires*).

Yes, he concedes, it is true that when agencies issue rules, they do not exercise the "legislative power," and when they conduct adjudications, they do not exercise the "executive power"—were the Court to hold those things to be anything other than exercises of the "executive power," they would plainly be unlawful.

> And yet . . . the citizen confronting thousands of pages of regulations—promulgated by an agency directed by Congress to regulate, say, "in the public interest"—can perhaps be excused for thinking that it is the agency really doing the legislating. And with hundreds of federal agencies poking into every nook and cranny of daily life, that citizen might also understandably question whether Presidential oversight—a critical part of the Constitutional plan—is always an effective safeguard against agency overreaching.[149]

This is radical stuff. The chief justice has previously expressed his concerns regarding executive control and accountability,[150] but this is something more. His dissent calls into question the constitutional basis of the administrative state, the idea that Congress need only provide an "intelligible" principle to guide the agencies in their exercise of their broad grants of authority.[151]

Less clear is what this has to with the question presented in *City of Arlington* and, in particular, the narrow way that the chief justice would resolve it. If the problem is standardless delegations of legislative authority, there is a doctrine for that to be plucked from near-desuetude.[152] What the chief justice seems to be saying, by combining a broad statement of principle with an exceedingly narrow rule of law, is that *enough is enough*.

---

[149] City of Arlington, 133 S. Ct. at 1879 (Roberts, C.J., dissenting) (ellipsis in original).

[150] E.g., Free Enter. Fund, 130 S. Ct. at 3156 (2010) ("The growth of the Executive Branch, which now wields vast power and touches almost every aspect of daily life, heightens the concern that it may slip from the Executive's control, and thus from that of the people.").

[151] See Whitman v. American Trucking Assocs., 531 U.S. 457, 472 (2001) ("*Congress* must lay down by legislative act an intelligible principle to which the person or body authorized to act is directed to conform." (emphasis in original) (quotation marks and citation omitted)).

[152] See Fed. Maritime Comm'n v. S.C. State Ports Authority, 535 U.S. 743, at 773–74 (2002) (Breyer, J., dissenting) (citing, *inter alia*, A.L.A. Schechter Poultry Corp. v. United States, 295 U.S. 495 (1935)).

IV. Final Thoughts

Really, it's anyone's guess as to whether Justice Scalia's renunciation of *Mead* will hold. In its favor are the departures of Justices Stevens and David Souter, who both favored the totality-of-the-circumstances approach that Justice Breyer is now left to defend alone. But it is too soon to say whether Justices Thomas and Ginsburg, who joined Scalia's majority opinion, necessarily embrace it in its entirety.[153] And to say that the Court's approach to agency deference has not been entirely consistent would be entirely accurate. Still, *Chevron* was an improvement in that respect, and *City of Arlington* may be one too. The fact that three of the Court's four "liberals"—Justices Ginsburg, Kagan, and Sotomayor—joined the majority suggests that, this time around, the Court's *Chevron* coalition may be more durable.

As for *City of Arlington's* headline holding on agency jurisdiction, it is certainly *relevant* to a number of current questions. May the FCC promote an "Open Internet" by prohibiting broadband providers from managing their networks by prioritizing certain traffic?[154] Must EPA regulate lead bullets as an environmental toxin?[155] May EPA regulate carbon-dioxide emissions from stationary sources under a statutory scheme that certainly does not contemplate anything of the sort?[156] May FERC regulate "demand response" (that is, utility customers drawing less electricity off the grid) as if it were a generating source?[157] And may the U.S. Army Corps of Engineers and EPA regulate a backyard puddle as "waters of the United States"?[158] While certainly helpful to defending agencies' positions on these questions, *City of Arlington* probably will not make much of a difference. In general, the real action in these cases was at *Chevron* step one, anyway. When agencies overstep their statutory bounds, it should

---

[153] Perhaps not. See, e.g., Christensen, 529 U.S. at 586–87 (Thomas, J.); Gonzales, 546 U.S. at 258–68 (Thomas, J.); Alaska Dept. of Environmental Conservation v. EPA, 540 U.S. 461, 487–88 (Ginsburg, J.).

[154] Verizon v. FCC, No. 11-1355 (D.C. Cir. filed Sept. 30, 2011).

[155] Trumpeter Swan Society v. EPA, No. 13-5228 (D.C. Cir. appeal filed July 24, 2013).

[156] Coal. for Responsible Reg., Inc. v. EPA, 684 F.3d 102 (D.C. Cir. 2012).

[157] Elec. Power Supply Assoc. v. FERC, No. 11-1486 (D.C. Cir. filed Dec. 23, 2011).

[158] See EPA & U.S. Army Corps of Engineers, Draft Guidance on Identifying Waters Protected by the Clean Water Act (Apr. 2011), available at http://water.epa.gov/lawsregs/guidance/wetlands/upload/wous_guidance_4-2011.pdf.

not matter much or at all whether their interpretations are addressed at the level of jurisdiction/interpretative authority or "substance."

And that, in turn, speaks to the final question: is *City of Arlington* good or bad for liberty? Prior to the decision, most conservatives and libertarians were rooting for a victory against the perceived excesses of the administrative state.[159] But that position raises the same question as the chief justice's impassioned dissent: is monkeying with the application of *Chevron* deference really the right way to achieve that result? As Justice Scalia's opinion suggests, if the courts are not appropriately cabining agency authority within statutory limits, that is a failure of statutory interpretation, not the standard of review for agencies' statutory constructions.[160] There is probably no reason to believe that a Court that, applying *Chevron*, upholds an agency's view that "up" means "down" or (less hypothetically) that "take" means "kill[] or injure[] wildlife by significantly impairing essential behavioral patterns, including breeding, feeding or sheltering,"[161] would necessarily reach a different result if the issue were framed as jurisdictional and the agency were afforded some lesser degree of deference. Scalia, after all, defers to agencies but is not "soft" on them; he undertakes the hard work of statutory construction to hold them to a "'permissible construction of the statute'" in each instance.[162]

At the same time, deference on jurisdictional matters may be welcome when an agency has declined to act or is reducing regulatory burdens, which was, after all, the reason that many conservatives initially took up the *Chevron* banner. Decisions like *Massachusetts v. EPA*—which rejected the EPA's view that it lacked jurisdiction to regulate greenhouse gas emissions—are a timely reminder that

---

[159] For example, the Cato Institute filed an amicus brief in support of the petitioner. Brief of Amici Curiae Cato Institute et al. in Support of Petitioners at 19, City of Arlington, Texas v. FCC, 133 S. Ct. 1863 (2013) (No. 11-1545). So did the author of this article. Brief of the Southern Company as Amicus Curiae in Support of Petitioners, City of Arlington, Texas v. FCC, 133 S. Ct. 1863 (2013) (No. 11-1545).

[160] City of Arlington, 133 S. Ct. at 1872 (citing Brown & Williamson Tobacco Corp., 529 U.S. 120).

[161] Babbitt v. Sweet Home Chapter Communities for a Great Oregon, 515 U.S. 687 (1995).

[162] Rapanos v. United States, 547 U.S. 715, 739 (2006) (quoting Chevron, 467 U.S. at 843, and rejecting the Army Corps of Engineers' interpretation of "the waters of the United States" to include "channels through which water flows intermittently or ephemerally, or channels that periodically provide drainage for rainfall.").

there are real risks to greater judicial engagement with the regulatory state. It would be short-sighted, as a matter of legal policy, to advocate a doctrine that depends entirely on having the right judges on the bench and enables endless mischief otherwise.[163] At least with *Chevron*, you know what you're getting, and only rarely is there any opportunity for judicial improvisation—certainly less than under de novo review. So long as administrative agencies' activity generally falls short of the full extent of their regulatory authority—as it surely must, by a large margin, given Congress's preference for capacious delegations and "moods"—*Chevron* at least stands as an obstacle to judicial decisions that push the agencies to undertake new missions that they would otherwise lack the political capital to carry out.

On that point, leave the last word to George Mason University law professor Michael Greve: Judge David Tatel on the D.C. Circuit is "smart and clever, and he decides more AdLaw cases in a month than the Supremes will see in a decade. You don't want to arm him."[164]

---

[163] See *supra* note 11 & surrounding text (discussing the judicial creation of the Prevention of Significant Deterioration program).

[164] Michael S. Greve, *City of Arlington*: Some Cheerful Thoughts, Liberty Law Blog, May 27, 2013, http://www.libertylawsite.org/2013/05/27/city-of-arlington-some-cheerful-thoughts.

Speech, Subsidies, and Traditions: *AID v. AOSI* and the First Amendment

Charles W. "Rocky" Rhodes*

Stating the issue in the term's only First Amendment case, *Agency for International Development v. Alliance for Open Society International, Inc.*,[1] suffices for most to agree with its holding: May the federal government, as a condition for a private entity to receive funds to implement a government program, require the recipient to pledge ideological support for government policies? As the Court held, of course not. While the government may impose limits on its grants to ensure that the funds are used appropriately, such limits can't regulate a private entity's speech outside the funded project. The government may set conditions on its programs and control the delivery of a government message, but must not repress recipients' expression (or their other constitutional rights and liberties) beyond the program's scope.[2]

Yet Justice Antonin Scalia's dissent—while continuing his too dismissive approach to the real threat to liberty from funding restrictions—raised a valid concern: the malleability of, and the constitutional source for, the Court's articulated distinction between conditions "inside" and "outside" the program.[3] The distinction between inside-program speech and outside-program speech is, as the majority admitted, "hardly clear."[4] This indefiniteness flags dangers of both underinclusiveness and overinclusiveness. The government must be checked from manipulating subsidies and the scope of its programs as a subterfuge to regulate its citizens' beliefs and commu-

* Professor of Law, South Texas College of Law. I'm indebted (as always) to my bride of 20 years, who once again provided her sage insight and advice.

[1] 133 S. Ct. 2321 (2013) [hereinafter AID v. AOSI].

[2] *Id.* at 2330–32.

[3] *Id.* at 2333–35 (Scalia, J., dissenting).

[4] *Id.* at 2328 (majority op.).

nications. On the other hand, the government in certain situations has a compelling need to consider outside viewpoints in selecting partners to accomplish its objectives.

These concerns can be alleviated, though, by recognizing that the inside/outside program classification is a useful analytical tool, but it's just that—a tool. The First Amendment provides the relevant limits on government-funding conditions. A core First Amendment principle is outlawing state regulation based on the ideas, messages, or viewpoints citizens express.[5] Although the government doesn't have to retain viewpoint neutrality with respect to its own speech and to further the objectives of its own undertakings, its imposition of viewpoint constraints on citizens effectively removes at least some of their speech from typical First Amendment protections. Just as the government can't exclude other types of expression from constitutional coverage without a historical warrant,[6] it shouldn't be allowed to leverage funding and other subsidies to withdraw core First Amendment safeguards from private expression without a supporting tradition. Enduring traditions authorize the government to fund speech within a public project to accomplish state purposes and to choose those funding recipients who will effectively accomplish the state's objectives. But no tradition allows the government either to control outside-program speech or to manipulate a program's scope to assert control over a traditional sphere of expression.

In this essay, I'll outline the Court's prior holdings on the constitutionality of conditions on government funding and other subsidies before turning to *AID v. AOSI*. While I applaud *AID*'s holding, its inside/outside program distinction, though appropriate in the presented context, can't govern every funding condition. The overarching appraisal should depend on continued judicial acquiescence in traditional government-funding practices. Inside-program limitations are one such tradition, but additional complementary traditions exist that must be taken into account—such as protecting traditional public forums and other expressive spheres—to check government overreach.

---

[5] See, e.g., Rosenberger v. Rectors & Visitors of Univ. of Va., 515 U.S. 819, 828 (1995); R.A.V. v. City of St. Paul, 505 U.S. 377, 386 (1992).

[6] United States v. Stevens, 130 S. Ct. 1577, 1585–86 (2010).

I. Existing First Amendment Limits on Conditioning Funds and Subsidies

The Spending Clause grants Congress discretion to tax and spend for the "general Welfare," allowing Congress to subsidize activities of—or fund programs implemented by—private entities.[7] As a condition for receiving such grants, Congress may establish limits to ensure their use in Congress's intended manner. The recipient doesn't have to accept the subsidy and the accompanying restrictions. But an assenting recipient typically must abide by the attached strings.

Such conditions may, in specific circumstances, constrain a recipient's expression. For example, if Congress offered a grant to private entities to advocate for democracy in the Middle East, the grant recipients could be barred from using the money to advocate for communism, monarchy, or any other form of government. Expressive conditions for obtaining funding or other subsidies don't violate the First Amendment when the limitations merely either refuse to fund specified expressive activities or are necessary to accomplish the objectives of a particular government program.

Regan v. Taxation with Representation of Washington provides an illustration.[8] A nonprofit public-interest corporation claimed that the government had unconstitutionally conditioned its receipt of tax-deductible contributions on its forbearance from undertaking substantial lobbying activities. The nonprofit urged that the government was therefore denying a benefit (tax-deductible contributions) because it was exercising an expressive right (to influence legislation). In rejecting this claim, the Supreme Court reasoned that the nonprofit hadn't been denied "any independent benefit on account of its intention to lobby."[9] The nonprofit could still lobby and receive tax-deductible contributions for its other activities through an affiliated organization; Congress merely ensured that the public fisc wasn't used to support its lobbying.[10] Moreover, the First Amendment doesn't compel government support of expressive activities, so Congress's decision

---

[7] See U.S. Const. art. I, § 8, cl. 1.
[8] 461 U.S. 540 (1983).
[9] *Id.* at 545.
[10] *Id.* at 544–45.

to subsidize most nonprofit activities while not subsidizing lobbying was well within its taxing and spending power.[11]

Rust v. Sullivan employed a similar rationale to uphold a funding restriction operating within a government program.[12] Health and Human Services departmental regulations barred physicians in a federally financed family-planning project that offered pre-conception counseling, education, and reproductive health services from counseling abortion as a method of family planning. The regulations didn't, however, prevent the project grantee from providing abortion counseling and even abortion services; the grant recipient just had to do so through programs separate from and independent of the funded project.[13] The Court held that the government was free to bar funding recipients from using project funds to counsel abortion:

> The Government can, without violating the Constitution, selectively fund a program to encourage certain activities it believes to be in the public interest, without at the same time funding an alternative program . . . . In doing so, the Government has not discriminated on the basis of viewpoint; it has merely chosen to fund one activity to the exclusion of the other.[14]

Such selective grants within public programs—along with mechanisms to ensure the funds are used in the intended manner—have a long history.[15] This tradition buoyed the constitutionality of the regulations challenged in *Rust*. Nonetheless, the Court acknowledged that subsidy conditions restricting the recipient's expression may sometimes run aground the First Amendment.[16]

The First Amendment is violated, for instance, if the government attempts to leverage a funding grant to regulate the recipient's speech beyond the program. *FCC v. League of Women Voters of California* addressed a challenge to a federal statute barring any

[11] *Id.* at 546–50.

[12] 500 U.S. 173 (1991).

[13] *Id.* at 196.

[14] *Id.* at 193.

[15] For an early example, see Act for the Relief of Sick and Disabled Seamen, 1 Stat. 605 (July 16, 1798) (allowing president to "direct" under his "general instructions" funding for the temporary relief of sick or disabled seamen).

[16] *Rust*, 500 U.S. at 197–200.

noncommercial broadcasting station receiving federal funds from editorializing.[17] One of the government's defenses to this challenge was that the ban merely refused to subsidize public broadcasting station editorials, as permitted by *Regan*.[18] But the Supreme Court disagreed. The challenged program wasn't simply a permissible refusal to expend public funds on editorializing by public broadcasting stations, but an absolute ban on such editorials by stations receiving any federal financial support.[19] Although the nonprofit in *Regan* could operate separate affiliates and thereby obtain the tax breaks for its non-lobbying activities while ensuring that the public didn't support its lobbying activities, no such mechanism existed in *League of Women Voters*.[20] A broadcasting station receiving any money from a federal grant—no matter how small a percentage of its operating funds—was absolutely barred from all editorializing, even when private funds solely supported the editorials.[21] While the government has no constitutional obligation to expend public money to support a private entity's expression, it can't exploit funding conditions to regulate or ban other expression by the recipient.

Moreover, the government is limited in regulating some traditional spheres of expression, even when the sphere is funded or subsidized by the government. Take traditional public forums, for instance. Private speakers using state-owned property historically open for expressive activity (such as parks, streets, and sidewalks) are granted a benefit that could be described as a subsidy from the government. But this subsidy doesn't allow the state to support only selected speakers or specified content or viewpoints on its property without demonstrating the necessity of doing so to serve a compelling government interest.[22] Government funding similarly doesn't allow state control over all expression of teachers and students in university classrooms and other university facilities.[23] Such historical enclaves or forums for expressive activity fall outside the typi-

---

[17] 468 U.S. 364 (1984).

[18] *Id.* at 399.

[19] *Id.* at 400.

[20] *Id.*

[21] *Id.*

[22] See Perry Educ. Ass'n v. Perry Local Educators' Ass'n, 460 U.S. 37, 45 (1983).

[23] See, e.g., Healy v. James, 408 U.S. 169, 187–88 (1972); Keyishian v. Bd. of Regents, 385 U.S. 589, 603–06 (1967).

cal tradition allowing the government to selectively fund certain expression.

A subsidy condition that distorts these historical spheres triggers First Amendment concerns. An illustration is *Legal Services Corporation v. Velazquez*.[24] Congress established the nonprofit Legal Services Corporation to distribute appropriated federal funds to local grantee organizations to use in hiring and supervising lawyers to represent indigent clients in noncriminal matters (such as proceedings for welfare benefits). Attorneys receiving these funds to represent an indigent client couldn't, however, assert any constitutional or statutory challenge to the validity of existing welfare laws in the course of their representation.[25] The government urged that this condition be upheld because it defined the contours of the federal program and merely declined to fund challenges to existing welfare laws—just as *Rust* upheld the government's refusal to fund abortion counseling.[26] But the Supreme Court disagreed with this analogy, reasoning that the LSC-funded attorneys, instead of promoting a government message as the physicians in *Rust* did, were to represent indigent clients *against* the government.[27] In other words, the government was providing funds for attorneys to represent the interests of indigent clients rather than to represent the government's interests or viewpoints. Congress's attempt to control attorneys' traditional representation of their clients' interests distorted the "usual functioning" of the legal system.[28] As this funding condition insulated existing welfare laws from challenge in contravention of traditional norms of expression and advocacy before the judiciary, the Court refused to accept this condition as merely defining the limits of the funded program: "Congress cannot recast a condition on funding as a mere definition of its program in every case, lest the First Amendment be reduced to a simple semantic exercise."[29]

The plurality in *United States v. American Library Association, Inc.* also considered the traditional usage of an expressive sphere in

---

[24] 531 U.S. 533 (2001).

[25] *Id.* at 536–37.

[26] *Id.* at 540–41.

[27] *Id.* at 542.

[28] *Id.* at 543.

[29] *Id.* at 547.

concluding that Congress could require libraries receiving federal subsidies for Internet access to install filtering software to block sexual materials.[30] The plurality explained that "public libraries have traditionally excluded pornographic material from their other collections," which indicated the reasonableness of Congress's establishing a parallel limitation on Internet subsidy programs.[31] While the plurality—which consisted of the *Velazquez* dissenters—subsequently continued to distinguish *Velazquez's* distortion rationale on a cramped basis,[32] the distinct traditions of each medium supported the disparate holdings. LSC funding interfered with the usual operation of expression in the legal system by banning attorneys representing welfare claimants from making a specified type of argument. In contrast, public libraries traditionally limited or barred access to pornographic material, so the funding limitation didn't interfere with the usual operations of libraries.

These decisions highlight the constitutionality of certain traditional expressive conditions on subsidies and grants. But instead of following these traditions, Congress enacted an anomalous ideological-commitment provision in the United States Leadership Against HIV/AIDS, Tuberculosis, and Malaria Act of 2003 (the "Leadership Act").[33] This commitment provision required organizations seeking funding from the federal government for overseas HIV and AIDS programs to adopt a policy explicitly opposing prostitution and sex trafficking.[34] This policy requirement was challenged by American organizations combating HIV and AIDS overseas who were concerned that adopting such a policy would require them to censor their privately funded communications and would detrimentally affect their programs by disrupting their efforts to assist prostitutes

---

[30] 539 U.S. 194, 210–13 (2003) (plurality op.).

[31] *Id.* at 212.

[32] See *id.* at 213. The plurality indicated that the distortion rationale didn't apply because public libraries didn't have a comparable role to attorneys that "pit[ted] them against the Government." *Id.* But *Velazquez* claimed support for analyzing the "accepted usage" of a particular medium from prior cases that likewise didn't involve an antagonistic role, such as broadcasting and student publications. 531 U.S. at 543. Unsurprisingly, then, no other member of the *American Library Association* Court joined the plurality's proffered distinction.

[33] Pub. L. No. 108-25, 117 Stat. 711, codified as amended at 22 U.S.C. §§ 7601–82.

[34] 22 U.S.C. § 7631(f).

and to collaborate with certain foreign governments. The Supreme Court resolved this constitutional challenge in *AID v. AOSI.*

II. Commitments and *AID*

The Leadership Act detailed a "comprehensive, integrated" strategy to combat the "pandemic" of HIV/AIDS (the fourth-highest cause of death worldwide at the time) and the associated hike in the spread of tuberculosis and malaria stemming from the compromised immune systems of those with the disease.[35] Part of this strategy authorized appropriations of billions of dollars in funding to nongovernmental organizations to assist in the worldwide fight against HIV/AIDS. In order to receive these funds, organizations didn't have to use or endorse a comprehensive approach to combating HIV/AIDS, nor did they need to support or participate in any religiously or morally objectionable program or activity.[36] But because Congress found that prostitution and sex trafficking contributed (along with numerous other identified factors) to the spread of HIV/AIDS,[37] it incorporated two related conditions in its Leadership Act funding grants. First, the funds couldn't be used "to promote or advocate the legalization or practice of prostitution or sex trafficking."[38] Second, in order to receive any funds, a group or organization had to "have a policy explicitly opposing prostitution and sex trafficking."[39] To fulfill this second condition, known as the policy requirement, the funding recipient had to pledge in the award document its opposition to "prostitution and sex trafficking because of the psychological and physical risks they pose for women, men, and children."[40]

Several groups receiving federal funding to battle the HIV/AIDS pandemic challenged the constitutionality of the policy

---

[35] *Id.* §§ 7601 & 7611(a).

[36] *Id.* § 7631(d)(1).

[37] *Id.* § 7601(23).

[38] *Id.* § 7631(e).

[39] *Id.* § 7631(f) ("No funds made available to carry out this chapter, or any amendment made by this chapter, may be used to provide assistance to any group or organization that does not have a policy explicitly opposing prostitution and sex trafficking, except that this subsection shall not apply to the Global Fund to Fight AIDS, Tuberculosis and Malaria, the World Health Organization, the International AIDS Vaccine Initiative or to any United Nations agency.").

[40] 45 CFR § 89.1(b).

requirement.[41] These organizations argued that, unlike the first grant condition banning the use of funds to support prostitution or sex-trafficking advocacy, the policy requirement didn't impose a condition on the *funds*, but instead impermissibly imposed a condition on the *recipient*, compelling its espousal of the government's viewpoint. This requirement effectively prevented the organizations from expressing their own viewpoints even with private funds, despite the fact that organizations were to combat a malady rather than to deliver a government message. The government protested that the policy requirement didn't entail legal compulsion, but was rather merely a mechanism to ensure that organizations receiving federal funds subscribed to the government's goal of eradicating prostitution and sex trafficking. Because this goal was an integral aspect of the Leadership Act, the government asserted that *Rust* governed. But the district court disagreed, issuing a preliminary injunction barring the government from cutting the organizations' funding or otherwise penalizing them for their privately funded speech.[42]

While the appeal was pending, the administering federal agencies developed new guidelines allowing a recipient organization to affiliate with a group that "engages . . . in activities inconsistent with the recipient's opposition to the practices of prostitution and sex trafficking" as long as the recipient maintained "objective integrity and independence from any affiliated organization."[43] The requisite independence depended on the totality of the circumstances, including but not limited to separate legal status, personnel, financial records, facilities, and outward identification.[44] The court of appeals remanded for reconsideration in light of these new guidelines, with the district court issuing a new but substantially similar preliminary injunction.[45] The

---

[41] Alliance for Open Society International, Inc., filed suit in 2005, with Pathfinder International joining as a plaintiff later that year. Alliance for Open Soc'y Int'l, Inc. v. U.S. Agency for Int'l Dev., 430 F. Supp. 2d 222, 237–38 (S.D.N.Y. 2006). In 2008, the Global Health Council and InterAction, which are associations of organizations that collectively include most U.S. organizations receiving funding under the Leadership Act, also joined as plaintiffs. Alliance for Open Soc'y Int'l, Inc. v. U.S. Agency for Int'l Dev., 570 F. Supp. 2d 533, 538, 550 (S.D.N.Y. 2008).

[42] 430 F. Supp. 2d 222, 278 (S.D.N.Y. 2006).

[43] 45 CFR § 89.3.

[44] *Id.* § 89.3(b)(1)–(5).

[45] 570 F. Supp. 2d 533, 550 (S.D.N.Y. 2008).

court of appeals then affirmed[46]—and was in turn affirmed by the Supreme Court in a 6–2 opinion by Chief Justice John Roberts.[47]

A. The AID Opinion

Chief Justice Roberts opened his legal analysis with first principles. The First Amendment blocks any government attempt to force citizens to pronounce a specific message or to endorse a particular idea or viewpoint.[48] The challenged policy requirement transgressed this basic principle by mandating that funding recipients agree to oppose prostitution and sex trafficking. A direct regulation sanctioning citizens or certain groups of citizens who didn't pledge their fealty to the government's policy on prostitution and sex trafficking undeniably would offend the First Amendment. The issue was whether the government could avoid this result by imposing the mandate as a funding condition rather than a direct regulation of speech.

Although acknowledging that funding conditions often affect expressive rights without violating the Constitution—such as in *American Library Association* and *Regan*—the Court highlighted that, in certain cases, such conditions unconstitutionally abridge protected First Amendment expression. Contrary to the dissent's misreading of the Court's prior precedents, unconstitutional funding conditions aren't merely those that are coercive or unrelated to the government program at issue. Rather, the Court interpreted the relevant precedential distinction as "between conditions that define the limits of the government spending program—those that specify the activities Congress wants to subsidize—and conditions that seek to leverage funding to regulate speech outside the program itself."[49] While conceding this line was "hardly clear," partially because "the definition of a particular program can always be manipulated to subsume the challenged condition," the Court reiterated its prior assurance that "'Congress cannot recast a condition on funding as a mere defini-

[46] Alliance for Open Soc'y Int'l, Inc. v. U.S. Agency for Int'l Dev., 651 F.3d 218, 240 (2d Cir. 2011) (2–1), reh'g en banc denied, 678 F.3d 127, 128 (2d Cir. 2012) (three judges dissenting).

[47] AID v. AOSI, 133 S. Ct. 2321 (2013). Justice Scalia, joined by Justice Clarence Thomas, dissented, while Justice Elena Kagan was recused.

[48] *Id.* at 2327.

[49] *Id.* at 2328.

tion of its program in every case.'"[50] The Court then outlined the precedential support from *Regan, League of Women Voters,* and *Rust* for distinguishing between conditions defining the federal program and those extending beyond the program's boundaries.[51]

Although the Court's distinction between inside- and outside-program speech is aptly supported by these precedents, that isn't the only relevant guidepost in determining the constitutionality of funding conditions. The Court at least implicitly acknowledged that other indicators existed by describing the difference between conditions operating within and without the government program as the relevant precedential distinction "[i]n the present context."[52] But the Court's narrow focus on this particular distinction might still be faulted—as the dissent pointed out—for lacking any stated connection to the First Amendment's underlying policies or foundational principles.[53] Without this grounding, the distinction, being dependent on the congressional definition of the program, is easily manipulated by the government. While reassuring that Congress couldn't merely recast funding conditions as program definitions "in every case," the Court didn't illuminate the principles that would preclude such manipulation beyond its citation to *Velazquez.*[54] On the positive side, though, at least the Court allowed itself leeway to establish further limitations in subsequent controversies while selecting the inside/outside program distinction as the appropriate guide under the presented circumstances.

The Court invalidated the policy requirement under this guide because it compelled "the affirmation of a belief that by its nature" couldn't be confined within the Leadership Act's scope.[55] The Court first explained that the policy requirement didn't operate merely to prevent the use of federal funds for promoting or supporting prostitution and sex trafficking; the other funding condition in the Leadership Act already accomplished this goal by specifically restricting funds from being used for such purposes. The policy requirement

---

[50] *Id.* (quoting Velazquez, 531 U.S. at 547).

[51] *Id.* at 2328–30.

[52] 133 S. Ct. at 2328.

[53] Cf. *id.* at 2333 (Scalia, J., dissenting).

[54] *Id.* at 2328 (quoting Velazquez, 531 U.S. at 547) (internal quotation marks omitted).

[55] *Id.* at 2332.

also was more than a means for selecting funding recipients, as it established an ongoing mandate on a recipient's expression, authorizing the government to terminate a grant based on the recipient's subsequent speech and activities. The Court regarded the policy requirement as not designed for the government "to enlist the assistance of those with whom it already agrees," but rather to oblige "a grant recipient to adopt a particular belief as a condition of funding."[56]

Requiring funding recipients to adopt the government's position on a civic issue as their own, the Court believed, inevitably affected protected expression outside the program's scope. The funding recipient had to comply with the pledge in all of its dealings; it couldn't profess support for eradicating prostitution and sex trafficking when spending Leadership Act funds, but then adopt another position while conducting operations "on its own time and dime."[57] This prohibition violated *Rust*'s principle that funding conditions may limit the *program*'s scope but can't restrict the *recipient*'s activities beyond the program.[58]

The affiliation guidelines didn't afford a lifeline for the policy requirement's constitutionality. The significance of affiliates in prior cases stemmed from their capacity to grant the funding recipient a means to exercise its expressive rights outside the program's scope. But that wasn't possible here when the government was compelling the recipient organization to adopt a particular belief as its own and then to adhere to that belief. A truly distinct affiliate wouldn't "afford a means for the *recipient* to express *its* beliefs," whereas a closely identified one would require the recipient organization to speak from both sides of its mouth in "evident hypocrisy."[59]

The government's final claims floundered on doctrinal and evidentiary grounds. The government protested that, without the policy requirement, the Leadership Act could be undermined if recipients used federal funds to conduct their operations and then funneled their other private funds to promote prostitution or sex trafficking. But the Court determined that neither proof nor precedential support

[56] *Id.* at 2330.
[57] *Id.*
[58] *Id.* at 2330–31 (citing Rust, 500 U.S. at 197).
[59] 133 S. Ct. at 2331 (empasis in original).

existed for this contention. The government offered no substantiation for its suggestion that federal funding would supplant private funding rather than pay for new programs or expand existing ones. Moreover, the government's argument contravened the holding in *League of Women Voters* and much of the analysis in *Regan* and *Rust*.[60] The policy requirement wasn't merely an attempt to ensure that the government program wasn't undermined, as the government maintained, but a requirement that the recipient organizations "pledge allegiance to the Government's policy of eradicating prostitution."[61] Such a required affirmation of belief "by its nature" couldn't be confined within the program's scope, and therefore violated the First Amendment.[62]

B. Dissenting from AID

Justice Scalia's dissent, joined by Justice Clarence Thomas, renewed his assault on First Amendment constraints on government-funding conditions.[63] His premise is that funding conditions only "abridge" First Amendment speech when they operate to compel, coerce, or ban expression.[64] Perhaps such conditions might also be unconstitutional when wholly unrelated to the federal program, although Scalia expressed serious doubts regarding whether every such "disadvantage is a coercion."[65] In general, as long as the government is merely offering a limited funding program that each organization can freely accept or reject, the First Amendment isn't, in his view, infringed by any attached conditions on the funds. It is merely "the reasonable price of admission to a limited governmental spending program."[66]

---

[60] *Id.*

[61] *Id.* at 2332.

[62] *Id.* at 2333.

[63] *Id.* at 2332 (Scalia, J., dissenting). For prior examples of similar protestations by Justice Scalia, see Velazquez, 531 U.S. at 552 (Scalia, J., dissenting); Nat'l Endowment for Arts v. Finley, 524 U.S. 569, 595–99 (1998) (Scalia, J., concurring); Ark. Writers' Project, Inc. v. Ragland, 481 U.S. 221, 236–37 (1987) (Scalia, J., dissenting).

[64] AID, 133 S. Ct. at 2335 (Scalia, J., dissenting); Velazquez, 531 U.S. at 552, 558 (Scalia, J., dissenting); Finley, 524 U.S. at 595–99 (Scalia, J., concurring); Ark. Writers' Project, 481 U.S. at 236–37 (Scalia, J., dissenting).

[65] AID, 133 S. Ct. at 2333 (Scalia, J., dissenting).

[66] *Id.* at 2335.

According to Justice Scalia, the Leadership Act's policy requirement was merely a method to select those organizations to implement the government's program to eradicate HIV/AIDS.[67] He urged that the government was allowed to discriminate on viewpoint in making such selections, enrolling those who support its policies while leaving the unsupportive on the sidelines. As is his wont, Scalia besprinkled his reasoning with colorful illustrations: The United States shouldn't have to use a domestic equivalent of Hamas to distribute food assistance overseas irrespective of the organization's distributive efficiency, and a healthy-eating public service program could exclude the American Gourmet Society, which is ambivalent about healthy foods.[68] The Leadership Act's policy requirement here, he contended, was likewise reasonable in selecting, as government-funded HIV/AIDS combatants, only those organizations believing in eradicating prostitution.[69]

But Justice Scalia's position ignores the pervasiveness of—and the threat to liberty from—the government's ability to leverage funding and other subsidy conditions to regulate speech. Such conditions can be used to effectively control expression as much as even so-called coercive regulations. Numerous forms of public discourse are funded or subsidized by the government. For instance, print media receive subsidized mailing rates, nonprofits enjoy tax-exempt status, and higher education and the arts obtain public financial support. Not to mention the thousands of grant programs the government operates: government agencies have an estimated 200,000 grant agreements and other contracts with approximately 33,000 human-service nonprofit organizations, with government funding providing almost two-thirds of all revenue for these organizations.[70] The threat to liberty if the government can leverage all of these subsidies and grants to require entities to pledge allegiance to government policies wouldn't be speculative, but a real abridgement on free expressive rights.

[67] Id. at 2332.

[68] Id

[69] Id. at 2333.

[70] Elizabeth T. Boris et al., Human Service Nonprofits and Government Collaboration: Findings from the 2010 National Survey of Nonprofit Government Contracting and Grants vii, 5–8 (Oct. 2010), available at http://www.urban.org/publications/412228. html.

Cato's amicus brief to the Supreme Court provided apt examples.[71] If the government, via the Leadership Act, could require funding recipients to pledge opposition to prostitution because prostitution contributed to HIV/AIDS, the government could also mandate that funding recipients pledge opposition to all organizations (even religious one) objecting to contraceptive use, as Congress found condom use to be effective in preventing the spread of HIV/AIDS.[72] Or, in the federal healthcare context, because Congress identified a national "policy objective" in expanding healthcare coverage,[73] the government could use Justice Scalia's logic to require, as a condition for physicians to receive Medicaid benefits or for private entities to run insurance exchanges, the recipients to pledge their support for the Affordable Care Act or other government interventions in health care. Or, because of findings that marijuana use may promote certain cancers and disrupt the immune system, Congress could require that research facilities and hospitals, in order to receive funding grants to fight cancer, adopt a policy opposing the legalization of marijuana.[74] Thousands of such government programs exist—and all are similarly manipulable to reward favored viewpoints while punishing disfavored ones.

Consider again the Leadership Act. The only policy required of funding recipients was opposition to prostitution and sex trafficking. But why? Why not a policy requiring the organization to promote contraceptive use, which was at least as (and likely more) integral to the Leadership Act's objectives than opposing prostitution?[75] But

---

[71] See Brief for Cato Institute as Amicus Curiae Supporting Respondents at 11, AID v. AOSI, 133 S. Ct. 2321 (No. 12-10).

[72] See 22 U.S.C. § 7601(35). Yet instead of adopting anything close to such a mandate, the Leadership Act took the exact opposite tact and specified that organizations didn't have to support or participate in any religiously or morally objectionable program or activity. *Id.* § 7631(d)(1). As discussed below, this in itself signifies the danger, as Congress was clearly favoring religious or moral points of view—even when such views contravened clear program objectives—while requiring a pledge regarding prostitution, which appeared no more central (and likely less so) to the program's objectives.

[73] See 42 U.S.C. § 18091(2)(C).

[74] See Brief of the Rutherford Institute as Amicus Curiae Supporting Respondents at 23, AID v. AOSI, 133 S. Ct. 2321 (No. 12-10).

[75] The policy requirement was a committee amendment to the Leadership Act by Representative Christopher Smith, whose primary purpose apparently was targeting

instead of requiring such a policy, Congress specified that funding recipients didn't have to either endorse a comprehensive approach to combating HIV/AIDS or support any religiously or morally objectionable program or activity.[76] Congress thereby allowed the participation of many not believing in all the program's objectives, while excluding only those not wanting to adopt a policy against prostitution and sex trafficking. And Congress wasn't finished playing favorites; it then waived the policy requirement for specified organizations.[77] The Leadership Act thus cherry-picked the application of a preferred political ideological pledge as the basis to award billions of dollars of funding, funding essential to many of the recipient organizations.[78] In the real world, that's an abridgement on expression.

Justice Scalia's dissent next took aim at the majority's inside/outside program distinction, asserting in part that it was unsupported by precedent.[79] He premised this argument, though, on a misreading of the Court's cases. He conjured a new rationale for *Rust's* discussion of the inside/outside program distinction,[80] dismissed aspects of *Regan* as "nonessential" footnoted material (even though the material was also contained in the opinion's text and has been cited

---

prostitution and sex trafficking in general rather than merely diminishing HIV/AIDS infections. See U.S. Leadership Act Against HIV/AIDS, Tuberculosis, and Malaria Act of 2003: Markup Before the H. Comm. on Int'l Relations, 108th Cong. 148–49 (statement of Rep. Christopher Smith). Smith's amendment barely passed the committee in a 24-22 vote. *Id.* at 160. This legislative history buttresses the inference from the act's text as a whole that the targeting of prostitution and sex trafficking—which was mentioned in just one of the act's 41 findings—wasn't as central as many other provisions. See 22 U.S.C. §§ 7601–82.

[76] 22 U.S.C. § 7631(d)(1).

[77] *Id.* § 7631(f) (excluding from the policy requirement all United Nations agencies, the International AIDS Vaccine Initiative, the World Health Organization, and the Global Fund to Fight AIDS, Tuberculosis and Malaria).

[78] See Boris, *supra* note 70, at vii, 5–8 (detailing that approximately 60 percent of all human-service nonprofit organizations obtained over half their funds from government, with government providing in the aggregate 65 percent of all nonprofit operating funds).

[79] AID, 133 S. Ct. at 2333–34 (Scalia, J., dissenting).

[80] *Id.* at 2333. Justice Scalia acknowledged that the distinction "was alluded to" in *Rust*, but was only relevant because *Rust* didn't involve an anti-abortion program. *Id.* But he cited no specific language from *Rust* for this proposition, and with good reason: *Rust's* discussion of subsidies operating within the program versus those operating on the recipient had no such limitation. Rust, 500 U.S. at 196–99.

as essential to the holding in subsequent cases),[81] and distinguished *League of Women Voters* by citing a segment of the opinion that addressed a wholly separate alternative argument.[82] Although inventive, his interpretation wasn't a fair reading of any of these cases, which, as mentioned previously, aptly support the majority's inside/outside program distinction.

Yet Justice Scalia also raised two more consequential objections to the inside/outside distinction, ones that the majority didn't fully answer. First, he highlighted its constitutional grounding: "I am at a loss to explain what this central pillar of the Court's opinion . . . has to do with the First Amendment."[83] Although he immediately turned in his next sentence to his (mis)reading of its precedential support, he had stumbled upon an important question: the First Amendment foundation for distinguishing between conditions operating within and without a government program.

He closed with a more pragmatic appeal. He maintained that it was "common" for the government to consider viewpoints in selecting those to accomplish its objections, but doubted that such ideological selections could be made after the Court's holding: "Ideological-commitment requirements such as the one here are quite rare; but making the choice between competing applicants on relevant ideological grounds is undoubtedly quite common. As far as the Constitution is concerned, it is quite impossible to distinguish between the two."[84] He therefore envisioned a rash of future challenges to funding decisions on ideological grounds.

---

[81] AID, 133 S. Ct. at 2334. Justice Scalia maintained that the fact that the nonprofit could operate a separate lobbying affiliate in *Regan* was "alluded to in a footnote" and "entirely nonessential to the Court's holding." *Id.* This is misleading because the affiliation opportunity was also discussed in the text of *Regan's* analysis, 461 U.S. at 544–45, and has been viewed as the basis of *Regan's* holding in subsequent cases, including one by *Regan's* author. See Rust, 500 U.S. at 197–98.

[82] AID, 133 S. Ct. at 2334. Justice Scalia's proffered distinction solely relied on a quote from page 397 of *League of Women Voters*. See *id.* This portion of *League of Women Voters*, however, addressed whether the government's editorializing ban was permissible as a direct regulation of speech and not the government's wholly alternative argument that its editorializing ban—even if an invalid direct regulation—was a valid funding condition. League of Women Voters, 468 U.S. at 399–401.

[83] AID, 133 S. Ct. at 2333.

[84] *Id.* at 2335.

His last two objections aren't without their merit, and deserve a fuller answer than was necessary for the majority to provide in resolving the case—so I offer a response in the following section. I'll first discuss a potential constitutional grounding for First Amendment limitations on funding conditions. Then I'll explain how this grounding both subsumes the majority's holding and provides a basis for appropriately resolving other controversies, allowing the government to make necessary selection choices while respecting expressive liberty.

III. First Amendment Traditions as Limits on Funding Conditions

Expressive conditions on funding and other subsidies highlight a tension between two fundamental First Amendment precepts: the viewpoint-neutrality mandate and government control of its own speech and undertakings. This tension may be reconciled, however, through longstanding American expressive traditions.

A. Viewpoint Neutrality and State Subsidies

A foundational First Amendment principle is that the government can't restrict speech based on the ideas, messages, or viewpoints expressed.[85] This tenet has been described by scholars as the cardinal concern of the First Amendment.[86] The Supreme Court appears to agree: "If there is a bedrock principle underlying the First Amendment, it is that the government may not prohibit the expression of an idea simply because society finds the idea itself offensive or disagreeable."[87]

This maxim even extends to categories of speech outside the First Amendment's typical coverage. For example, although fighting words, threats, fraud, obscenity, and similar traditional unprotected categories of utterances may be outlawed without offending the First

[85] See, e.g., Rosenberger v. Rectors & Visitors of Univ. of Va., 515 U.S. 819, 828–29 (1995); R.A.V. v. City of St. Paul, 505 U.S. 377, 386 (1992); Police Dep't v. Mosley, 408 U.S. 92, 95 (1972).

[86] See, e.g., Joseph Blocher, Viewpoint Neutrality and Government Speech, 52 B.C. L. Rev. 695, 696 (2011); Kathleen M. Sullivan, Artistic Freedom, Public Funding, and the Constitution, in Public Money and the Muse: Essays on Government Funding for the Arts 80, 89–90 (Stephen Benedict ed., 1991).

[87] Texas v. Johnson, 491 U.S. 397, 414 (1989).

Amendment, the government can't pick and choose favored view-points within these otherwise unprotected categories.[88] To take an-other example, while the government is allowed almost free rein to limit speech or make content choices on state-owned property that hasn't been traditionally or intentionally opened for the public's indiscriminate expressive use, viewpoint discrimination within these nonpublic fora is still prohibited.[89] This mandate of state regulatory neutrality in ideas and messages—even in areas outside the First Amendment's typical protections—is necessary to ensure the vigorous public discourse between speakers and audiences on which democratic self-government and the marketplace of ideas depend.

But despite this viewpoint-neutrality regulatory mandate, the government has to make viewpoint choices with respect to its own speech and undertakings. The First Amendment simply can't demand that the state acts in a viewpoint-neutral manner when operating within its own managerial sphere to accomplish its objectives. The government often must select certain viewpoints in expressing its own messages to the public—the health hazards of smoking, the benefits of a healthy diet, the need for particular legislation, the means for preventing forest fires, and strategies to prevent HIV/AIDS. The government also adopts certain viewpoints when it designs programs for private partners to express its messages or to support its undertakings. A blanket prohibition on viewpoint discrimination with respect to the government's own speech and undertakings is neither possible nor desirable.[90] So even though government can't "burden the speech of others in order to tilt public debate in a preferred direction," it can express its views through its own speech, undertakings, and associations with private parties.[91]

But a real concern arises because every time the government makes a choice to subsidize a particular message, that choice "has the effect of 'singling out a disfavored group on the basis of speech

[88] R.A.V., 505 U.S. at 386.

[89] See, e.g., Rosenberger, 515 U.S. at 829–30; Perry Educ. Ass'n v. Perry Local Educators' Ass'n, 460 U.S. 37, 46–49 (1983).

[90] See Robert C. Post, Between Governance and Management: The History and Theory of the Public Forum, 34 UCLA L. Rev. 1713, 1825 (1987) (positing government might "grind to a halt were the Court to seriously prohibit viewpoint discrimination in the internal management of speech").

[91] Sorrell v. IMS Health, Inc., 131 S. Ct. 2653, 2671 (2011).

content,' namely the group that does not receive the subsidy because it seeks to express a different message."[92] Moreover, government's unique access to and control over speech avenues—and its trillions of dollars of financial resources—risk unduly influencing public discourse and distorting the marketplace of ideas. State involvement with speech is pervasive: providing public forums, subsidizing mailing rates, authorizing tax breaks, and funding numerous activities wholly or partially involving expression. Many of these government-subsidized benefits have traditionally been accorded without reference to viewpoint and are relied on by private parties.[93] The government must be checked from interfering with private speech in all these spheres to ensure state accountability, to safeguard individual liberty, and to foster the independent expression of ideas.

Subsidized private speech thus can't always be immune from the viewpoint-neutrality mandate. And the Court's precedents acknowledge as much. Otherwise, governments could exclude individuals from public property based on the messages expressed;[94] publicly funded libraries could remove books based on viewpoint;[95] public universities could bar student groups based on their objectionable perspectives;[96] public art grants could be awarded based on favored government themes;[97] and public universities could fire professors with unorthodox beliefs.[98] But still, sometimes the government has

[92] David Cole, Beyond Unconstitutional Conditions: Charting Spheres of Neutrality in Government-Funded Speech, 67 N.Y.U. L. Rev. 675, 690 (1992).

[93] See, e.g., Hannegan v. Esquire, Inc., 327 U.S. 146, 151–52 & n.7 (1946) (discussing the longstanding history of special postage rates based on objective criteria for specified classes of publication and their importance to the publishing industry).

[94] But see Rosenberger, 515 U.S. at 829–31 (holding university engaged in impermissible viewpoint discrimination by excluding religious perspectives from its student publication funding); Perry Educ. Ass'n, 460 U.S. at 49 (recognizing that viewpoint discrimination is prohibited in even nonpublic fora).

[95] But see Bd. of Educ. v. Pico, 457 U.S. 853, 870–72 (1982) (plurality op.) (concluding books couldn't be removed from a school library due to partisan or ideological ideas).

[96] But see Healy v. James, 408 U.S. 169, 187–88 (1972) (holding public university couldn't deny school affiliation to a student group because the school found "the views expressed by [the] group to be abhorrent").

[97] But see Nat'l Endowment for the Arts v. Finley, 524 U.S. 569, 583–87 (1998) (indicating that "directed viewpoint discrimination" or "penalt[ies] on disfavored viewpoints" in public arts funding would violate the First Amendment).

[98] But see Rust, 500 U.S. at 200 (recognizing that a university is a "traditional sphere of free expression so fundamental to the functioning of our society" that First

to make funding choices based in part on viewpoint, such as funding a center for democracy (but not communism). The difficulty is drawing a principled line, grounded in the First Amendment, between permissible and impermissible viewpoint-based funding.

The inside/outside program distinction is helpful here, but it can't reconcile all the Court's precedents. Consider *Velazquez* again.[99] The LSC regulations there, as Justice Scalia explained in dissent, allowed "funding recipients to establish affiliate organizations to conduct litigation and other activities that fall outside the scope of the LSC program."[100] In other words, the regulations only operated within the program and didn't constrain the recipient. Yet the Court still invalidated it. More than the inside/outside principle was—and still is—afoot.

So consider a broader perspective. The concern with viewpoint-based government funding arises when the conditions affect citizens' expression. Such viewpoint constraints effectively remove at least some speech from the very heart of the First Amendment, that is, its ban on state favoritism toward certain ideas and messages. In other situations in which the Court has allowed analogous government incursions into core First Amendment principles, a supporting historical tradition has been required.[101] The basic premise is that such a history demonstrates that the First Amendment was never intended to serve as a shield against the government action at issue.[102] The presumption is that the First Amendment's typical restraints apply unless the government establishes a tradition to the contrary. As developed more fully below, an analogous presumption appears appropriate for government-funding conditions imposing viewpoint restraints.

Amendment freedoms limit the government's ability to constrain speech); Keyishian v. Bd. of Regents, 385 U.S. 589, 603 (1967) (holding that the First Amendment "does not tolerate laws that cast a pall of orthodoxy over the classroom").

[99] 531 U.S. 533 (2001).

[100] *Id.* at 556 (Scalia, J., dissenting).

[101] United States v. Stevens, 130 S. Ct. 1577, 1585–86 (2010).

[102] See Charles W. "Rocky" Rhodes, The Historical Approach to Unprotected Speech and the Quantitative Analysis of Overbreadth in *United States v. Stevens*, 2010 Emerging Issues 5227 (LexisNexis July 2010); Nadine Strossen, *United States v. Stevens*: Restricting Two Major Rationales for Content-Based Speech Restrictions, 2009-2010 Cato Sup. Ct. Rev. 67, 82–83 (2010).

B. Historical Exceptions to Prohibiting Speech Discrimination

Government neutrality in speech regulation is a core First Amendment principle, as speech regulations that discriminate on either a content or viewpoint basis are typically invalid.[103] The content-discrimination ban nullifies state regulations favoring or disfavoring certain subject matters or speakers, unless the regulation is necessary to serve a compelling government interest.[104] The viewpoint-discrimination ban outlaws "an egregious form of content discrimination" occurring when the government targets "the specific motivating ideology or the opinion or perspective of the speaker."[105] Both of these types of expressive discrimination pose inherent (and intolerable) risks of suppressing ideas and manipulating public discourse.[106]

Despite these risks, though, "certain well-defined and narrowly limited classes of speech" may be prohibited or punished on a subject-matter or content basis.[107] These classes—such as incitement of illegal activity, fighting words, true threats, obscenity, fraud, and speech integral to criminal conduct—thus fall outside the normal First Amendment ban against content discrimination. Until recently, a common understanding was that these so-called unprotected categories of speech were identified through a balancing test, which compared communicative value with associated harms.[108] Relying on this balancing approach in a case decided three terms ago, the government in *United States v. Stevens* contended that animal cruelty depictions should likewise be excluded from the content-discrimination

---

[103] Ashcroft v. ACLU, 535 U.S. 564, 573 (2002).

[104] See, e.g., Citizens United v. FEC, 558 U.S. 310, 340–41 (2010); United States v. Playboy Entm't Group, Inc., 529 U.S. 803, 811–13 (2000).

[105] Rosenberger, 515 U.S. at 829.

[106] Turner Broad. Sys. v. FCC, 512 U.S. 622, 641 (1994).

[107] Chaplinsky v. New Hampshire, 315 U.S. 568, 572 (1942).

[108] See Strossen, *supra* note 102, at 70–71 (detailing examples from legislatures, courts, and litigants). See also Chaplinsky, 315 U.S. at 572 (describing unprotected speech classes as "of such slight social value to the truth that any benefit that may be derived from them is clearly outweighed by the social interest in order and morality"). This formulation has been oft-repeated. See, e.g., R.A.V., 505 U.S. at 382–83; New York v. Ferber, 458 U.S. 747, 763–64 (1982); Beauharnais v. Illinois, 343 U.S. 259, 256–57 (1952).

ban.[109] But the *Stevens* Court spurned the government's cost-benefit premise as "startling and dangerous."[110]

Stevens instead held that, for a category of speech to be outside the content-discrimination ban, a longstanding historical tradition of its exclusion from the principles of free expression is necessary.[111] The mere fact that speech is adjudged valueless, or an ad hoc judicial appraisal of its costs outweigh its benefits, is insufficient to remove it from this constitutional safeguard.[112] A "simple cost-benefit analysis"—representing a "freewheeling authority" to declare speech unprotected because the speech is just "not worth it"—dishonors the American people's judgment expressed in the First Amendment.[113] Only when words or utterances have never been considered as within the First Amendment should they be removed from the guarantee's typical protections.

This historical approach has normative appeal because it prevents judges from arbitrarily weighing the costs and the benefits of new forms or subject matters of speech. If the associated costs of the speech are sufficiently significant, the government might perhaps establish that a content-based regulation is necessary to further a compelling government interest. But the judiciary shouldn't summarily excise some speech from core First Amendment protections based on a case-by-case weighing of the costs and benefits of the expression. The First Amendment is too sacrosanct to entrust to such ad hoc balancing.

This sacredness counsels against confining the historical prerequisite to content-based regulations while continuing to engage in ad hoc appraisals of viewpoint-based funding conditions. Through viewpoint-based funding conditions, the government favors certain ideas and messages while disfavoring others. Simply because the government has "purchased" favored views, rather than punishing

---

[109] 130 S. Ct. 1577, 1584–85 (2010).

[110] *Id.* at 1585.

[111] *Id.* at 1584, 1586. As Professor Strossen highlighted, in order to adopt this historical approach, *Stevens* had to "significantly recast" almost seven decades of precedent. See Strossen, *supra* note 102, at 69. The Court has since, though, adhered to the historical approach. See, e.g., United States v. Alvarez, 132 S. Ct. 2537, 2544–47 (2012) (plurality op.); Brown v. Entm't Merch. Ass'n, 131 S. Ct. 2729, 2734–35 (2011).

[112] Stevens, 130 S. Ct. at 1585–86.

[113] *Id.*

disfavored ones, doesn't pardon transgressing the First Amendment's command against obliging orthodoxy in public ideals, especially in light of government's vast financial resources. Targeting one side or perspective in the public discourse is "an egregious form of content discrimination."[114] So just as *Stevens* held that the First Amendment prevents a "freewheeling authority" to create new exceptions to the content-discrimination ban "simply on the basis that some speech is not worth it,"[115] the government shouldn't be free to impose viewpoint-based subsidy conditions simply because the government defines a funding program to encompass them. Instead, the government should only be authorized to impose viewpoint-based funding conditions when falling within a traditional managerial sphere in which government has employed analogous conditions to achieve government objectives.

This traditional prerequisite would preclude the government from attempting to use viewpoint-based funding conditions in subsidized venues that have long been open to a variety of viewpoints, such as public forums, the postal service, public broadcast editorials, public grants for the arts, publicly funded adversarial advocacy, or public university student groups. In these traditional "domains of public discourse," the government's attempts to leverage subsidies or other government benefits to control private expression would violate the First Amendment.[116] Only those funding conditions comparable to historic "baselines," in which the government has traditionally employed viewpoint-based funding conditions to accomplish government objectives, would be valid.[117]

The Court's prior decisions addressing viewpoint-based funding are consistent with this approach. *Velazquez* emphasized that the funding condition preventing challenges to welfare laws contravened the traditional norms and usual functioning of the legal system.[118] And while not discussed in the opinion, *Rust* might be defended as being within longstanding traditions allowing the gov-

---

[114] Rosenberger, 515 U.S. at 829.

[115] Stevens, 130 S. Ct. at 1585–86.

[116] See Robert C. Post, Subsidized Speech, 106 Yale L. J. 151, 157–58 (1996).

[117] Cf. Seth F. Kreimer, Allocational Sanctions: The Problem of Negative Rights in a Positive State, 132 U. Pa. L. Rev. 1293, 1359–63 (1984).

[118] Velazquez, 531 U.S. at 543.

ernment to specify the available services in a public health program and to ensure that its funds are used for those services.[119] The government may adopt viewpoint-based funding conditions to ensure the appropriate delivery of its expressive messages—for example, that smoking is hazardous to your health, or that democracy is preferable to communism—as the government has historically exercised managerial viewpoint control over those compensated to engage in a governmentally funded enterprise to project certain messages to the populace.

This traditional approach also authorizes the government to employ funding limitations based on content and speaker status, as long as the constraints aren't viewpoint-based and any conditions are on the funding, not the recipient. Government grants and subsidies historically have depended on content and speaker status. Take mailing subsidies: From the beginning of our nation, Congress has provided special rates for certain classes of publications. Initially, Congress granted this special rate just to newspapers, with magazines and pamphlets added shortly thereafter.[120] These rates have always been based on the content and form of the publication—such as different rates for public-interest newspapers and other periodicals than for books or for advertising publications—but not on the quality or viewpoints within the publication.[121] The Court has tacitly approved these longstanding content classifications in mailing subsidies, while warning that differentiating on "economic or political ideas"

[119] See Act for the Relief of Sick and Disabled Seamen, 1 Stat. 605 (July 16, 1798). This act authorized the executive branch to issue "instructions" to local physicians working in private boarding residences in locales without a marine hospital. These instructions included such matters as qualifying seamen to the program, permissible stay lengths, and treatable conditions. See Gautham Rao, Sailors' Health and National Wealth, 9 Common-place (Oct. 2008), available at http://www.common-place.org/vol-09/no-01/rao. But while a longstanding tradition thus supports defining limits on a public-health program's scope (such as the *Rust*'s program confinement to preconception family planning), the portion of *Rust* upholding muzzling a doctor's advice arguably is of a different ilk. Although governments in America have provided funds to private entities for specifically defined public health purposes since even before the Revolution, and these defined health purposes can encompass delivering a specific message to the populace, my research hasn't revealed any indication that such programs limited physicians' advice to patients. See Steven Rathgeb Smith & Michael Lipsky, Nonprofits for Hire: The Welfare State in the Age of Contracting (1993).

[120] See Act of February 20, 1792, 1 Stat. 232, 238; Act of May 8, 1794, 1 Stat. 354, 362.

[121] See Hannegan v. Esquire, Inc., 327 U.S. 146, 151–52 (1946).

would raise "grave constitutional questions."[122] Similarly, *Regan* approved the traditional practices of Congress since the enactment of the income tax in defining tax exemptions by content and speaker status.[123] *Regan* accordingly upheld denying tax-deductible contributions for nonveteran organizations engaged in substantial lobbying activities (even though this ruling favored veterans' groups over other speakers), while indicating that the result would be different if the exemptions were to "discriminate invidiously" to suppress "dangerous ideas."[124] The Court likewise expressed in *League of Women Voters* that Congress could deny funding to public broadcast editorializing while funding other public broadcasting programs. The constitutional difficulty in that case was that Congress prohibited stations receiving any federal financial support from all editorializing, even with private funds.[125] These cases confirm that *content-based* funding conditions are constitutional as long as the restrictions are on the funding, not the recipient. But *viewpoint-based* funding restrictions require a more searching analysis.

That jurisprudence accords with the Court's approach to nonpublic fora. State-owned property that isn't by tradition or design a channel for public communication can be reserved by the government to its dedicated purposes.[126] The government is free to discriminate based on content or speaker status in such nonpublic fora, but it can't discriminate on viewpoint.[127] Government funding is somewhat comparable: the government's money (rather than other types of property) is dedicated to accomplishing certain objectives. In general, this money can be reserved for its dedicated purposes, allowing the government to discriminate based on content or speaker status. Yet when the government uses this funding or other subsidies to discriminate based on viewpoint, a tradition of comparable viewpoint-based conditions to accomplish government objectives should be required before removing typical First Amendment protections.

---

[122] *Id.* at 155–56.

[123] See, e.g., Regan, 461 U.S. at 546–48; Cammarano v. United States, 358 U.S. 498, 503–07, 513 (1959).

[124] Regan, 461 U.S. at 545–51 (internal quotations omitted).

[125] League of Women Voters, 468 U.S. at 400.

[126] Perry Educ. Ass'n v. Perry Local Educators' Ass'n, 461 U.S. 37, 46 (1983).

[127] See, e.g., Perry Educ. Ass'n, 461 U.S. at 46–53; Greer v. Spock, 424 U.S. 829, 838–40 & n.10 (1976).

This will sometimes be a difficult analysis. As one example, consider public funding to private educational facilities, a practice existing since colonial times.[128] Government viewpoint-based subsidies are impermissible mechanisms to control student organizations or to dampen intellectual freedom,[129] but funding conditions related to other educational aspects, such as curriculum, resource allocation, and nondiscrimination policies, have been allowed.[130] Any education-funding condition based on viewpoint, then, would necessitate a consideration of the appropriate traditional analogue. And of course, similar classification difficulties would arise in other contexts, which would be especially vexing when ascertaining the correct historical analogue for any new forms of subsidies and grants without an existing tradition. Yet this inherent difficulty exists in all historical analyses, including those necessary after *Stevens* for categorical exclusions from the content-discrimination ban. And such an effort is warranted when considering its benefits.

These benefits include harmonizing the Court's analytical approach to departures from the First Amendment's core principles. A traditions-based prerequisite provides leeway for the government to employ viewpoint-based conditions when necessary to accomplish its managerial objectives, while still protecting traditional spheres of subsidized public discourse necessary to check government overreach, to safeguard individual expressive autonomy, and to preserve the independence of the marketplace of ideas. This requirement subsumes the Court's prior holdings on funding conditions, on a basis grounded in the underlying principles of the First Amendment. For good measure, it even provides a principle to address Justice Scalia's concerns regarding the occasional need for viewpoint to be considered in selection criteria, as illustrated by revisiting *AID* under a historical approach.

---

128 See Lester M. Salamon, Partners in Public Service: Government-Nonprofit Relations in the Modern Welfare State 35 (1995).

129 See, e.g., Healy v. James, 408 U.S. 169, 187–88 (1972); Keyishian v. Bd. of Regents, 385 U.S. 589, 603 (1967).

130 See, e.g., Rosenberger, 515 U.S. at 833; Grove City College v. Bell, 465 U.S. 555, 575–76 (1984).

C. Subsidy Traditions and AID

By mandating that funding recipients agree to oppose prostitution and sex trafficking due to psychological and physical risks, the policy requirement challenged in *AID* entailed a viewpoint-based endorsement of a specific government message.[131] The lack of any analogous viewpoint-based ideological pledge imposed by Congress—apparently ever!—aptly illustrates that this wasn't a necessary condition to obtain a government objective in a traditional managerial government sphere. Neither the government's briefing in *AID* nor that of any of its amici identified a comparable condition ever imposed as a condition to obtain federal funding for a project.[132] At oral argument, the government likewise failed to point to any specific examples of a similar condition in any government program, much less a public-health program.[133] Because no tradition supported such a viewpoint-based ideological pledge, the normal rules of the First Amendment should apply—including the nearly absolute prohibition on state compulsion of personal beliefs.[134]

But does this mean, as Justice Scalia asserted, that the government would have to allow a domestic equivalent of Hamas to distribute food assistance overseas?[135] I think not. First, my intuition here (shared perhaps ironically by Justice Scalia) is that the government could establish a tradition of selecting overseas grant recipients in part on their ability to foster American goodwill abroad, which is of course an overarching goal of any foreign aid program.[136] But even if we both are wrong, I still think that the government could satisfy strict scrutiny—especially in light of *Holder v. Humanitarian Law Proj-*

---

[131] AID, 133 S. Ct. at 2327.

[132] See, e.g., Brief for the Petitioners at 32–33, AID v. AOSI, 133 S. Ct. 2321 (No. 12-10) (suggesting hypothetical statutes that in the government's view would be constitutional without providing any actual legislative examples).

[133] See Transcript of Oral Argument at 8–10, AID v. AOSI, 133 S. Ct. 2321 (No. 12-10). In response to Justice Ruth Bader Ginsburg's query whether there was "anything else quite like this where you make a pledge to the government," Deputy Solicitor General Sri Srinivasan didn't identify any such program, but instead sought to explain why "this kind of requirement makes sense in this particular context."

[134] See, e.g., W. Va. State Bd. of Educ. v. Barnette, 319 U.S. 624, 642 (1943).

[135] AID, 133 S. Ct. at 2332 (Scalia, J., dissenting).

[136] Id. at 2335 (assuming that selecting "competing applicants on relevant ideological grounds is undoubtedly quite common").

ect's teaching regarding the provision of nonviolent material support to terrorist organizations[137]—by demonstrating that allowing such an organization to participate would undermine foreign relations and impede the program's objectives.

Justice Scalia may be right that a healthy-eating public-service program couldn't exclude the American Gourmet Society simply because of its ambivalence toward healthy eating—at least assuming that the society could establish that it was otherwise superiorly qualified to promote a government message through a public-service program, which perhaps is unlikely.[138] I wouldn't envision that some tradition supports such a viewpoint-based selection criteria in a domestic public-service program, and the government probably couldn't satisfy strict scrutiny. But I'm not troubled by this result, assuming that an organization has the technical proficiency, qualifications, and experience to achieve the program's objectives without undermining them. So although I believe that there is some room for viewpoint-based selection criteria when either historical traditions support them or the government can establish their necessity to prevent the undermining of its programs, the government shouldn't enjoy carte blanche to select funding recipients based on viewpoint. Such a government power would risk a dangerous state-imposed orthodoxy that the First Amendment is designed to prevent.

Conclusion

AID v. AOSI is a victory for free speech, individual liberty, and limited government. The Court's holding—and general approach—was aptly supported by its prior precedents, and I commend the result. While the Court didn't exhaust the considerations that should govern the constitutionality of funding conditions, it appropriately granted itself leeway to establish further limitations in subsequent controversies. These further limitations should depend on the traditions-based prerequisite outlined in this article, which would both encompass its existing doctrine and serve as a useful future guide for invalidating those funding conditions infringing on private expressive liberty.

---

[137] 130 S. Ct. 2705, 2725–28 (2010).
[138] AID, 133 S. Ct. at 2332 (Scalia, J., dissenting).

Looking Ahead: October Term 2013

Howard J. Bashman*

After two consecutive years when much of the nation's attention was riveted on the Supreme Court, awaiting long-anticipated rulings on the final day of the Court's term, it is far too soon to know whether we will again find ourselves similarly transfixed on electronic media and the Court's own website once the final day of the October 2013 term arrives in June 2014. Nevertheless, the coming term is already off to quite an auspicious start. Before departing on its summer vacation, the Supreme Court had granted review in 47 cases for its next term, which after some consolidations of similar cases will produce a total of 44 hours of oral argument.

If the Court's workload in each of the last three years is any indication, the Court may have already granted review in more than half of the cases that will be decided on the merits during the October 2013 term—in line with Chief Justice John Roberts's wish to front-load oral argument a bit more to give himself and his colleagues more time to write those final opinions. Or perhaps the term will mark an increase in the Court's merits workload after several terms in which the Court's workload has either declined or held relatively steady.

I begin this essay by taking a look at a baker's dozen of the most important and interesting cases on the Court's docket for the upcoming term. Then I conclude by examining three other cases that may sooner or later make it onto the Court's docket and one potential development that could capture the attention of Court-watchers as the October 2013 term approaches its conclusion.

---

* Howard J. Bashman is a nationally known attorney and appellate commentator whose practice focuses on appellate litigation at the Law Offices of Howard J. Bashman in Willow Grove, Pennsylvania. His blog, *How Appealing*, is hosted by ALM and is regularly visited by U.S. Supreme Court justices and many other federal and state appellate judges, appellate lawyers, members of the news media, and other interested readers.

Separation of Powers

Recess Appointments

From its origin in 1789, the U.S. Constitution has provided that: "The President shall have Power to fill up all Vacancies that may happen during the Recess of the Senate, by granting Commissions which shall expire at the End of their next Session."[1] Although presidents have used their recess appointment powers numerous times to fill vacancies in the executive and judicial branches, the U.S. Supreme Court has never been called on to conclusively determine when that power may lawfully be exercised. Until now.

In *NLRB v. Noel Canning*, the Court has agreed to review a recent ruling by the U.S. Court of Appeals for the D.C. Circuit that severely limited the nature and availability of the president's recess appointment power.[2] Attempting to thwart President Barack Obama's ability to make certain recess appointments, the Senate avoided declaring formal recesses and instead convened every few days in so-called pro forma sessions. After President Obama nevertheless proceeded to make recess appointments of individuals to serve on, among other places, the National Labor Relations Board, companies adversely affected by NLRB decisions began challenging the legality of the composition of that agency's board.

Eventually, one such dispute made its way to the D.C. Circuit, where the majority on a divided three-judge panel held not only that a president is limited to exercising his recess appointment power during a formal intersession recess of the Senate, but also that the recess appointment power can only be exercised with respect to a vacancy that arose during the same recess in which the appointment was made. Taken together, the D.C. Circuit's ruling represented a significant and largely unexpected limitation on the president's recess appointment power that made Supreme Court review a foregone conclusion.

NLRB v. Noel Canning offers something for every possible method of approaching a constitutional conundrum. The plain language of the original text of the U.S. Constitution is implicated, of course. In addition, the recess appointment power has a long history of having

---

[1] U.S. Const., art. 2 § 2, cl. 3.

[2] 705 F.3d 490 (D.C. Cir. 2013), cert. granted, 133 S. Ct. 2861 (June 24, 2013) (No. 12-1281).

been exercised, so justices who care to examine the historical understanding of a constitutional provision will have much history to examine. And the purpose that the recess appointment power was originally intended to serve may prove important, as may the purpose that the power has come to serve now that compromise has become especially rare in the nation's capital. Finally, justices who value a pragmatic approach to judging may feel conflicted between enabling the president to use the recess appointment power to fill vacancies and encouraging the opposing political parties to pursue compromise nominees acceptable to both parties, which could be a consequence of upholding the D.C. Circuit's rigorous limits.

The judiciary is far from an uninterested observer in the battle over the legality of recess appointments. The three most recent recess appointees to the U.S. Supreme Court remain well-known today: Chief Justice Earl Warren and Associate Justices William Brennan and Potter Stewart. President George W. Bush named two recess appointees to the federal appellate bench: Charles Pickering Sr. and William Pryor Jr. Although the Senate never confirmed Judge Pickering, it did confirm Judge Pryor, who continues to serve on the U.S. Court of Appeals for the Eleventh Circuit. And some may recall that President Bill Clinton, shortly before leaving office, used a recess appointment to place Roger Gregory on the U.S. Court of Appeals for the Fourth Circuit. In a gesture of bipartisanship—which proved futile given the battles attending his later nominees—President George W. Bush thereafter nominated Judge Gregory to a lifetime post on the Fourth Circuit, where he continues to serve thanks to the Senate confirmation that followed.

It is next to impossible to predict the ultimate outcome of the recess appointment case at the Supreme Court, but I would be very surprised if the D.C. Circuit's ruling emerged entirely intact. The decision could provide one more noteworthy opportunity for comparing and contrasting the justices' varied approaches to constitutional construction.

Bankruptcy Courts Exercising Article III Jurisdiction

In *North Pipeline Construction Co. v. Marathon Pipe Line Co.*, the Supreme Court examined the adjudicatory limitations applicable to bankruptcy courts created by Congress under Article I of the Constitution, presided over by judges who lacked life tenure and the other protections constitutionally guaranteed to judges who preside over the courts created pursuant to Article III.[3] The Court returned to this issue most recently in *Stern v. Marshall*, a case made all the more interesting because it tangentially involved Anna Nicole Smith.[4]

In the upcoming term, the Court will again reexamine the limits of the adjudicatory powers of Article I bankruptcy courts. The newly pending case, *Executive Benefits Insurance Agency v. Arkison*, calls on the Court to resolve, among other things, whether litigants can consent through their conduct to a bankruptcy court's exercise of power otherwise reserved to an Article III court.[5]

Given the continuing economic uncertainties plaguing both businesses and American workers, bankruptcy remains a busy area of practice for the courts. Although Congress, in a fairly expeditious manner, fixed the flaws in the bankruptcy system that the Supreme Court identified in *Northern Pipeline*, Congress has yet to fully remedy the additional flaws that the Court more recently identified in *Stern v. Marshall*. The Court has, in the past, almost jealously guarded the Article III judicial power to ensure that it is exercised only by officials who possess the attributes of Article III judges. In the *Executive Benefits* case, the justices will have the opportunity to further confront these issues in the context of uncertainty that has arisen in the aftermath of the *Stern* ruling.

Individual Rights

State Affirmative Action Bans

Sometimes, a potential Supreme Court blockbuster can fizzle out, as was the case with the Court's ruling in the 2012 term case of *Fisher v. University of Texas at Austin*.[6] That case potentially could have prohibited—but ultimately did not do so—as a matter of federal constitutional law using race or national origin as a ground for giving minorities an advantage in admissions to state colleges and universities.

Like a moth to a flame, however, in the 2013 term the Court will again return to this same controversial subject matter, this time in

[3] 458 U.S. 50, 58 (1982) (plurality opinion).

[4] 131 S. Ct. 2594 (2011).

[5] 702 F.3d 553 (9th Cir. 2012), cert granted, 133 S. Ct. 2880 (June 24, 2013) (No. 12-1200).

[6] 133 S. Ct. 2411 (2013).

the context of examining the constitutionality of an amendment to Michigan's constitution that prohibits, as a matter of state law, race- and sex-based discrimination or preferential treatment in public-university admissions decisions, government contracting, and public employment.

The en banc Sixth Circuit, by a vote of 8-7 over several heated dissents, ruled that the Michigan Civil Rights Initiative, which Michigan voters approved as a state constitutional amendment in 2006, violated the Equal Protection Clause of the U.S. Constitution by denying minorities a "fair political process."[7] In *Schuette v. Coalition to Defend Affirmative Action*—pronounced "shoo-tee"—the Supreme Court will review not just this controversial ruling, but that little-used and much-misunderstood "political process" doctrine.

If a majority on the Supreme Court views the MCRI not as an obstacle to protection against unequal treatment, but only as prohibiting preferential treatment, then the Court is likely to reverse the Sixth Circuit and uphold the constitutionality of the Michigan provision. But if the en banc Sixth Circuit's sharply divided views on this case offer any insight, the nearly unanimous outcome that the Supreme Court reached in *Fisher* may be difficult to replicate here. On the other hand, to this point only California and Michigan have enacted these types of state constitutional affirmative action bans, so the ultimate impact of this case—whatever it turns out to be—may initially be rather limited.

Legislative Prayers and the Separation of Church and State

In *Town of Greece v. Galloway*, the Supreme Court will again return to the always-controversial subject of separation of church and state. The Town of Greece, New York—located just outside Rochester—has a practice of allowing citizens to volunteer to give the invocation at the beginning of town board meetings. In that regard, this small New York State town has much in common with many other local governments throughout the nation.

After two town residents challenged the constitutionality of the town's legislative prayer practices, the U.S. Court of Appeals for the

---

[7] Coal. to Defend Affirmative Action v. Regents of Univ. of Mich., 701 F.3d 466 (6th Cir. 2012) (en banc), cert. granted sub nom. Schuette v. Coal. to Defend Affirmative Action, 133 S. Ct. 1633 (Mar. 25, 2013) (No. 12-682).

Second Circuit applied an "endorsement" test and concluded that the proportion of Christian prayers to non-Christian prayers could be viewed by an "ordinary, reasonable observer" as affiliating the town with the Christian faith.[8] The Supreme Court has now granted review to resolve whether constitutional challenges to legislative prayer practices should be analyzed under a historical test, whereby the practices will ordinarily be held lawful, or instead under an "endorsement" test, which is the approach the Second Circuit used in ruling against the Town of Greece.

Although the vast majority of the U.S. citizenry is probably unconcerned and unaware whether its local governmental bodies have any practices or policies regarding legislative prayer, the issue at the heart of *Town of Greece* remains likely to stir passions in people who have strong feelings on where the line separating church from state should be drawn. The composition of the Supreme Court has changed somewhat since the Court sharply divided over the legality of various Ten Commandments displays located on government property.[9] But it would not be a surprise if the Court were still divided on the subject of how to evaluate the constitutionality of challenged legislative prayer practices. The most anyone who values clarity in the law can hope for is a decision announcing clear principles joined in by a majority of the justices.

Abortion and the Speech Rights of Anti-Abortion Protestors

Another perennially controversial subject at the Supreme Court is abortion. Before even formally opening the 2013 term, the Court has accepted for review not one but two cases implicating that politically fraught issue.

Abortion was necessarily going to be in the news in 2013, as this year marks the 40th anniversary of the Court's ruling in *Roe v. Wade*,[10] which has unquestionably become one of the Court's all-time controversial rulings. Moreover, a number of states appear to be in a contest to see which can enact the most restrictive abortion-access law

[8] Galloway v. Town of Greece, 681 F.3d 20, 29–30 (2d Cir. 2012), cert granted, 133 S. Ct. 2388 (May 20, 2013) (No. 12-696).

[9] McCreary County v. American Civil Liberties Union of Ky., 545 U.S. 844 (2005); Van Orden v. Perry, 545 U.S. 677 (2005).

[10] 410 U.S. 113 (1973).

imaginable, in an effort to continue to provide the Supreme Court with opportunities to revisit and perhaps overrule earlier decisions recognizing a woman's substantive due process right to terminate her pregnancy.

Some had thought that perhaps medical advances might ultimately render the right to an abortion less controversial, as abortions induced by medications began to replace the need for a surgical procedure. As the Supreme Court's grant of review in *Cline v. Oklahoma Coalition for Reproductive Justice* demonstrates, however, states are equally capable of attempting to place obstacles in the path of medication-induced abortions.[11]

On June 27, 2013, when the Supreme Court granted review in *Cline*—slipping this in while the news cycle was consumed with the previous days' rulings on voting rights and gay marriage—the Court immediately certified several state-law questions to the Supreme Court of Oklahoma for resolution before the U.S. Supreme Court would address the *Cline* case on the merits. The U.S. Supreme Court's order asks Oklahoma's highest court to address whether the challenged Oklahoma statute "prohibits: (1) the use of misoprostol to induce abortions, including the use of misoprostol in conjunction with mifepristone according to a protocol approved by the Food and Drug Administration; and (2) the use of methotrexate to treat ectopic pregnancies."[12]

Presumably, if the Oklahoma court were to answer "no" to both of those questions, the case now pending before the U.S. Supreme Court would largely disappear. However, if the state court answers "yes" to one or both of those questions, then the federal high court would need to decide whether the Oklahoma law unconstitutionally infringes on the federally recognized abortion right.

There is no timetable for the Supreme Court of Oklahoma to act, so it is unclear right now whether the U.S. Supreme Court will itself actually decide this case on the merits in the October 2013 term if a decision on the merits turns out to be necessary.

The continued controversial nature of the Supreme Court's abortion jurisprudence is regularly driven home to the justices not just

---

[11] Cline v. Okla. Coal. for Reproductive Justice, 292 P.3d 27 (Okla. 2012), cert. granted, 133 S. Ct. 2887 (2013) (Jun. 27, 2013) (No. 12-1094).

[12] *Id.*

by annual protests outside the Court's windows, but also by a steady stream of cases challenging on First Amendment grounds the restrictions placed on anti-abortion protestors who picket, chant, and often directly confront people outside the offices of physicians who provide abortions. In *McCullen v. Coakley*, the Court will examine the constitutionality of a Massachusetts law that makes it a crime for speakers to enter or remain on a public way or sidewalk within 35 feet of an entrance, exit, or driveway of a reproductive health care facility.[13]

The anti-abortion protestors challenging the law argue that it violates their rights under the First and Fourteenth Amendments and that the law is particularly suspect because it solely targets those who wish to speak out against abortions. In general, speech restrictions based on the content of what is being said are subject to more rigorous scrutiny than content-neutral restrictions.[14] The Court has also agreed to address, if necessary, whether the Court's 6-3 ruling in 2000 in *Hill v. Colorado*[15]—that the First Amendment right to free speech was not violated by a Colorado law limiting protest and distribution of literature within eight feet of a person entering a healthcare facility—should be overturned.

Cases involving a conflict between access to abortion services and the exercise of freedom of speech are difficult because they involve a battle between two constitutionally recognized rights. Although Justice Sandra Day O'Connor's departure from the Court, and her replacement by Justice Samuel Alito, cause many to think that the existence and scope of the federal substantive due process right to an abortion rest on a 5-4 margin—depending on the views of Justice Anthony Kennedy in any given case—the Court's lineup in *Hill* was a little different. Although the vote in *Hill* was 6-3, those six votes for the majority included both O'Connor and Chief Justice William Rehnquist; Justice Kennedy was among the dissenters. Accordingly, it is the man who replaced Rehnquist, Chief Justice Roberts, who may hold the key vote in deciding whether *Hill* should be overruled—though he may do all he can to avoid having to reach that question.

[13] 708 F.3d 1 (1st Cir. 2013), cert granted (June 24, 2013) (No. 12-1168).

[14] See, e.g., Charles W. "Rocky" Rhodes, Speech, Subsidies, and Traditions: *AID v. AOSI* in Context, 2012-2013 Cato Sup. Ct. Rev. 363, 364 (2013).

[15] 530 U.S. 703 (2000).

Political Contribution Limits

Federal law places limits on the amount of money that can be contributed to candidates and so-called "non–candidate committees"—a term that describes national and subnational political party committees and political action committees ("PACs")—both to each candidate and committee and in the aggregate by one donor. In *McCutcheon v. Federal Election Commission*, the Court has agreed to decide the constitutionality of those aggregate limits.[16]

Critics of the Court's recent campaign-finance jurisprudence are already warning that *McCutcheon* may be the next *Citizens United*, which perhaps means that a ruling in favor of the petitioners in *McCutcheon* will give wealthy donors greater political power at the expense of those with more modest means. To be clear, though, this case is not about corporate speech, super PACs, "social welfare organizations," or any of the other independent advertising vehicles that have controversially entered the campaign space in recent election cycles. *McCutcheon* simply asks whether the federal limits on *aggregate* contributions by one donor (currently $123,200, divided among candidates, parties, and PACs) are constitutional. With one limited exception that was swept away by *Citizens United*, the Supreme Court has only ever accepted one justification for limits on political speech: quid pro quo corruption or the appearance thereof. The Court will now decide whether those aggregate limits are justified by that concern.

Or it may not. As one commentator suggests, the Court "may ultimately decide to strike down or uphold the overall limits, but there is also a middle path. The court could find the overall limits to be generally constitutional, but their level to be unconstitutionally low."[17]

McCutcheon is scheduled for oral argument on October 8, 2013, but given the complexity of the case and the strong passions on both sides of this issue that the justices have previously expressed, a decision may not issue until late in the term.

---

[16] 893 F. Supp. 2d 133 (D.C. Cir. 2012), cert. granted, 133 S. Ct. 1242 (Feb. 19, 2013) (No. 12-536).

[17] Paul Blumenthal, Next Citizens United? McCutcheon Supreme Court Case Targets Campaign Contribution Limits, Huffington Post, Jul. 31, 2013, http://huffingtonpost.com/2013/07/31/mccutcheon-supreme-court_n_3678555.html.

Personal Jurisdiction

As every first-year law student recalls with some trepidation, the Supreme Court frequently considers cases raising the issue of when a defendant with little to no contact with a particular state may be sued in that state's judicial system. This term already presents two such cases, both from the embattled (at the Supreme Court) U.S. Court of Appeals for the Ninth Circuit.

First, in *DaimlerChrysler AG v. Bauman,* the Court has agreed to decide whether a court may exercise general personal jurisdiction over a foreign corporation based solely on the fact that an indirect corporate subsidiary performs services on behalf of the defendant in the forum state.[18] "General jurisdiction" means that the lawsuit need not concern the defendant's actual activities within the state, or even be targeted toward the state, in which the defendant is being sued. At issue here is whether Daimler may be sued in California for alleged human-rights violations committed in Argentina by an Argentine subsidiary against Argentine residents. The Ninth Circuit answered "yes." Chances are that a majority of the Supreme Court will disagree.

The second case, *Walden v. Fiore,* involves a lawsuit against a Georgia police officer who was working at the Atlanta airport as a deputized agent for the Drug Enforcement Agency.[19] Several professional gamblers who were traveling with $97,000 in cash sued the police officer who seized the cash pending receipt of documentation showing that the money had been legitimately obtained. After the U.S. Attorney's office for the Northern District of Georgia determined that probable cause did *not* exist to forfeit the funds, the money was returned to the gamblers in March 2007.

This case wouldn't have reached the Supreme Court except for the fact that the gamblers filed their suit in federal district court in Nevada—where they resided—rather than in Georgia. The police officer moved to dismiss the suit, arguing that his actions were in no way directed toward Nevada and that the events and omissions giving rise to the gamblers' claims occurred entirely in Georgia. The

[18] DaimlerChrysler AG v. Bauman, 644 F.3d 909 (9th Cir. 2011), cert. granted, 133 S. Ct. 1995 (Apr. 22, 2013) (No. 11-965).

[19] Walden v. Fiore, 688 F.3d 558 (9th Cir. 2012), cert granted, 133 S. Ct. 1493 (Mar. 4, 2013) (No. 12-574).

district court granted the motion to dismiss, but a divided three-judge panel of the Ninth Circuit reversed and reinstated the lawsuit. The unusual facts giving rise to an exercise of personal jurisdiction in this case, and the unusual facts that give rise to the *Daimler* case, make it quite possible that the oft-reversed Ninth Circuit will suffer at least two more reversals in the 2013 term.

Criminal Law

Fourth Amendment and a Co-Tenant's Consent to Search

Seven years ago, in *Georgia v. Randolph*, the Supreme Court considered the legality under the Fourth Amendment of the search of a residence when one tenant consents to the search but not the other.[20] The defendant had declined the police request to search his residence for evidence of drug use, but the man's estranged wife, who also lived there, consented to the search. The Court ruled that the consent of one co-tenant could not overcome the denial of consent by another co-tenant.

In the 2013 term, the Court has agreed to examine a case arising from a somewhat similar fact pattern. In *Fernandez v. California*, the defendant had refused to give the police permission to search his residence.[21] After the defendant was arrested, the police asked his co-tenant for permission to search the residence, and the co-tenant granted permission. The question presented in *Fernandez* is whether a co-tenant who objects, *but is thereafter arrested and removed from the scene* (although not for the purpose of preventing an objection), loses his constitutional objection when a co-tenant consents to the police entry and search.

The vote in *Randolph* was 5-3, with Justice Alito not participating. Accordingly, if the outcome in *Fernandez* is anything other than 5-4 in favor of the criminal defendant, it will come as a surprise.

Criminal Forfeiture and the Right to Counsel

A federal statute allows a district court, acting on an *ex parte* motion of the United States, to restrain an indicted defendant's assets that are subject to forfeiture upon conviction. Such a restraining

[20] 547 U.S. 103 (2006).

[21] 208 Cal. App. 4th 100 (Cal. App. 2d Dist., 2012), cert granted, 133 S. Ct. 2388 (May 20, 2013) (No. 12-7822).

order, however, will often preclude the defendant—due to lack of available funds—from retaining the defense counsel whom he wishes to retain. In *Kaley v. United States*, the Supreme Court will consider whether, under these circumstances, the Fifth and Sixth Amendments require a pretrial, adversarial hearing at which the defendant may challenge the evidentiary support and legal theory of the underlying charges.[22]

The Court's earlier rulings in this area have not been particularly friendly to the criminal defendants involved.[23] However, *Kaley* merely asks whether a criminal defendant is entitled to a pre-deprivation hearing before he is precluded from using funds previously under the defendant's control—but which may have been fruits of the criminal enterprise—to hire legal counsel of his choice. The Court may be willing to allow an accused to enjoy this limited degree of procedural protection of his right to counsel, recognizing that in the vast majority of cases the restraint on the use of the funds at issue is likely to be upheld even after a hearing.

Criminal Victim Restitution

Many victims of childhood sexual abuse continue to be victimized as the images of child pornography that their abusers created remain in wide circulation despite federal criminal laws banning their possession and distribution. In *Paroline v. United States*, the question presented is "what, if any, causal relationship or nexus between the defendant's conduct and the victim's harm or damages must the government or the victim establish in order to recover restitution" under the relevant federal statute entitling crime victims to recover for their losses.[24]

Advocates for the children depicted in these images have argued that each person convicted of possessing or distributing the images should be held jointly and severally liable for the full amount of the victims' damages. Thus, a defendant convicted of possessing only a single image could be required to pay over a million dollars, if

---

[22] 677 F.3d 1316 (11th Cir. 2012), cert. granted, 133 S. Ct. 1580 (Mar. 18, 2013) (No. 12-464).

[23] See, e.g., Caplin & Drysdale v. United States, 491 U.S. 617 (1989); United States v. Monsanto, 491 U.S. 600 (1989).

[24] 701 F.3d 749 (5th Cir. 2012), cert granted, 133 S. Ct. 2885 (June 27, 2013) (No. 12-8561).

the defendant can afford to pay that much, to the victims of these crimes.[25] On the opposing side, the convicted defendants themselves have argued that the most any one of them should be responsible for paying in restitution is the share of the loss, if any, that the victim has sustained as the result of the specific individual defendant's criminal offense. This approach would prevent any one defendant from being liable for the entirety of the aggregate losses that the victims have suffered.

The vast majority of the federal appellate courts that have confronted this issue have ruled in favor of the criminal defendants and against the victims. A divided en banc Fifth Circuit, however, held that a district court must award restitution against the criminal defendant for the full amount of the victim's losses, without regard to whether that defendant proximately caused all of them.[26] On the final day of the October 2012 term, again upstaged by that week's big rulings, the Supreme Court decided to review that ruling and resolve this circuit split.

Federalism

The Scope of the Treaty Power

No lawyer worth his or her salt would ever advise a client to attempt to use dangerous chemicals to poison a rival for the romantic attention of the client's spouse. Nevertheless, having a client who engaged in that legally prohibited conduct appears to be the recipe for periodic visits to address the justices in the Supreme Court's courtroom—at least if you're a superstar Supreme Court advocate.

In the forthcoming term, the case captioned *Bond v. United States* makes its return visit to the Court.[27] In its previous incarnation, the Supreme Court held that the woman charged with attempting to poison her romantic rival for her husband's affections had standing to object to Congress's enactment of legislation alleged to violate the

---

[25] See Emily Bazelon, Money Is No Cure, The N. Y. Times Sunday Magazine, Jan. 27, 2013, available at http://www.nytimes.com/2013/01/27/magazine/how-much-can-restitution-help-victims-of-child-pornography.html.

[26] In re Amy Unknown, 701 F.3d 749 (5th Cir. 2012) (en banc).

[27] Bond v. United States, 681 F.3d 149 (3rd Cir. 2012), cert. granted, 133 S. Ct. 978 (Jan. 18, 2013) (No. 12-158).

Tenth Amendment's limitations on federal power.[28] On remand to the U.S. Court of Appeals for the Third Circuit, Bond argued that Congress had overstepped the bounds of its authority to make criminal the purely local poisoning attempt at the heart of the criminal charges against her. Relying on dictum from the Supreme Court's ruling in *Missouri v. Holland*—which suggests that Congress has the power to enact implementing legislation in furtherance of a lawfully approved treaty even if that legislation broadens Congress's constitutional power—the Third Circuit rejected Bond's challenge.[29]

Now, on its return visit to the Supreme Court, Bond is asking the justices to hold that the federal government's approval of a treaty— here an international chemical weapons convention—does not authorize it to assume police powers to turn what otherwise would have been an offense under state law—here, assault or attempted murder—into a federal crime. Although the structural limitations on federal power are important, as the Supreme Court recognized most recently in *NFIB v. Sebelius*,[30] this case appears to present an especially vexing question.

State and local governments are of course powerless to enter into international treaties. Because the treaty power of necessity resides exclusively with the federal government, perhaps the states can be understood to have ceded to the federal government the ability to encroach on what would otherwise ordinarily be state prerogatives where necessary to implement a lawful treaty. Or perhaps the Supreme Court will hold that federalism principles render the federal government unable to fully implement treaties that require such encroachment on state power.

One thing is for sure: the case is bound to be very well argued, as former Solicitor General Paul Clement will represent Bond in this appeal, just as he did in his client's previous victorious visit to the Court. Although the outcome of this case is far from clear, my suspicion is that a majority consisting of the ordinarily pragmatic justices are likely to prevail in holding that the Constitution's treaty

[28] Bond v. United States, 131 S. Ct. 2355 (2011). See also John C. Eastman, Will Mrs. Bond Topple *Missouri v. Holland?*, 2010-2011 Cato Sup. Ct. Rev. 185 (2011).

[29] United States v. Bond, 681 F.3d 149 (3rd Cir. 2012) (citing Missouri v. Holland, 252 U.S. 416, 432 (1920)).

[30] 132 S. Ct. 2566 (a.k.a. the "Obamacare case").

power does give Congress the ability to encroach on state prerogatives where necessary to implement a treaty. Yet even such a holding, however broad, would do little to justify the seemingly aberrant
decision of federal prosecutors to treat Mrs. Bond's bizarre offenses
as federal crimes.

Certiorari Pipeline and Beyond

Federal appellate courts have recently divided over whether for-
profit, secular corporations may claim a religious exemption from providing employees with certain methods of contraception as required
under the federal healthcare mandate in the Patient Protection and Affordable Care Act.[31] Given the existence of a circuit split on this issue,
and given the importance of the issue, the Supreme Court is likely to
agree to hear and resolve the question in relatively short order.

A second issue that is destined for Supreme Court resolution in
the near future involves whether the Fourth Amendment requires
the police to obtain search warrants to access either the contents of
cell phones or tracking information revealed by a person's cell phone.
Lower courts have already reached conflicting outcomes on these issues.[32] Given the ubiquitous nature of cell phones in modern life, the
Court will be unable to avoid deciding this question for much longer.

Next, after a conclusion to the October 2012 term that gave supporters of same-sex marriages much to applaud, the Supreme Court may
soon have to confront a different question regarding homosexuals
and their right to serve on juries. The Supreme Court has previously
recognized that excluding individuals from jury service solely based
on race, gender, or national origin is unconstitutional. A case now
pending in the Ninth Circuit asks whether excluding a juror on the
basis of his or her sexual orientation is likewise unconstitutional.[33]

[31] Compare Hobby Lobby Stores, Inc. v. Sebelius, No. 12-6294, 2013 WL 3216103
(10th Cir. Jun. 27, 2013) (en banc), with Conestoga Wood Specialties Corp. v. Secretary
of U.S. Dept. of Health and Human Services, No. 13-1144, 2013 WL 3845365 (3d Cir.
Jul. 26, 2013).

[32] See, e.g., United States v. Wurie, 2013 WL 2129119 (1st Cir. May 17, 2013); In re
Application of United States for Historical Cell Site Data, 2013 WL 3914484 (5th Cir.
Jul. 30, 2013); State v. Earls, 2013 WL 3744221 (N.J. Jul. 18, 2013).

[33] See Adam Liptak, Court to Decide if Lawyers Can Block Gays From Juries, The
New York Times, Jul. 30, 2013, available at http://www.nytimes.com/2013/07/30/
us/court-weighs-exclusion-of-jurors-because-theyre-gay.html.

Finally, and unavoidably, at the end of the October 2013 term attention will surely turn again to the retirement plans of Justice Ruth Bader Ginsburg. One consideration may be that congressional midterm elections will occur in November 2014. The party in control of the White House typically loses congressional seats in a midterm election, so the composition of the Senate is likely to be different in January 2015 from what it is now. The Republicans may even take control of the upper chamber, thus making it more difficult for President Obama to confirm more controversial judicial nominees.

Although Justice Ginsburg shows no signs of being interested in voluntarily departing from the Court, no one can remain on the Court forever. Surely it is important to Justice Ginsburg that the president who nominates her replacement will be someone likely to nominate a justice with views similar to hers. The most certain way to ensure such a replacement is for Justice Ginsburg to retire during the Obama presidency, and the most certain way to obtain confirmation of such a replacement is for the confirmation process to occur during the current Senate, rather than with a Senate of unknown composition that will exist in 2015–2016 (and the run-up to another presidential election).

* * *

The upcoming term does not yet rival the past two terms with regard to the likelihood of capturing the general public's attention, but that of course remains subject to change depending on the cases that are added once the Court returns in October. What is already certain is that the term will be far from boring, as many cases already accepted for review implicate the hot-button legal and societal issues of our time. The addition of one or two more especially riveting cases, or a justice's surprise retirement announcement, could make the October 2013 term one that will be long remembered.

Contributors

Kenneth Anderson is a professor of law at Washington College of Law, American University, in Washington. He is also a visiting fellow of the Hoover Institution, Stanford University, and a member of its Jean Perkins Task Force on National Security and Law; and a non-resident senior fellow of the Brookings Institution. Prior to joining the American University law faculty, he was general counsel to the Open Society Institute and director of the Human Rights Watch Arms Division. Professor Anderson's scholarly work focuses on international law, both public international law and private international economic law. He has written extensively on international organizations, and particularly their relationship with international nongovernmental organizations and global civil society; his book, *Living with the UN: American Responsibilities and International Order* (Hoover Institution Press) appeared in 2012. He has also written extensively on the laws of war and national security; his new book, with the Brookings Institution's Benjamin Wittes, is *Speaking the Law: The Obama Administration's Addresses on National Security Law* (Hoover Institution Press 2013). His recent work has focused on the law of war and robotics, including drone warfare and targeted killing, and emerging technologies of weapons automation; his articles in this area have appeared in *Commentary*, *Policy Review*, the *Weekly Standard*, and other journals, as well as academic journals. Professor Anderson grew up in California, and received his B.A. from UCLA and his J.D. from Harvard Law School; following graduation from law school, he clerked for Justice Joseph Grodin of the California Supreme Court and was an associate at Sullivan & Cromwell. He blogs at the *Volokh Conspiracy* and the international law blog *Opinio Juris*; a longtime contributor to the *Times Literary Supplement* and editorial board member of the *Journal of Terrorism and Political Violence*, Professor Anderson serves as the reviews editor of the national security website *Lawfare*.

Howard J. Bashman is an appellate lawyer with his own practice in suburban Philadelphia who appears regularly before the U.S. Court of Appeals for the Third Circuit and Pennsylvania's state appellate courts. Bashman graduated from Columbia College, where he was named a John Jay National Scholar and won the George William Curtis Prize in Oratory. He received his J.D. with distinction from the Emory University School of Law, where he served as managing editor of the *Emory Law Journal* and received the Emory University School of Law Merit Scholarship. Following law school, Bashman had a two-year clerkship for Judge William D. Hutchinson of the U.S. Court of Appeals for the Third Circuit. Since December 2000, Bashman has written a monthly column on appellate developments for *The Legal Intelligencer*, Philadelphia's daily newspaper for lawyers. ALM Media's law.com hosts his popular appellate-related Web log, *How Appealing*. Previously, Bashman served as co-chair and then chair of the appellate courts committee of the Philadelphia Bar Association. Bashman has been profiled by the Associated Press, the *ABA Journal, Legal Times, Pennsylvania Super Lawyers Magazine*, and the *Daily Journal*, a California-based legal newspaper. He has published essays about appellate issues in the *Los Angeles Times* and *Slate*. Bashman is admitted to practice law in Pennsylvania, New Jersey, the U.S. Supreme Court, and in numerous federal courts of appeals.

Erin C. Blondel is an associate at Robbins, Russell, Englert, Orseck, Untereiner & Sauber LLP. She graduated *summa cum laude* in 2009 from Duke Law School, where she was an executive editor of the *Duke Law Journal*. She served as a law clerk to the Honorable Sandra L. Lynch for the U.S. Court of Appeals for the First Circuit and then as a litigation associate at Wachtell, Lipton, Rosen & Katz. Blondel received a Master of Studies, with distinction, in English Language and Literature from Oxford University in 2006. She received a B.A. *magna cum laude* in 2005 from the University of Notre Dame, where she was a member of the University Honors Program.

Paul D. Clement is a partner at Bancroft PLLC. He served as the 43rd Solicitor General of the United States from June 2005 until June 2008. Before his confirmation as solicitor general, Clement served as acting solicitor general for nearly a year and as principal deputy solicitor general for over three years. He has argued more than 65 cases before the U.S. Supreme Court, including *McConnell v. FEC, Tennessee v. Lane, Rumsfeld v. Padilla, Credit Suisse v. Billing, United States v. Booker, MGM v. Grokster, McDonald v. Chicago,* and *NFIB v. Sebelius.* He has argued before the Supreme Court 16 times in just the last two terms, an unprecedented number for a lawyer in private practice. Indeed, Clement has argued more Supreme Court cases since 2000 than any lawyer in or out of government. He has also argued many important cases in the lower courts, including *Walker v. Cheney, United States v. Moussaoui,* and *NFL v. Brady.* He was recognized as the 2012 Lawyer of the Year by the D.C. Bar Association and was selected by the National Law Journal in 2013 as one of the 100 most influential lawyers in America. Clement received his bachelor's degree *summa cum laude* from the Georgetown University School of Foreign Service, and a master's degree in economics from Cambridge University. He graduated *magna cum laude* from Harvard Law School, where he was the Supreme Court editor of the *Harvard Law Review.* Following graduation, Mr. Clement clerked for Judge Laurence H. Silberman of the U.S. Court of Appeals for the D.C. Circuit and for Associate Justice Antonin Scalia of the U.S. Supreme Court. After his clerkships, Mr. Clement served as chief counsel of the U.S. Senate Subcommittee on the Constitution, Federalism and Property Rights. Clement has been an adjunct or visiting professor at the Georgetown University Law Center since 1998, where he teaches a seminar on the separation of powers. He also serves as a senior fellow of the Law Center's Supreme Court Institute.

William S. Consovoy is a partner at Wiley Rein LLP whose practice focuses on federal constitutional and statutory issues. In particular, Consovoy advises clients on issues involving the First Amendment, the Commerce Clause, the Fourteenth and Fifteenth Amendments, the Communications Act, the Voting Rights Act, and the Federal Arbitration Act. He represents clients primarily before the U.S. Supreme Court, federal appellate and districts courts, as well as before federal agencies. Since 2011, Consovoy has been the co-director of the George Mason University School of Law Supreme Court Clinic. He also is a former law clerk for Supreme Court Justice Clarence Thomas, Judge Edith Jones of the U.S. Court of Appeals for the Fifth Circuit, and the 17th Judicial Circuit of Virginia. Consovoy is a member of the Edward Coke Appellate Inn of Court and was named by

Law360 as a "rising star" in appellate law for 2013. Consovoy earned his B.A. from Monmouth University, and his J.D. *magna cum laude* from George Mason University School of Law. He is a member of the Virginia and D.C. bars.

Gregory Dolin is a law professor at the University of Baltimore Law School. Dolin is also co-director of the Center for Medicine and Law, a partnership a partnership between UB Law and the Johns Hopkins University School of Medicine. The center supports collaboration between experts in the fields of both medicine and law, and focuses its efforts on an examination of medical and legal issues from the perspective of the health care practitioner. Prior to joining UB Law, Dolin held a position at the George Washington University Law School as a Frank H. Marks Visiting Associate Professor of Law and administrative fellow in the intellectual property program. He was a law clerk to the Hon. Pauline Newman of the U.S. Court of Appeals for the Federal Circuit and the late Hon. H. Emory Widener Jr. of the U.S. Court of Appeals for the Fourth Circuit. He served as a John M. Olin Fellow in Law at Northwestern University School of Law, and as an associate in the intellectual property group of Kramer, Levin, Naftalis, and Frankel LLP. He received his B.A. from Johns Hopkins University, his J.D. from Georgetown University Law Center, and his M.D. from State University of New York at Stony Brook School of Medicine.

Daniel Epps is a Climenko Fellow and a Lecturer on Law at Harvard Law School. He received his A.B. *summa cum laude* with highest distinction in philosophy from Duke University in 2004 and his J.D. *magna cum laude* from Harvard Law School in 2008. At Harvard, he served as articles co-chair of the *Harvard Law Review* and won the John M. Olin Law & Economics Prize. After law school, he clerked for Justice Anthony M. Kennedy on the Supreme Court of the United States and Judge J. Harvie Wilkinson III on the U.S. Court of Appeals for the Fourth Circuit. He then was an associate at King & Spalding in Washington, where he litigated a number of appeals in the Supreme Court and the federal appellate courts. While in practice, he also served as a lecturer at the University of Virginia School of Law, where he co-taught a course about the Supreme Court.

Andrew M. Grossman is an associate at the Washington office of Baker & Hostetler LLP. He has represented states in challenges to the constitutionality of federal statutes and the legality of federal environmental regulations, and is also active in commercial litigation. He is experienced in Supreme Court practice, authoring or contributing to many certiorari-stage filings, merits briefs and amicus briefs, and frequently "mooting" the nation's top Supreme Court litigators and state solicitors general before their oral arguments. Before joining BakerHostetler, Grossman was a senior legal analyst for the Center for Legal and Judicial Studies at the Heritage Foundation where his research focused on law and finance, bankruptcy, national security law, and the constitutional separation of powers. Grossman has testified before the House and Senate Judiciary Committees on a variety of issues and is a frequent commentator on radio and television, having appeared on Fox News, CNN, MSNBC, CNBC, NPR and its affiliates, and elsewhere. His legal commentary has also appeared in dozens of magazines and newspapers, including the *Wall Street Journal, USA Today, Washington Post, Washington Times, CQ Researcher,* and many others. Grossman has written and published research on criminal law and "overcriminalization," constitutional law, civil liberties and privacy, domestic intelligence operations, the legal aspects of economic regulation and civil justice reform. He served as a judicial clerk to Chief Judge Edith H. Jones of the U.S. Court of Appeals for the Fifth Circuit. In 2007, the Burton Foundation and the Library of Congress presented Grossman with the Burton Award for Legal Achievement, citing his research on federal evidentiary law and Internet communications technologies. In addition to his litigation practice, Grossman serves as a legal fellow at the Heritage Foundation, where he continues to write on constitutional law and advise members of Congress on complex legal and policy issues. He is a member of the D.C. Bar.

Joshua D. Hawley is an Associate Professor of Law at the University of Missouri School of Law. He is a former clerk to Chief Justice John G. Roberts Jr. of the U.S. Supreme Court, and to Michael W. McConnell of the U.S. Court of Appeals for the Tenth Circuit. He is a graduate of the Yale Law School, where he served as articles editor for the *Yale Law Journal* and as president of the Yale Federalist Society. He earned his A.B. from Stanford University with distinction and highest honors. Hawley returned to his native Missouri to join the University of Missouri Law School in 2011 following several years in the national appellate practice of Hogan Lovells US LLP, in Washington. At Hogan, Hawley briefed cases in multiple federal circuit courts, state courts and the U.S. Supreme Court. Hawley currently serves as Of Counsel to the Becket Fund for Religious Liberty, where he has helped litigate ground-breaking First Amendment cases, including *Hosanna-Tabor v. EEOC*. At the University of Missouri, he teaches constitutional law, torts, and legislation. His scholarship focuses on constitutional law and law and religion. He is the author most recently of "The Transformative Twelfth Amendment," "Theodore Roosevelt's Constitution," and *Theodore Roosevelt: Preacher of Righteousness*, a book-length study on TR's political thought published by Yale University Press.

Gail Heriot is professor of law at University of San Diego School of Law and a member of the U.S. Commission on Civil Rights. She teaches and writes in the areas of civil rights, employment discrimination, product liability remedies, and torts. Heriot clerked for the Honorable Seymour F. Simon on the Illinois Supreme Court. Before entering academia, she practiced with Mayer, Brown & Platt in Chicago and Hogan & Hartson in Washington. She also served as civil rights counsel to the U.S. Senate Committee on the Judiciary and as associate dean and professor of law at the George Mason University School of Law. She joined the USD law faculty in 1989. Heriot earned her B.A. from Northwestern University and her J.D. from the University of Chicago. She was an editor of the *University of Chicago Law Review* and also a member of Phi Beta Kappa and Order of the Coif. She sits on the board of directors of the National Association of Scholars and the California Association of Scholars. Heriot's publications include "Lights! Camera! Legislation!: Grandstanding Congress Set to Adopt Hate Crimes Bill that May Put Double Jeopardy Protections in Jeopardy" in *Engage*; "Affirmative Action in American Law Schools" in the *Journal of Contemporary Legal Issues*; and "The Politics of Admissions in California" in *Academic Questions*. As a frequent contributor to popular media outlets, her writing has been featured in the *Wall Street Journal* and the *Philadelphia Inquirer*.

Thomas R. McCarthy is a partner at Wiley Rein LLP. McCarthy has significant litigation experience on a wide array of issues in federal trial and appellate courts across the country, especially in the U.S. Court of Appeals for the D.C. Circuit and the U.S. Supreme Court. He also represents clients before the Federal Communications Commission and various other federal agencies. McCarthy's recent cases before the Supreme Court involve issues relating to federal preemption, the Administrative Procedure Act, the dormant Commerce Clause, the Equal Protection Clause, the Federal Arbitration Act, patent law, voting rights, and criminal law. Since 2011, McCarthy has been the co-director of the George Mason University School of Law Supreme Court Clinic. He also is a former law clerk for D.C. Circuit Judge David Sentelle and Judge Frank Bullock of the U.S. District Court for the Middle District of North Carolina. McCarthy earned his B.S. from the University of Notre Dame, where he was a Notre Dame Scholar, and his J.D. *magna cum laude* from George Mason University School of Law. He is a member of the Virginia and D.C. bars.

Mark Moller, is an associate law professor at the DePaul College of Law, where he teaches and writes in the area of civil procedure and complex litigation. He received a J.D. with honors from the University of Chicago Law School, an LL.M. with first class honors from the University of Cambridge, and a bachelor's degree *magna cum laude* from Duke University. Prior to joining DePaul, Moller was an associate in the appellate and class action groups at Gibson Dunn & Crutcher in Washington, where he served on the team that successfully litigated *Bush v. Gore*. Following private practice, he was a senior fellow at the Cato Institute's Center for Constitutional Studies, where he oversaw Cato's Supreme Court amicus program, was editor-in-chief of the *Cato Supreme Court Review*, and appeared frequently as a legal commentator in print and on television and radio.

David S. Olson is an associate professor at Boston College Law School. He teaches patents, intellectual property, and antitrust law. Olson researches and writes primarily in the areas of patent law and copyright. Olson came to Boston College from Stanford Law School's Center for Internet and Society, where he researched in patent law and litigated copyright fair use impact cases. Before entering academia,

he practiced as a patent litigator at the law firm of Kirkland & Ellis
LLP. Olson clerked for Judge Jerry Smith of the U.S. Court of Appeals
for the Fifth Circuit. He earned his B.A. from the University of Kansas and his J.D. from Harvard Law School.

Roger Pilon is the founder and director of Cato's Center for Constitutional Studies, which has become an important force in the national debate over constitutional interpretation and judicial philosophy. He is the publisher of the *Cato Supreme Court Review* and is an adjunct professor of government at Georgetown University through The Fund for American Studies. Prior to joining Cato, Pilon held five senior posts in the Reagan administration, including at State and Justice, and was a National Fellow at Stanford's Hoover Institution. In 1989 the Bicentennial Commission presented him with its Benjamin Franklin Award for excellence in writing on the U.S. Constitution. In 2001 Columbia University's School of General Studies awarded him its Alumni Medal of Distinction. Pilon lectures and debates at universities and law schools across the country and testifies often before Congress. His writing has appeared in the *Wall Street Journal*, the *Washington Post*, the *New York Times*, the *Los Angeles Times*, *Legal Times*, *National Law Journal*, *Harvard Journal of Law & Public Policy*, *Stanford Law & Policy Review*, and elsewhere. He has appeared on ABC's *Nightline*, CBS's *60 Minutes II*, Fox News Channel, NPR, CNN, MSNBC, CNBC, and other media. Pilon holds a B.A. from Columbia University, an MA and a Ph.D. from the University of Chicago, and a J.D. from the George Washington University School of Law.

Charles W. "Rocky" Rhodes is a professor of law at South Texas College of Law, where he teaches constitutional law, First Amendment law, state constitutional law, civil procedure, and complex litigation. He is the author or co-author of three texts on constitutional law, *Cases and Materials on Constitutional Law*, *The Texas Constitution in State and Nation*, and *Skills & Values: The First Amendment*. His writings also include over 20 journal articles and book chapters on a wide variety of constitutional and procedural issues, such as constitutional interpretation, due process rights, free speech protections, state constitutionalism, the judicial confirmation process, personal jurisdiction, federal practice and procedure, mandamus proceedings, and appellate procedure. His articles, books, and chapters have been cited hundreds of times in judicial decisions, treatises, textbooks, law journals, and legal briefs. He is a frequent media commentator, including television and radio appearances on CNN, NPR's *Morning Edition* and *Day to Day*, BBC Radio's *World Business News*, and Bloomberg Radio, along with interviews in newspapers and magazines across the United States. He earned his undergraduate degree *summa cum laude* while on a National Merit Scholarship at Baylor University before enrolling at Baylor Law School, where he was editor-in-chief of the *Baylor Law Review*, the President's Award recipient as the outstanding third-year student, and valedictorian of his graduating law school class. Before becoming a professor, he served as a briefing attorney for Justice Raul Gonzalez and as a staff attorney for Justice Greg Abbott at the Supreme Court of Texas, practiced appellate law at a national law firm, and earned his board certification in civil appellate law by the Texas Board of Legal Specialization.

Ilya Shapiro is a senior fellow in constitutional studies at the Cato Institute and editor-in-chief of the *Cato Supreme Court Review*. Before joining Cato, he was a special assistant/advisor to the Multi-National Force in Iraq on rule of law issues and practiced international, political, commercial, and antitrust litigation at Patton Boggs and Cleary Gottlieb. Shapiro has contributed to a variety of academic, popular, and professional publications, including the *Wall Street Journal*, *Harvard Journal of Law & Public Policy*, *Los Angeles Times*, *USA Today*, *National Law Journal*, *Weekly Standard*, *New York Time Online*, and *National Review Online*, and from 2004 to 2007 wrote the "Dispatches from Purple America" column for *TCS Daily.com*. He also regularly provides commentary for various media outlets, including CNN, Fox News, ABC, CBS, NBC, Univision and Telemundo, *The Colbert Report*, NPR, and American Public Media's *Marketplace*. Shapiro has provided testimony to Congress and state legislatures and, as coordinator of Cato's *amicus* brief program, filed more than 100 "friend of the court" briefs in the Supreme Court. He lectures regularly on behalf of the Federalist Society and other groups, is a member of the Legal Studies Institute's board of visitors at The Fund for American Studies, was an inaugural Washington Fellow at the National Review Institute, and has been an adjunct professor at the George Washington University Law School. Before entering private practice, Shapiro clerked for Judge E. Grady Jolly of the U.S. Court of Appeals for the

Fifth Circuit, while living in Mississippi and traveling around the Deep South. He holds an A.B. from Princeton University, an M.Sc. from the London School of Economics, and a J.D. from the University of Chicago Law School, where he became a Tony Patiño Fellow. Shapiro is a member of the bars of New York, the District of Columbia, and the U.S. Supreme Court. He is a native speaker of English and Russian, is fluent in Spanish and French, and is proficient in Italian and Portuguese.

Ilya Somin is professor of law at George Mason University School of Law. His research focuses on constitutional law, property law, and the study of popular political participation and its implications for constitutional democracy. He is the author of *Democracy and Political Ignorance: Why Smaller Government is Smarter* (Stanford University Press, forthcoming September 2013), and coauthor of *A Conspiracy Against Obamacare: The Volokh Conspiracy and the Health Care Case* (Palgrave Macmillan, forthcoming November 2013). His work has appeared in numerous scholarly journals, including the *Yale Law Journal, Stanford Law Review, Northwestern University Law Review,* and *Georgetown Law Journal.* Somin has also published articles in a variety of popular press outlets, including the *Los Angeles Times*, the *New York Times* Room for Debate website, *USA Today,* the *Wall Street Journal OpinionJournal.com, National Law Journal,* and *Reason.* He has been quoted or interviewed by the *New York Times, Washington Post,* NPR, BBC, Al Jazeera and the Voice of America, among other media. He recently testified on the use of drones for targeted killing in the War on Terror before the U.S. Senate Judiciary Subcommittee on the Constitution, Civil Rights, and Human Rights. In July 2009, he testified on property rights issues at the U.S. Senate Judiciary Committee confirmation hearings for Supreme Court Justice Sonia Sotomayor. Somin writes regularly for the popular *Volokh Conspiracy* law and politics blog. From 2006 until mid-2013, he served as co-editor of the *Supreme Court Economic Review,* one of the country's top-rated law and economics journals. Somin has been a visiting professor at the University of Pennsylvania Law School, as well as the University of Hamburg, Germany, and the University of Torcuato Di Tella in Buenos Aires, Argentina. Before joining the faculty at George Mason, Somin was the John M. Olin Fellow in Law at Northwestern University Law School in 2002-2003. In 2001-2002, he clerked for the Hon. Judge Jerry

E. Smith of the U.S. Court of Appeals for the Fifth Circuit. Somin earned his B.A., *summa cum laude*, at Amherst College, M.A. in political science from Harvard University, and J.D. from Yale Law School.

Elizabeth B. Wydra is Constitutional Accountability Center's chief counsel. She frequently participates in Supreme Court litigation and has argued several important cases in the federal courts of appeals. She joined CAC from private practice at Quinn Emanuel Urquhart & Sullivan in San Francisco, where she was an attorney working with former Stanford Law School Dean Kathleen Sullivan in the firm's Supreme Court/appellate practice. Previously, Wydra was a supervising attorney and teaching fellow at the Georgetown University Law Center appellate litigation clinic, a law clerk for Judge James R. Browning of the U.S. Court of Appeals for the Ninth Circuit, and a lawyer at Shaw Pittman, a law firm in Washington. Elizabeth has appeared as a legal expert for NBC, ABC, CNN, Fox News, the BBC, Fox Business Channel, Current TV, and NPR, among other outlets. She has been quoted extensively in the print media and is a regular contributor to the ABA's Preview of United States Supreme Court Cases. Her writings have appeared in the *New York Times*, Reuters, *USA Today*, *Politico*, *Slate*, and on numerous political and legal blogs, such as *Huffington Post*, *Grist*, and *ACSblog*. She has also published in the *UCLA Journal of Environmental Law & Policy*, *Syracuse Law Review*, and the *Yale Journal of International Law*. Wydra is a graduate of Yale Law School.

Ernest A. Young is Alston & Bird Professor of Law at Duke Law School, where he teaches constitutional law, federal courts, and foreign relations law. He is one of the nation's leading authorities on the constitutional law of federalism, having written extensively on the Rehnquist Court's "Federalist Revival" and the difficulties confronting courts as they seek to draw lines between national and state authority. Young also is an active commentator on foreign relations law, where he focuses on the interaction between domestic and supranational courts and the application of international law by domestic courts. He has been known to dabble in maritime law and comparative constitutional law. A native of Abilene, Texas, Young joined the Duke Law faculty in 2008, after serving as the Charles Alan Wright Chair in Federal Courts at the University of Texas at Austin School of

Law, where he had taught since 1999. He graduated from Dartmouth College and Harvard Law School. After law school, he served as a law clerk to Judge Michael Boudin of the U.S. Circuit Court of Appeals for the First Circuit and to Justice David Souter of the U.S. Supreme Court. Young practiced law at Cohan, Simpson, Cowlishaw, & Wulff in Dallas and at Covington & Burling in Washington, where he specialized in appellate litigation. He has also been a visiting professor at Harvard Law School and Villanova University School of Law, as well as an adjunct professor at Georgetown University Law Center. Elected to the American Law Institute in 2006, Young is an active participant in both public and private litigation in his areas of interest. He has been the principal author of *amicus* briefs on behalf of leading constitutional scholars in several recent Supreme Court cases, including *Medellin v. Texas* (concerning presidential power and the authority of the International Court of Justice over domestic courts) and *Gonzales v. Raich* (concerning federal power to regulate medical marijuana).